On Resentment:
Past and Present

Edited by

Bernardino Fantini, Dolores Martín Moruno and Javier Moscoso

On Resentment: Past and Present,
Edited by Bernardino Fantini, Dolores Martín Moruno and Javier Moscoso

This book first published 2013

Cambridge Scholars Publishing

12 Back Chapman Street, Newcastle upon Tyne, NE6 2XX, UK

British Library Cataloguing in Publication Data
A catalogue record for this book is available from the British Library

ISBN (10): 1-4438-4772-0, ISBN (13): 978-1-4438-4772-8

TABLE OF CONTENTS

Part III: Look Back in Anger

Part IV: Coming into Conflict: Resentment, Wars and Revolutions

Part V: Resentment and Collective Identities

INTRODUCTION

ON RESENTMENT:
PAST AND PRESENT

In *A Room of One's own*, an essay published in 1929, Virginia Woolf explores the connections between women and literary creation, describing a type of sublimated anger mixed with indignation to portray the emotional universe surrounding the seventeenth-century female poet Anne Finch, the Countess of Winchilsea. In the eyes of Woolf, resentment appeared as a necessary step in women writers' emancipation, as personalities like Finch could only realise their oppressed identity by means of the recognition of their negative feelings against Patriarchal Civilisation:

> Yet it is clear that could she have freed her mind from hate and fear and not heaped it with bitterness and resentment, the fire was hot within her ... It was a thousand pities that the woman who could write like that, whose mind was turned to nature and reflection should have been forced to anger and bitterness. But how could she have helped herself? I asked, imagining the sneers and the laughter, the adulation of the toadies, the scepticism of the professional poet. She must have shut herself up in a room in the country to write, and been torn asunder by bitterness and scruples perhaps, though her husband was of the kindest, and their married life perfection.[1]

For Woolf, the poetry of Anne Finch, "the melancholy lady," embodied female resentment against men, a combination of hate and fear that emerged primarily in women because they were trapped in a way of life that was imposed on them by their husbands, a life devoid of freedom in the public and in the private sphere.[2] Men were superior, argued Woolf while she dissected the interior life of Finch, because they had the power

---

[1] Virginia Woolf, *A Room of One's Own* (London: The Hogarth Press, repr. Oxford University Press, 1998), 77.
[2] Woolf, 79.

to forbid what women wanted really to do, making them perfect wives and mothers but never writers. What Woolf was pointing out about resentment was that it was not only a poisonous mindset that led Finch to acute depression at the end of her life, but furthermore, and most importantly, the fact that it acted as a way of denunciating social injustices, which required a spectator to be able to feel sympathy towards the victim that had suffered violence.

This public dimension of resentment, which had already been pointed out by Adam Smith in his *Theory of Moral Sentiments* (1759), related this emotional experience to our capacity to feel indignation, "which boils up in the breast of the spectator, whenever he thoroughly brings home to himself the case of the sufferer."[3] By contrast to further nineteenth-century interpretations, such as those of Friedrich Nietzsche and Max Scheler, who would stress the pathological proportions of resentment or more exactly of what they called *ressentiment*, Adam Smith focused on the importance of this social passion as a mechanism of retributive justice when an innocent victim was wrongly injured.

Some questions immediately arise from these two different perceptions of resentment: were Adam Smith and Friedrich Nietzsche referring to the same emotion or were they speaking about fundamentally different experiences? Even though contemporary historians such as Marc Ferro have identified the presence of resentment from Greek Antiquity up to the twenty-first-century terrorist attacks of radical Islam, can we argue that this experience has remained unchanged throughout history?[4] In other words, can we take the meaning of resentment for granted as it has always been understood under the same linguistic definition and had the same social appreciation in the past?

These were some of the concerns which originally inspired our project "On Resentment," launched in September, 2010 as an initiative put forward by the HIST-EX "Emotional Studies" research group (Centre for Human and Social Sciences, Madrid) in collaboration with the Institute for the History of Medicine and Health at the University of Geneva. The choice of this topic of research responds, on the one hand, to the multifaceted nature of our working group, which brings together more than eighteen researchers from the fields of cultural history, anthropology, history of science, philosophy, literature and sociology, as well as artists

---

[3] Adam Smith, *The Theory of Moral Sentiments* (Edinburgh: A. Millar, A. Kincaid and J. Bell, 1767), 127. It is also interesting to consult John Rawls, *A Theory of Justice* (Cambridge: Harvard University Press, 1971), 533, to see how resentment has been reintroduced in the modern theory of justice.

[4] Marc Ferro, *Resentment in History* (Cambridge: Polity Press, 2010).

from photography and cinema. In this respect, the project "On Resentment" provided us with a common field in which it was possible to encourage a dialogue expressing ideas from very different perspectives to explore the diverse representations through which this affective experience has been crystalized throughout history.

On the other hand, our interest in studying an emotion such as resentment comes from the fact that our individual research projects are mainly focused on the history of nineteenth- and twentieth-century emotional communities and, therefore, we were looking for an emotion which could help us to trace discontinuities between codes, norms and institutions that ruled ancient and modern societies. In our view, resentment was a good example of how affective experiences are not irremediably psychological, but rather how they have been shaped in particular cultural and social contexts such as the French Revolution, the Romantic Era, the Latin American independence movement or the World Wars.

Our starting point was, contrary to that supported by Ferro, to consider that resentment has a history which could be reconstructed by paying attention to the evolution of common patterns of feeling in a wide range of modern social currents, such as the nineteenth-century working class and women's liberation movements. In this way, our project "On Resentment" follows the main lines of the multidisciplinary programme of research, which has been called by some scholars "the History of Emotions."[5] This new way of understanding the emotional life of the past has gained increasing interest during the last three decades thanks to the publication of books exploring the history of particular emotions such as Peter N. Stearns' *Jealousy: the Evolution of an Emotion in American History* (1989), Patricia M. Spacks' *Boredom: the Literary History of a State of Mind* (1995), Barbara Rosenwein's *Anger Past* (1998), Joanna Bourke's *Fear: A Cultural History* (2005), Elena Pulcini's *Invidia: La passione triste* (2011) and Javier Moscoso's *Pain: A Cultural history* (2012).

The historical evolution of resentment can be perceived through a careful analysis of the changing meaning of the term used to describe this affective experience, which did not acquire a moral connotation until the second half of the eighteenth century, when it began to be understood as a sentiment rooted in a deep sense of injury that arises against the author of an injustice.[6] To write the history of resentment, however, also necessitates

---

[5] Jan Pampler, "The History of Emotions: An interview with William Reddy, Barbara Rosenwein and Peter Stearns," *History and Theory* 49 (2010): 237–265.

[6] David Hume, *An Enquiry into the Principles of Morals* (London: A. Millar, 1751).

an examination of the rise of a plethora of cultural expressions, revolutions and counter revolutions, which vindicated their preaching of equality as a form of hatred mixed with fear and indignation directed against an oppressor.[7] Therefore, we cannot understand the history of resentment as a mere invention of certain philosophers such as Friedrich Nietzsche or Max Scheler. If resentment became a major topic of cultural discussion in the nineteenth century, this was not because intellectuals cultivated its philosophical expression, but rather because certain cultural conditions promoted its emergence as a defining emotional feature of modern society. According to this, our initial hypothesis was to understand the history of resentment as being intimately linked to the transformations that occurred in late eighteenth-century societies following the impact of the French Revolution on world politics, a period that was marked by the promise of a merit-based society in which, for the first time, individuals were conceived as having the opportunity to fulfil their expectations under the same social conditions.

From this point of view, resentment appears not only as the exclusive property of women but of all individuals, groups and national communities that have defined their identity through the denunciation of their suffering and misery, and by the accusation of the aggressor that had transformed them into victims. Seen in this light, resentment flourishes among those "who are reduced to total powerlessness" in the context of what Hannah Arendt called a politics of pity assuming "different forms depending on the position within the structure of domination occupied by the groups which embody it."[8] However, this emotion may not only be considered as an attribute of the "unfortunate victims," as its influence has also been frequently exhibited by powerful figures in the history of politics. As the Spanish physician Gregorio Marañón suggested in his study of the life of Tiberius, resentment was a passion of the mind associated to those people who, despite attainment of considerable power, suffered from an inferiority complex. Thus, resentful people who became important political leaders such as Caesar Tiberius, used their power to unleash resentful elements of their cruel and violent personalities in conducting a type of personal revenge motivated by the humiliations that they had endured in their past. In these terms, resentment—observed Marañón—was produced by an

---

[7] For a recent history of indignation, see Anne Claude, Ambroise Rendu & Christian Delporte, *L'Indignation: histoire d'une émotion, XIXe–XXe siècle* (Paris: Nouveau Monde, 2008).

[8] Luc Boltanksi, *Distant Suffering: Morality, Media and Politics* (Cambridge University Press, 1999), 133; See also Hannah Arendt, *On Revolution* (New York: Viking Press, 1965).

accumulation of suffering that led to a "fermentation of feeling that breaks out, when it is least expected, in some arbitrary form of conduct."[9]

Here lies the intricate nature of this emotion—it acts in silence, as its expression is blocked by forces such as fear, anxiety and intimidation and, therefore, it should be depicted as a repressed reaction, which attempts to avoid direct confrontation with superiors, authority figures, as well as with sexual partners.[10] This aspect is exactly what distinguishes resentment from hate or effective anger—that frustration lies at the heart of the first, giving rise to strong feelings of bitterness. This characterisation of resentment as a repressed reaction explains why resentful people can neither act, nor forget, as the effects of this emotion become more virulent as time goes by.[11]

In contrast to other emotional experiences that have very often been described as synonymous with resentment, such as rancour, the former establishes an intimate relationship with temporality, as it needs to be constantly cultivated by memory. Unlike rancour, resentment implies the renewal of the original suffering which is caused by the traumatic event. It even modifies our perception of time as it chains us to a permanent past; a past full of dark memories that prevent us from living in the present and looking with hope towards the future. The only future that can be imagined in the context of resentment is one that is brought into being by the obsessive desire of revenge oriented towards the destruction of all persons, communities and systems that are considered potential enemies. Furthermore, the persistent sense of hostility involved in resentment seems to respond to a cyclical pattern, which defines this emotion in clinical terms together with other pathological symptoms such as anxiety, depression and, notably, embitterment.[12] This aspect of resentment, which emphasises the obsessive repetition of past memories, was reinforced by

---

[9] Gregorio Marañón, *Tiberius: A Study in Resentment* (London: Hollis and Carter, 1956), 8.
[10] Robert C. Solomon, *The Passions: Emotions and the Meaning of Life* (Indianapolis: Hackett Publishing, 1976), 291.
[11] Michael André Bernstein, *Bitter Carnival and the Abject Hero* (Princeton University Press, 1992), 108.
[12] Among the notable studies conducted in contemporary psychiatry and psychology, which reveal the presence of negative emotions such as resentment in personality disorders, is Michael Linden, *Embitterment: Societal, Psychological and, Clinical Perspectives* (New York : Springer, 2011) and A. Fossati, E. S. Barrat, I. Carreta, B. Leonardi, F. Graziolli & C. Maffei, "Predicting Borderline and Antisocial Personality Disorder features in Non-Clinical Subjects using Measures of Impulsivity and Aggressiveness," *Psychiatry Research* 125 (2) (2004): 161–170.

means of the popularisation of the French term *ressentiment* in nineteenth-century European literature and, notably, in the German language, which introduced a stronger connotation with memory and a peculiar nuance of lingering hate in comparison with its English counterpart, along with other German words such as *Groll*, meaning grudge, or *Schadenfreude* that means joy at the suffering of others.

As various studies have shown, this French word was widely used by the German élite at least from the eighteenth century, probably as a result of the impact of the French Enlightenment movement on the intellectual Prussian milieu.[13] However, it is not until the early nineteenth century that we can start to perceive how resentment became a central concern in science as well as in aesthetics. On the one hand, the medical expression of resentment was extensively studied by anatomical and psychological models such as Franz Joseph Gall's phrenology, a scientific movement that explained human behaviour according to the different forms of the skull, as well as by means of an identification of each part of the brain with a moral disposition. Some supporters of Gall's theory such as the Scottish George Combe interpreted resentment as a basic reaction to violence, which was present not only in the human but also in the whole of the animal realm. From this perspective, this passion was understood as a type of self-defence, "the result of wounded Self-esteem, aided by destructiveness."[14]

On the other hand, resentment would become a central topic in early nineteenth-century Romantic aesthetics as is shown by the work of poets such as John Keats (1795–1821) and Heinrich Heine (1797–1856) or writers such as René François de Chateaubriand (1768–1848), who appealed to this expression to describe their inner experiences, which were profoundly embedded with envy, pride and malignity against the political model of civilisation that had been introduced during the French Revolution, and that was later imposed all over Europe with the rise of the

---

[13] See Kurt Kepler, "Problems of German-English Dictionary Making," *The Modern Language Journal* 41 (1) (1957): 26–29; Rüdiger Bittner, "Ressentiment," in *Nietzsche, Genealogy, Morality: Essays on Nietzsche's Genealogy of Morals*, edited by Richard Sacht (Berkley and Los Angeles, California: University of California Press, 1994). According to *Littré*'s dictionary the prefix "re" included in *ressentiment* originally functioned only as an intensifier rather than a word, which attempted to depict repetition. Before the eighteenth century in, for example, Francois de la Rouchefoucauld, "Lettre à Mme. Sablé," in *Maximes, suivies des Réflexions diverses, du Portrait de La Rochefoucauld par lui-même, et des Remarques de Christine de Suède sur les Maximes* (Paris: Garnier, 1967) 558; the term *ressentiment* appears as a synonym of "*a sentiment de reconnaissance.*"

[14] Georges Combe, *Essays on Phrenology* (Edinburgh: John Anderson, 1830), 170.

Napoleonic Wars.[15] In this respect, Thomas Pfau has recently observed that *ressentiment* always appeared to be related to melancholy in the context of European Romantic culture, as both emotions:

> arise from a deeply felt alienation and aversion to the emergent hegemony of the nation—an imagined community of middle class, professionally trained, gentile subjects—justifying and reinforcing its specious coherence by worshipping the image of a national literature.

Melancholy cannot be imagined without a careful cultivation of painful *ressentiment*, which was not only the mirror through which the romantic projected their aversion against the contemporary world—as past times were always better—but also "the veritable affective signature of the 19th century German culture after Waterloo."[16]

Even before Nietzsche spread the French word *ressentiment* as a *terminus technicus* in his philosophy, Soren Kierkegaard had pointed out this emotion as a key concept for explaining the dynamics of culture. As he explained in *The Present Age* (1846), his own time was marked by the rise of a particular envy, which he termed *ressentiment*, a social phenomenon that generally happens when people consider themselves as equals and thereby mediocrity becomes the criteria for measuring individuals' achievements. For Kierkegaard, the best cultural expression of *ressentiment* was a "passionless, sedentary, reflective age" dominated by "envy and abstract thought" in which all creativity was stifled.[17] In Kierkegard's work, as would also be the case in Nietzsche and Scheler's further philosophy, the notion of *ressentiment* seems not only to have introduced a peculiar connotation of malice in its meaning, but also a fundamentally different conception to the eighteenth-century Scottish definition of this social passion in politics. From the nineteenth-century perspective, resentment lost its significance as a central social passion linked with justice, which is implanted in human nature for "salutary purposes" to evolve into an expression of the bad conscience of certain individuals and groups who turned their inner suffering into a strategy of revenge.[18] What differs between these two representations is the development of a suspicion about the morality of pity which began to be understood as a

---

[15] Nicholas Roe, *Keats and History* (Cambridge: Cambridge University Press, 1995).

[16] Thomas Pfau, *Romantic Moods: Paranoia, Trauma, and Melancholy, 1790–1840* (Baltimore: John Hopkins University Press, 2005), 26.

[17] Soren Kierkegaard, *The Age of Revolution and the Present Age. A Literary Review* (London: Oxford University Press, 1970), 23–4.

[18] Hume, *An Enquiry into the Principles of Morals*, 264.

mere expression of resentment. Thus, the transformation of resentment into *ressentiment* showed not only that this emotion should be understood in connection to the rise of the egalitarian ideology but also as a symptom of abnormal behaviour closely linked with psychological and psychiatric troubles of the modern self.

As Nietzsche explained in *The Genealogy of Morals* (1887), *ressentiment* was a dark passion caused by affects such as "anger, pathological vulnerability and impotent lust for revenge," which revealed not only a sign of weakness in certain individuals, but moreover the moral disease of Western culture—Nihilism. Like a kind of physician, he provides in his biographical essay *Ecce Homo* (1908) a detailed description about how the physiological mechanism of this emotion worked. It was equally traditionally associated with stomach problems as resentment was, according to Ancient Greek medicine, included in the group of choleric emotions such as anger, frustration and envy, controlled by the gall bladder.

> Nothing burns one up faster than the affects of *ressentiment* … no reaction could be more disadvantageous for the exhausted; such affects involve a rapid consumption of nervous energy, a pathological increase of harmful excretions—for example the gall bladder into the stomach.[19]

Following the genealogical method, Nietzsche portrayed the psychological type of the man who harbours *ressentiment* as embodying the mental attitude of the weak and powerless—the *schelechtwegekommene*—against their more fortunate fellow men, their aristocratic masters.[20] As slaves cannot revolt against noble men openly, they try to discredit them and their achievements, leading to a falsification of all genuine sensations and compensating "themselves with an imaginary revenge," which gave birth to values such as God and the Devil.[21] In this sense, the slave revolt began when *ressentiment* became creative and established its own code of morality, which is particularly represented in Christian morality, as a vengeance upon aristocratic masters. However, not only are Christians

---

[19] Friedrich Nietzsche, *Ecce homo*, in *Basic Writings of Nietzsche*, edited by Peter Gay & Walter Kaufmann (New York: The Modern Library, 2000), 686.

[20] Nietzsche described the man of *ressentiment* in *The Genealogy of Morals* as follows: "While the noble man lives in trust and openness with himself, the man of *ressentiment* is neither upright, nor naïve, nor honest with himself … His spirit loves hiding places, secret paths and back doors; everything covert entices him as his world, his security, his refreshment, he understands how to keep silent, how to not forget, how to wait, how to be provisionally self-deprecating and humble."

[21] Nietzsche, *The Genealogy of Morals*, 472.

included in Nietzsche's list of resentful people, but also all personalities "watching for danger and advantage everywhere" such as Anarchists, Anti-Semites and intellectuals, who are the most brilliant practitioners of literary and philosophical *ressentiment* as the conceptual systems that they have elevated only reveal their evil motivation and revenge against the instinct of preserving life.[22]

While for Nietzsche *ressentiment* was definitively a pathological disposition, associated with a particular psychological type, Max Scheler would understand its emergence as a typical modern phenomenon "accumulated by the very structure of society," which is largely independent of the individual temperament. For Scheler, this kind of existential envy particularly appeared in modern democratic societies "where equal rights or former social equality go hand in hand with wide factual differences in power, property and education."[23] Although Scheler was not directly focused on the historical genealogy of this emotion in his 1915 investigation *Das Ressentiment im Aufbau der Moralen* with the historical, he pointed out how the core of Christian ethics has not grown on resentment, but rather that of "bourgeois morality, which gradually replaced Christian morality" from the thirteenth century onwards, and "culminated in the French Revolution" demanding supreme rights of the majority of civil society.[24]

The sociological groups subject to resentful feelings included women, the industrial proletariat, but also the disappearing class of artisans belonging to the petty bourgeoisie. All these groups cultivated a kind of romantic nostalgia towards the past. Scheler concluded by explaining *ressentiment* as a particular emotional attitude that describes the sociological type of "the common man," who felt a profound insecurity and weakness as a permanent condition of their existence, being constantly divided between their object of desire and themself.[25] As the sociologist René Girard would observe in his mimetic theory, resentment is anthropologically inscribed in our subjective identity as a result of the dynamics of desire that rule our modern societies. Thus, from a Girardian point of view, our desire to be other than we are is always at the heart of this particular suffering.[26]

---

[22] Robert C. Solomon, *The Passions*, 291.

[23] Max Scheler, *Ressentiment* (Milwaukee: Marquette University Press, 1994), 28. See also Jack M. Barbalet, *Emotion, Social Theory and Social Structure: A Macrosociological Approach* (Cambridge: Cambridge University Press, 1998).

[24] Scheler, 53.

[25] Scheler, 23.

[26] René Girard, *Il risentimento* (Milan: Raffaello Cortina, 1999).

This preliminary overview does not expect to be an exhaustive account of what has been written about resentment, but rather to shed light on its most important transformations since the second half of the eighteenth century up to contemporary society. In a broader sense, these changes in the representation of resentment, that should be considered fundamental moments in order in writing its history, also reveal the main cultural changes which have shaped our modern society, such as the belief that all individuals are equal and, therefore, they have the same right to education and job opportunities. Drawing on these considerations, the following contributions attempt to explore discontinuities and continuities in the history of resentment, providing new perspectives to Emotion Studies coming from the history of art, photography, war and culture studies and, even, the history of science. As will be shown throughout this collection of essays, resentment has not only inspired philosophical treatises, but also paintings, photographs depicting the brutalisation of the enemy during the Great War, the modernisation of chemical industry during World War I, novels such as Samuel Richardson's *Clarissa*, and nineteenth-century women's manifestos that claimed resentment as way of emancipation. Resentment is not only introduced as a polyhedric experience, but it will also be elucidated throughout this volume with the help of recent analytical tools provided by historians of emotions such as "emotional communities" or "emotional styles" to make the particular cultural and social conditions which prompted its emergence visible.

The first section of the present volume, which we have entitled "How to Write the History of Resentment," brings together various contributions aimed at examining the changing representation of resentment and its French relative *ressentiment* in eighteenth- and nineteenth-century Western societies. In the first chapter, Javier Moscoso addresses the question of the material expression of resentment, according to the "social passion" definition proposed by Adam Smith, which was communicated to our fellow man by our natural sympathy. Following the eighteenth-century Scottish moral tradition, Moscoso interprets the famous painting of Théodore Géricault, *Le radeau de la Méduse* (1818), as embodying the subjective experience of political and moral resentment. As he argues, Géricault's work does not attempt to enhance the viewer's approval towards the figure of the "benefactor," but rather to suggest sympathy with the hatred of the victims towards the perpetrators of their misfortune, and thereby aims at showing resentment rather than compassion, as it involves an implicit accusation and a craving for justice.

In chapter two, Yamina Oudai Celso proposes a reflection about Friedrich Nietzsche's *ressentiment* in order to explore the nineteenth-century cultural forces that nourished his moral interpretation. However, Celso interprets Nietzsche's *ressentiment* not as a mere philosophical concept that can help us to understand the origins of Western morality, but rather as a "symbolic language of emotions" that requires philosophical, psychological and even medical knowledge in order to be explained. In turn, the third chapter, written by Patrick Lang, sheds light on the role of *ressentiment* within the entire work of the phenomenologist Max Scheler. A comparative analysis between *Das Ressentiment im Aufbau der Moralen* (1912) and *Der Geist und die ideellen Grundlagen der Demokratien der großen Nationen* (1916), led to him to conclude that this emotion was not only understood as a consequence of social inequalities, but equally as a specific combination of inequality and equality, linked to the unawareness of the hierarchy of values.

As the title of the second section suggests, "Gendered Resentment" deals with the representation of this emotion both as a way of expressing female opposition to male authority, as well as the male response when the patriarchal model encountered historical contestation. On the one hand, Lina Minou's contribution seeks to demonstrate how resentment underwent a change within an eighteenth-century British context by means of conducting an investigation into its embodiment within the female protagonists of the sentimental literary tradition. Whilst in seventeenth-century English literature, resentment appears to be associated with the experience of having a true feeling, in eighteenth-century literature it can be associated to a more empathic view, tied to injury. Drawing on the ethical discourse on anger of that time, Minou deduced that current expressions associated with resentment such as "to take ill" or "stifling one's resentment" involved intricate considerations about women's topics such as decorum, virtue, honour or social status.

On the other hand, Susanna Ferlito proposes the examination of the question of gendered resentment in "Responding to Injury—on the Shadow Economy of Female Resentment" as expressed in the writings of one of Italy's most devoted Risorgimento patriots: Cristina di Belgiojoso (1807–1871). This case of female theorising and aesthetic channelling of resentment addresses the question of how nineteenth-century women strove to be heard in their expression of strong feelings of social and sexual injustice without being dismissed as overly emotional. Finally, Elise Dermineur's contribution deals with the understanding of what she calls "gender resentment," a social mechanism, which she identifies in eighteenth-century rural France, which was a result of men's feeling of inferiority towards women. In this case, resentment mirrored the increasing economic power of women in rural areas, such as those located in the South of Alsace. As these women became gradually more involved in economic activities, a reaction toward this breach in the patriarchal system followed, which is reconstructed by means of a detailed analysis of local judicial records that inform the reader about the prevailing emotions ruling in these rural communities from 1680 to 1789.

The third section of the book, which we have entitled "Look Back in Anger," inspired by John Osborne's play, addresses the issue of resentment as a particular form of hostility directed at the person identified as the cause of one's frustration in the context of interpersonal relationships, which includes those created in a medical as much as in a political context. Pilar León Sanz's essay explores the pathological dimension of resentment in the so-called school of psychosomatic medicine, as it was developed in the United States between 1930 and 1960. From this clinical perspective, resentment appeared as a central emotional aspect together with deception and seduction in the therapeutic relation established between physician and patient. It was also seen as one of the features defining psychosomatic diseases.

As Juan Manuel Zaragoza-Bernal argues in the following chapter, resentment frequently arose in intimate relationships and, particularly, when one of the members of a couple suffers from a chronic disease and the other becomes a caregiver. Drawing on the case of Arthur Conan Doyle's biography, Zaragoza-Bernal demonstrates to what extent resentment shapes not only the experience of disease, but furthermore the creation of the social identity of both the caregiver and the sick. This section, based around stories of resentment, is completed with Joseph Maslen's contribution in which he proposes parallels between the history of emotions and the political biography of Margaret Thatcher, Conservative Prime Minister of the United Kingdom from 1979 to 1990. Thus, he approaches Thatcher's biography considering that she was a victim of shaming practices earlier in her career, and how those experiences were related to resentment between social classes. Maslen concludes by pointing out how the dynamics of resentment describe perfectly not only Thatcher's life and her relationship with British political culture, but moreover the emotional politics of class in contemporary British history.

The fourth section "Coming into Conflict: Resentment, Wars and Revolutions" brings together a series of exciting contributions focused on analysing how this affective experience has worked as a cohesive element unifying the masses against a common enemy in the history of modern warfare. Following this approach, Manuel Lucena's essay explores some of the ways in which this emotion was a slogan that was vindicated in the age of Atlantic revolutions, from the independence of the United States in 1776 to the French Revolution in 1789, the Haitian Revolution and the foundation of the first black republic of the world in 1804, and the independence of Portuguese and Spanish America in 1824. Lucena explains that resentment was used by the Creole elites to justify their rebellion against the kings and the monarchies and, furthermore, how it also served mixed races, free blacks, slaves and poor whites to convey their political aspirations for social changes.

Taking the relationship between war and emotions as starting point, Javier Ordóñez attempts to analyse the role played by resentment in modern warfare in his study. With this aim in mind, he suggests interpreting the emotional background of WWI through analogy to the production of synthetic components by the modern chemical industry, an hypothesis that led him to understanding the creation of a modern type of hatred in relation to the scientific concept of *Ersatz*. Ordóñez views the emotional chemistry produced during World War I as being intended as a way of unifying the different societies in conflict. By replacing natural emotions for "synthetic" ones, the continuity of the conflict could be ensured. Finally, in her essay, Beatriz Pichel examines other aspects of the Great War from the point of view of visual culture studies—how resentment became a powerful tool for constructing national propaganda in France. As Pichel explains, resentment was portrayed in the French press as the feeling that justified the fight against the German population, achieved through the production of a particular type of photograph that portrayed German prisoners, as well as crimes such as the destruction of churches.

The last section, "Resentment and Collective Identities," stresses how resentment has been a powerful force in the creation of social and national identities, as in the case of the twentieth-century working class, or in the definition of international political relationships such as those maintained between Lebanon and Syria. Firstly, Stefano Tomelleri proposes approaching the question of resentment by discussing classical and contemporary views in sociological theory to set out his own interpretation of this emotion according to the main cultural transformations of modernity. For Tomelleri, resentment should be conceived as a relational form, crystallised in concrete historical processes such as the crisis of the hierarchy, the individualization of social manoeuvring and the liberalisation of desire.

In the following chapter, María Garrido emphasises the relevance of emotions such as resentment, shame and indignation in contemporary sociological and political research, stressing that they are not solely processes controlled by rational decisions. From the point of view of the theories of recognition, Garrido seeks to comprehend the emotional experience of the twentieth-century working class as a way of restoring the dignity of those who suffer by means of transforming their individual experiences into a collective reality. In the final essay of this volume, Elisabeth Meur looks at emotions as being at the heart of world politics. The imbalanced structure of the international system can generate anger, feelings of unfairness, frustration, envy and also resentment. By relying on emotion regulation theory and the concept of coping, Meur examines the Lebanese-Syrian relationship as a case study, which reveals how resentment can be understood as a mechanism that prevents violent conflicts in the context of international politics.

The majority of the contributions included in this volume were originally presented at the International Workshop "On Resentment," which the took place at the *Louis Jeantet Auditorium* (Geneva), October 26–28, 2011 thanks to the financial support of the Swiss National Foundation. The celebration of this workshop organised by the Institute of Philosophy of The Spanish Scientific Council (Madrid) in partnership with the Institute for the History of Medicine and Health based at the University of Geneva, provided us the opportunity of discussing our initial hypothesis on the history of resentment, as well as our ideas about the future of the history of emotions with other scholars from around the world. Since the celebration of this workshop, we are delighted to see a growing fascination towards the elucidation of this complex emotional experience and its multiple psychological, cultural and social expressions as shown by the celebration of the Symposium "Resentment's Conflicts," organised by the Department of Spanish, Italian and Portuguese at the University of Illinois at Urbana-Champagne and the recent publication coordinated by Antoine Grandjean and Florent Guénard at the University of Nantes.[27]

The present book is the fruit of our particular way of understanding the History of Emotions not only as an intellectual but also a moral and political exercise, which is moved by the firm belief that to elucidate the changes perceived in the representation of resentment means to also shed light on embodied cultural transformations, which are crucial to understanding our contemporary world. Even though the present book attempts to write the history of resentment as a modern phenomenon;, further work is needed to carry out a comparative study between this emotion and other affective experiences, such as Aristotelian anger or the concept of *nemesis*.[28] We hope that this book can contribute to what

---

[27] Antoine Grandjean, Florent Guénard, *Le ressentiment, passion sociale* (Rennes: Presses Universitaires de Rennes, 2012).

[28] Susanna Braund, Glenn W. Most, *Ancient Anger: Perspectives from Homer to Galen,* (Cambridge. Cambridge University Press, 2003).

Nietzsche conceived as a history of the human passions, oriented towards showing how our past philosophical treatises, judicial records, artistic creations and moral systems are only cultural expressions of our most intimate affects.

Dolores Martín Moruno
Geneva, December 17, 2012.

Works Cited

Arendt, Hannah. *On Revolution*. New York: Viking Press, 1965.

Barbalet, Jack M. *Emotion. Social Theory, and Social Structure: A Macrosociological Approach*. Cambridge: Cambridge University Press, 1998.

Bernstein, Michael André. *Bitter Carnival and the Abject Hero*. Princenton: Princenton University Press, 1992.

Boltanski, Luc. *Distant Suffering: Morality, Media and Politics*. Cambridge: Cambridge University Press, 1999.

Bourke, Joanna. *Fear: A Cultural History*. London: Virago, 2005.

Braund, Susanna & Glenn W. Most. *Ancient Anger: Perspectives from Homer to Galen*. Cambridge: Cambridge University Press, 2003.

Claude, Anne, Rendu, Ambroise & Delporte, Christian. *L'indignation: histoire d'une emotion, XIXe–XXe siècle*. Paris: Nouveau Monde, 2008.

Combe, Georges. *Essays on Phrenology*. Edinburgh : For John Anderson, 1830.

Ferro, Marc. *Resentment in History*. Cambridge: Polity Press, 2010.

Fossati, A., E. S. Barrat, I. Carreta, B. Leonardi, F. Grazioli & C. Maffei. "Predicting Borderline and Antisocial Personality Disorders Features in Non-Clinical Subjects using Measures of Impulsivity and Aggressiveness." *Psychiatry Research* 125 (2) (2004): 161–170.

Girard, René. *Il risentimento*. Milan: Raffaelo Cortina, 1999.

Grandjean, Antoine & Florent Guénard. *Ressentiment, une passion sociale*. Rennes : Presses Universitaires de Nantes, 2012.

Hume, David. *An Enquiry into the Principles of Morals*. London: for A. Millar, 1751.

Kepler, Kurt. "Problems of German-English Dictionary Making." *The Modern Language Journal* 41 (1) (1957): 26–29.

Kierkegaard, Soren. *The Present Age and Two Minor Ethico-Religious Treatises*. Oxford: Oxford University Press, 1940.

La Rouchefoucauld, François. *Maximes, Suivies des Réflexions Diverses, du Portrait de La Rochefoucauld par lui-même, et des Remarques de Christine de Suède sur les Maximes.* Paris: Garnier, 1967.

Linden, Michael. *Embitterment: Societal, Psychological, and Clinical Perspectives.* New York: Springer, 2011.

Marañón, Gregorio. *Tiberius: A Study in Resentment.* London: Hollis and Carter, 1956.

Moscoso, Javier. *Pain: A Cultural History.* Basingstoke: Palgrave Macmillan, 2012.

Nietzsche, Friedrich. *Basic Writings of Nietzsche.* New York: The Modern Library, 2000.

Pampler, Jan. "The History of Emotions: An interview with William reddy, Barbara Rosenwein and Peter Stearns." *History and Theory* 49 (2010): 237–265.

Pfau, Thomas. *Romantic Moods: Paranoia, Trauma, and Melancholy. 1790–1840.* Baltimore: John Hopkings University Press, 2005.

Pulcini, Elena. *Invidia: La passione triste.* Bologna: Il Mulino, 2011.

Rosenwein, Barbara. *Anger's Past: The Social Uses of an Emotion in the Middle Ages.* Ithaca and London: Cornell University Press, 1998.

—. "Worrying about Emotions in History." *The American Historical Review*, http://historycooperative.rg/journals/ahr/107.3/ah0302000821. html (accessed June 13, 2012).

Rawls, John. *A Theory of Justice.* Cambridge Mass.: Harvard University Press, 1971.

Roe, Nicholas. *Keats and History.* Cambridge: Cambridge University Press, 1995.

Sachts, Richard. *Nietzsche, Genealogy, Morality: Essays on Nietzsche's Genealogy of Morals.* Berkley and Los Angeles: University of California Press, 1994.

Scheler, Max. *Ressentiment.* Milwaukee: Marquette University Press, 1994.

Smith, Adam. *The Theory of Moral Sentiments.* Edinburgh: A. Millar, A. Kincaid and J. Bell, 1767.

Solomon, Robert C. *The Passions: Emotions and the Meaning of Life.* Indianapolis: Hackett Publishing, 1976.

Spacks, Patricia M. *Boredom: the Literary History of a State of Mind.* Chicago: The University of Chicago Press, 1996.

Stearns, Peter N. *Jealousy: the Evolution of an Emotion in American History.* New York: New York University Press, 1989.

Woolf, Virginia. *A Room of One's Own.* Oxford: Oxford University Press, 1998.

PART I:

HOW TO WRITE THE HISTORY OF RESENTMENT

CHAPTER ONE

THE SHADOWS OF OURSELVES: RESENTMENT, MONOMANIA AND MODERNITY

JAVIER MOSCOSO

Introduction[1]

Resentment is not an easy word. Neither is it an easy reality. On the contrary, its meaning is fuzzy and its referent unclear. In the most important repository of the emotions of antiquity, Aristotle's *Rhetoric*, there is no mention of any feeling or affection that, one way or another, would resemble what we mean by this term today.[2] On the other hand, our contemporary understanding of the word very often refers to nothing more than residual and lasting hatred. The *Oxford English Dictionary* defines the word as "a sense of grievance; an indignant sense of injury or insult received or perceived, a feeling of ill will, bitterness or anger against a person or a thing." The *Dictionary of the Spanish Academy* (DRAE) does not even consider within its semantic field any moral of affective sense.

---

[1] This chapter has been undertaken under the research project "Historical Epistemology: History of Emotions in the Nineteenth and Twentieth Centuries," funded by the Spanish MICINN FFI2010-20876.
[2] David Konstan, "Ressentiment ancien et ressentiment moderne," in *Le ressentiment*, ed. Pierre Ansart (Brussels: Bruylant, 2002) 259–76. On the historicity of emotions, see also David J. Konstan: "Y-a-t'il une histoire des émotions?" *ASDIWAL: Revue Genevois d'Anthropologie et d'Histoire des Religions* 1 (2006): 23–35; revised and expanded version under the title "Haben Gefühle eine Geschichte?" (trans. Regina Höschele), in *Pathos Affekt Emotion. Transformationen der Antike*, eds. Martin Harbsmeier, Naomi Kubota & Sebastian Möckel (Frankfurt a. M.: Suhrkamp, 2009), 27–46; revised French version in *Mythes, rites et emotions*, ed. Philippe Borgeaud (Geneva: Librairie Droz 2009), 15–28.

On the contrary, it equates its signification with a pain or ailment that does not simply go away.[3]

In this chapter, I do not mean to enquire into the semantic variations of this word, but to face and comment on the changing reality of this moral and political passion. In the next few pages, I will attempt to draw some connections between the cultural history of emotions and the political history of psychiatry. Resentment, on the one hand, and monomania, on the other, will serve to explore the cultural forms of modern subjectivity, the conditions that make both the salience of a particular mental disorder and the intellectual reflection on a highly sophisticated social passion possible. I will argue that resentment and monomania came about in the same cultural and political space and that, in a sense that should become clear later, neither could have developed without the presence of the other. I will focus on a famous artist and an even more famous painting to illustrate this. However, before I get into the details, a few methodological clarifications are in order. In the first place, it might be wise to mention that my approach does not share the tenants and assumptions of the seminal work of Marc Ferro.[4] Unlike this French historian, who defended resentment as a key and constant element in the revolutionary processes of any type and any period, from Antiquity to contemporary societies, I consider resentment as a passion of modernity, whose first systematic treatment was provided by Adam Smith in the mid-eighteenth century, and whose birth depended on highly embedded social roots. Of course, we may find here and there emotional reactions that, one way or another, resemble the basic features of modern resentment. Historians are fully aware of these of continuities or discontinuities within the cultural history of emotions.[5] Resentment, however, is not a universal emotion, but a highly intellectual passion linked to the denial of fortune as a form of retribution, to the promise of an equalitarian and meritocratic society and to the democratization of mental illnesses.[6]

With regard to the history of monomania, I do share some assumptions with the recent and not so recent readings in the social and cultural history of mental disorders. The works of Jean Goldstein, Marcel Gauchet and

---

[3] The Spanish *Diccionario de Autoridades*, in volumen III, published in 1737, defines "Resentimiento" as "la muestra o seña de sentirse o quebrantarse alguna cosa."

[4] Marc Ferro, *Resentment in History* (Malden: Polity Press, 2010).

[5] See, for example, Ute Frevert, *Emotions in History. Lost and Found* (Central European University Press, 2011).

[6] On this last point, see Lennard J. Davis, *Obsession* (Chicago and London: The University of Chicago Press, 2008).

Gladys Swain have confronted some of the connections between mental illness, subjectivity and modernity.[7] More recently, Laure Murat, in the *L'homme qui se prenait pour Napoléon*, has also drawn interesting suggestions regarding the political history of monomania before and after the events of the French Revolution.[8] My approach, however, also differs from theirs in that my reading is primarily concerned with the relation between distorted experiences and inflated passions. I am not so much interested here in the layers of the modern identity, as Goldstein was, or in the romantic bio-politics of the self, as Gauchet and Swain proposed, following Foucault. I intend to shed some light on the historicity of human experiences and, in particular, on the salience of moral and political resentment. This "historical epistemology of experience," as I would like to call it, following the work of Lorraine Daston, Ian Hacking or Arnold Davidson, will lead me to suggest, in the case of resentment, a few cognitive and cultural conditions that made its formulation and inclusion within a theoretical framework possible.[9]

I would argue that the formation of the resentful consciousness rested on two different social and epistemic virtues. First of all, resentment took place within the dramatic setting of modern theatricality. It demanded not just the presence of victims and offenders, but also the attentive eye of an "emancipated spectator," a figuration very similar to what the philosopher Adam Smith referred to as simply "the spectator," the "bystander" or the "witness."[10] These witnesses shared with the victims their thirst for vengeance and their desire for justice. Without being the most affected persons, they

---

[7] Jan Goldstein, *Console and Classify: The French Psychiatric Profession in the Nineteenth Century* (New York: Cambridge University Press, 1987); J. Goldstein, *The Post-revolutionary Self* (Cambridge, Mass.: Harvard University Press, 2005); Marcel Gauchet & Gladys Swain, *Madness and Democracy. The Modern Psychiatric Universe* (Princeton: Princeton University Press, 1999).

[8] Laure Murat, *L'Homme qui se prenait pour Napoléon. Pour une histoire politique de la folie* (Paris: Gallimard, 2011).

[9] Lorraine Daston, *Biographies of Scientific Objects*, Chicago y Londres (Chicago: Chicago University Press, 2000); Ian Hacking, *Historical Ontology* (Cambridge, Mass.: Harvard University Press, 2002); Arnold Davidson, *The Emergence of Sexuality. Historical Epistemology and the Formation of Concepts* (Cambridge, Mass.: Harvard University Press, 2001). For a more recent approach, see Javier Moscoso, *Pain: A Cultural History* (London: Palgrave-Macmillan, 2012).

[10] All references to Adam Smith are taken from his *The Theory of Moral Sentiments*, eds. Raphael y A. L. Macfie (Indianapolis: Liberty Fund, 1982). On Smith, see Fonna Forman-Barzilai: "Sympathy in Space(s). Adam Smith on Proximity," *Political Theory* 33 (2005): 189–217, 192. For a more contemporary account, see Jacques Rancière, *The Emancipated Spectator* (London: Verso, 2011).

assumed as their own the circumstances and disgrace of others; they sympathized with the bitterness of others. This is the reason why re-sentiment was not truly a sentiment, but a re-sentiment, made from the remains, emotions, shadows or shades of others.

In the second place, resentment came about as a consequence of the new correlation in the distribution of merit; a quality fully shared with the outburst of monomania, and in particular with the monomania of ambition. Far from being a low passion of the heart it was regarded as a high perception of the mind and, in particular, of the imagination. Its emotional qualities came about as the cultural expression of social inequality and implied the political denial of fortune to explain and justify social differences. The presence of this passion called into question the merits of those who enjoyed a privileged situation. Their position was very often regarded as a consequence of usurpation or corruption. To resentful eyes, the status and the honours of many others were not the result of their own deeds, but the corollary of a succession of social manoeuvres that turned them into vulgar usurpers.

The economy of modern resentment is built on a *tableau vivant* which, denying the upheavals of the medieval and early modern fortune, takes the stand to show neither compassion nor hatred but a third inter-subjective value: denunciation. This is one of the meanings that, in fact, the *Oxford English Dictionary* confers to the word: "an act of feeling or perceiving something," very close to the similar word "discernment," in the sense of appreciation or understanding of something. Adam Smith called this kind of discernment "imaginary resentment." For the Scottish philosopher, as for many other defenders of empathetic agreements, our feelings of compassion, impotence, indignation, shame or lewdness always were, first of all, generated from vicarious emotions. When seeing the criminal in the dock, he argued, we "place ourselves in his situation, conceive ourselves enduring all the same torments, we enter, as it were, into his body, and become in some measure the same person with him."[11] This quality of the imagination was in use, of course, during the punitive procedures of the Ancien Régime, and therefore during its rituals of retribution, but it equally applied to the contemplation of the misfortunes and tragedies of other victims, not necessarily guilty; victims whose lives had been lost, for example, as a consequence of an event that, like a shipwreck, could no longer be regarded as a natural disaster, but as the result of mischievous and malignant actions.

---

[11] Adam Smith, *Theory of Moral Sentiments*, 9. See also Norman S. Fiering: "Irresistible compassion: An aspect of eighteenth century sympathy and humanitarianism," *Journal of the History of Ideas* 37 (1976): 200–202.

It is precisely the representation of a shipwreck that I will use here as an exemplification of the material expression of moral and political resentment. Discredited in Nietzsche's genealogy, misrepresented very often by close emotions —like rage, hatred, or envy— this emotional perception has lost part of its political and moral value. For Adam Smith, however, resentment was a natural reaction, a kind of sympathy that we, the witnesses, showed not so much towards the victim, but towards the hatred that victims professed toward their enemies: "In the same manner, as we sympathize with the sorrow of our fellow-creature whenever we see his distress, so we likewise enter into his abhorrence and aversion for whatever has given occasion to it"; or more specifically: "If the injured should perish [in the quarrel], we not only sympathize with the real resentment of his friends and relations, but with the imaginary resentment which in fancy we lend to the dead, who is no longer capable of feeling that or any other human sentiment."[12] From this perspective, resentment will not simply be linked to feelings or emotions traditionally considered negative, as envy or meanness, but to some others like solidarity, empathy or objectivity; that is to say, linked to other emotional and cognitive attitudes that reflect a political and ideological commitment.

To clarify this point, I will examine the work of the French painter Thédore Géricault and in particular his *Radeau de La Méduse* (*The Raft of the Medusa*), an oil painting produced in 1818 and exhibited for the first time in the Salon of the same year in Paris. This extraordinary painting focuses on the distant eye of the spectator who, rather than commiserate in front of the other's disgrace, or forget their outrageous fortune, holds an attentive gaze and forces us to look at the crudest and most discarnate result of appalling behaviour. In this case, as in others referred to later, resentment is not simply a feeling, but a perception, a moral reaction caused by a sort of suffering triggered by a disproportion between realities and expectations or, in particular, the harm of broken promises.

The Shipwreck

The French frigate *La Méduse* departured towards the coast of Senegal on June 18, 1816. Along with the members of the Colonial Government and the main employees of this French protectorate, the vessel transported around four hundred people between officials, seamanship and other passengers.[13] On July 2, it began to collapse and, after five days of intense

---

[12] Adam Smith, *Theory of Moral Sentiments*, 70.
[13] See Jonathan Miles, *The Wreck of the Medusa. The Most Famous Sea Disaster of the Nineteenth Century* (New York: Grove Press, 2007).

work to keep it afloat, it was finally abandoned. Without enough boats to evacuate the crew and the passengers, almost one hundred and fifty people were set adrift on a raft. Although the initial idea was that the rescue boats drag the raft, the captain, who had given his word to bring the passengers to firm land, gave orders to cut the ties, leaving the raft in the open sea. Thirteen days later, the *Argus* rescued fifteen survivors, among them Jean-Baptiste-Henri Savigny, a surgeon who in 1818 published his *Observations on the Effects that Hunger and Thirst had Produced on La Méduse after its Shipwreck.*[14] This text explained in great detail how those one hundred and fifty men were abandoned with twenty five pounds of bread, wet from seawater, and a few barrels of wine. The situation was so dramatic that on the first night twelve of them disappeared. On the second day, as a consequence of the strong swell, another sixty-three people died, many killed at the hands of their own fellows. On the fourth day some of the survivors began to devour the cadavers of the corpses trapped on the raft. Though Géricault was certainly impressed by this outburst of cannibalism, and even considered the possibility of rendering this scene rather than others, he finally opted to present the public with another part of the story. On the fifth day a new upheaval left only thirty survivors. On the ninth day, the remaining fifteen began to drink their own urine to combat the lack of water. Some among them showed clear signs of madness. According to Savigny, those who had refused to eat the "*viandes sacrilèges*" died within a few days: "Meantime the night came, and its gloomy shades revived in our minds the most afflicting thoughts. We began to feel an invincible disgust at the flesh which had till then, scarcely supported us; and we may say that the sight of it inspired us with a sentiment of terror, which was doubtless produced by the idea of an approaching destruction."[15]

From a political point of view, the liberal opposition used the case of *La Méduse* against the monarchic government. To sympathize with the fate of the victims seemed to question the monarchy of Louis XVIII. The election of the subject allowed the empathetic identification with those who died, but also the scorn and resentment against the executioners, and dislike for the incompetence and wickedness of all those who, either by action or by omission, were responsible for the tragedy. Géricault, who was not entirely alien to the liberal agenda, could have very well used the *Méduse affaire* as a way to show his sympathy for the government's

---

[14] Jean-Baptiste Savigny, *Observations sur les effets de la faim et de la soif éprouvés après le naufrage de la frégate du Roi, La Méduse*, en 1816 (Paris, 1818).
[15] Savigny, English trans. (London, 1821), 134–135.

critics, but his interest in this story was actually more profound.[16] On the one hand, he was convinced that he should avoid the rather limited style of the portrait and approach instead the historical gender. He knew well that there was no artist of prestige who had not directed their paintbrush to the immediate history, usually as a result of a work commissioned by different political authorities. Historians of art have compared *Le radeau de la Méduse* with the painting that Antoine-Jean Gros produced of Napoleon and his visit to the plague camp. In both cases, the election of the historical motif placed the spectator in the position of contemplating the spectacle of tragedy. This new shipwreck with spectator, as the philosopher Hans Blumenberg would have called it, placed the witnesses in the position of observing, face to face, the misfortune of others.[17] In the case of Géricault, however, what the spectator feels when contemplating the scene doesn't have anything to do with either delight or compassion. For Delacroix in 1855, for example: "The impression it gave me was so strong that as I left the studio I broke into a run, and kept running like a fool all the way back to the rue de la Planche, where I lived then, at the far end of the Fauburgh Saint-Germain." This is a run of almost four kilometres.[18]

More important than this interest in the historical record was Géricault's disposition to study the expressive forms of emotional states. His position forms part of the cultural climate that looked into the lines, colours and textures of human skin in search of inner passions and affections as a manifestation of the human character. Without being entirely indebted to Caspar Friedrich Lavater, or Charles le Brun, and without arriving at the positions later defended by Charles Darwin or Paolo Mantegazza, Géricault shared the point of view of, for example, the physiologist Charles Bell, for whom the study of the geography of the body should not lead to an ideal model, bound to classicism, but to the truth of the here and the now, to the real human flesh, with its imperfections, failures and brutality.[19] For Géricault, as for the physiologist Xavier Bichat, it was necessary to study death in order to understand the living; it was

---

[16] Lorenz E. Eitner, *Géricault, His Life and Work* (London, Orbis Press, 1983), 137. See also Jean Sagne, *Géricault* (Paris: Fayard, 1991); Germain Bazin, *Théodore Géricault, étude critique, documents et catalogue raisonné*, vols. I–VII (Paris, Wildenstein Institute: la Bibliothèque des arts, 1988–1997).

[17] Hans Blumenberg [1979], *Shipwreck with Spectator. Paradigm of a Metaphor for Existence*, English trans. (Cambridge, Mass: MIT Press, 1997).

[18] Eitner, *Géricault*, 179.

[19] Charles Bell, *Essays in the Anatomy of Expressions in Painting*, 1808. See also Jean-Jacques Courtine y Claudine Haroche, *Histoire du visage, xviiième-début xixième siècle* (París: Éditions Rivages, 1988).

compulsory to observe the pathological to gather the norm; it was necessary to look at the most common citizens to envision the most heroic actions.[20] His technique addressed him to the careful examination of the expressive features of madmen, but also animals or cadavers. For someone like him, who spent most of his life obsessed with horses and their anatomy, the difference between humans and animals was rather limited. Like Bichat, he was convinced that the increase in aneurysms and heart ailments was related to the evils of the Revolution. The famous physiologist defended that whereas anger accelerated the circulation of the blood, multiplying the efforts of the heart, terror, conversely, debilitated the vascular system and by preventing the blood flow from reaching the capillary vessels caused pallor of the face.[21] The transparent faces and rouged cheeks that proliferated during the reign of Louis XV, the same faces painted by Gerard David, grew pale as a result of anxiety, resentment, fear, and revenge.

Unlike David, who found his source of inspiration in great historical deeds, or Delacroix who would later look at the images of the classical tradition, Géricault was interested in the immediate reality, in those events that took place in front of his eyes. Along with the election of the subject, he faced the problem of the representation of morbid deformations. Their enterprise began with the obsessive accumulation of testimonies. He managed to talk with the survivors and made portraits of some of them. He also found one of the carpenters of the raft and gave instructions to build a scale model that he completed with anatomical figures in wax. He decided to leave his study of *la rue des martyrs* and find another, slightly bigger one. In the words of Clément, one of his first biographers, he found a place in which he could study "all faces of human suffering, from the most visible grimaces to the most excruciating agony, along with the features that they all imprint in the human body. He has been able to find models who, even without any gesture, show all the ailments of physical suffering and moral anguish, the evils of disease and the terrors of death."[22]

This relation between the visible and the invisible, human passions and their physical manifestations, though present in the whole of Gericault's work, has been studied mainly in relation to the five paintings that he produced in 1822 on the mental condition known then as "monomania."

---

[20] Rita Susan Goodman, *Theodore Gericault's Portraits of the Insane: Art, Psychiatry and the Politics of Philantrophy*, PhD. Dissertation (UMI, 1996).

[21] Xavier Bichat, *Physiological Researches on Life and Death*, trans. by Gold (London: Longman, Hurst, Rees, Orme and Browne, 1815), 62 *ff.*

[22] Cited by Cadinouche, *La médecine dans l'œuvre de Géricault* (Paris, Marcel Vignés, 1929), 23.

These works, produced in cooperation with the doctor Étienne-Jean Georget, a psychiatrist interested, after Pinel and Esquirol, in the systematic study of mental illnesses based on clinical evidence, included not just the observed behaviour of the sick, but also their physical and physiognomic features. Previously, Jean-Étienne Dominique Esquirol had managed to gather a monumental collection related to the physical features of mental diseases. The collection included around two hundred plasters models of patients and around six hundred cranes.[23] Géricault, who had always been interested in medical matters, and who would develop an interest in the physical appearance of the destitute, paid frequent visits to the Paris hospital of Beaujon. He knew well that among the general symptoms of mental diseases, the skin, for example, became dry, its colour brownish, and that this change in the colour could not be attributed the action of the sun, since it took place equally in winter.[24] Within this universe of shadows, which many of his contemporaries found even monochromatic, the use of colour in his painting was something very well thought out. After all, the colour was a sign and a symptom within the medical understanding of the human passions. For Esquirol, for example: "The physiognomy of monomaniacs is animated, expansive, and very mobile: the eyes are lively, sometimes enflamed and brilliant. The complexion is coloured and even very red; the features of the face are contracted and concentrated: the eyes stare vacantly; the complexion is yellow or pallid."[25]

The similarity between monomania and the resentful does not lay, however, in their physical appearance. Neither does it rest on the uniformity of expressive signs. The first and most important link between mental disease and moral passion is that both were initially concerned with an observational attitude. None of them could exist without the attentive eye, without the fixed idea that crossed, once and again, the border between discernment and denunciation. Even though the most characteristic symptoms of mental disease referred to the obsessive nature

---

[23] R. Hunter & I. Macalpine, *Three Hundred Years of Psychiatry* (London, 1963), 737.
[24] Eitner, *Géricault*, 245: "*elle devient brune, cuivreuse, sans qu'on puisse attribuer ce changement à l'action du soleil, puisqu'il a également lieu l'hiver comme l'été.*" See also Georget, *De la folie, ou aliénation mentale*, (extrait du dictionnaire de médecine), Paris, De l'imprimerie de Rignoux, 1823, and Georget, *Des maladies mentales, considérés dans leur rapports avec la législation civile et criminelle* (Paris : Imprimerie de Cosson, 1827), 38–45.
[25] Esquirol, "Monomanie," in *Dictionnaire des sciences médicales* 34, 1819, 115.

of the patient's behaviour, the compilation of its many medical histories points to a very different cultural and medical origin.

Le Radeau was presented to the public in the Salon of 1819. This exhibition contained more than 1,300 works, mainly oil paintings of medium size, portraits, still natures, landscapes and so on. There were also many historical and religious subjects. Surrounded by *madonnas*, by biblical scenes and paintings of national exaltation, mostly produced by mediocre authors or by disciples of David, then in the exile, *Le Radeau* was not only the biggest work of the exhibition, it also broke all rules and violated all conventions: "in an exhibition dominated by flattery or amusement, it affronted authority, spurned official piety and popular taste, and offered nothing to national pride."[26] The history of *La Méduse* was a materialization of some of the most radical human passions; the very same passions that Esquirol had distinguished among the moral causes of madness: anger, rage, jealousy, envy, unsatisfied expectations or failed ambitions, and of course hatred and the wish of vengeance. In the words of the doctor Savigny: "Pity was painted in every face and compassion drew tears from all who cast their eyes on us. Let the reader imagine fifteen unfortunate men, almost naked; their bodies and faces disfigured by the scorching beams of the sun; ten of the fifteen were hardly able to move; our limbs were excoriated, our sufferings were deeply imprinted on our features, our eyes were hollow, and almost wild, and our long beards rendered our appearances still more frightful; we were but the shadows of ourselves."[27]

Monomania

Coined by the French alienist Esquirol in 1810, the word "monomania" was well in use by the 1830s. As a transient entity, the illness was called into question by the 1850s and faded away in the second half of the nineteenth century.[28] During its short life it became one of the most frequently diagnosed illnesses for patients entering French asylums. Between 1826 and 1829, for example, forty-five percent of the inmate

---

[26] Eitner, *Géricault*, 188.

[27] Savigny, 1818, 139.

[28] On the historicity of mental illnesses, see Ian Hacking, *Mad Travellers. Reflections on the Reality of Transient Mental Illnesses* (Charlottesville and London: University Press of Virginia, 1998); and I. Hacking, *Rewriting the Soul: Multiple Personality and the Sciences of Memory* (Princeton, Princeton University Press, 1995).

population entering Charenton was diagnosed with the disease.[29] Defined as a chronic cerebral affection, unattended by fever, and characterized by a limited lesion of the intelligence, affections or will, monomania was a partial delirium in which the patient seized upon a false principle, which they pursue without deviating from logical reasoning, and from which they deduced legitimate consequences which modify their affections and the acts of their will.[30] Though this fixed idea could be fed by a great variety of passions, it was very often related to ambition. Among the causes of the disorder the experts numbered a large amount of triggering factors, including "all moral affections that hinder unexpectedly one or several functions of the living economy, the violent passions, the news of an unforeseen death, the loss of freedom, the commotions of a pusillanimous consciousness, fright, exaggerated fears, all burning passions which meet invincible obstacles; the elated love towards the fine arts, religious dreams, the sadness of avarice, the disorganized wishes of arrogance and ambition, the diseases of self-esteem and intelligence, the joy of a big satisfied hope."[31]

The fixed idea of the monomaniac was a pathological ambition that Esquirol considered his duty to control for the benefit of the whole French Nation. Along with the natural causes, like climate, age, gender or character, this doctor considered some social causes as triggering factors. In the first place, he pointed to all those peoples who, as a consequence of their profession, abandoned themselves to the fire of their imagination. Those who gain their intelligence either through a lively curiosity or through an interest in theories, hypothesis or speculative ideas, also have a tendency to mental alienation.[32] Studying, however, did not in principle lead to madness; it was rather the wish of distinction: "I have seen, wrote Esquirol, very many students who, guided by the desire to emulate or surpass their peers, have fallen into both masturbation and madness."[33] The same applies to novelists and writers, musicians and artists, the military and the civil servants. Whereas in the countryside most mental illnesses originate in simple passions, such as love, wrath, or domestic

---

[29] See Jan Goldstein, *Console and Classify: The French Psychiatric Profession in the Nineteenth Century* (New York: Cambridge University Press, 1987), 154.

[30] Georget, *Des maladies mentales, considérés dans leur rapports avec la législation civile et criminelle* (Paris : Imprimerie de Cosson, 1827), 10–12.

[31] Georget, *De la folie, ou aliénation mentale* (extrait du dictionnaire de médecine) (Paris : De l'imprimerie de Rignoux, 1823), 11.

[32] Esquirol, *Des maladies mentales, accompagnées de 27 planches gravées*, 2 vols; vol. I, 41 (Paris : Chez J.B. Baillière, 1838).

[33] Ibid., 42–43.

quarrels, in cities and urban sites madness comes about as the result of wounded self-esteem, ambitions cut short and reversals of fortune.

In the first clinical case that Esquirol examined in his *Medicine of Passions*, the French psychologist described the story of a military officer whose life did not run according to his own expectations. Once he was sent to Paris, perhaps dreaming of a promotion, his professional career did not follow the path traced by his wishful thinking. His imagination became so excited that he left his premises at midnight, wandering the streets of Paris. While passing the palace of Louis XV he could not find the column Vendôme erected there, even though it was 3.60 m in diameter and 44 metres tall; he simply could not see it. He became convinced that a group of rebels had pulled it down and were also threatening the government. He then made a stand on the bridge and barricaded himself, preventing anyone from crossing. He remained there, defending his position against the enemies of the country, until he was arrested by the national army, though not without a fight in which he became injured. Though Esquirol relates this story to an error of perception, one of the prevailing symptoms of madness, what triggered the disease was a perceptual mistake of a more refined nature. The fact that our officer could not see the column Vendôme and imagined instead that the country had been taken over by insurgent forces is nothing but a physical symptom of a previous and deeper perceptual mistake. As in many other similar cases, the illness depended on a lack of symmetry between reality and expectation. In the words of Esquirol himself, our official had not been received as he expected (*"n'est pas reçu comme il l'espérait"*) or, in other words, had been given what he thought he deserved.

Throughout the pages of early nineteenth century books on madness, there are plenty of similar stories. In one case, a young artist, an admirer of Jean-Jacques Rousseau, who had failed to win a prize of sculpture, developed a surprising hatred towards humanity as a whole. He began to walk on all fours as a dog; he refused to sleep in a bed, rejected all food and attempted to feed himself on the small fruits he found on the soil. In another case, a young chemist, after a breakdown from his intense and desperate work, threw himself through a window. The very last sentence he uttered before his death was "I believe that I must give up my expectations." In all cases, monomania is linked to the urban conditions and possibilities of the new bourgeoisie, to its desire of glory and its longing for *grandeur*. Like resentment, monomania also began with a partially wrong judgment, with an attentive eye forced to discern and denounce. It was a form of madness that rested on the yearning for distinction and recognition: "These monomaniacs," wrote Esquirol, "are convinced that they have been taken to the highest honors; that everyone should pay them respect; that they inhabit a superior region where they will remain forever."[34]

Conclusions

In his detailed study of distant suffering, the sociologist Luc Boltanski identifies three expository forms that, with all their historical variations, serve to account for the spectacle of violence. The first two, he tells us, may take the form of accusation or philanthropy. The first, accusation, stems from the idea, as old as humanity itself, that it is easier to construct a moral system when an agreement is reached as to who is directly responsible for the evil being denounced. In this case, the observer not only looks on but also condemns. In the second, on the other hand, where sympathy toward benefactors is greater than hatred toward executioners, the action is directed toward philanthropy rather than revenge. There is a final possibility, however. In this third aesthetic form, the observer cannot be drawn toward denouncement nor do they succumb to sentimentality. On the contrary, they keep their gaze steady in the face of horror and do not blink in the face of truth.[35] In the world in which we live, nothing seems stranger than this connection between what we today call the sphere of aesthetics and the world of politics. From the eighteenth century onwards, however, the relationship between both elements has not been merely episodic. It has come from a concept of justice that, defined as an individual virtue rather than a system of laws, is based on a visual attitude that, without being located in a specific place, has no point of reference or perspective and, therefore, can at least in principle be universal, objective and disinterested.[36] Its logic and economy is based on observation, denunciation and prosecution. It does not accept differences between citizens based on the lack of fortune; on the contrary, it firmly defends a model of society based on merit and virtue.

Within the tragedy of *La Méduse*, Géricault decided finally to not depict the most dramatic scenes of the story, such as the revolts, fights and cannibalism. He concentrated instead on the arrival of the rescuers, the

---

[34] Ibid., 13.

[35] Luc Boltanski, *Distant Suffering. Morality, Media and Politics* (Cambridge, Cambridge University Press, 1999), 116.

[36] Michael L. Frazer, *The Enlightenment of Sympathy: Justice and the Moral Sentiments in the Eighteenth Century and Today* (Oxford, OUP, 2010), 104. This work by Smith, along with Burke's work, continues the tradition started by Hutchenson in his *Inquiry into the Original of Our Ideas of Beauty and Virtue*.

moment of hope. He changed his perspective, however, in such a manner that the second version of this experience considerably reduced the size of the rescue ship. As he was digging into this aesthetic judgement, he left hope aside to concentrate on the decomposition of the survivors and the imaginary resentment of those already dead. He portrayed a flagrant injustice that could not be attributed to a reversal of fortune. On the contrary, it was the result of a human action that deserved to be denounced. Far from being a residual feeling, resentment exploded as the political and moral expression of two previous injustices that could be neither hidden nor ignored.

In the mid-nineteenth century, Géricault's *Radeau* was taken, by the Scottish historian Thomas Carlyle, as a metaphor for the whole French nation. Its bodies seemed to reflect the hope of the French people and their struggle for survival. In 1845, when Esquirol published his *Mental Maladies*, he made a similar comparison between the world and the asylum. The similarity between the early nineteenth century society and the wards that gave shelter to the mentally ill did not rest simply on the fact that the latter, the asylum, could be regarded as a consequence of the former. For Esquirol, the *maison de fous*, more than being a reflection of the world, was a scale model of society. Each one of them contained the same ideas, the same passions, the same misfortunes that could be found anywhere beyond its walls. Like society, the asylum had its gods, priests, congregations, fanatics, kings and queens and emperors, courtiers and ministers, generals, academics and civil servants. Among its members, there was always one who claimed to be God and another who believed to be endowed with the genius of a Newton or the eloquence of a Bossuet.

If resentment and monomania preyed equally on academics and artists, if it affected musicians, military officers and civil servants, it was because all of them were persuaded that that their position, their economic and social position, depended on merit and not birth; it was because they all felt that the promise of an equalitarian society had been broken; it is because all of them had seen their expectations betrayed.. The question that inspires both resentment and monomania is: Why not me? Why wasn't I delivered from this unjust fate? Why could not I count myself among the survivors of this shipwreck? Why couldn't I be a military commander, the Emperor of France, or Napoleon himself?

Of course, I do not mean to say that monomania and resentment always took place in the same person and at quite the same time. What I mean to suggest is that political and moral resentment and monomania of ambition belong to the same cultural niche. They are both related to the revolutionary promise of a political space and a form of social organization based on equalitarian measures. They are both related to a form of meritocracy that also postulates a secular distribution of justice, wealth and honour independent of birth or fortune. It might well be true that the judgement that feeds both the passion and the illness is mistaken, but in both cases that judgement takes the form of a fixed idea, of an obsession with a broken promise.

Works Cited

Bazin, Germain. *Théodore Géricault, étude critique, documents et catalogue raisonné*, vols. I–VII. Paris, Wildenstein Institute: la Bibliothèque des arts, 1988–1997.

Bell, Charles. *Essays in the Anatomy of Expressions in Painting.* 1808.

Bichat, Xavier. *Physiological Researches on Life and* Death. Translated by Gold. London, Longman, Hurst, Rees, Orme and Browne, 1815, 62 *ff.*

Blumenberg, Hans. *Shipwreck with Spectator. Paradigm of a Metaphor for Existence.* Cambridge, Mass.: MIT Press, 1997.

Boltanski, Luc. *Distant Suffering. Morality, Media and Politics.* Cambridge: Cambridge University Press, 1999.

Cadinouche. *La médecine dans l'œuvre de Géricault.* Paris: Marcel Vignés, 1929, 23.

Courtine, Jean-Jacques & Claudine Haroche. *Histoire du visage, xviiième-début xixième siècle.* París: Éditions Rivages, 1988.

Daston, Lorraine. *Biographies of Scientific Objects.* Chicago and London: Chicago University Press, 2000.

Davidson, Arnold. *The Emergence of Sexuality. Historical Epistemology and the Formation of Concepts.* Cambridge, Mass.: Harvard University Press, 2001.

Hacking, Ian. *Historical Ontology.* Cambridge, Mass.: Harvard University Press, 2002.

Davis, Lennard & J. Davis. *Obsession.* Chicago and London: The University of Chicago Press, 2008.

Eitner, Lorenz E. *Géricault, His Life and Work.* London: Orbis Press, 1983.

Esquirol. "Monomanie." In *Dictionnaire des sciences médicales* 34, 1819.

——. *Des maladies mentales, accompagnées de 27 planches gravées*, 2 vols. Paris, Chez J.B. Baillière, 1838.

Ferro, Marc. *Resentment in History.* Malden: Polity Press, 2010.

Fiering, Norman S. "Irresistible compassion: An aspect of eighteenth century sympathy and humanitarianism." *Journal of the History of Ideas* 37 (1976): 200–202.

Forman-Barzilai, Fonna. "Sympathy in Space(s). Adam Smith on Proximity." *Political Theory* 33 (2005): 189–217

Frazer, Michael L. *The Enlightenment of Sympathy: Justice and the Moral Sentiments in the Eighteenth Century and Today.* Oxford: OUP, 2010.

Frevert, Ute. *Emotions in History. Lost and Found.* Central European University Press, 2011.

Gauchet, Marcel & Gladys Swain. *Madness and Democracy. The Modern Psychiatric Universe.* Princeton: Princeton University Press, 1999.

Georget. *De la folie, ou aliénation mentale* (extrait du dictionnaire de médecine). Paris: De l'imprimerie de Rignoux, 1823,

——. *Des maladies mentales, considérés dans leur rapports avec la législation civile et criminelle.* Paris: Imprimerie de Cosson, 1827.

Goldstein, Jean. *Console and Classify: The French Psychiatric Profession in the Nineteenth Century.* New York: Cambridge University Press, 1987;

——. *The Post-revolutionary Self.* Cambridge Mass.: Harvard University Press, 2005.

Goodman, Rita Susan. *Theodore Gericault's Portraits of the Insane: Art, Psychiatry and the Politics of Philantrophy.* PhD. Dissertation, UMI, 1996.

Hacking, Ian. *Mad Travellers. Reflections on the Reality of Transient Mental Illnesses.* Charlottesville and London: University Press of Virginia, 1998.

——. *Rewriting the Soul: Multiple Personality and the Sciences of Memory.* Princeton: Princeton University Press, 1995.

Hunter, R. & I. Macalpine. *Three Hundred Years of Psychiatry*, London, 1963, 737.

Konstan, David. "Ressentiment ancien et ressentiment moderne," in Pierre Ansart, ed. *Le ressentiment*, 259–76. Brussels: Bruylant, 2002.

——. "Y-a-t'il une histoire des émotions?" *ASDIWAL: Revue Genevois d'Anthropologie et d'Histoire des Religions* 1 (2006): 23–35; revised and expanded version under the title "Haben Gefühle eine Geschichte?" in *Pathos Affekt Emotion. Transformationen der Antike*, edited by Martin Harbsmeier, Naomi Kubota and Sebastian Möckel, 27–46. Frankfurt: a. M.: Suhrkamp, 2009; revised French version in *Mythes, rites et emotions*, edited by Philippe Borgeaud, 15–28. Geneva: Librairie Droz, 2009.

Miles, Jonathan. *The Wreck of the Medusa. The Most Famous Sea Disaster of the Nineteenth Century.* New York, Grove Press, 2007.

Moscoso, Javier. *Pain: A Cultural History.* London, Palgrave-Macmillan, 2012.

Murat, Laure. *L'Homme qui se prenait pour Napoléon. Pour une histoire politique de la folie.* Paris: Gallimard, 2011.

Rancière, Jacques. *The Emancipated Spectator.* London: Verso, 2011.

Sagne, Jean. *Géricault.* Paris: Fayard, 1991.

Savigny, Jean-Baptiste. *Observations sur les effets de la faim et de la soif éprouvés après le naufrage de la frégate du Roi, La Méduse,* en 1816, Paris, 1818.

Smith, Adan. *The Theory of Moral Sentiments,* edited by Raphael y A.L. Macfie. Indianapolis: Liberty Fund, 1982.

CHAPTER TWO

NIETZSCHE:
THE "FIRST PSYCHOLOGIST"
AND GENEALOGIST OF *RESSENTIMENT*

YAMINA OUDAI CELSO

A Psychological and Philosophical Notion

Among all the possible and varied interpretative keys, it strikes me as very useful and appropriate to approach Nietzsche's theory of *ressentiment* from the point of view of the genealogical method employed in its elaboration, paying special attention to Nietzsche's psychological observations about self-deception and false consciousness. As we will see in the following pages, Nietzsche's psychological construction of *ressentiment* stems from crucial contributions from many different sources, such as: (1) the psychological science of Nietzsche's time, namely positivist psychiatry, dynamic psychiatry and Darwinian psychology;[1] (2) the French moralist literature and novel tradition[2] of Montaigne, La Rochefoucauld, Flaubert, Stendhal etc. and, in particular, the French translation of Dostoevsky's work (*L'esprit souterrain* 1864), from which Nietzsche[3] borrows the word *ressentiment*; (3) the *Baseler Kreis*,[4] as it is

---

[1] Paul Katsafanas, "Nietzsche on Agency and Self-Ignorance," in *The Oxford Handbook of Nietzsche*, eds. John Richardson & Ken Gemes (New York: Oxford University Press, 2010); Robert Pippin, *Nietzsche, Psychology and First Philosophy* (Chicago: Chicago University Press, 2010); Paul Laurent Assoun, *Freud et Nietzsche* (Paris: PUF, 1982); Henri Frédéric Ellenberger, *The Discovery of the Unconscious. The History and Evolution of Dynamic Psychiatry* (New York: Basic Books, 1970); Dirk Robert Johnson, *Nietzsche's Anti-Darwinism* (Cambridge: Cambridge University Press, 2010).
[2] Franco Volpi, *Nietzsche e le sue fonti francesi* (Bologna: Il Mulino, 1995).
[3] Friedrich Wilhelm Nietzsche, *On the Genealogy of Morals*, trans. Walter Kaufmann and R. J. Hollingdale (New York: Vintage Books, 1989); *The Anti-*

known, and its approach to ancient Greek thought, which is essential to an understanding of Nietzsche's notion of aristocracy and aristocratic morals; (4) positivist "material idealism" (influenced by French sensism and neo-Kantian psychology),[5] which allows Nietzsche to emphasize all the physiological and instinctual forces involved in the dynamics of the *ressentiment* felt by priests and slaves against the nobles/warriors (*Wohlgerathener*, or of good birth). As the keystone of Nietzsche's deconstruction of morality, the mechanism of *ressentiment* shows, above and beyond external appearances, the snares of a universal, moralizing law that makes "mistrust of the instincts second nature," as the author claims in *Ecce Homo*. In Nietzsche's thought, morals themselves are conceived as a "symbolic language of the emotions,"[6] to be analyzed by bringing in philosophy, psychology and even medicine. Therefore, unlike other recurring literary or even philosophical uses of this term, *ressentiment* is not, in Nietzsche's view, a simple passing feeling or a restricted event, but rather rises to the rank of a true theoretical system. In other words, it becomes the root of a particular vision of the world, a real *episteme*, with all its "thousand-year lies" and its damaging metaphysical misunderstandings, or the false moral values marking what goes by the name of *décadence*. And against this reversal of values produced by *ressentiment*—namely the replacement of the instinct for strength and happiness with the blame and guilt attributed to all drives—Nietzsche proclaims the very necessity of a new *Umwertung aller Werte*. In this perspective, I will highlight the differences between Nietzsche's notion of *ressentiment*, the common category of "resentment" and other similar German terms such as *Groll* or *Verstimmung*. Furthermore, we will see that Nietzsche conducts his analysis of *ressentiment* as a very strong feeling of inferiority and a source of mystification (according to the "ascetic ideals" created by priests) by the very peculiar "genealogical"

Christ, Ecce Homo, Twilight of the Idols (and other writings), eds. Aaron Ridley and Judith Norman, trans. Judith Norman (Cambridge: Cambridge University Press, 2005); *Beyond Good and Evil*, trans. by Helen Zimmern (Charleston, SC: *BiblioBazaar*, 2007); *Daybreak: Thoughts on the Prejudices of Morality*, trans. R. J. Hollingdale (Cambridge; New York: Cambridge University Press, 1982); *The Will to Power: In Science, Nature, Society and Art*, trans. Walter Kaufmann & R. J. Hollingdale (New York: Random House, 1968).

[4] Michael Worbs, *Nervenkunst: Literatur und Psychanalyse im Wien der Jahrhundertwende* (Frankfurt a/M.: Athenäum Verlag, 1988).

[5] Maurizio Ferraris (ed.), *Nietzsche* (Bari: Laterza, 1999).

[6] *"Eine Zeichensprache der Affekte"*: Friedrich Wilhelm Nietzsche, *Beyond Good and Evil*, V, 187. See also Jean Granier, "Le Statut de la philosophie selon Nietzsche et Freud," *Nietzsche Studien* 8 (1979): 210–24.

method. "Genealogy" is not a historical method as such, because Nietzsche is not interested in the chronological or specific aspects of different ages, but rather in a selection of psychological and physiological factors determining the origin of a phenomenon like *ressentiment* across the whole of human history. In this sense, Nietzsche can describe himself as the "first psychologist"[7] (or *der erste große Psychologe*) in the history of philosophy. After a very brief examination of the commonest anti-Semitic misunderstandings about Nietzsche's notion of *ressentiment*, this essay will also provide an interpretation of this theory in connection with Nietzsche's polemic against Darwin's evolutionism. More specifically, Nietzsche's *ressentiment* might be considered[8] as the most acute and insidious objection to Darwin's idea of "fitness" and, at the same time, as an attempt to solve one of the hardest of Nietzsche's dilemmas, namely: how could the herd (of priests and slaves) defeat the Overman? Analysing the famous passage about lambs and eagles,[9] we will see that Nietzsche seems to introduce an important difference between "evolution" (in a Darwinian sense) and "progress." According to Nietzsche, each person must try to satisfy their self-preservation instinct not by using treacherous, revengeful and repressive mechanisms, such as those of *ressentiment*, to fight other people, but rather by adopting the attitudes of *will to power* and *amor fati*; in other words, he has to overcome his human condition by rising to the superior, aristocratic status of the Overman (also symbolized by Dionysus versus the Crucified). Thus, as I will further argue, the theory of *ressentiment* brings out by contrast the virtues of Nietzsche's *Übermensch* without any requirement for a true, concrete political or juridical proposal, but with many references to the crucial scientific Darwinian debate of the late nineteenth century, and also with all the limits and advantages of a magnificent "utopia."

The Lexical Choice and the "Hammer" of Psychological Analysis

In Nietzsche's whole *Weltanschauung*, the notion of *ressentiment* represents just one of many examples—maybe the most outstanding or emblematic—of a typical way of using the instrument of psychological inquiry to deconstruct or dismantle long-lasting moral disbeliefs. Even the

---

[7] See also Walter Arnold Kaufmann, *Nietzsche, Philosopher, Psychologist, Antichrist* (Princeton: Princeton University Press, 1974).

[8] Johnson, *Nietzsche's Anti-Darwinism*.

[9] Nietzsche, *On the Genealogy of Morals*, I, 13.

choice of the French, italicized version of this word appears significant, and for several reasons. First of all, the French *ressentiment* had been perfectly understandable, if not for the ordinary person in the street, for German élites since the seventeenth century and, as noted by one commentator,[10] this lexical choice should be considered as an expression of a typical German Enlightenment taste for French vogues (obviously previous to Nietzsche). At the same time, it was also a way[11] for the author to underline his Europeanist vocation, as opposed to the Hegelian tendency to nationalize and Germanize the philosophical lexicon. But the term *ressentiment,* of which we may detect as many as sixty-seven occurrences[12] in Nietzsche's *opera omnia*, is also evidence of this author's well-known preference for French literature, especially the writings of essayists and moralists (such as La Rochefoucauld, Montaigne, Flaubert, Stendhal and many others). Nietzsche himself reveals, in a letter to Franz Overbeck dated February 21, 1887 (the *Genealogy of Morals* was to be written the following summer), a very special, highly valued literary source, just discovered a few weeks before: *L'esprit souterrain* ("Notes from Underground"), a novel by Dostoevsky, in one of its many different French editions (such as "Mémoires écrits dans un souterrain," "Le sous-sol," "Les carnets du sous-sol," "Manuscrit du souterrain" etc.). It is precisely from the description of the main character, Anton Antonovich, from his psychological[13] inclination to frustration and bitterness, that Nietzsche borrows the term *ressentiment*.[14]

It is no coincidence that Antonovich shows a strong feeling of inferiority and inadequacy towards his fellow men. Indeed, he envies their success, appearance and intelligence, and the behaviour arising from such feelings is not so different, as we will see, from the attitude of the priest

---

[10] Andrea Orsucci, *La "Genealogia della Morale" di Nietzsche. Introduzione alla lettura* (Roma: Carocci, 2001), 58–65; Remo Bodei, *Destini personali. L'età della colonizzazione delle coscienze* (Milano: Feltrinelli, 2002), 114–116.

[11] Kaufmann, *Nietzsche, Philosopher, Psychologist, Antichrist.*

[12] We find the word *ressentiment* not only in Nietzsche, *Genealogy of Morals* (I 10, 11, 13, 14, 16; II 11, 17; III 11, 14, 15), but also in many passages of Nietzsche, *Twilight of the Idols, Antichrist, Ecce Homo* and *Posthumous Fragments.*

[13] In 1888, Nietzsche wrote in section 45 of *Twilight of the Idols*: "Dostoevsky, [is] the only psychologist, incidentally, from whom I had something to learn; he ranks among the most beautiful strokes of fortune in my life, even more than my discovery of Stendhal...."

[14] Carlo Gentili, *La filosofia come genere letterario* (Bologna: Pendragon, 2003), 205; Orsucci, *La "Genalogia della Morale" di Nietzsche.*

Nietzsche described in *Genealogy of Morals* where we find the most systematic and accomplished treatment of the notion of *ressentiment*.

It is precisely in this book that the origin of morals is proposed as an out-and-out history of *ressentiment*, namely as a set of false values devised by a specific social category (*die Priester* or the priests) as a reaction to a feeling of inferiority towards another group of individuals (the nobles, i.e. the warriors or masters).

In the first of the three dissertations composing the *Genealogy of Morals*, Nietzsche outlines some important elements of *ressentiment* illustrating the difference between ordinary "resentment" and the particular attitude evoked by the French term:

> The slave revolt in morality begins when *ressentiment* itself becomes creative and gives birth to values: the *ressentiment* of natures that are denied the true reaction, that of deeds, and compensate themselves with an imaginary revenge. While every noble morality develops from a triumphant affirmation of itself, slave morality from the outset says No to what is "outside," what is "different," what is "not itself"; and *this* No is its creative deed. This inversion of the value-positing eye—this *need* to direct one's view outward instead of back to oneself—is of the essence of *ressentiment;* in order to exist, slave morality always first needs a hostile external world; it needs, physiologically speaking, external stimuli in order to act at all—its action is fundamentally reaction.

First of all, this passage supports the view, mentioned at the beginning, that not all cases of resentment can be classified as *ressentiment*. To have *ressentiment*, it is necessary for the people who feel it to have built a true system of values, or rather an *episteme*, moving from their own emotions. Unlike simple resentment, indeed, *ressentiment* generates a vision of life, a rigid grid of antinomies, such as good/bad and right/wrong.

It is precisely from the wish to challenge these moral categories (perfectly symmetrical to the metaphysical ones), namely from the need to destroy them with a metaphorical "hammer,"[15] that Nietzsche starts his analysis of *ressentiment*, as the source that generates these false beliefs. The "no" ("this no"), i.e. the denial and repression that resentful people express against vital instincts, will be the perfect counterpart, as we will see, to the Overman's values of "yes to life" and *amor fati*, intended by Nietzsche as a physiological, non-repressive immersion in the flow of things.

---

[15] The hammer is even mentioned in the subtitle of Nietzsche's *Twilight of the Idols* ("How to Philosophize with a Hammer"), published in 1889 but written in 1888, just a year later than *Genealogy of Morals*.

Actually, the same word, in its English version "resentment," would have appeared much more exotic in a German context than its French variant, and would have had a much more sarcastic tone,[16] evoking the same difference as between the terms "genre" (French) and "kind" (English) from the point of view of a German reader.

On the contrary, the two German variants *Groll*[17] and *Verstimmung*, which also appear in Nietzsche's opus, assume a number of much more non-technical meanings than *ressentiment*, and are consequently more general and more context-based. In particular, *Verstimmung*[18] is understood in the wider and global sense of "discontent," "bad mood" or "irritation," while *Groll*[19] is more literally translated as "rancour" or "hatred."

In neither case do we find anyone who gets to build a "world," meaning a system of values typical of *ressentiment* and such a peculiar, wholly "creative" reactivity seems to be lacking. That is why resentful people will also be defined as *Hinterweltlern*, a term commonly translated with "those in backwaters" but actually and literally indicating "those who are attached to the rear side of the world." According to Nietzsche, they have conceived a sort of second world[20] in addition to the real one.

Thus, in order to question the system of values produced by *ressentiment* and to be able to obtain an *Umwertung aller Werte* (transvaluation of all values), Nietzsche's genealogical[21] method, as it is called, implies that moral notions, just like metaphysical or philosophical ones, are not to be considered as absolute or valid entities *per se*, but on the contrary as the result of historical, physiological[22] and, above all, psychological conditionings.

---

[16] Robert C. Solomon, "One Hundred Years of *Ressentiment*: Nietzsche's *Genealogy of Morals*," in *Nietzsche, Genealogy, Morality: Essays on Nietzsche's On the Genealogy of Morals*, ed. Richard Schacht (Berkeley: University of California Press, 1994), 95–126.

[17] This term is also employed by Max Scheler who tries to adopt Nietzsche's notion of *ressentiment* but in the context of a diametrically opposite conception of Christianity. Other religious implications of *ressentiment* inspired by Nietzsche's analysis were also to be theorized by Max Weber.

[18] There are eighteen occurrences of this term in Nietzsche's *Human Too Human; Daybreak; Beyond Good and Evil; Genealogy of Morals* and *Posthumous Fragments*.

[19] We find this word seven times in Nietzsche's *Schopenhauer as Educator; Preface to Unwritten Works* and *Posthumous Fragments*.

[20] This attitude is the opposite of Overman's "meaning of the earth."

[21] *Mutatis mutandis* this method has been borrowed by many other authors, such as Foucault.

[22] Concerning the physiology of *ressentiment* and the physical suffering it entails, see Nietzsche, *Genealogy of Morals* III, 15.

Therefore, unlike the historian, the genealogist does not worry about the chronological succession of single events, nor is he interested in their specific conjunctures or other details; he only analyzes general phenomena by selecting particular aspects of them, namely the physiological[23] and psychological dynamics involved.

This orientation is inspired precisely by the material idealism or metaphysical naturalism deriving from a neo-Kantian background and setting out to explain moral phenomena by analyzing them from a naturalistic point of view, that is by tracing them back to the physiological drives on which they are grounded.

This approach has to do with what Freud would have defined as the "economic point of view" (*der oekonomische Standpunkt*), i.e. the investigation of the intensity of instinctual strengths involved in psychic phenomena. In this sense, in *Beyond Good and Evil* Nietzsche was able to define morals as a "symbolic language of the emotions" (*eine Zeichensprache der Affekte*).[24]

This is the reason why Nietzsche was, repeatedly and emphatically, to underline the crucial value of psychological analysis.

We could cite countless aphorisms or passages in Nietzsche's work in which the value of psychological knowledge is emphasized and the author describes himself as the best specialist in this discipline, and which to some extent suggest that psychology is something of a keystone of his philosophical endeavour. In *Ecce Homo*, for example, Nietzsche writes:

> What philosopher before me was a *psychologist* instead of his opposite, "a higher fraud," an "idealist"? Psychology did not exist until I appeared? It can be a curse to be first here, it is at any rate a destiny: *because you are also the first to despise* ... My danger is *disgust* with people ....[25]

In *Beyond Good and Evil* we read:

> All psychology hitherto has run aground on moral prejudices and timidities, it has not dared to launch out into the depths ... nobody had yet

---

[23] As we mentioned at the beginning, Nietzsche's emphasis on physiological mechanisms is also linked to the influence of French sensism, which he considers as the best heritage of the French Enlightenment. This is why he quotes Condillac and Destutt de Tracy among the masters of Stendhal, in his opinion the best French writer of nineteenth century. In addition, it was in the wake of Locke and empiricism that French sensism was to conceive of ideas and mental concepts as the product of elementary sensations.

[24] Nietzsche, *Beyond Good and Evil*, V, 187.

[25] Nietzsche, *Ecce Homo*, XV, 6.

harboured the notion of psychology as the morphology and *development-doctrine of the will to power*, as I conceive of it. The power of moral prejudices has penetrated deeply into the most intellectual world, the world apparently most indifferent and unprejudiced, and has obviously operated in an injurious, obstructive, blinding, and distorting manner ... Psychology shall once more be recognized as the queen of the sciences, for whose service and equipment the other sciences exist. For psychology is once more the path to the fundamental problems.[26]

This final definition of psychology as the "queen of the sciences [and] the path to fundamental problems" may itself be considered to be a typical case of Nietzsche's *Umwertung* or transvaluation. Indeed, the expression "queen of the sciences," from the Latin *regina scientiarum*, is exactly the same position of priority that Scholastic philosophers attributed to metaphysics. Thus, psychology, instead of metaphysics, implies a reversal of perspectives marked by Nietzsche's usual rhetorical strategy of estrangement. What I mean is that he uses this strategy to emphasise that psychology is the main tool for the deconstruction of metaphysics itself, or the hammer mentioned in *Twilight of the Idols*.

But as we will see in the next paragraph, Nietzsche's conception of morals as a "symbolic language of the emotions" is also connected to his attempt to reduce the complexity of values or theoretical (and therefore ethical) constructions to the basic, elementary structure of physiological and biological mechanisms. In other words, Nietzsche prefigures the contemporary "revaluation" of the cognitive role of the emotions,[27] foreseeing their centrality in the intellectual and decisional trials that human beings face. In his opinion, the contiguity between emotions and corporeality is no longer to be understood as a limit or a flaw in comparison to a presumed "purity" of speculative abstractions but, on the contrary, as a confirmation of the biological and materialistic (in Lange's sense, following in the footsteps of one of his main philosophical influences) paradigm on which Nietzsche's ontology is founded.

---

[26] Nietzsche, *Beyond Good and Evil*, I, 23.

[27] From the terminological point of view, it seems that Nietzsche "tends to refer to affects [*Affekte*], passion [*Leidenschaft, Passion*] and feeling [*Gefühl, Empfindung*] interchangeably" (Erika Kerruish, 2009, "Interpreting Feeling: Nietzsche on the Emotions and the Self," in *Minerva: An Internet Journal of Philosophy* (2009), 1–27.

Instinctive and Reactive Dynamics of *Ressentiment*: "To Make Mistrust of the Instincts Second Nature."[28]

Some interpreters[29] have argued that the (obviously unconscious) psychological attitude of people affected by *ressentiment* could be summarized using the analogy of the famous tale of the fox and the grapes, first narrated by Aesop and then by La Fontaine. In the same way that the fox, whose desire to reach the grapes being frustrated, reacts by despising the qualities of the fruit, the priests (and, accordingly, the slaves), being unable to share the strength and vitality of the *Wohlgerathener*, decide to debase and defame those qualities by creating an alternative and opposite system of values.

In this sense, the attitude of "resentful" people may be considered as reactive: they try to provide a remedy to a condition of frustration, or rather to a feeling of inferiority.

Actually what specifically characterizes *ressentiment* is not the simple fact of having suffered unfair treatment; to be "resentful," in Nietzsche's sense, it is also necessary to have a feeling of inadequacy.

To fully understand Nietzsche's notion of *ressentiment* as a negative or dysfunctional moral paradigm, namely as a polemical target (and, not for nothing, "a polemical tract" is precisely the subtitle of *Genealogy of Morals*), it will be useful to consider the positive reference model adopted by Nietzsche by way of contrast. As indicated in the passage quoted in the last paragraph, "every noble morality develops from a triumphant affirmation of itself." The model of such aristocratic morals is rooted in Nietzsche's youthful philological past, at the time of his *Valediktionsarbeit* at Pforta, and it is identified with the Greek[30] poet

---

[28] Nietzsche, *Ecce Homo*, IV, 8. In the original, "um das Misstrauen gegen die Instinkte zur zweiten Natur zu machen."

[29] Rüdiger Bittner, 1994, "Ressentiment," in *Nietzsche, Genealogy, Morality: Essays on Nietzsche's On the Genealogy of Morals*, ed. Richard Schacht (Berkeley: University of California Press, 1994), 127–138.

[30] Nietzsche, along with his contemporaries Schopenhauer, Rohde (one of his friends and sparring partners), Bachofen and Burckhardt, is considered one of the main representatives of the *Baseler Kreis*, as it is known (a definition coined by historian Michael Worbs, see Worbs, *Nervenkunst*), a group of university professors all teaching at the University of Basel, characterized by a sort of complementaristic approach to a number of crucial concepts of ancient Greek thought, revisited in a new dialectic relationship, such as *Es/Ich*, feminine/masculine, archaic/classical, *chaos/logos*, *soma/psyche*, Mycenae/Athens, animal/divine or, in Nietzsche's terms, Apollonian/Dionysian.

Theognis of Megara Iblea (VI–V BC). Nietzsche borrows from Theognis the idea that happiness does not come from the observance of moral rules. Conversely, it is happiness itself that produces ethical rectitude. From an aristocratic perspective, discipline is never imposed from the outside but is a natural consequence for a person inspired by a passionate drive towards performance.[31] The features attributed by Nietzsche to the masters, namely to the *Wohlgerathener*, in *Genealogy of Morals*, come precisely from this Greek background. They are the nobles or the warriors expressing a natural physical and/or intellectual superiority over other social categories. Their habit is to face enemies as a challenge, to manifest their thoughts and desires explicitly and, above all, to live in tune with their own vital instinct. In doing so, they act in the present and tend towards forgetfulness of the past and of wrongs they have suffered. On the contrary, the slaves have the tendency to dwell on negative thoughts and to cultivate silently in themselves a wish to be redeemed. Their slavery is not[32] necessarily the result of a state of economic or social inferiority, as we see, for instance, in the *Posthumous Fragments* where Nietzsche mentions slave categories such as the monk, the Prussian officer and even the scholar. Their discontent and their *ressentiment* are cleverly exploited by a third category—the priests— rightly defined as, in a way, direction-changers of *ressentiment* ("the priest alters the direction of *ressentiment*").[33] The priests, acting in a sneaky, hypocritical way, with an attitude quite similar to that of Molière's Tartuffe, provide the slaves with an explanation (obviously false and deceptive) of their suffering, by making them feel guilty about their desires.[34] In other words, they build, as we said, a fictitious world

---

[31] Nietzsche, *Genealogy of Morals*, I.

[32] Bittner, *Ressentiment*.

[33] Nietzsche, *Genealogy of Morals*, III, 15.

[34] This relationship between morals and repression of instincts is usually linked by interpreters to Freud's definition of civilization's discontent (*das Unbehagen in der Kultur*): on this point see Oudai Celso, *Freud e la filosofia antica. Genealogia di un fondatore* (Torino: Bollati Boringhieri, 2006), chapter 6. We lack the space here even to enumerate the many theoretical and textual connections between Nietzsche and Freud, but we can hardly avoid citing the fact that Freud explicitly takes from Nietzsche, through the mediation of Groddeck, the use of the neuter pronoun *Es* to define the set of all unknown and uncontrollable forces acting deeply and secretly in each man. These forces characterize him as the result of a naturalistic necessity. Readers have thus proposed many theoretical parallels (actually not always well founded, but sometimes forced or arbitrary) between their respective psychological issues, especially between Freudian *Libidotheorie* and Nietzsche's notion of "Will to Power," between Eternal Recurrence and *Wiederholungszwang* or compulsive

in which the vital instincts are denied by the affirmation of antithetical values (for instance, the exaltation of suffering, so-called holiness etc.) disguised in a positive form:

> This dominating sense of displeasure is combated, first, by means that reduce the feeling of life in general to its lowest point. If possible, will and desire are abolished altogether; all that produces affects and "blood" is avoided (abstinence from salt: the hygienic regimen of the fakirs); no love; no hate; indifference; no revenge; no wealth; no work; one begs; if possible, no women, or as little as possible; in spiritual matters, Pascal's principle "il faut s'abêtir" is applied. The result, expressed in moral-psychological terms, is "selflessness," "sanctification;" in physiological terms: hypnotization—the attempt to win for man an approximation to what in certain animals is hibernation, in many tropical plants estivation, the minimum metabolism at which life will still subsist without really entering consciousness. An astonishing amount of human energy has been expended to this end—has it been in vain?[35]

In the fictitious world built by priests and Christian morals, or in the so-called "Kingdom of Heaven,"[36] it is possible to keep the hope of future compensation alive, namely a chance for the slaves to be avenged and rewarded in the end. This is why Christian morality represents the most resounding and abominable example of *ressentiment*, and the different prerogatives of nobles and priests can be symbolized by the opposition between Dionysus and the Crucified.[37]

However, how can the priests manage to instil ascetic ideals into slaves? What is the psychological mechanism allowing *ressentiment* to prevail?

In fact, the process works in the same way from both the moral and the metaphysical point of view. In both cases, the real source of our convictions has to be identified in our drives and in our instinctual nature.

---

repetition (a comparison authorized, at least from a purely terminological point of view, by Freud himself), between *décadence* and civilization's discontent and so on. Some people (for instance Assoun, *Freud et Nietzsche*) have even talked about a real "Nietzscheofreudism" existing in the first half of the twentieth century.

[35] Nietzsche, *Genealogy of Morals*, III, 17.

[36] As remarked by Bittner, *Ressentiment*, this faith in a "fantasy world" needs to be slowly enforced across the centuries and generations by a sort of collective madness. The tendency of priests to store up worldly goods and power may be interpreted as an early lack of confidence in a future reward.

[37] Nietzsche, *Ecce Homo*, IV, 9.

For these reasons, in the following (and very famous) passage of *Twilight of the Idols* Nietzsche talks about a causal instinct or a causal drive, the *Ursachentrieb*:

> Most of our general feelings—every kind of inhibition, pressure, tension, and explosion in the play and counterplay of our organs, and particularly the state of the nervus sympaticus—excite our causal instinct [*Ursachentrieb*]: we want to have a reason for feeling this way or that—for feeling bad or for feeling good. We are never satisfied merely to state the fact that we feel this way or that: we admit this fact only—become conscious of it only—when we have furnished some kind of motivation [*eine Art Motivierung*] ... The psychological explanation of this. To derive something unknown from something familiar [*Etwas Unbekanntes auf etwas Bekanntes zurückführen*] relieves, comforts, and satisfies, besides giving a feeling of power [*ein Gefühl von Macht*]. With the unknown, one is confronted with danger, discomfort, and care; the first instinct is to abolish these painful states ... That which is new and strange and has not been experienced before, is excluded as a cause ... Consequence: one kind of positing of causes predominates more and more, is concentrated into a system and finally emerges as dominant, that is, as simply precluding other causes and explanations. The banker immediately thinks of "business," the Christian of "sin," and the girl of her love.[38]

We find here the most typical of Nietzsche's criticisms of teleology, i.e. of Aristotle's classic causal paradigm. On this view, the connection between cause and effect (*Ursache/Wirkung*) is the basic or elementary grammar on which every metaphysical architecture is founded, and it is exactly symmetrical to the guilt/penalty (*Schuld/Strafe*) pair that we find on the moral level.[39] In that case, as well as in the passage we have seen, Nietzsche notes a psychological impulse (the causal instinct or drive, the *Ursachentrieb*), a sort of anxiety, an instinct of fear or self-conservation (fear as the "secret instinct of science", as Nietzsche calls it at other times). In this sense, Nietzsche clearly claimed elsewhere[40] that morals are a "symbolic language of the emotions" (*eine Zeichensprache der Affekte*).

Instinct is always "good," is never "wrong," because even when it deceives the person, even if it is badly oriented, it is always an expression—or almost an ingenuous or *naïve* expression—of will to power, i.e. of the attitude by which each individual aims to preserve and then to assert themself, to impose themself, to master in some way or other

---

[38] Nietzsche, *Twilight of the Idols*, V, 4–5

[39] Nietzsche, *Genealogy of Morals*, I, 10 (*ressentiment* of priests against warriors)

[40] Nietzsche, *Beyond Good and Evil*, V, 187. See also Granier, *Le statut de la philosophie selon Nietzsche et Freud*.

the mysterious reality around him. In *The Will to Power*, Nietzsche clearly states:

> The subjective compulsion not to contradict here is a biological compulsion: the instinct for the utility of inferring as we do infer is part of us, *we almost are this instinct*—But what *naïveté* to extract from this a proof that we are therewith in possession of a "truth in itself"!-?[41]

Just as in physics or other branches of scientific knowledge, Nietzsche believes that psychology works like a sort of double-edged sword, because it is both the language of demystification and also the language by which we construct our self-deceptions, with a perverse use of psychology itself, like that of priests or metaphysical philosophers. If we preserve ourselves from becoming, if we try to make reality predictable, we are not expressing our will to power in the best way, because we preclude a useful, unprejudiced investigation of reality. For this reason, according to Nietzsche,[42] people who lack any experience or knowledge of psychology are passive and unwittingly driven by their instincts.

Conversely, psychology brings us closer to the actual experience of human life than any other branch of science, because it does not produce artificial worlds or rigid classifications, nor does it exercise violence against becoming; on the contrary, it reveals the instinctual and material nature of human beings. This instinctual, material nature is exactly the core argument of Nietzsche's analysis. His use of psychology in an anti-metaphysical sense is possible precisely because his approach is inspired by the promptings of dynamic psychiatry and, at the same time, by his material-idealistic[43] background, whereby we may doubt everything, but the material consistence of the world, of human and animal life, is beyond doubt.[44] In the same way that the world is, in a typical positivist approach, a "monster of matter and force," our mind is a bundle of instincts and desires behind which the inner nature of human life is hidden. This instinctual nature is nothing other than the sheer force of will, or the will to power.

---

[41] Nietzsche, *Will to Power*, §515.

[42] Nietzsche, *Will to Power*, §585 A.

[43] It is very close to the metaphysical naturalism mentioned by Mathias Risse, "Origins of *Ressentiment* and Sources of Normativity," in *Nietzsche-Studien*, (2003), 30, 142–70.

[44] See on this point Ferraris, *Nietzsche*, VI. In the same chapter, especially 192–202, the author also explains that Heidegger's misunderstanding of Nietzsche's thought depends precisely on the confusion between axiological nichilism and ontological nichilism; the latter has been warded off by material-idealism itself.

This is why, in *Genealogy of Morals'* first dissertation, Nietzsche asserts the necessity of adopting a method of inquiry that will wed philosophy, psychology and medicine.

Ressentiment as an Adaptive Strategy: the Herd, the Overman and the Argument against Darwin

When sketching the psychological features of people affected by *ressentiment*, Nietzsche very often underlines their high level of intellectual elaboration and sharp-wittedness. Indeed, the author often betrays a sort of admiration for the complex, sophisticated nature of their "reaction" as compared with the much simpler, less complicated psychology of nobles. The relationship between weakness and strength should be precisely understood in terms of a struggle for survival, in which the "inferior" species legitimately tries not to be overwhelmed.

Framing the problem this way situates the discourse at a naturalistic level very close to that of Darwin's remarks, namely to the theories of the "English psychologists" collectively cited by Nietzsche. The reference is especially evident in the famous passage concerning the relationship between lambs and birds of prey:

> But let us return: the problem of the other origin of the "good," of the good as conceived by the man of *ressentiment*, demands its solution. That lambs dislike great birds of prey does not seem strange: only it gives no ground for reproaching these birds of prey for bearing off little lambs. And if the lambs say among themselves: "these birds of prey are evil; and whoever is least like a bird of prey, but rather its opposite, a lamb – would he not be good?" there is no reason to find fault with this institution of an ideal, except perhaps that the birds of prey might view it a little ironically and say: "we don't dislike them at all, these good little lambs; we even love them: nothing is more tasty than a tender lamb."[45]

In the metaphor under discussion, the lambs, according to Nietzsche, represent the "weaker species" while the birds of prey are the "stronger species" corresponding to nobles and warriors. The former are portrayed with the psychological features typical of priests and slaves, namely the tendency to denigrate the birds of prey by criticizing and stigmatizing their aggressive instinct. Actually this is an instinct present in every living being engaged in the struggle for survival.

---

[45] Nietzsche, *Genealogy of Morals*, I, 13.

Obviously it is a simple allegorical projection in which the author takes an imaginative example vaguely inspired by animal[46] psychology to illustrate how, in his opinion, *ressentiment* is almost similar to what Darwin would have considered the fitness and/or the adaptation of living beings. In other words, by acting as polished, evolved "animals," priests and slaves cleverly try to avoid a direct clash with the stronger species by creating an overturned system of values and using sideways attacks to fight their enemies. This is why the lambs denigrate the birds of prey but not vice versa.

Leaving the metaphor aside and drawing its ultimate meaning, I have to note that Nietzsche aims here to underline the adaptive value of *ressentiment* and its successful match with what he thinks might be Darwin's evolutionary paradigm

Regardless of the reliability[47] of Nietzsche's version of Darwinism, and since it is not possible to retrace the complex relationship between Nietzsche and evolution theory in detail here, it is, however, interesting to note that the author of the *Genealogy of Morals* makes a very apposite, subtle objection[48] to it. Although the man marked by *ressentiment* appears, in fact, successful in his struggle for survival, and if he defeats his enemies, at least in terms of the assertion of ethical principles as he builds an anti-vital model of society, his efficient adaptation to the environment cannot, nevertheless, be considered as the best expression of human nature. Indeed, *ressentiment*, as I have already noted, with its "no" to life, humiliates and mortifies each person's instincts and best energies. Therefore, the evolution of the species, or its fitness and adaptation, are not to be confused, according to Nietzsche, with the progress of humanity: the latter must, rather, aim for the growth of its own *Wille zur Macht* or *will to power*.

In this way, as I mentioned at the beginning, Nietzsche implicitly succeeds in resolving the dilemma about the relationship between the weaker and the stronger people, the gregarious and the heroes or, in the last analysis, between the herd (composed of slaves and headed by priests) and the Overman, i.e. the ideal model to which the whole of humanity

---

[46] Nietzsche, *Genealogy of Morals*, III, 20.

[47] According to Claire Richter, *Nietzsche et les théories biologiques contemporaines* (Paris: Mercure de France, 1911), for instance, Nietzsche confused Darwin's theories with Lamarck's and was a Lamarckian in spite of himself. Furthermore, Solomon (*One Hundred Years of Ressentiment*) rightly objects to Nietzsche's assumption of weakness and strength as defining characteristics of a biological species.

[48] Johnson, *Nietzsche's Anti-Darwinism*.

must tend. Thus, for the very reason that evolution is not to be identified with progress, it is possible that the herd and *ressentiment* prevail in the history of humanity. However, if the slaves' victory is a matter of fact, man can and must rise to higher values: man's future, his sunset and his going beyond, the fitting anthropological model, namely individual self-affirmation, must be oriented in the opposite direction to that of *ressentiment*. As I remarked in the previous section, the survival instinct in itself, like any instinct, is never wrong. People who act according to it may make mistakes, but these mistakes are not to be ascribed to the instinct in itself, but rather to their dealing with it in the wrong way; in other words, to an action oriented to a "no" rather than a "yes" to life.

Contrary to what might be assumed, Nietzsche absolutely does not[49] advocate anti-democratic individualism or violent ill-treatment of the weak by the strong. As we noted while discussing Theognis and aristocratic morals, the Overman acts according to superior values and draws his graceful way of relating to others from his "happiness." The main feature of the Overman is a utopian aspiration based on the values of the mythical past of Greek tragedy but not identified with any concrete political project or positive legal order.

Nietzsche himself mentions the various historical recurrences,[50] namely the alternation between eras (such as the Renaissance or Napoleon's ascent) marked by the primacy of aristocratic morals and other ages (for instance the Reformation and the Counter-Reformation) in which the paradigm of *ressentiment* prevailed. Therefore, neither a particular age, nor a legal system, nor, least of all, a race, is better able than others to embody the model of nobility, that of the Overman.

In particular, we must reject and deny all interpretations aiming to find support for anti-Semitic leanings in Nietzsche's theory of *ressentiment.* The notion that Nietzsche was pro-Nazi, pro-Aryan and anti-Semitic is fully disproven beyond all doubt by several passages of his writings. First of all, in a letter dated June 5, 1887[51] and written to his sister, Elizabeth Förster (who, it is well known, altered some of her brother's writings to support Nazi propaganda), Nietzsche clearly states that any German person claiming any superiority over a Jew, should—for that very reason—be considered a buffoon, if not an utter madman. And in addition to his own general disgust for the anti-Semites (voiced, for instance in a letter to Theodor Fritsch dated 1887), Nietzsche is inclined to place Jews

---

[49] Nietzsche, *Genealogy of Morals*, III, 23.
[50] Nietzsche *Genealogy of Morals*, III, 41.
[51] The same opinions are also expressed in another letter to Elizabeth dated June 11, 1865.

and Germans on the same footing because of their common tendency to *ressentiment*, and he even thinks that, in his day, *ressentiment* is primarily a feature of "the anarchists and the anti-Semites."[52]

Thus Nietzsche is not intending to propose a tyrannical or anti-democratic project as an alternative to *ressentiment*, but rather wants to underline the potential inherent in human beings, their capacity to emancipate themselves from their "human, too human" instincts by endeavouring to rise to the status of Overman. In the rest of Nietzsche's work, the Overman's alternatives to *ressentiment* will therefore consist, at times, in heroic individualism, and at other times in the artistic and creative life, and especially in rejecting (moral and metaphysical) false certainties, plunging into the flow of becoming and exploring the contradictions and eternal conflict or *polemos* between interpretations.

Works cited

Assoun, Paul Laurent. *Freud et Nietzsche*. Paris: PUF, 1980.

Bodei, Remo. *Destini personali. L'età della colonizzazione delle coscienze*. Milano: Feltrinelli, 2002.

Bittner, Rüdiger. "Ressentiment." In *Nietzsche, Genealogy, Morality: Essays on Nietzsche's On the Genealogy of Morals*, ed. Richard Schacht, 127–138. Berkeley: University of California Press, 1994.

Ellenberger, Henri Frédéric. *The Discovery of the Unconscious. The History and Evolution of Dynamic Psychiatry*. New York: Basic Books, 1970.

Ferraris, Maurizio (a cura di). *Nietzsche*, Bari: Laterza, 1999.

Gentili, Carlo. *La filosofia come genere letterario*, Bologna: Pendragon, 2003.

Granier, Jean. *Le Statut de la philosophie selon Nietzsche et Freud*. *Nietzsche Studien* 8 (1979): 210–24.

Johnson, Dirk Robert. *Nietzsche's Anti-Darwinism*. Cambridge: Cambridge University Press, 2010.

Katsafanas, Paul. "Nietzsche on Agency and Self-Ignorance." In John Richardson/Ken Gemes (eds.), *The Oxford Handbook of Nietzsche*. New York: Oxford University Press, 2010.

Kaufmann, Walter Arnold. *Nietzsche, Philosopher, Psychologist, Antichrist*. Princeton: Princeton University Press, 1978.

Kerruish, Erika. "Interpreting Feeling: Nietzsche on the Emotions and the Self." *Minerva: An Internet Journal of Philosophy* 1–27, 2009.

---

[52] Nietzsche, *Genealogy of Morals*, II, 10.

Nietzsche, Friedrich Wilhelm. *On the Genealogy of Morals* (1887). Translated by Walter Kaufmann and R. J. Hollingdale. New York: Vintage Books, 1989.

—. *The Anti-Christ, Ecce Homo, Twilight of the Idols (and other writings)*, edited by Aaron Ridley and Judith Norman, translated by Judith Norman. Cambridge: Cambridge University Press, 2005.

—. *Beyond Good and Evil* (1886), translated by Helen Zimmern. Charleston, SC: BiblioBazaar, 2007.

—. *Daybreak: Thoughts on the Prejudices of Morality* (1881), translated by R. J. Hollingdale. Cambridge; New York: Cambridge University Press, 1982.

—. *The Will to Power: In Science, Nature, Society and Art* (1901), translated by Walter Kaufmann with R. J. Hollingdale. New York: Random House, 1968.

Orsucci, Andrea. *La "Genealogia della Morale" di Nietzsche. Introduzione alla lettura*. Roma: Carocci, 2001.

Oudai Celso, Yamina. *Freud e la filosofia antica. Genealogia di un fondatore*. Torino: Bollati Boringhieri, 2006.

Pippin, Robert. *Nietzsche, Psychology and First Philosophy*. Chicago: Chicago University Press, 2010.

Richter, Claire. *Nietzsche et les théories biologiques contemporaines*. Paris: Mercure de France, 1911.

Risse, Mathias. "Origins of Ressentiment and Sources of Normativity." *Nietzsche-Studien* 30 (2003): 142–70.

Solomon, Robert C. "One Hundred Years of *Ressentiment*: Nietzsche's *Genealogy of Morals*." In *Nietzsche, Genealogy, Morality: Essays on Nietzsche's On the Genealogy of Morals*, edited by Richard Schacht, 95–126. Berkeley: University of California Press, 1994.

Volpi, Franco. 1995. *Nietzsche e le sue fonti francesi*. Bologna: Il Mulino.

Worbs, Michael. 1988. *Nervenkunst: Literatur und Psychanalyse im Wien der Jahrhundertwende*. Frankfurt a/M.: Athenäum Verlag.

CHAPTER THREE

MAX SCHELER'S ANALYSIS OF RESSENTIMENT IN MODERN DEMOCRACIES

PATRICK LANG

Whereas Edmund Husserl (1859–1938) is now fully recognized as the founder of phenomenology, the decisive and at least equally original contribution to this philosophical current by Max Scheler (1874–1928) remains far less appreciated. It is Scheler, not Husserl, who applied the phenomenological method to the systematic analysis of emotions; he repeatedly refers to his project of a "phenomenology of the emotional life"[1] which (due to his early death) remained incomplete, important writings like *The Nature of Sympathy*[2] or *Shame and Feelings of Modesty*[3] being part of its elaboration. Opposing the philosophical tradition that defines the human primarily as the subject of knowledge and pure reason, Scheler stresses love as the fundamental act of the spirit, and the ultimate source of all intellectual and voluntary powers.

---

[1] M. Scheler, *Der Formalismus in der Ethik und die materiale Wertethik* (1913/1916) (Bern: Francke, 1980); (*Gesammelte Werke* [Collected Works], vol. 2), 331. I quote according to this reference edition (hereafter *GW*, followed by the volume number), always offering my own translation of the quoted passages. (*Formalism in Ethics and Non-Formal Ethics of Values*, trans. M. Frings & R. Funk (Evanston: Northwestern University Press, 1973.)

[2] M. Scheler, *Wesen und Formen der Sympathie* (1923) (Bern: Francke, 1973) (*GW* 7). (*The Nature of Sympathy*, trans. P. Heath [1954], Piscataway [NJ]: Transaction Publishers, 2011.) In the foreword to the second edition of this book (1923), Scheler announces a systematic study about *Die Sinngesetze des emotionalen Lebens* ("The Meaning Laws of the Emotional Life"), of which the book itself is to be considered a part (cf. *GW* 7, p. 10).

[3] M. Scheler, *Über Scham und Schamgefühl* (1913), in *Schriften aus dem Nachlass Bd. 1* (Bonn: Bouvier, 1986), (*GW* 10), 65–164. (*Shame and Feelings of Modesty*, trans. by M. Frings, in *Person and Self-Value. Three Essays*, Dordrecht: Nijhoff, 1987, 1–85.)

One of Scheler's earliest studies in this field, *Das Ressentiment im Aufbau der Moralen* ("The Ressentiment in the Construction of Moralities," first published in 1912[4]), translated into English under the simplified title *Ressentiment*,[5] definitely raised "ressentiment"[6] to the dignity of a philosophical concept. It critically examines Nietzsche's famous "discovery," according to which morals, and especially Christian morals, are the production of the ressentiment nourished by the slaves against the masters and rests on a "falsification of value tables." Far from adopting this thesis, Scheler sharply distinguishes and contrasts two notions erroneously identified by his predecessor: Christian morality and modern bourgeois morality. He wishes to demonstrate[7] that bourgeois morality, having gradually replaced Christian morality since the thirteenth century and culminating in the Revolution of 1789, is indeed rooted in ressentiment, and that Nietzsche, in this regard, was right; but also, secondly, that ressentiment is in no way involved in the authentic core of Christian morality which, according to Scheler, was best embodied in feudal chivalry. By means of a tight argumentation, thoroughly nourished by biblical, theological and historical references, Scheler presents[8] the authentic morality of the Gospels as a strictly aristocratic and individualistic morality, not at all opposing the values of the Nietzschean overman, but coinciding with them. On the other hand, Scheler admits that Christian values are more likely than others to be "taken over" by ressentiment, as it is the case in modern "philanthropy" or "humanitarianism."[9]

My purpose is to give a brief account of Scheler's contribution to the understanding of the role of ressentiment in modern democratic and

---

[4] M. Scheler, *Das Ressentiment im Aufbau der Moralen*, in *Vom Umsturz der Werte. Abhandlungen und Aufsätze* (Bern & Munich: Francke, 1972 (*GW* 3), 35–147.

[5] M. Scheler, *Ressentiment*, trans. W. Holdheim (1961) (Milwaukee: Marquette University Press, 1994).

[6] As "ressentiment" is a French loan-word, introduced by Nietzsche as a philosophical term in German, its meaning is not exactly equivalent to the English word "resentment." Scheler's most eloquent advocate in the English-speaking world, the late Manfred Frings, therefore maintained the use of the original term, as I do in this chapter.

[7] This is the subject of chapters IV and V of Scheler's book.

[8] Cf. *Das Ressentiment* ..., chapter III, and the study by W. H. Ng, *Die Leidenschaft der Liebe. Schelers Liebesbegriff als eine Antwort auf Nietzsches Kritik an der christlichen Moral und seine soteriologische Bedeutung* (Frankfurt: Peter Lang, 2009).

[9] Cf. chapter IV. Scheler relativizes the impact of this analysis in *Wesen und Formen der Sympathie* (*GW* 7), 108–111.

capitalistic societies. I shall recall, at first, the connection of the "phenomenology of ressentiment" (developed by the first chapter of his essay) with the axiological background that Scheler himself considered to be the crux of his entire work. Thus, we shall be equipped for a better appreciation of the social, political and economic analyses that follow.

I. The Emotive Structure of Ressentiment in the Context of Scheler's Non-formal Axiology

The phenomenological analysis characterizes ressentiment as the unity of a lived experience (*Erlebnis*), namely that of a "permanent psychic self-poisoning," which by the systematic repression of certain emotional discharges causes a "distortion in the sense of values and in valuation judgements." Values are attached to things, facts, actions etc. that we call "goods"; but they must not be confused with these goods. Normally, Scheler holds, values are evident objects given to us not through reason, but through specific emotive experiences which he names "intentional feeling"; and they are related to each other in a way that can be described as an immutable *a priori* hierarchy, which consists of four independent levels[10]: the lowest value modality is that of sensuous values (agreeable/disagreeable); then comes the modality of vital values (noble/vulgar); the next higher rank are spiritual values (among which the aesthetic: beautiful/ugly; the juridic: right/wrong; and the cognitive: true/false); finally and highest we find the values of holiness (holy/unholy). The moral values good and evil appear in personal acts of choosing and realizing respectively positive and negative values on each of these levels, and in personal acts of choosing and realizing respectively a value of a higher or lower level. Moral values are therefore primarily values of the person (*Personwerte*), in contrast to values of things (*Sachwerte*).[11] This order, given in the intuitive evidence of preference, is "an absolute ethic reference system, on the background of which all moral judgements, norms, variation of ethos and moralities in history take

---

[10] Scheler, *Der Formalismus*, GW 2, 122–126.

[11] "The core of good or evil as pure personal values is seen in the person's *be-ing* good or *be-ing* evil, not in seeking good and evil as objects—although Scheler does not object to the latter as a secondary form of realizing a good." (M. Frings, *The Mind of Max Scheler*, Milwaukee: Marquette University Press, 1997, 44.) The second section of the present chapter will highlight Scheler's concept of the person in the context of a specific issue.

place."[12] The order of values is correlated with the order of feelings. Kant had erroneously restrained *a priori* knowledge to pure reason and had therefore identified "*a priori*" with "rational" and "formal," "*a posteriori*" with "sensuous [*sinnlich*]" and "material"; Scheler brings out an "emotional *a priori*," i.e. an order and hierarchy of feelings that has, as Blaise Pascal put it, "reasons of its own" that reason doesn't know, and that Scheler also calls *ordo amoris*,[13] "order of love."

This axiology is recalled here only insofar as it is necessary for a thorough understanding of Scheler's developments about ressentiment. The latter is an inability to prefer or to realize a value, which nevertheless one cannot refrain from recognizing as such. Ressentiment entails value detraction, i.e. the action of "pulling down," denying and slandering values which should normally, due to their high level, attract us and arouse our approval; conversely, the areas not related to this inability are exalted and enhanced. The resulting reversal and falsification of the order of values is merely illusory, though, insofar as the subject of ressentiment nevertheless continues to perceive the original order, as by "transparency," behind the screen of the disturbed apprehension that he interposes. In this respect, Scheler calls "organic mendacity" [*organische Verlogenheit*][14] the attitude of constantly lying to oneself, which prefigures the "bad faith" subsequently analysed by Sartre in *Being and Nothingness*.

Scheler intends to study not only the genealogy of such *axiological illusions*, but also the conditions for their expansion and success. The etiology of ressentiment reveals two main sources: (1) the combination of (a) a desire for revenge and (b) a sense of powerlessness, which durably inhibits the satisfaction of that desire, while moving it towards more and more distant and indeterminate objects. This first source had already been identified and described by Nietzsche; (2) envy and the propensity to compete (*Konkurrenzstreben*). This second source, which determines political and economic ressentiment, is an original contribution of Scheler to the analysis of this passion. He specifies that the genealogy of ressentiment is primarily related to innate human aptitudes, and only secondarily to the structure of the society in which people live, this structure itself being determined by the hereditary factors of the human type who dominates in it, and by the way this dominant type apprehends

---

[12] M. Frings, *Max Scheler. A Concise Introduction into the World of a Great Thinker*, (Milwaukee: Marquette University Press, 1996), 79.

[13] M. Scheler, *Ordo amoris* (1916), *GW* 10, 345–476. (*Ordo amoris*, in *Selected Philosophical Essays*, trans. David R. Lachterman, Evanston: Northwestern University Press, 1973.)

[14] Scheler, *Das Ressentiment*, *GW* 3, 67.

values.[15] Thus social structure can well be a cause that promotes the formation of ressentiment, but it can also be partly a consequence of the deterioration of the sense of values by ressentiment; in other words, ressentiment produces structures conducive to its perpetuation and its propagation, which partially explain the "highly contagious" character of this "psychic poison."[16] Some of these social aspects will now be considered in more detail.

II. Is Striving for Equality Always Valuable?

The causes of the accumulation of ressentiment in individuals and groups should be sought in a social structure that combines equality of rights with inequality of conditions:

> This psychic dynamite will spread with the *discrepancy* between the legal status and public recognition of a group as determined by politics and constitution or by tradition, and its *factual* power ... The most extreme load of ressentiment is therefore to be found in a society in which, like in ours, approximately equal rights (political and otherwise) or formal social equality, publicly recognized, go hand in hand with wide factual differences in power, property, and education; a society where each has the "right" to compare himself to everyone else, without being able "to do so in fact."[17]

To do justice to the impact of this analysis (which remains marginal within the *Ressentiment* essay), we shall bind it to the more comprehensive reflection developed by Scheler about the relationship between democracy and equality.[18] The concept of democracy remains purely formal as long as one doesn't connect it to various cultural spheres, which alone give it contents and make it a political and social reality. To account for this connection, Scheler introduces a distinction between "democratism" as a sociological worldview and "democracy" as the name of a political current. *Democratism* is a sociological conviction claiming that in all possible groups, it is the large number which determines the values and

---

[15] Ibid., 52.
[16] Ibid., 41.
[17] Ibid., 43.
[18] M. Scheler, *Der Geist und die ideellen Grundlagen der Demokratien der großen Nationen* ["The Spirit and the Ideal Foundations of Democracies in the Great Nations"] (1916), in *Schriften zur Soziologie und Weltanschauungslehre* (Bonn: Bouvier, 1986), (*GW* 6), 158–186. (This essay has not been translated into English.)

sets the norms; such a belief is opposed to "aristocratism," according to
which it is a minority of personalities (examples and leaders[19]) that
introduces, in whatever group, the norms ensuring its cohesion.[20] This first
couple of concepts must be distinguished from a second terminological
pairing: democracy indicates the party of those who, inside one of the
sociological convictions previously evoked, choose to commit to an
increase in equality in some sphere of goods[21]; this current or political
party is opposed not only to liberalism which gives freedom the priority
over equality, but also to other currents which emphasize fraternity or
love. As the commitment to democracy combines with a "democratist" or
"aristocratist" world view, it will take different, liberal or conservative
colourings; this explains the diversity of the historical democracies in
various cultural spheres, for example in England, France, Russia and
Germany.

According to Scheler's analyses, English democracy is chiefly
characterized by the privilege given to liberty and rights of social
individuals at the cost of all other forms of equality. French democracy
mainly strives for the equalization and standardization of spirit and culture,
more than for equality of material wealth. On the opposite side, Russian
democracy, grounded on the idea of revolutionary fraternity, is eager to
achieve equality of possession.[22] German democracy is a mixture of these
types, its main concern being freedom and diversity in the spiritual life of
persons.

If democracy as a political reality is thus essentially bound to a group
activity aiming at an increase of equality in society, it remains to be
specified to which sphere of goods this increase should relate. Scheler
does not underestimate the importance of the issue, as it is usually put—is
it about increasing the equality of material possessions, of instruction, of
political rights and duties, etc.? In other words, is it a question of
establishing a social, cultural or political democracy? Yet the philosopher

---

[19] M. Scheler, *Vorbilder und Führer, GW* 10, 255–344. ("Exemplars of Person and
Leaders," in *Person and Self-Value. Three Essays,* trans. M. Frings, Dordrecht:
Nijhoff, 1987, 125–198.)
[20] In this sense, Scheler professes aristocratism; he holds that a society's ethos
always stems from a minority, even if it eventually "contaminates" the majority.
As we shall see, capitalist societies are imbued with the values of a particular type
of people, the "bourgeois."
[21] This somewhat peculiar definition of democracy reveals the influence of
Tocqueville (whom Scheler seldom cites in other writings).
[22] Scheler's description was published in 1916, i.e. before the Russian revolution
which was to take place in October 1917.

recommends asking beforehand a formal question, which brings us back to the hierarchy of values. What is the value level affected by the goods on which the egalitarian effort is supposed to focus? Indeed, it is one thing to promote equal access to goods covered by the values of the useful and the pleasant; it is something quite different to promote such access to goods falling under the values of justice, truth, or beauty. Here Scheler's position reveals its full originality:

> I consider it as a principle open to rigorous ethical foundation [*Begründung*] that people must become all the more equal as the (positive) values concerned by the comparison are lower [in the hierarchy], and all the more unequal as these values are higher.[23]

In order to understand the rationale leading to this proposition, we have to take a detour into Scheler's notion of "person." Both against Kant's assumption of person as the subject of an activity of (mainly practical but also theoretical) reason, equal in all individuals, and against scholastic heritage treating person as a substance, Scheler claims that the concrete person (who can never be objectified, and is therefore to be sharply distinguished from "ego" or "consciousness") is *per definitionem* and originally unique. "Person is the concrete, self-essential unity of the being of acts of different nature, which in itself ... precedes all essential differences of acts,"[24] i.e. perceiving, knowing, judging, remembering, wanting, feeling, loving, hating, etc.[25]: "The qualitative peculiarity of the how of acting out acts is that which makes every person unique."[26] The whole (trans-spatial, trans-temporal and trans-causal) sphere of acts, i.e. of intentionality and meaningfulness, is named "spirit" [*Geist*]; person being the essentially necessary and only form of the existence of concrete spirit.[27] Thus the spiritual person (*Geistesperson*) appears to be the ultimate bearer of supreme moral values, both individual ("self-hollowing" [*Selbstheiligung*]) and universal ("charity" [*Nächstenliebe*]). Three implications of this theory are of interest for our issue.

---

[23] Scheler, *Der Geist und die ideellen Grundlagen ...*, GW 6, 160.

[24] Scheler, *Der Formalismus ...*, GW 2, 382.

[25] "'Act' has the common phenomenological meaning of an activity of the mind in which there is 'consciousness-of-something.' But in the Schelerian sense, the term extends it to include pre-conscious acts of feeling and preferring." (M. Frings, *The Mind of Max Scheler*, 43.)

[26] Frings, *Max Scheler ...*, 98.

[27] Scheler, *Der Formalismus ...*, GW 2, 389.

(1) Scheler emphasizes that the aim of all society and of the historical process is the being of the person.[28] As the powers of solidarity of interests through labour organization and production techniques tend to relieve person and spirit of tasks that can be realized by non-personal, non-spiritual powers, Scheler states as a first ethical principle:

> All positive values which, according to their nature, can be realized by non-personal and non-spiritual forces should be realized so. To put it briefly: All mechanizeable should be mechanized.[29]

This makes it clear that genuine ethical personalism has nothing to do with "romantic" and reactionary theories that believe that the personal principle and spiritual activity should be preserved at the expense of solidarity of interests, collective organization and machines.

(2) The phenomenology of emotions sketched out in Scheler's *Formalism* distinguishes four different strata of feelings: sensuous feelings (e.g. pain), body or vital feelings (e.g. exhaustion), psychic feelings (e.g. sadness), and spiritual feelings (e.g. despair).[30] Along with this classification runs a decreasing hierarchy of wilful control—sensuous feelings are the most and spiritual feelings the least subject to mastering, removal, and practical change. This is a second matter of ethical importance, as all feelings are tokens of values and disvalues, and as only the spiritual feelings originate from the "sphere of the person" itself. Hence the value and moral importance of happiness feelings are inversely proportional to their accessibility through willing and acting; only the joys that are lowest in value can be influenced by all possible reforms of social and legal systems and, in general, by socio-political action; conversely, the deeper the stratum to which a joy or a suffering belongs, the less it is susceptible to practical influence. Thus only the causes of sensuous pleasure are subject to immediate practical guidance; "in the scope of socio-ethical activity, for example, [this means] in the first place the property situation."[31]

(3) The essential law according to which the feasibility of values by will and action is inversely proportional to their height leads to the conclusion that the highest value (i.e. the holiness of the person) can be realized only if it is not an intentional object of the will; in fact, personal

---

[28] Ibid., 494–495.
[29] Ibid., 496.
[30] Ibid., 334 sq.
[31] Ibid., 339.

value cannot even be given through "being wanted" or "being aimed at."[32] Ethical personalism claims that spiritual persons are fundamentally unequal with regard to the moral ideal because they have, as ultimate bearers of any moral value, an individual and unique value. The assumption of equivalence (in the sense of equality in value) of persons is legitimate only if related to a particular area of tasks. In terms of this area, for example economic subjects or bearers of civil rights and duties, they may be considered equal, but, assuming some ideal state where all organic, psychic and external circumstances were equal, each person would ethically behave in a different way, thus showing their unique personal value.

> As a result of our investigations may actually be regarded the proposition: People should all the *more* become equal and therefore be considered equivalent, as the goods and tasks in relation to which they are taken as subjects of property (for the former) and as subjects of commitment (for the latter) are *lower* and *more relative* within the ranks of the value order.[33]

Hence the difference in the individual value of each person can only appear as their instinctual needs are satisfied in their order of urgency; the goods and the tasks corresponding to more urgent needs should thus be more and more equally distributed between people, precisely in order to ensure that the difference in their capacities concerning goods and tasks of higher axiological range does not remain hidden.

> Only the establishment of *maximally uniform conditions for the being and life of persons, in terms of distribution of goods subject first to the utility value* and second to the vital value, can bring to the fore the *inner* differences of the bearers of *higher* values and provide the basis for their self-explication in actions and works.[34]

Scheler thus combines "aristocracy in heaven" with "democracy on earth," taking the exact opposite course to the tradition of the Enlightenment, which associated transcendental universalism (all men are equal as subjects of reason) with empirical aristocracy (as for material and sensitive well-being, men must, or at the very least can, be unequal). The clue of his whole reasoning is the idea (stemming from Schleiermacher) that the individuality of the being and value of a person grow with the purity of their spirituality, whereas the eighteenth century considered individuals

---

[32] Ibid., 495–497.
[33] Ibid., 500.
[34] Ibid., 508.

being equal with regard to their essence (reason), individuation being provided only by the body or the inductively ascertainable contents of the psychic life. The "individualism" of the Enlightenment absorbed the individual person into the social person. On one side, Kant, in particular, identified the person with the subject of public law, i.e. the citizen of the state, while on the other side the English philosophers identified the person with the subject of economy and private-law contracts. Scheler makes it clear that both were wrong, but claims that the person as subject of private law should be conceived in terms of submission to the person as citizen, for the state deals with the rational ruling of the will to live and with the suitable distribution of life goods among a community, whereas private law deals with the values of the useful and the agreeable, whose rank is inferior to vital values. Especially, Scheler holds, it should be clear that all so-called laws of economics are nothing but a set of technical rules which the person as member of the state, i.e. the citizen, can use for their purposes; economic liberalism is therefore no more a "principle" than protectionism.[35]

These analyses help us to understand (from a normative point of view) why Scheler rejects a social structure that combines equality of civil and political rights (belonging to a higher value level) with inequality of material and vital situations (belonging to a lower level). It also makes clear (from a descriptive point of view) that social ressentiment does not follow from inequalities as such, but merely from a specific combination of inequality and equality, related to the unawareness of the hierarchy of values. To a certain extent, Scheler's analysis joins the Marxist criticism according to which the bourgeois society bestows formal rights on all its members to ideologically mask the interests of the economically dominant class; but, by reference to an immutable order of values, independent from any *de facto* social ethos and from any class interest, Scheler shows that this Marxist criticism is itself the expression of a contingent ressentiment, resulting from a society structured by a distorted appreciation of this order. As he was to put it some years later:

> What is properly antihuman in capitalism is … not at all, as Marx believes, a systematically unfair distribution of capital profit among entrepreneurs and workers … but the nourishing of capital at the expense of man and of a meaningful life of man in general.[36]

---

[35] Ibid., 502 with note 1.

[36] M. Scheler, *Christlicher Sozialismus als Antikapitalismus* ("Christian Socialism as Anti-capitalism") (1919), in *Politisch-pädagogische Schriften* (Bern: Francke, 1982 [*GW* 4], 640).

III. Ressentiment and the Genesis of Capitalism

This leads us to the second aspect by which our modern Western societies are conducive to the formation of ressentiment—the principle of rivalry and competition on which the market economy relies. Former societies (Scheler evokes the Middle Ages) were pervaded by the idea of a fixed "place" or "state" allotted to everyone by God or nature; our "competing" societies arose from the prevalence acquired by a certain type of individual, the "pusher" or "arriviste" (*Streber*):

> An arriviste is a person for whom the fact of being more, being worth more etc. in a possible comparison with others, as the ultimate goal of his striving, intervenes between him and any qualified thing value; for whom any matter is only an indifferent pretext to abolish the crushing feeling of inferiority which arises from these comparisons.[37]

The "system of competition" is characterized by the spread of this form of apprehension of values: "… all concrete tasks and their values depend on the respective claims to be more and to be worth more than anyone."[38]

This evolution has a threefold consequence: (1) it affects the stability of social order by introducing a permanent mobility where each "state" is nothing more than "a transitional point in the scramble," and where the time flow of the lives of individuals and communities is apprehended in terms of "progress"; (2) by dissolving the connection of desire to concrete things and qualitative values, it denies any limit to desire and thus creates in the individual a feeling of perpetual dissatisfaction; (3) it leads to understand goods in kind (*Sachgüter*) in terms of merchandise, i.e. objects of exchange expressed in monetary value:

> Of course we can still enjoy qualitative values, but our enjoyment—and indeed its very possibility—is now limited to goods which are most immediately recognized as units of merchandise value.[39]

These considerations are part of the broader context of Scheler's reflection about the essence and genesis of capitalism.[40] This concept is, in his eyes,

---

[37] *Das Ressentiment* …, *GW* 3, 48. See also *Der Formalismus…*, *GW* 2, 355, note.

[38] *Das Ressentiment…*, *GW* 3, 48.

[39] Ibid., 49.

[40] Like his counterparts Max Weber, Werner Sombart and Ernst Troeltsch, Scheler was durably worried by this question. See in particular *Drei Aufsätze zum Problem des kapitalistischen Geistes* ("Three Essays on the Problem of the Capitalist Spirit") (*GW* 3, 341–395), *Prophetischer oder marxistischer Sozialismus?*

not just economic or sociological, but ethical and axiological. It means the hierarchical relationship of evaluation, for a given group of humans, between economy and its goods, on one hand, and all other goods, contents of desire and values, on the other.[41] A constant thesis runs trough all relevant Schelerian writings—it was not technical forms of production and social forms of organization, nor an immutable "human nature" seeking to maximize its advantages by minimizing its efforts, which ended up producing a "capitalist spirit"; it was on the contrary the capitalist spirit—or bourgeois spirit—which led to the introduction of a capitalist order of society.[42] Hence Scheler strives to clarify the origin of this "spirit" as a "form of evaluation [*Wertungsform*]," i.e. to understand how greed, despised by the pre-capitalist societies (where any desire to acquire was limited by the idea of a "maintenance befitting the rank [*standesgemäßer Unterhalt*]"[43]), could become subject to moral approval and even prescription.[44] The essay on *Ressentiment* is a first attempt in this direction, and the logical order of the genesis of capitalism is the following: (1) a particular form of the comparison of values generates the characterological type of the arriviste; (2) the social predominance of this type[45] (after a process that Scheler only evokes in terms of "contagion") leads to the socio-economic system of competition, i.e. to a social organization (a) inducing unlimited needs, and (b) where goods which could satisfy the desires are first treated as merchandise (in Marxian terminology, their value in exchange taking precedence over their value in use). As a result, consumer society exhausts itself in a paradox—the increasingly massive and fast production of goods intended for enjoyment requires a pace and type of work which reduces the human capacity for

---

("Prophetic or Marxist Socialism?") (*GW* 6, 259–272), as well as the summary of the theses that are being discussed here, in *Die Ursachen des Deutschenhasses* ("The Causes for the Hatred of Germans"), *GW* 4, 297.

[41] Scheler, *Christlicher Sozialismus ...*, *GW* 4, 616.

[42] E. Kiss, "Max Schelers 'Umsturz der Werte' als Kritik der europäischen Moderne," in *Vom Umsturz der Werte in der modernen Gesellschaft*, ed. G. Pfafferott (Bonn: Bouvier, 1997), 129–140; and M. Barber, *Guardian of Dialogue. Max Scheler's Phenomenology, Sociology of Knowledge, and Philosophy of Love* (London/Toronto: Associated University Presses, 1993), 37–42.

[43] M. Scheler, *Der Bourgeois* (1914), *GW* 3, 348.

[44] *Christlicher Sozialismus ...*, *GW* 4, 622.

[45] "The social prevalence of the arriviste type must not be understood in quantitative terms; it is decisive in the rise of the capitalist spirit that the '*morals of the 'poor'* ... has become the morals *of those who in fact are rich*, i.e. precisely the *ruling minority*" (*Die Zukunft des Kapitalismus* ["The Future of Capitalism"] [1914], *GW* 3, 386–387).

enjoyment; this is some perverted form of asceticism, as opposed to ancient asceticism, which aimed at maximizing the capacity for enjoyment, even with a minimum of material wealth.

In these "grotesque"[46] anomalies of contemporary societies, Scheler diagnoses a "disturbance in the order of values"—if our ideal is, in full nonsense, a "minimum of enjoyment *vis-à-vis* a maximum of pleasant and useful things,"[47] it is because we subordinate the value of the agreeable to the value of utility and, even worse, to the useful the vital values, whereas the axiological hierarchy shows us, in its lower part, that the useful is always relative to the pleasant, and the pleasant always relative to the vital. More generally, the specific "disorder of the heart" of our time, induced by ressentiment, consists of three essential axiological illusions according to which: (1) moral value only applies to what one acquires by their own work,[48] whereas we saw that moral distinction among persons is constituted neither by intentions and willing nor by established purposes, but by the "qualitative direction" of the persons' acts which can always be changed for the better by the attraction of moral exemplars[49]; (2) values are not considered worth objectively, but only as they are recognized by all,[50] the endeavour for general recognition being "meant to compensate for the absence of objective values and their ranks"[51]; (3) moral value only applies to what is quantifiable and calculable, i.e. to what corresponds to the values of utility.[52]

IV. Conclusive Assessment

Let us finish with a somewhat broadened perspective. It would be useful to explore what these analyses owe to nineteenth century writers like Thomas Carlyle (whom Scheler sometimes quotes) or John Ruskin (whom he doesn't seem to have mentioned). The latter wrote:

> The production of effectual value ... always involves two needs: first, the production of a thing essentially useful; then the production of the capacity

---

[46] Ibid.
[47] Ibid., 130–131.
[48] Ibid., 117 sq.
[49] M. Frings, *The Mind of Max Scheler*, 164.
[50] *Das Ressentiment ...*, *GW* 3, 122 sq.
[51] Frings, *The Mind of Max Scheler*, 166.
[52] *Das Ressentiment ...*, *GW* 3, 126 sq.

to use it. *Where the intrinsic value and acceptant capacity come together there is Effectual value, or wealth.*[53]

In other words, "Wealth is ... the possession of the valuable by the valiant."[54] Ruskin denounces the systematic destruction of that valiant acceptant capacity by industrial capitalism.

On the other hand, Scheler's diagnosis finds a remarkable resonance in some modern economists, starting with the most distinguished of them, John Maynard Keynes, who stated in October 1930, several months after the beginning of the great global economic crisis, that this crisis is due not to scarcity but to an excessively rapid growth of abundance, which economic actors have failed to manage. The Keynesian thesis, according to which markets, left with themselves, produce harmful imbalances, is well known. Far less well known is this statement (relayed nowadays, among others, by Patrick Viveret[55])—for millennia, mankind was obsessed with shortage and scarcity; modern economy and technology have allowed us to overcome these limitations, and here we are faced with a problem of abundance and overproduction that we are unable to handle, "for we have been trained too long to strive and not to enjoy."[56] It's about time, according to Keynes, to put back in place the scale of values: "Do not let us overestimate the importance of the economic problem, or sacrifice to its supposed necessities other matters of greater and more permanent significance."[57] Having resolved the problem of scarcity, man, for the first time since his origins, faces "his real, his permanent problem—how to use his freedom from pressing economic cares, how to occupy the leisure, which science and compound interest will have won for him, to live wisely and agreeably and well."[58] The article which is presented in the form of an essay in futurology over one century (1930–2030), states forecasts that are perhaps as worthy as recommendations heard this very day:

---

[53] J. Ruskin, *Munera Pulveris*, Essay I, § 14, in *The Works of John Ruskin*, Library Edition (*LE*), edited by E. T. Cook & A. Wedderburn, vol. 17, 154. (London: George Allen, 1905).

[54] J. Ruskin, *Unto this Last*, Essay IV, § 64, in *LE*, vol. 17, 88. See my study "La signification existentielle du travail. Considérations inactuelles inspirées par une lecture de John Ruskin," in *Cahiers Simone Weil* XXXII (4) (2009): 478–479.

[55] Cf. P. Viveret, *Reconsidérer la richesse* ("Reconsidering Wealth") (Paris: Éditions de l'Aube, 2003).

[56] J. M. Keynes, "Economic Possibilities for Our Grandchildren," in *Essays in Persuasion* (New York & London: W. W. Norton, 1931), 368.

[57] Ibid., 373.

[58] Ibid., 367.

... there will be great changes in the code of morals. We shall be able to rid ourselves of many of the pseudo-moral principles which have hag-ridden us for two hundred years, by which we have exalted some of the most distasteful of human qualities into the position of the highest virtues ... We shall once more value ends above means and prefer the good to the useful. We shall honour those who can teach us how to pluck the hour and the day virtuously and well ... Meanwhile there will be no harm in making mild preparations for our destiny, in encouraging, and experimenting in, the arts of life ....[59]

Will Max Scheler's analysis of ressentiment be considered as part of a strategy used by social elites in order to disqualify popular protest and struggle for equality?[60] I hope to have shown that his position is more subtle, providing an unexpected ethical foundation to the claim for social justice and welfare state. By identifying the primary source of ressentiment in individual characterological types, Scheler's conception probably fails to understand the social origin and nature of this passion.[61] But it has the undeniable merit of linking most concrete economic and social problems to the core of philosophical ethics, and to make us understand that the challenge we face in the contemporary world is not merely production of more wealth but rather the capacity to use it wisely; the lack of such capacity being related to a philosophical tradition that never took into account the pre-rational *a priori* order of feelings.

Works Cited

Works by Max Scheler

Gesammelte Werke [Collected Works] in 15 vols., edited by Maria Scheler (1954–1969) and Manfred S. Frings (1970–1997), Berne/Munich: Francke (1954–1985); Bonn: Bouvier (since 1986).

---

[59] Ibid., 369–373, *passim*. See also L. Pecchi & G. Piga (eds), *Revisiting Keynes: Economic Possibilities for Our Grandchildren* (Cambridge (MA): The MIT Press, 2008).

[60] Albert O. Hirschman, *The Rhetoric of Reaction: Perversity, Futility, Jeopardy* (Cambridge (MA): Harvard University Press, 1991).

[61] A. Grandjean & F. Guénard (dir.), *Le Ressentiment, passion sociale* (Rennes: Presses Universitaires de Rennes, 2012).

Other works

Barber, M. *Guardian of Dialogue. Max Scheler's Phenomenology, Sociology of Knowledge and Philosophy of Love*. London/Toronto: Associated University Presses, 1993.

Frings, M. S. *Max Scheler. A Concise Introduction into the World of a Great Thinker*, 2nd ed. Milwaukee: Marquette University Press, 1996.

—. *The Mind of Max Scheler*. Milwaukee: Marquette University Press, 1997.

Grandjean, A. & F. Guénard (dir.). *Le Ressentiment, passion sociale*. Rennes: Presses Universitaires de Rennes, 2012.

Hirschman, A. O. *The Rhetoric of Reaction: Perversity, Futility, Jeopardy*. Cambridge (MA): Harvard University Press, 1991.

Keynes, J. M. "Economic Possibilities for Our Grandchildren." In *Essays in Persuasion*. New York & London: W. W. Norton, 1931.

Kiss, E. "Max Schelers 'Umsturz der Werte' als Kritik der europäischen Moderne." In G. Pfafferott (ed.), *Vom Umsturz der Werte in der modernen Gesellschaft*, Bonn: Bouvier, 1997, 129–140.

Lang, P. "La signification existentielle du travail. Considérations inactuelles inspirées par une lecture de John Ruskin." In *Cahiers Simone Weil* XXXII (4) (2009): 473–495.

Ng, W. H., *Die Leidenschaft der Liebe. Schelers Liebesbegriff als eine Antwort auf Nietzsches Kritik an der christlichen Moral und seine soteriologische Bedeutung*. Frankfurt: Peter Lang, 2009.

Pecchi, L. & G. Piga (eds.). *Revisiting Keynes: Economic Possibilities for Our Grandchildren*. Cambridge (MA): The MIT Press, 2008.

Ruskin, J. *The Works of John Ruskin*, "Library Edition" in 39 vol., ed. by E. T. Cook & A. Wedderburn. London: George Allen, 1903–1912.

Viveret, P. *Reconsidérer la richesse*. Paris: Éditions de l'Aube, 2003.

PART II:

GENDERED RESENTMENT

CHAPTER FOUR

TO TAKE ILL:
RESENTMENT IN EIGHTEENTH-CENTURY
CONTEXT

LINA MINOU

Definitions

The first line of enquiry for the historian of emotions, or the student of cultural phenomena of past periods, is the way they were defined. As Barbara Rosenwein notes, 'many words and ideas have only fuzzy equivalents in the past.'[1] Consequently, the way we use them in analyses may obscure, instead of shed light on, the concepts they describe. In addition, even if an emotion is defined in recognizable ways, an analysis of its use in the past needs to account for the intricate nuances of meaning that it holds for the certain period of study and which may be lost to us. This endeavour cannot be pursued without attention to emotional terms themselves and their relevance to the contexts in which they occur. For this reason, this discussion of resentment in an eighteenth-century context begins by acknowledging its lexical background.

The primary sense of 'resentment' as given in the *OED* is: 'a sense of grievance, an indignant sense of injury or insult received or perceived; (a feeling of) ill will, bitterness, or anger against a person or thing.' It is in this sense that one usually recognises the emotion of resentment; as born of injury and insult, humiliation or suffering. However, entries in early-modern dictionaries (prior to and to some extent informing Johnson's definitive work) show that the word itself did not always carry solely negative connotations or strict connections to injury and insult. Thomas Blount's *Glossographia* of 1661 defined 'ressentiment' as 'a full taste, a

---

[1] Barbara Rosenwein, 'Problems and Methods in the History of Emotions' http://www.passionsincontext.de/index.php?id=557 (accessed June 13 2012). The article delineates a methodology for the history of emotions and a relevant framework of study.

true feeling, a sensible apprehension of, a resentment.'[2] In 1678, Edward
Philips's *The New World of Words* offered the far-reaching definition of
'Resentment or Ressentiment' as 'a sensible feeling or true apprehension
of any thing.'[3] In 1694, the dictionary of the French academy defined the
word 'ressentiment' as 'a sense of injury received' (*'sentiment d'un mal
qu'on a eu'*) and as the remembrance not only of injuries but also of
beneficial, kind deeds (*'le souvenir qu'on garde de bienfaits ou des
injures'*).[4] Dictionaries of the early eighteenth-century, or subsequent
editions of the seventeenth-century ones, often gave similar definitions of
the word and its derivatives. This element of repetition or similarity of
definition is, in part, a characteristic of early-modern lexicography.
Lexicographers would look back to earlier works and include, with some
modifications, older, and accepted, ways of definition in their works. This
practice can be helpful in determining changes in the perception of the
concepts defined. One can assume that an older definition would be
abandoned when it was felt to be no longer useful, accurate or popular.
Hence, when in 1730, Nathan Bailey defined resentment as 'a sensible
apprehension of an Injury offered, or a revengeful Remembrance of it,' he
emphasized a difference in the perception of the word.[5] This difference
does not indicate that Bailey was articulating a new meaning of the word
since its meaning as a sense of grievance was there all along. Rather,
Bailey's definition indicates the abandonment of one of the word's
meanings and the emerging predominance of another. Eventually, this
change was articulated by Samuel Johnson in his *Dictionary of the English
Language* (1755-6) who felt obliged, when giving the definition of the
verb 'to resent', to designate its most usual sense for the time: 'To resent:
1. To take well or ill 2. To take ill; to consider as an injury or an affront.
This is now the most usual sense.'[6]

When Frances Sheridan's virtuous heroine, Miss Sidney Bidulph,
refers to her 'resenting heart' she uses the term in the broader sense of

---

[2] Thomas Blount, *Glossographia; or, a Dictionary Interpreting all such Hard
Words* (London: by Tho. Newcomb, 1661).
[3] Edward Philips, *The New World of Words*; *or, a General English Dictionary*
(London: for Robert Harford, 1678).
[4] 'Ressentiment', in Dictionnaire de l' Académie Française (1694), *The ARTFL
Project: Dictionnaires d'autrefois* artflx.uchicago.edu/cgi-bin/dicos/pubdico1look.
pl?strippedhw=ressentiment (accessed May 14, 2012).
[5] Nathan Bailey, *Dictionarium Britannicum; or, a more Compleat Universal
Etymological English Dictionary than any Extant* (London: for T. Cox, 1730).
[6] Samuel Johnson, *A Dictionary of the English Language: in which the Words are
Deduced from their Originals*, 2nd edn, 2 vols (London: by W. Strahan, 1755–6).

'feeling' heart: a heart susceptible to sensible apprehensions.[7] Sheridan's use of the word 'resenting' may be viewed as an anachronism, since her novel appeared in 1761, a time when the meaning of the word 'resent' was predominantly connected to a sense of injury. However, it might also be argued that her use of the term is in keeping with the time of the story in the novel. The narrated events take place in the early eighteenth century, beginning in 1703, when the word still bears a wider meaning. Such instances of the use of an emotional term, as in Sheridan's novel, indicate that familiarity with the relevant emotional vocabulary of the time is necessary to fully appreciate early-modern works. Without a clarification of the phrase by the editors of the novel, the phrase 'resenting heart' would appear confusing and even oxymoronic, being expressed, as it is, by an exemplary sentimental heroine. Historical information on the various senses of an emotional term, though, allows for a more nuanced interpretation. That is not to say that the definition of an emotional term is a sufficient premise on which to base an interpretation of an instance of the emotion signified. What is more important is how this primary sense of a term becomes varied, or even acquires a new meaning, through context. For example, Sheridan's heroine imputes to her resenting heart the fact that she feels obliged to reject Faulkland's marriage proposal even though she is a widow, and he has always been her true choice. Sidney's rejection of Faulkland is a perplexing act because it is not required. Having fulfilled her filial duty in marrying a suitor approved by her mother and also her wifely duty in being a respectful and loyal wife even during her husband's adultery and consequent financial distress, Sidney can now choose on her own. This rejection is not an act required by the eighteenth-century female codes of honour. It is an act that goes above and beyond them and is based on Sidney's own interpretation of these codes which, she admits, others may find too scrupulous. Sidney's 'resenting heart' means that she is susceptible to those feelings associated with delicacy and female virtue to a heightened degree.

It becomes apparent, then, that the consideration of the way in which an emotional term is defined and the context in which it appears can provide fruitful insights into a work. The verb 'resent' and its derivatives 'resenting', 'resentment', or 'resentful' become progressively associated with a cluster of words that includes: 'injury', 'offence', 'anger', 'long retained anger', and also 'malice' and 'revenge'. Depending on the context, these terms can acquire further modifications. One of the most

---

[7] Frances Sheridan, *Memoirs of Miss Sidney Bidulph*, eds. Patricia Köster & Jean Coates Cleary (Oxford: Oxford University Press, 1995), 316. See also the relevant editors' note, 476.

influential of such modifications is articulated within the discourse of ethics at the time in Butler's sermon 'Upon Resentment' (1726). In this sermon, Butler identifies the injury that causes resentment with moral injury. In doing so, he also modifies resentment from a 'negative' emotion to a feeling that is approved or even required at cases; there are injuries which ought to be resented. Yet, the claim to resentment is more complicated. Considering resentment within an ethical or philosophical work is different from considering it within the context of an eighteenth-century novel that is also concerned with, and informed by, cultural and conduct codes such as the extent to which a wife may express her resentment of her husband's adultery and maltreatment, or a maid's resentment of a man's advances. It is also different to consider the expression of resentment within such contexts as men in apprenticeship or in letter-writing and other social interactions.

In order, then, to understand resentment in its eighteenth-century contexts, and to better appreciate what it means 'to take ill', it is important to examine its representation in various instances and what the claims made in them may be. It is also important to consider what claims are denied when the word used is not 'resentment' but a synonym. Synonyms can help further elucidate a complex concept and with regard to the concept of resentment the word 'stomachfulness' is of particular interest. Characteristically older-sounding and with clear connections to visceral theories of emotion that locate the passions in the belly or the stomach, 'stomachful' begins to be defined as 'resentful': 'Stomachful: resentful, dogged, and loth to submit.'[8] The relevant verb 'stomach' is also defined as a synonym: 'stomach: to resent'[9], or 'Stomach: to resent, be angry at, displeased with.'[10] In light of the above, what follows is an analysis of the representation of resentment in various instances and within various eighteenth-century sources, with special notice to the expression of women's resentment as it is a matter of concern in many of the studied sources.

Feeling Resentment and being Resentful

Discussions of the passions in the eighteenth century do not always demand their condemnation, as being opposite to reason. Some follow a

---

[8] *A Pocket Dictionary; or, Complete English Expositor* (London: for J. Newbery, 1753).
[9] Ibid.
[10] Thomas Dyche, *A New General English Dictionary*, 4th edn (London: for Richard Ware, 1744).

more moderate approach.[11] Analysts cannot deny the fact that the passions, especially violent ones such as anger or negative ones such as envy or malice, are part of human nature. However, this was a time that sought to emphasize notions such as the moral sense or benevolence and needed to reconcile these with the existence of such emotions as anger, envy or resentment. Writers on the passions find a way out of this conundrum by stressing the imperfection of the human state and the negative emotions as its consequence. In other words, they modify bleak conceptions of human nature, as posited by Hobbes and Mandeville, by stating that negative emotions are implanted in human nature for a reason, mostly for self-preservation, and when used within carefully circumscribed bounds they are acceptable or even required. That is, instead of presenting violent passions as the 'state' of human nature, they make them the 'circumstance' and claim that there are cases that call for them. In other words, it is because there is injury, in this imperfect world, that there is also anger.

In the case of the emotion of resentment, ethical discussion modifies injury to moral injury. Butler's sermon 'Upon Resentment' makes a very important distinction between the hasty and sudden passion of anger and settled and deliberate anger or resentment. Sudden anger, he writes, can be raised to resist 'Sudden force, Violence and opposition', in a state of self-defence, 'without Regard to the Fault or Demerit of him who is the Author of them.'[12] On the other hand, resentment is raised in cases of moral wrong: 'it seems in us plainly connected with a sense of Virtue and Vice, of Moral good and Evil.'[13] He further notes 'that it is not natural, but moral Evil; it is not Suffering but Injury, which raises that Anger or Resentment, which is of any continuance.'[14] For Butler, resentment is not a negative or evil passion in itself. He recognises that it can be perverted but in its due bounds it is appropriately directed towards a wrongdoer in order to check and extirpate moral injury and not to harm from malign motives. Moreover, one of the most important, and also counterintuitive, points in Butler's analysis is the assignment of a positive social role to this emotion. Resentment fulfils a social purpose in that it is raised communally against vice and wickedness. That is, it is felt by all people

---

[11] For a consideration of the different attitudes to the idea of the subjection of passions to reason at the time, see Thomas Dixon, *From Passions to Emotions*, especially chapter 3, section on reason and passion, 72.

[12] Joseph Butler, 'Upon Resentment', in *Fifteen Sermons Preached at the Rolls Chapel upon the Following Subjects* (London: for J. and J. Knapton, 1726), pp.137–154, 142.

[13] Butler,143–4.

[14] Butler, 145.

who are bound by the same moral standards when confronted with cases of injustice and moral injury. The fear of provoking this common feeling of resentment is a deterrent to injurious action and further confirms the social benefit of this emotion.

In connecting resentment to 'settled and deliberate' anger instead of 'hasty and sudden' anger, Butler also distinguishes resentment from that description of anger that presents it as 'short madness'.[15] Although the passions, in general, may be perceived as in conflict with reason anger, in particular, is more conspicuously so. It is connected to disorder, to madness and frenzy; it signifies excess and loss of control and is pictured emblematically as an earthquake, a storm, a torrent or as wild animals. Suspension of reason can be perceived either in a fit of anger, very intense but short in duration, or in a state of being blinded to reason due to an intense desire for revenge. In between these states, though, there is an aspect of resentment that is amenable to reason. The most important criterion for reasonable resentment is its cause. William Webster, writing on the consequences of immoderate anger, states that we can take the 'Course of law for any injuries done to our *good Name*, *Estates*, or *Person*, where the injury is of consequence enough to justify our resentment.'[16] Accordingly, resentment can be deemed reasonable because one can present the case, the instance of resentment to others, and also within a formal institution such as a court as is suggested here, and validate it as such. Certainly, it can be argued that anger can also have judicial legitimacy. However, Butler's distinction between hurt or harm as the cause of anger and injury or injustice as that of resentment connects, in a more direct way, resentment with notions of reasonableness and acceptability.

The analysis, though, pertains to the emotion of resentment and not to being resentful which is never justifiable. Resentment is an emotion whereas being resentful signifies emotional disposition. An instance of resentment can be discussed according to certain points of reference that in turn determine whether the emotion itself and its expression is within bounds or unjustifiable. When, for example, texts seek to determine

---

[15] I am interested here in this distinction between hasty or instinctive anger and deliberate anger as resentment and its implications. For a full account of Butler's discussion on resentment see also the following sermon IX 'Upon Forgiveness of Injuries' (Butler makes the point in the preface of the 1729 edition that the account of resentment is 'introductory' to it) and relevant comments in the sermon VI 'Upon Compassion'.

[16] William Webster, *A Casuistical Essay on Anger and Forgiveness* (London: for William Owen, 1750), 67.

between rightful or sinful anger they do so by considering good cause; appropriateness of expression (even with a good cause anger cannot be expressed disproportionately), and duration (it should not be retained longer than needed or after the cause has been removed). Being resentful on the other hand, denotes a person who is, as Johnson notes, 'Malignant, easily provoked to anger and long retaining it.'[17] It is defined in the sense of a state, one 'is' resentful, that is, one bears a tendency to resentment that negates the points above. It is not bound by cause, and exceeds, by definition, the criteria of appropriateness both as to expression and duration. It is, moreover, doubly unsettling because it means that one is incapable of forswearing resentment, either through satisfaction of injuries or through forgiveness of injuries as Butler advocates, and this goes against the very purpose of ethical writings.

These are some of the basic premises laid out in the philosophical and ethical discussion of resentment. However, the articulation of emotion always goes beyond the descriptive bounds designated in writings about the passions. The more or less standardized discussion of resentment would have to be modified by the caveats that the same writers pose. Readings of instances of resentment, fictional or other, must also be sensitive to an articulation of this emotion that may even contradict the premises of the ethical discourse.[18] Studies of emotions, such as Barbara Rosenwein's edition of the study of the social uses of anger,[19] clearly demonstrate that social uses of the emotions often unsettle or even contradict descriptive terms that traditional accounts assign to them. Anger is not always, and very often not at all, connected to violence and irrationality. In the same way, resentment is very often not about moral injury or it is not defined retrospectively as the retained memory of an injury. As the discussion will show, resentment can be about the present and can be raised by a variety of causes, with or without connections to morality.

Resentment and Submission

Resentment's connections to reason and morality allow for it to be considered in different terms from anger. For this reason, resentment can

---

[17] Johnson, *A Dictionary*.
[18] See Alice MacLachlan, 'Unreasonable Resentments', *Journal of Social Philosophy*, 41(2010), 422–41 for an argument on 'the descriptive inadequacy of the philosophical paradigm of resentment.'
[19] *Anger's Past: The Social Uses of an Emotion in the Middle Ages*, ed. by Barbara Rosenwein (Ithaca, N.Y.; London: Cornell University Press, 1998).

be an 'acceptable' feeling for women. Although women's anger is rarely justifiable, resenting a moral injury can be acceptable and even required as a sign of a virtuous character. In this sense it is often used by female characters within early texts that are published as 'novels' or would have been perceived as such. Within this context, showing resentment can be a sign of virtue. In the opening episode of *The Prude* (1724), a young man boldly addresses a company of women. Their guardian, Emelia, reacts quickly and, as the narrator informs us, 'with Looks which express'd her Resentment much more than her Words, said, Sir, have these Ladies or I given you any Offence, that you presume on these unusual Liberties with us [?]'[20] In this case, resentment is defined firmly in the present, more specifically to the moment, and through signifiers in the face ('looks') and Emelia's words. It is not a harboured emotion but an instant response that comes close to anger. This sentiment is also expressed by Samuel Richardson in his influential work *Clarissa* (1747-8). In order to prove that her heart is free, and thus negate the accusation that she rejects the suitor her parents propose on grounds other than principle, Clarissa gives her private letters to her mother for inspection. The letters are exchanged between her and Lovelace, a known rake and dangerous man. Admittedly, this correspondence is blameable, and Clarissa herself perceives it as such, but it began with the family's approbation, when Lovelace was in good standing with them, and was continued to prevent the consequences of the resentment between her brother and Lovelace. Her mother returns the letters saying she finds nothing objectionable, adding: 'you have even kept a proper dignity and decorum: And you have resented, as you ought to resent, his menacing invectives.'[21] Instances like the above show that resentment can operate within the pattern of notions that designate female conduct such as decorum and decency as they are perceived at the time. In this sense, resentment becomes open-ended in definition and manifestation. Although both cases above use the term, what constitutes resentment in both and how it is to be expressed is variable: it can be a look, a reproach or a spirited letter. Moreover, in the first case, that of Emelia's reaction, to resent the man's advances does not need to be a sincere emotion but a culture-coded response. Further on in the episode, the young man casts aspersions on Emelia's character, implying that she is not as virtuous as she seems. Consequently, Emelia's reaction can be said to have more of a semiotic function: she has to show that she resents a kind of behaviour to be perceived as virtuous. However, we can be sure that Clarissa's resentment

---

[20] MA. A, *The Prude; a Novel* (London: for J. Roberts, 1724), 2.
[21] Samuel Richardson, *Clarissa, or, the History of a Young Lady*, ed. Angus Ross (London: Penguin, 1985), 100.

of Lovelace's behaviour, in the case quoted and in others within the novel, is genuine. And this is not the silent, inward, retrospective emotion that we usually perceive as resentment. In a way, resentment in these cases comes closer to anger. It is instant, conspicuous in the body or face and articulated as an 'angry response'. However, despite the similarities, resentment occupies a specific lexical and moral ground that is different from that of anger.

For this reason, it is significant that the word 'resentment' is used when there is a question of submission to unlawful authority. Eliza Haywood's novel *The Distress'd Orphan* (1726) presents the story of Annilia, a virtuous young woman in the care of her paternal uncle. As an accomplished woman and heiress to her late parents' fortune, Annilia's marriage prospects are very promising. However, her uncle plans to marry her to his own son for the purpose of promoting his financial interests by joining their two fortunes. It is essential to the success of this plan that Annilia is denied social interaction with Marathon, a suitor preferable in terms of character and status to her cousin, and much to her liking. When her uncle forbids her to receive a letter which he thinks is from Marathon, and insists on calling his son her prospective husband, Annilia loses patience: 'He is not yet so, *answered she*, and to whatever Subjection I may be destined after Marriage, I take it ill that my liberty should be restrained till then.'[22] Such a response goes against the conduct codes of the time. Even if he is not her father, her paternal uncle and ward has the right to demand from her the equivalent of filial obedience. However, Annilia refuses to recognise such authority in him because he has forfeited the obligations that come with it by selfishly promoting his interests over hers and restricting her even though she has not behaved indecorously. This comes close to an account of resentment that confirms it as deriving from a position of inferiority and an awareness of humiliation (Annilia also resents being treated as a child and denied agency), but it is far from the notion of it as an inward, self-consuming emotion that festers without being articulated.

Another such instance occurs in Richardson's *Clarissa*. The virtuous Clarissa is caught between the schemes of a rake who involves her in his plans to effect revenge to the family, and an overly strict parental authority that through fear and anger becomes excessively oppressive. The family, in the interests of preserving its honour, and also aggrandizing itself economically, insists on marrying Clarissa to a man whom she dislikes, not only personally but on grounds of moral principle. As the situation

---

[22] Eliza Haywood, *The Distress'd Orphan; or, Love in a Mad-House* (London: for J. Roberts, 1726; repr. AMS, 1995), 21–2.

becomes more and more fraught, Clarissa seeks the advice of her friend, Anna Howe. Anna responds: 'Only, let me advise you, to pull up a spirit, even to your uncle, if there be occasion. Resent the vile and foolish treatment you meet with, in which he has taken so large a share, and make him asham'd of it, if you can.'[23] Here, the imperative 'resent' involves actions such as to speak up against the vile treatment, to expose it as vile, to make the offender ashamed of it. In these cases, resentment goes beyond self-defence and attempts to define an exception from the strict rules that bind eighteenth-century female conduct and experience. The passages suggest that there are circumstances when submission to parental authority is not required but actually questioned. However, Clarissa's resentment, as well as Annilia's, is bound by the codes of filial obedience exactly as it seeks to question their binding force. No matter what the nature of the injury is, there are certain people whose authority supersedes any claim to resentment. William Webster noted that we ought not to be angry with:

> Parents and Governors, in the Exercise of their just Authority; because such inward Emotions of Resentment are inconsistent with the inward Reverence which is due to that particular relation, and with the external Obedience which is due to their commands; which do not lose their binding force whenever their Authority is improperly exercised.[24]

The comment above shows that, although the necessary conditions exist for a moralized claim to resentment, women's resentment is always subject to different interpretations. It is very easy to move from a framework of appropriate resentment to that of being resentful. That is, instead of interpreting resentment as expressed in line with notions of virtue and sense of dignity to interpret it as a sign of disposition to resentment. For instance, whereas the virtues and the rhetoric of Clarissa firmly locate her resentment within a moralized framework, her family imputes her behaviour to obstinacy. She is often referred to as 'obstinate', 'perverse' and 'sullen' and her distress is constantly devalued and misinterpreted. It is worth mentioning here that 'sullenness' was defined in 1744 as 'a disposition that carries resentment high, that refuses to speak.'[25] This is particularly resonant when one considers that the very core of Clarissa's incompliance is that she does not speak, that is, she does not express consent. However, Clarissa's silence, as Kathlyn Steele points out,

---

[23] Richardson, *Clarissa*, 279.
[24] Webster, *A Casuistical Essay*, 37.
[25] Dyche, 1744.

is a rhetorical silence.[26] She remains silent so that her words cannot be made into consent. Moreover, when Clarissa's servant comments that she lately subsides on nothing but air, Clarissa's sister is reported as saying that: 'stomachfulness, had swallowed up [her] stomach; and that obstinacy was meat, drink, and cloth to [her].'[27] The comment devalues Clarissa's claim to resentment as the word suggests that Clarissa's behaviour is visceral and detached from principle. The difference between the terms 'resentment' and 'stomachfulness' is significant. One cannot talk about resentment without invoking the concept of injury. But when one talks of 'stomachfulness' the emphasis shifts clearly to disposition and character. Thomas Dyche defined 'stomachful' as 'angry, dogged, cross, peevish, proud, loth to submit or comply.'[28] The repetition of words that suggest anger and the term 'loth' used in Dyche's definition suggest that to be stomachful is to be unnecessarily incompliant and that is a quality that unsettles both the notion of sociability that pervades eighteenth-century thought and the notion of filial duty. The word 'resentment' brings into question the family's cruel behaviour but the word 'stomachfulness' centres on Clarissa, revealing her as the defiant daughter whose behaviour breaches filial obedience not out of principle but out of stubbornness.

The unwillingness to assign resentment to Clarissa derives from the fact that resentment retains enough connections to anger to be considered subversive in the way it characterises behaviour as insulting or injurious. To claim action that comes from people of authority, such as parents, husbands or governors, as injurious is also to question the lawfulness of their authority. When Haywood's Betsy Thoughtless decides to leave her husband after a series of incidents of maltreatment and his committing adultery with a guest at their house, she is certain that her action conflicts neither with 'divine nor human law.'[29] She feels justified in this action because although she has observed her wifely duties her husband's behaviour is a breach of his duties towards her. But even if Betsy's own arguments, condoned by other virtuous characters in the novel, present a solid case for resenting abusive behaviour, she still expresses doubts: 'she could not quite assure herself, that a Breach of that solemn covenant [the covenant of marriage] was to be justified by any provocations; nor whether the worst usage on the part of the husband could authorize

---

[26] Kathlyn Steele, "Clarissa's Silence," *Eighteenth-Century Fiction* 23 (2010): 1–34.

[27] Richardson, *Clarissa,* 265.

[28] Dyche, 1744.

[29] Eliza Haywood, *The History of Miss Betsy Thoughtless*, 4 vols (London: by T. Gardner, 1751), 4, 226.

Resentment in that of a wife.'[30] Betsy's uncertainty over the acceptability of her emotion indicates that notions of female virtue at the time operate upon restraints that involve the silencing of emotions that are considered subversive or their channelling into prescribed responses.

To stifle one's Resentment and to Take Ill

If eighteenth-century conduct codes made it difficult for women to express resentment, additional considerations made the matter of forswearing resentment not one of obedience but one of choice. Conduct books that formed a popular part of literature at the time and were used as guides to social interaction would advise their readers that it is beneficial to stifle their resentment. In 1740 a conduct book aimed at young people in apprenticeship advertised resentment as one of the topics on which it gave advice. Barnard's *A Present for an Apprentice* was reprinted frequently and was advertised as useful to young people in general. In the book, resentment appears as a concern from the small matter of telling a joke that might offend to social interactions and marriage. Under the heading 'Dissimulation of Injuries', the writer argues that it makes financial sense to stifle one's resentment because otherwise a person 'shuts the door to opportunities.'[31] In 1743 the *Lady's Preceptor* similarly advised women that:

> It is frequently very advantageous to appear Blind to what gives us offence: Suppose a Female Acquaintance should complain of your having done her an Injury, and begin her revenge by loading you with Reproaches; why if you stifle your Resentment, and take no notice of them, she'll be quickly appeased, and you'll have an Enemy the less.[32]

This kind of advice is not tied to ethical considerations, but is purely a matter of interest. As economic practices change to favour commercial action, good reputation becomes associated not only with concepts of honour but also with trustworthiness in economic exchange. Under this consideration, the emotions are subjected to interests, financial and other. The argument posited by the *Lady's Preceptor* is that stifling one's resentment is a way of, ultimately, protecting one's reputation, as fewer enemies means fewer people who could damage one's reputation by

---

[30] Haywood, *Betsy Thoughtless*, 248.

[31] Sir John Barnard, A *Present for an Apprentice; or, a Sure Guide to Gain both Esteem and Estate* (London: F. Gogan, 1741), 49.

[32] Abbé d'Ancourt, The *Lady's Preceptor; or, a Letter to a Young Lady of Distinction upon Politeness*, 2nd edn (London: for J. Watts, 1743), 24.

venting their displeasure. Within this framework there is no consideration of what constitutes resentment, its psychological effects, or its consequences in terms of ethics. Resentment is not discussed here as part of a process that seeks to achieve virtue, or at least a degree of moral wisdom, by making one capable of forswearing the emotion and practice forgiveness of injuries. Instead, the reader is encouraged to 'appear blind', to 'stifle' resentment, to 'dissemble the very feeling'[33] of injuries. In short, as Barnard puts it, to act 'as if' there is no cause for resentment.

Conversely, it can be the case that cultural and social codes would encourage the opposite behaviour; to show resentment even if the cause does not justify it. A good case in point comes from a source that is representative of eighteenth-century social exchange: letter-writing. The eighteenth century saw the proliferation of letters and letter-writing from a means of everyday communication to its exploration as a narrative technique. Accordingly, many works appeared that were compilations of types of letters, offered as guides to proper letter-writing. In one such compilation, Charles Hallifax poses as the editor of a substantial number of letters of a deceased relative that he has decided to publish for their instructional value. In addition to letters, the work also includes models of cards. These were short notes to be exchanged in social interactions such as invitations or refusals of them. Hallifax assembles the cards that are to be used in positive social interaction, such as invitations to dinners, airings and exchange of compliments or trivial information, under the heading 'cards of politeness.'[34] In contrast, he uses the heading 'cards of resentment'[35] to group those cards that expressed disruption in a social relationship. Despite the mildness of the injury–the cases described are minor transgressions of etiquette, such as keeping a lady waiting for too long, or a misunderstanding between two gentlemen on revealing supposed amorous feelings to a woman–the language used is generally sharp (especially in the gentlemen's case). Words such as 'slighted', 'neglected' and 'insulted' are not only used in them but also designated for use in similar exchanges for which these cards serve as models. This discrepancy between the diction of the cards and the relative insignificance of the injury marks the resented behaviour as inappropriate because it is discordant with the codes that inform polite social exchanges and with the status of the eighteenth-century gentleman and lady. In this case the focus

---

[33] Barnard, 48, the sentiment is expressed in more or less similar wording in other editions of the work.

[34] Hallifax, Charles, *Familiar Letters On Various Subjects of Business and Amusement* (London: for R. Baldwin, 1754), 197.

[35] Hallifax, 205.

is less on the injury itself than in the very capacity of someone to resent. Indeed, the phrase 'to take ill', used by Johnson, does not reveal anything about the nature of the injury. Rather, it suggests a frustration in one's expectations about a behaviour that they feel is due to them. Butler's discussion actually recognised this aspect of resentment for he noted that the term injury comprehends   'not only the more gross and shocking instances of wickedness, but also contempt, scorn, neglect, any sort of disagreeable behaviour towards a person, which he thinks other than what is due to him'.[36] In its turn, this expectation of what is due to one involves intricate considerations of the notions of honour, virtue and social status as they operated at the time and, essentially, an act of self-identification with regard to these.

***

The study of emotions in history, especially in the way it has been redefined by recent work in the field,[37] ultimately provides an insight into past cultural and social phenomena. As Rosenwein notes, people express emotions for what they assess as either valuable or harmful to them.[38] Accordingly, changing attitudes to what is considered valuable or harmful are always at the core of social and cultural transformation. A historical account of resentment is, in this light, especially fruitful because of its diversity. Resentment does not suggest a definite affective response: there are many ways in which it can be experienced, manifested or discussed. Older definitions of resentment include a neutral meaning while later perceptions may be positive or wholly negative. It may be a sign of moral degeneracy (in its denial of forgiveness or in being resentful), or a sign of virtue and moral standing (in being a response against injustice). Consequently, it may be petty, bitter and powerless or significant and powerful and also gendered on the basis of this distinction. In eighteenth–century context, resentment is often used interchangeably with anger.

---

[36] From the preface to the 1729 edition of the *Fifteen Sermons* (London: for J. and J, Knapton, 1729), xxiii.

[37] See Barbara Rosenwein, 'Problems and Methods'. Also by the same author, 'Worrying about Emotions in History', *The American Historical Review*, http://historycooperative.rg/journals/ahr/107.3/ah0302000821.ht ml (accessed June 13, 2012). Thomas Dixon, *From Passions to Emotions: The Creation of a Secular Psychological Category* (Cambridge: Cambridge Unversity Press, 2003) and other publications by the same author, as well as other relevant sources suggested in the bibliography.

[38] Rosenwein, "Problems and Methods," 11.

However, through its connections to moral injury after Butler's influential discussion, it is also defined in a lexical, ethical and cultural space that differentiates it from the discourse on anger in important ways. This allows for resentment to be articulated in ways that conform to social expectations or are in opposition to them. In addition, resentment's affinities to concepts with social and political resonance, such as injury, insult and injustice, make the discussion of this emotion a concern for important cultural realms as the sources studied here show, such as ethics, polite social interaction, the world of economic exchange, and domesticity. In delineating the conditions of justified resentment in each of these realms, writers also reveal principal social norms of the time and the challenges they undergo.

Within the social realm, resentment is akin to the concepts that define the social positions of a lady or a gentleman. The cards of resentment essentially provide a way of laying claim to a social position by resenting even the minor transgression that can be taken as disregard of the etiquette attached to it. However, it is also a way that marks a difference in social codes. To resent an affront necessarily invokes, for the eighteenth-century gentleman, the concept of male honour, and this carries with it the threat of violence, that is, resolution of the situation by a duel. In Hallifax's cards, the misunderstanding between the gentlemen occasions strong language and there is a threat of physical violence but it is never realised as the conflict remains a matter of intense but written exchanges. A card of resentment, then, suggests a new form of emotional outlet at a time when writings against duelling and its consequences are a main part of the call for social, and male, reformation. It allows both for the expression of resentment and the confirmation of the status of the gentleman but avoids violence. Characteristically, after the resolution of the misunderstanding the gentleman apologizes, asks for the cards of resentment he had sent to 'be burnt, and the contents of them forgotten.'[39] This suggests that instead of multiplying the injury, as happens in a duel, a card of resentment bears the potential to 'undo' it: the burning of the papers being the tangible erasure of the offence. In the workspace, Barnard's advice seems to qualify resentment as being closer to anger and he seeks to moderate the venting of displeasure, that is, the outburst that would reveal a character as immoderate and thus untrustworthy. Here the discourse on resentment becomes differentiated according to gender. Resentment, for a man, is a concern for the workplace in the ways it hinders the prospects of economic advantage. For a woman, as sources from fiction and conduct books reveal, it becomes a major concern in the domestic realm.

---

[39] Hallifax, 207.

Indeed, the domestic realm, in the ways it operated in the eighteenth-century, is most relevant to an account of the emotion of resentment because it brings together two important factors that generate it. Firstly, it is a space invested with value. For a patriarchal society, women's most valuable roles, those of wife and daughter, operate within domesticity. Secondly, and most importantly with regard to resentment, because this value is defined in ways that translate as suppression or emotional restraint for women, the domestic realm is also the space of injury and insult. Within this context, resentment stems from the discrepancy between the demands of wifely and filial duties and the woman's sense of dignity. For instance, Betsy feels that despite demands for wifely obedience her husband's cumulatively injurious behaviour should not be tolerated because it is essentially degrading. In the cases of Annilia and Clarissa, it stems from the discrepancy between duty and principle when authority becomes oppressive and thus cruel or, even, unlawful. The expression of resentment in these cases is primarily verbal. Annilia declares her resentment directly ('I take it ill') and Clarissa is encouraged to 'resent', that is, to speak up against maltreatment. This is fittingly so because resentment here is part of the argument against oppressive rules of female conduct. In essence, Clarissa argues for an exception to the social and cultural codes that bind female behaviour. The general rule is that children owe obedience to their parents and in no other case is this notion of filial duty more binding than that of a daughter's marriage. However, while parental authority is binding, it is also bound by obligations towards the children, and it can become unlawful when oppressive.[40] When Clarissa is encouraged to resent her family's treatment expressed in anger, pressure and confinement, her resentment will also confirm this behaviour as vile and consequently her own behaviour will not be a breach of the laws of filial duty but a justified exception from them. In its turn, this argument for an exception from applying social codes is also to challenge them, to expose their oppressive characteristics and to argue for the limitation of their binding force. Hence, in what possible ways a historical account of resentment may evolve, the part that studies women's resentment must overcome its representation as a petty, bitter emotion of powerlessness. Certain considerations, such as concern with female reputation, may suggest its articulation in ways that confirm existing social codes or its repression. However, the cases that call for its expression do so in

---

[40] For a discussion of the codes of parental authority informing *Clarissa,* see Thomas Keymer, 'Casuistry in Clarissa', in *Richardson's Clarissa and the Eighteenth-Century Reader* (Cambridge: Cambridge University Press, 1992), 85–141, especially pages 98–120.

assertive ways. As a part of the rhetoric against oppression, women's resentment can be a powerful and subversive response. In no way is this aspect of their resentment more confirmed than in the cases when the claim to it is denied, either by female characters expressing doubt as to whether they have a right to it, as Betsy does, or by the use of a word that negates its connections to morality such as 'stomachfulness,' as in *Clarissa*.

I wish to thank Dr Dolores Martin Moruno for her encouragement and valuable suggestions and Dr Nick Freeman for offering his opinion and help. I am especially grateful to Professor Bill Overton for reading and commenting upon earlier versions of this paper with his usual support and astute discernment All the comments and critical attention of the named persons and of the members of the audience on the day of presentation are greatly appreciated.

Works Cited

A Pocket Dictionary; or Complete English Expositor. London: for J. Newbery, 1753.

Barnard, Sir John. *A Present for an Apprentice; or, a Sure Guide to Gain both Esteem and Estate*. London: for F. Gogan, 1741.

Bailey, Nathan. *Dictionarium Britannicum; or, a More Compleat Universal Etymological English Dictionary than any Extant*. London: for T. Cox, 1730.

Blount, Thomas. *Glossographia; or, a Dictionary Interpreting all Such Hard VVords*. London: by Tho. Newcomb, 1661.

Butler, Joseph. "Upon Resentment." In *Fifteen Sermons Preached at the Rolls Chapel*. London: for J. and J. Knapton, 1726, 137–154.

d'Ancourt, Abbé. *The Lady's Preceptor; or, a Letter to a Young Lady of Distinction upon Politeness*, 2nd edn. London: for J. Watts, 1743.

Dictionnaire de l'Académie Française (1694). The ARTFL Project: Dictionnairesd'autrefoisartflx.uchicago.edu\cgibin/dicos/pubdicollook .pl?strippedhw=ressentiment (accessed May 14, 2012).

Dixon, Thomas. *From Passions to Emotions: The Creation of a Secular Psychological Category*. Cambridge: Cambridge University Press, 2003.

Dyche, Thomas. *A New General English Dictionary*, 4th edn. London: for Richard Ware, 1744.

Hallifax, Charles. *Familiar Letters on Various Subjects of Business and Amusement*. London: for R. Baldwin, 1754.

Haywood, Eliza. *The Distress'd Orphan; or, Love in a Mad-House.* London: for J. Roberts, 1726; reprint AMS, 1995.

—. *The History of Miss Betsy Thoughtless*, 4 vols. London: by T. Gardner, 1751.

Johnson, Samuel. *A Dictionary of the English Language: in which the Words are Deduced from their Originals*, 2nd edn, 2 vols. London: by W. Strahan, 1755–6.

Keymer, Thomas. *Richardson's Clarissa and the Eighteenth-Century Reader.* Cambridge: Cambridge University Press, 1992.

MacLachlan, Alice. "Unreasonable Resentments." *Journal of Social Philosophy* 41 (2010): 422–41.

Philips, Edward. *The New World of Words, or A General English Dictionary.* London: for Robert Harford, 1678.

Richardson, Samuel. *Clarissa, or, the History of a Young Lady*, edited by Angus Ross. London: Penguin, 1985.

Rosenwein Barbara (ed.). *Anger's Past: The Social Uses of an Emotion in the Middle Ages.* Ithaca, N.Y.; London: Cornell University Press, 1998.

—. 'Problems and Methods in the History of Emotions' http://www.passionsincontext.de/index.php?id=557 (accessed June 13, 2012).

—. 'Worrying about Emotions in History', *The American Historical Review*,http://historycooperative.rg/journals/ahr/107.3/ah0302000821.html (accessed June 13, 2012)

Sheridan, Frances, *Memoirs of Miss Sidney Bidulph*, edited by Patricia Köster and Jean Coates Cleary. Oxford: Oxford University Press, 1995.

Steele, Kathlyn. "Clarissa's Silence." *Eighteenth-Century Fiction* 23 (2010): 1–34.

Webster, William. *A Casuistical Essay on Anger and Forgiveness.* London: for William Owen, 1750.

CHAPTER FIVE

RESPONDING THE INJURY: ON THE SHADOW ECONOMY OF FEMALE RESENTMENT IN CRISTINA DI BELGIOJOSO'S "ON THE PRESENT CONDITION OF WOMEN AND THEIR FUTURE" (1866)

SUSANNA F. FERLITO

Introduction

Of all the emotions (love, anger, hate, jealousy, compassion, etc.), resentment has least inspired critical discussion or visual portrayal. Rooted in the memory of a past wound that cannot (or should not) be forgotten, resentment both resists visual representation and explicit affective behaviour, and yet is all about making others "feel" the wound and the injustice done to them. Resentment is typically vilified as a deeply antisocial emotion, both petty and soul consuming, and as such is an emotion that is often gendered as female. Immanuel Kant, for example, described the ideal woman as characterized by "sympathetic sensations, good-heartedness and compassion," as well as *"very delicate feelings in regard to the least offence."*[1] He described women as "naturally" susceptible to petty offence. In his view, resentful women held on to their grudges and bitterness. As the emotion of unforgiving, female resentment thus signalled a woman's normative failure to be compassionate and forgiving. Nietzsche's later portrayal of resentment as a poisonous emotion thriving in the damp and moist corners of the weak and slave-like soul added a

---

[1] Immanuel Kant, *Observations on the Beautiful and the Sublime* (Berkeley: University of California Press, 1960) (emphasis mine).

female-gendered topography.[2] Popular understandings of resentment's nastiness stem from Nietzsche's influence. Resentment, however, is not wholly negative. Philosophers have depicted resentment as a powerful response to personal or collective injury and injustice.[3] In his *Dictionary of Synonyms* (1848), the Dalmatian-Italian linguist Niccoló Tommaseo defined resentment as: "that insult which stems from receiving an injustice, real or imagined. Men can, due to impatience or intolerance, or violence, become angry. Resentment stems from that same sense of injury. It is more or less strong but it never becomes anger or rage."[4] More importantly, "a people resents the violence it is subjected to not by getting angry but by *making it felt* that *it feels* the injustice and this suffices for a people to do prodigious things."[5] Tommaseo's definition of resentment foregrounds this emotion's capacity for patience, tolerance and control, despite a sense of injury to the self or to the collective. It is an emotion that affectively moves other people or even nations to feel injustice. Thus, it works through representation and metaphor instead of violence, rage or revenge. From Tommaseo's perspective, as in Adam Smith's *Theory of Moral Sentiments* (1759), the expression of righteous resentment can become a powerful political weapon for an individual or collective to move a society to share in the feeling of a grievous injustice. Understood as a powerful response to injustice, resentment has been largely gendered as male. Scholars have recently begun to examine male resentment as the emotional precursor to righteous acts of revolt on the part of victims, whether as individuals or as societies, but have overlooked the social and political role of women's resentment.[6] Feminist literature has focused on

---

[2] On the relationship between resentment and forgiveness, see Thomas Brudholm, *Resentment's Virtue: Jean Améry and the Refusal to Forgive* (Philadelphia: Temple University Press, 2008); also see Friederich Nietzsche, *On the Geneaology of Morals; Ecce Homo,* trans. and ed. Walter Kaufmann (New York: Vintage, 1989).

[3] See: Joseph Butler, *Butler's Fifteen Sermons Preached at the Roll's Chapel; and, a Dissertation of the Nature of Virtue,* ed. J.H. Bernard and Tom Aerwyn Roberts (London: Society for Promoting Christian Virtue, 1970); David Hume, *An Inquiry Concerning Human Understanding: with a Supplement, an Abstract of a Treatise of Human Nature,* ed. Charles W. Hendel (Indianapolis: Bobs-Merrill Educational Publishing, 1955); Adam Smith, *A Theory on Moral Sentiments* (Edinburgh: J Bell, 1759); Brudholm; and Margaret Urban Walker, *Moral Repair: Reconstructing Moral Relations after Wrongdoing* (Cambridge: Cambridge University Press, 2006).

[4] Niccoló Tommaseo. *Dizionario dei Sinonimi della lingua Italiana* (Milan: Vallardi, 1848), 422.

[5] Tomaseo, *Dizionario,* 422 (emphais mine).

[6] Stefano Tomelleri, *La società del risentimento* (Rome: Meltemi, 2010); Mark Ferro, *Resentment in History* (Cambridge, UK: Polity, 2010).

women's anger and bitterness but not on resentment as a powerful emotional response to injustice.[7] Yet, as I show through the case of the nineteenth-century Italian patriot and political activist Cristina di Belgiojoso (1807–1871), resentment offers a rich ground for investigating how women, constrained by normative gender expectations of compassion, forgiveness, and self-abnegation, found different emotional strategies and an effective means for protesting the injustice of their subjugation and oppression.

Much has been written about nineteenth-century female hysteria as the "female malady" of the century that gave symptomatic expression to women's unhappiness and to their protest against oppression.[8] But were emotions of protest like resentment and anger always subject to a medicalizing narrative, or did women also find ways to make their resentful protest felt by others in politically, culturally and socially effective ways? To date, the study of nineteenth-century female physical and emotional responses to injustice seems to fall either into the medicalized purview of hysteria studies or into socio-political studies of organized women's emancipationist practices and movements. Yet, this polarized understanding of women's protest leaves out many who were neither strictly speaking hysterical nor emancipationists but who shared with their peers profound feelings of resentment against social and political oppression and desired to affect political, social and cultural change. Cristina di Belgiojoso's essay "Della presente condizione delle donne e del loro avvenire" [On the Present Condition of Women and their Future] (1866), written for the first issue of the Italian journal *Nuova antologia*, offers us a key to understanding the emotion of resentment as a political and social problem, rather than as an existential or medicalized expression of the injured (ill, mad, bitter, aged) self.[9] Her unleashing of resentment's representational capacity to move others to feel injustice works within an emotional economy typically passed over by critical inquiries focused on visible signs (street demonstrations, meetings, etc.) or symptomatic readings of female protest. My reading of Belgiojoso's essay

---

[7] Marilyn Frye, "A Note on Anger," in *The Politics of Reality: Essays in Feminist Theory* (Trumansburg, N.Y: Crossing Press.1983); Sue Campbell, *Interpreting the Personal: Expression and the Formation of Feelings* (Ithaca, N.Y.: Cornell University Press, 1997); Naomi Scheman, "Anger and the Politics of Naming," *Women and Language in Literature and Society,* ed. Sally McConnell-Ginet, Ruth Borker & Nelly Furman (New York: Praeger, 1980), 174–187.

[8] Elaine Showalter, The *Female Malady: Women, Madness and English Culture, 1830–1980* (New York: Pantheon Books, 1985).

[9] Cristina Belgiojoso, "Della presente condizione delle donne e del loro futuro," *Nuova Antologia di scienze, lettere e arti* 1 (1) (1866): 6–24.

goes against a tradition of scholarship that deems it an essay of her "old age," a disappointing, belated, and intellectually modest piece of writing "pervaded by melancholic resignation," a refusal to call for political and legal reforms, and a revealing personal document of the author's grudges and memories of her experiences of gender discrimination.[10] Such critical perspectives stem from the justifiable attempt to understand and explain why an influential political activist like Belgiojoso failed, in her essay, to support the emancipationist call for an immediate end to women's oppression. Furthermore, focused as they are on a biographical approach to the essay, these critical readings also presuppose that emotions are universal, biological and psychological feelings that are deeply private and personal. My reading of the essay takes as its point of departure an understanding of emotions as affective expressions shaped by and within a social, political and emotional economy. From this perspective it makes a difference to, as Daniel Gross argues, "not only what sort of passions are distributed to whom, but also how they are hoarded and monopolized and how their systematic denial helps produce political subjects of a certain kind."[11] For my purpose here, the gendering of women's resentment as a "natural" feeling of petty offence helps to, in other words, produce women as a certain kind of political subject lacking representational and emotional power to make their resentment matter to others. While I agree with Daniela Chiarito that resentment is a key emotion in Belgiojoso's essay, it is not merely symptomatic of her "old age" or her private emotional world. Rather, what is at stake is an emotional economy of resentment that Belgiojoso deploys to make women's responses to injustice matter, both politically and socially.

Belgiojoso's emotional deployment of women's resentment cannot be separated from the political, social, economic and cultural context that led to Italian national unification in 1860 after decades of divisive violence, political conspiracies and wars of independence against foreign oppression. Belgiojoso's essay, I argue, stems from a desire to resolve a crucial

---

[10] Aldobrandino Malvezzi dé Medici, *La principessa Cristina di Belgiojoso,* (Milan: Fratelli Treves, 1937), 383; Ginevra Conti Odorisio,"La questione femminile nell'Ottocento e Cristina di Belgiojoso," in *Cristina di Belgiojoso: politica e cultura nell'Europa dell'Ottocento*, eds. Ginevra Conti Odorisio, Cristina Giorcelli & Giuseppe Monsagrati (Casoria [NA]: Loffredo University Press, 2010), 384; D. M. Chiarito, "Gli scritti della vecchiaia," in *La prima donna d'Italia: Cristina Trivulzio di Belgiojoso tra politica e giornalismo,* eds. Mariachiara Fugazza & Karoline Rörig (Milano: F. Angeli, 2010), 209.

[11] Daniel M. Gross, *The Secret History of Emotion: From Aristotle's Rhetoric to Modern Brain Science* (Chicago: University of Chicago Press, 2006), 49.

theoretical and practical question: how might one imagine a radical reform of Italian society, a righteous collective revolt on the part of both victims and oppressors against the "monstrous injustice" done to women without this revolt undermining the political and social fragility of the newly-formed Italian nation?[12] Belgiojoso's desire to radically reform society must be read alongside her equally strong desire to protect Italy's hard-won but extremely fragile national unity. In my view, this double-orientation of thought is not a failure of attitude or commitment towards women's emancipation. Rather, it reflects a modern understanding of political and moral questions facing societies or nations transitioning away from a past of oppression, war, mass-atrocities and grievous violence to social and political justice for all. Modern transitional justice societies face the dilemma of how to reconcile oppressors and victims in order to build a collective social and political trust in the nation and its future.

My point here is not that the violence experienced, for example, in apartheid South Africa or former Yugoslavia should be compared to that in Italy during the nineteenth-century nation-building process known as the *Risorgimento*, but that some of the questions facing these societies are similar. How does a society reconcile victims and oppressors, repair moral relations and re-build trust in political system? How does a people respond collectively and privately to grievous injustice, recognize appropriate compensation for the victims and recognize its freedom to express a variety of "negative emotions" (anger and rage, and resentment)?[13] What is at stake in Belgiojoso's essay, as it is for most emancipationist writers, is the quest of undoing a form of violence and oppression that has been a foundation of society since "the dawn of time."[14] It is an oppression that, as Belgiojoso points out, has become so seemingly "natural" that a majority of women and men not only do not understand women's subjugation as problematic, but they do not even see it as such. This blindness to women's oppression, in the Italian case, mirrors a similar blindness about what was then Italy's recent emergence from a centuries-long history of foreign oppression. In her treatise *Osservazioni sullo stato attuale dell'Italia e del suo avvenire [observations on the present State of Italy* and on its Future] (1868), Belgiojoso urges Italians to reflect on the wounds left by their long history of oppression in order to leave the past behind. Without this reflection, without understanding the legacy of one's oppression, she argues, the past will continue to haunt the present. Barely eight years into national unification, Belgiojoso is most aware of the need

---

[12] Belgiojoso, "Condizione," 6.
[13] On the emotions and transitional justice societies, see Brudhlom.
[14] Belgiojoso, "Condizione," 6.

for Italians to rethink their relation to past oppression. Cutting the "chains of slavery" is simply not enough. As she puts it: "our principle work must at this point be to shed all the lethal influence of the past [oppression]. Let us remember that our past was one of slavery, and that a people educated to slavery must transform itself, if it wants to be able to enjoy freedom and independence."[15] Thus, both the woman-question and the nation-consolidation question are, in Belgiojoso's writing, linked by a shared history of oppression and the question of how to overcome this history and transition to a new future based on a just and equal society for both men and women. In her essay on women, she attempts to imagine how this transition might be accomplished without destroying the bio-political, necessary relation between men and women and thereby destabilizing the nation's future.

Belgiojoso tackles the question of imaging a new social foundational structure free from oppression and subjugation with moral strength, political courage, practical sense, and an understanding of the power of emotions in re-educating a people and culture. Resentment, understood as a just weapon of protest, offers her a representational tool for moving both men and women to feel that the time has come to end women's subjugation. It also shows her modern-oriented understanding that true and affective emancipation cannot simply be based on the advent of new laws and legal reform but rather on a profound transformation of how men and women as a society re-present, feel and emotionally/cognitively experience freedom and independence. What is at stake for her, given the political fragility of the nation, is prioritizing a new form of militancy, which in recognizing the desire for freedom and the political reality aims first at an affective and cultural transformation of experience of freedom.[16]

From Personal to Political

Not everyone has the power to make others feel injustice and injury. Cristina di Belgiojoso was perhaps one of the few Italian women of her generation who did have such power. Born in 1807 into an influential Milanese aristocratic family, the Trivulzio, she married at sixteen and four

---

[15] Belgiojoso, *Osservazioni*, 73.

[16] Belgiojoso's writing here might be fruitfully thought of alongside Michel Foucault's affirmation of affective power: "Do not think that one has to be sad in order to be militant, even though the thing one is fighting for is abominable. It is the connection of desire to reality (and not its retreat into the forms of representation) that possesses revolutionary force." Cited in Brady Thomas Heiner, *The Passions of Michel Foucault* (Durham, NC: Duke University Press, 2003), 45.

years later left her philandering and syphilitic husband and lived the rest of her life as an independent (married but separated) woman, head of her own household which included an only child, a daughter born in 1838 in Paris. Belgiojoso had class privilege, beauty, intelligence and riches on her side, and she was well aware of her power. For decades she was persecuted by the Austrian government ruling in Northern Italy who sought to curtail her anti-Austrian political sympathies by holding her finances hostage. She fled Italy in 1830 and lived in exile in Paris for ten years (1830–1840) and then commuted between Italy and France in the 1840s. After participating in the failed Roman revolution of 1849, she fled from political persecution and lived in exile in Turkey for five years with her then thirteen year old daughter (1850–1855). During her life, Belgiojoso's accomplishments included a highly successful experiment in social reform in the village of Locate, important treatises on Italian politics and history and religion, and a life-long sustained financial and intellectual commitment to founding and directing European-oriented journals aimed at promoting the Italian national movement. Belgiojoso thought of herself as an intellectual, a political journalist and an activist. Relentlessly courageous and stubborn, she sought, throughout her life, to be taken seriously and not marginalized by the male dominated nation-building process. Belgiojoso was both exceptional and typical, responding symptomatically to gender oppression while fighting for increased power, recognition, and a space in the public world of politics.[17]

Given Belgiojoso's transgressive life, it is reasonable and important to wonder why in her essay on women she positions herself against the emancipationist calls for action. Should she not have spear-headed the emancipationist movement? Should she not have used her power and influence to call for political and legal reforms? Belgiojoso's explicit self-distancing from and desire to turn down the volume on the "the deafening declamations of the emancipationists" won immediate favour among her moderate peers but has subsequently failed to win her any approval or critical interest.[18] According to Ginevra Conti Odorisio, Belgiojoso did not want to risk losing her hard won political authority by too vigorously advancing the emancipationist cause.[19] What is most disappointing to Conti Odorisio is that, unlike other emancipationist women, Belgiojoso did not offer any concrete initiatives for reform. There are "no [calls for] associations, no initiative that could be unpopular, no political action. For

---

[17] See Susanna Ferlito, "Hysteria's Upheavals: Emotional Fault Lines in Cristina di Belgiojoso's Health History," *Journal of Modern Italy* 17 (2) (2012): 157–170.
[18] Belgiojoso, "Condizione," 20.
[19] Conti Odorisio, 66.

Cristina the only valid path was individual, to follow the example of exceptional women, of those who despite everything could demonstrate that the female mind was not naturally and necessarily inferior to the virile mind."[20] Daniela Maldini Chiarito, equally disappointed with the essay, focuses on it as a document of biographical interest, which "reveals much more about herself and her life than she would have wanted to."[21]

Yet, these biographical and ageist perspectives fail as explanations when one compares her reflections on Italy's political and economic needs in the post-unification period. Belgiojoso's *Osservazioni* (1868), written two years after her essay on women, is deemed by scholars to be an acute assessment of Italy's post-unification state. Belgiojoso, in this political treatise, urges her fellow Italians to heal the wounds left by the chains of centuries-long enslavement.[22] She exudes a sense of urgency about the quickening speed of modernity and urges her fellow Italians to not remain crushed by "the wheels progress."[23] She writes: "we have entered the sphere of continuous progress, of perpetual movement, of the always faster."[24] Belgiojoso's experience of the acceleration of time brings her to urge Italy to move ahead in the process of nation-consolidation so as not to be left behind by more modern nations, like England and France. The emphasis on speed advocated in *Osservazioni* contrasts dramatically with the slowness she advocates in her earlier essay on women. Yet, in my view, it would be a critical mistake to equate a call for speed on the one hand with a modern outlook and the call for a slower process of reform on the other, with a conservative or even moderate commitment to reform. Time, temporality and reflecting on the legacy of the past in the present and future are the essence of both works. What is important to underline from this brief comparison of the two texts is that the slowness Belgiojoso imagines as necessary to radically reforming women's condition has nothing to do with (her) age, but rather stems from her adopting a different tactical, political, and cultural approach to the question of radically reforming women's condition of subjugation. In this essay, she doesn't adopt the more typical language of emancipation discourses (wheels of progress, cutting the chains of slavery, healing the wounds of oppression) because, in my view, she understands this language of break or rupture as being dependent on a militant practice that, in the case of "the woman

---

[20] Conti Odorisio, 66
[21] Chiarito, 211.
[22] Belgiojoso, *Osservazioni*, 91.
[23] Ibid., 85.
[24] Ibid., 85.

question," would threaten rather than promote social transition to a just society for all. Breaks, rupture, war and militancy are more easily called for when what is at stake is fighting foreign oppression. Indeed, the call for war often strengthens the building of a community identity and internal relations of trust within this community, as it did during the *Risorgimento*. But how does one fight an oppression that is internal to and constitutive of a society of men over women? This kind of foundational oppression, Belgiojoso recognizes, cannot be destroyed in the same way. In her words: "so many things are based on this female condition [of subjugation] that it cannot be destroyed at once without creating immense damage to society."[25] In order to clarify how she imagines this radical reform taking places, she explains:

> It is better instead to walk slowly, to take out one by one the stones which can be taken out from the current social edifice without causing it to collapse; it is better in fact to place some solid props so as to keep it standing straight as little by little the stones of which it is built are taken out to be used in the erection of a new building in which the needs of all men and all women find equal satisfaction.[26]

Belgiojoso's desire to represent her imagined process of reform comes towards the end of her essay after she has weighed all the arguments for and against it. Her image has, perhaps, slipped under the radar of critical attention because of its seeming banality. Yet, I argue, it offers a key to thinking about what her essay attempts to do, rather than simply say. If historically the language of emancipation has imagined the future as radically breaking away from the past, as an event that "cuts" or "ruptures' the ties between what is past and present, Belgiojoso's image offers a very different perspective on temporality, history, past and future. Her image describes an old edifice being shored up while being dismantled to construct a new foundation upon which the needs of men and women will find "equal satisfaction." This double image of deconstruction and reconstruction of the social edifice raises a number of problems, such as its strange temporal co-presence of past and future, the slowness and quietness of the deconstructive-reconstructive process of building, the imagined maleness of the professional expertise required (builders and architects), and its emotional economy based on "equal satisfaction." Belgiojoso's image works to keep the past and present operative and sustainable while the future is being constructed. All the while nothing is

---

[25] Ibid., 21.
[26] Ibid., 21.

lost, broken, cut or wasted; no brick touches the ground. The scene of this radical reform is eerily quiet, un-peopled, and hygienic, with no construction noise, no dust or debris, no waste, no need for a clean-up. As if in a silent film, the image exudes silence not sound, suggesting a process that is as fluid as it is almost imperceptible. Here, past and future exist side by side, one shrinking in matter and size as the other grows. It is an image highly productive of change without being disruptive. Like Marx's definition of how value transits from one form to another: "The constant continuity of the process, the unobstructed and fluid transition of value from one form into the other, or from one phase of the process into the next, appears as a fundamental condition for production based on capital."[27] Yet in Marx's continuous process, value is transferred rather than radically altered. In Belgiojoso's vision, old parts of the social edifice are re-used to build the new. Nothing seems to be wasted and nothing seems to be lost, but the end result is a society that is radically different because it is not founded on women's oppression. What is fascinating about this image is also how it enables Belgiojoso to distance the question of women's oppression from the medicalized language adopted in emancipationist and nation-building discourses. Here her reference to "social edifices" and "shoring up, rebuilding" keeps the focus on structural issues. There the nation becomes a patient needing to be healed, the national skin suffering from the putrefying wounds inflicted by the tight chains of slavery and (mostly) foreign oppression. What she seems to suggest is that the solution to radically overcoming women's oppression does not lie in a pathologizing of women as wounded or as wounds needing nurturing and healing. In other words, the problem of oppression lies not with or in women; what is needed is time to transform a culture of oppression in which women are compliant participants of their oppression and to which they have become so habituated to not feel the need for change. What her image of a construction site makes visible is that both women as victims and men as their oppressors must feel and share in the desire to end oppression. This affective process cannot take place overnight nor, in Belgiojoso's view, does it need to, since women are well trained in the seductive arts and know they can make their power felt through pleasing men and flattery. She writes: "a woman may be the slave of social norms but she is not, or only in a few cases, slave to the will of her husband."[28] A similar point had been made by David Hume when he argued that a woman's power over man lay in her "insinuation, charm and

---

[27] Cited in Jonathan Crary, *Suspensions of Perception: Attention, Spectacle, and Modern Culture* (Cambridge, Mass: MIT Press, 1999), 11.

[28] Belgiojoso, "Condizione," 20.

address" or her ability to "withhold her charm."[29] By recognizing and referring to women's limited sexual power, Belgiojoso aims merely to temporize with those emancipationists who demand immediate action and resolution of oppression. Seduction is, in her view, a temporary tactic that women are forced to use in order to exert some power over their oppressors and be understood by men. It is not through seduction and emotional manipulation that Belgiojoso seeks to promote a radical reform of society. Nor is it, however, through legal requests, petitions, the constitution of women associations, or "the deafening declamations" of emancipationist protests. Her image of social de-and re-construction suggests that a different logic is at stake, an emotional economy of making resentment work politically through affect. For radical gender reform, society at large must be collectively brought to resent the unjust foundational and structural oppression that renders the founding building block of society, the partnership between husbands and wives, false and unequal. What is most suggestive in Belgiojoso's choice to imagine radical reform as an on-going site of re-construction rather than as an "event" (as in revolution) or "moment" (as in conversion) is it's resonance with the temporal logic of resentment.[30] Holocaust survivor and writer Jean Améry describes how his resentment upsets the "natural-time sense" that sees the past as "already over."[31] Resentment's "twisted sense of time" upsets the natural-biological understanding of time as naturally leaving behind the past for the sake of the future.[32] By shoring up the edifice that needs to be torn down, Belgiojoso marks it as a site of ongoing structural (affective) work. The scaffolding both keeps the building standing and yet marks it, and makes it visible, as unusable and unsafe. This worksite requires a collaborative process of moving towards a future that both men and women find desirable. In this sense, this image of a construction site brings the process of undoing the past while making the future into view. Resentment's most intimate desire, as Améry argues, is not the desire for revenge, violence or punishment (the destruction of the past or even worse the forgetting of past injustice), but rather the joining together of oppressor and oppressed in a shared desire to turn back time and undo the past. He writes: "two groups of people, the overpowered and those who

---

[29] Cited in Annette C. Baier, "Hume on Resentment," *Hume Studies* 6 (2) (1980): 11.

[30] See, Hannah Arendt, *On Revolution* (New York: Viking Press, 1963).

[31] Jean Améry, "Resentments," *At the Mind's Limits: Contemplations by a Survivor on Auschwitz and Its Realities* (Bloomington: Indiana University Press, 1980), 72.

[32] Améry, 72.

overpowered them would be joined in the desire that time be turned back, and with it, that history become moral."[33]

The Portrait

One of Belgiojoso's greatest challenges, as she perceives it, consists of maintaining a semblance of impartiality and distance while making a passionate case for radical reform. Obviously, in the eyes of her future critics and readers she failed since her essay has been deemed so disappointing. Before trying to understand why it failed, I will examine how she attempts to make her case. What is at stake behind her explicit assumption of an impartial perspective and her practice throughout her essay of weighing the pros and cons of the emancipationist question? Belgiojoso's opening lines of her essay stage some mixed emotions: "I have always shied away from discussing the rights and duties of women in modern society ... because I am convinced that a woman discussing these issues is never seen as impartial and disinterested."[34] What has subsequently, to critics, appeared as personal hesitation about entering the heated fray for fear of losing her hard-won political influence or "revealing too much of herself" can be read more productively as rhetorical, authorial self-positioning.[35] In order for her critique of oppression to have any moral standing she must immediately raise the question of partiality and interest and proceed to construct her case as if from a non-gendered (hence male) perspective. She must not seem to be writing out of self-interest or personal resentment. Her strategy is to keep her critique of women's oppression on the high moral ground so that it cannot be dismissed as the personal gripe of an old woman. Ironically, this is exactly how it will be read by scholars, an irony that, as I will argue later, makes visible how our critical tools for recognizing radical reform and militancy perhaps differ from the past. Positioning herself as an impartial spectator, Belgiojoso proceeds to list the reasons for and against women's freedom from oppression. At the heart of her presentation, which with its pros and cons mimics the doing and undoing work of a construction site, Belgiojoso unleashes a powerfully affective portrait of society's heart of darkness—the bourgeois family. What this family portrait does is to place and represent women's oppression as constituting the basic building block of the modern nation. Her portrait of the mother

---

[33] Améry, 78.
[34] Belgiojoso, "Condizione," 5.
[35] Chiarito, 211.

and wife as a "derelict wife" is extraordinary and uniquely brutal.[36] While most of her emancipationist peers remained faithful to the nation-building discourse and bourgeois ideology of family life as idyllic, her portrait emerges as a fundamental critique of discourses exalting women as Angels of the House. Her portrait shows how women, the presumed female agents of moral redemption and regeneration, the presumed protectors, educators, and healers of society, are in fact mere slaves. This portrait, I argue, is meant to move both men and women to feel the feeling of grievous injustice.

In Belgiojoso's portrait of marriage and the family, women's marriages are for the most part experiences of loss, humiliation, a shameful sense of inferiority, and growing resentment. Loss is immediately defined as a physical loss of health that comes as a consequence of repeated pregnancies, the resulting illnesses, and the burdens of domestic duties.[37] Women's bodies thus consumed lose their beauty. Husbands, disenchanted by what they see, turn away from their now less-than-young wife to seek "pastures more suited to their mature intelligence."[38] What is remarkable is that for Belgiojoso the husbands abandon their "derelict wives" not for sex but because their wife cannot satisfy the needs of their "mature intelligence."[39] In other words, women are abandoned because of their lack of a serious intellectual education. Education is a key point in all women's emancipationist discourses and the point of departure from which most programs of reform start. Belgiojoso's argument is no different. In her view, women must have access to the same educational system as men. In Belgiojoso's portrait, the wife/mother's ignorance is the main reason she is abused, humiliated and shamed. It underlies her state of victimization and leads her to a tragic end. Her male children, Belgiojoso argues, quickly learn to sneer at their mother's inferiority and consider her to be of a different and inferior species. While her children continue to love her, Belgiojoso writes: "they love her as a part of the past, without any effect on the future."[40] Mothers are relegated to history, to the child's memory of its infancy, and as such remain as effective and as visible in their children's present and future as a scar, a reminder of a first great emotional investment in the wrong subject—the slave, the victim, the downtrodden ignorant. "Fortunately," as Belgiojoso puts it, "it is rare that a mother understands and fully grasps the humiliation of this [her child's]

---

[36] Belgiojoso, "Condizione," 11.
[37] Ibid.
[38] Ibid.
[39] Ibid.
[40] Ibid.

affection; but an indefinite feeling of diffidence and timidity colors the immense love she has for her children and *renders it bitter.*"[41] Within the dynamics of this portrait, the mother's bitterness remains unarticulated, a barely perceived sensation, but read from the perspective of the "impartial spectator" it produces knowledge and feeling; the feeling of pity and resentment against such humiliation, dismissal, and injustice.

Belgiojoso's portrait utterly undermines the *Risorgimento*'s national-patriotic cult of a mother's sacred mission to raise and morally guide their male children to become the virile citizens and patriots, soldiers and martyrs of the new Italian nation. From Belgiojoso's perspective, once mothers have reared their young through their first years, their children see them as a relic of the past only to be restored to a momentary emotional viability when, and if, the child experiences a great tragedy. Belgiojoso examines the mother's emotional response: "but does the mother receive pleasure from that return of trust and love procured through immense suffering? No of course not, she would prefer to give away her few remaining days of life so as to see her son be cold and indifferent, but happy."[42] Through self-abnegation, self-sacrifice and emotional death, mothers reach the limits of a tolerable existence. One is reminded of what Foucault has defined as a "limit-experience" that "has the function of wrenching the subject from itself, of seeing to it that the subject is no longer itself, or that it is brought to its annihilation or its dissolution."[43] Belgiojoso's portrait does not end with the death of the maternal subject but reflects upon the slow dissolution and transformation of the aged woman to a puppet, easily manipulated by a professionally trained listener, the priest. In his hands, the older derelict woman becomes an easy victim of his desire to control her family. She confesses to him all the practices of her family and he quickly becomes "the absolute king over her tortured and timorous soul."[44] Her complete and tragic downfall is only a step away. Encouraged by her new master, the poor woman starts to raise the banner of rebellion against her family expecting them to listen to her. She writes:

> And so one will see that same woman who had *up to that moment* constantly accepted the notion of her own inferiority towards her husband and sons, raise to their face the banner of rebellion, judging them and condemning them and presuming to impose on them her own opinions; and

---

[41] Ibid., 12 (my emphasis).
[42] Ibid.
[43] Cited in Heiner, 25.
[44] Belgiojoso, "Condizione," 13.

the husband and sons merely distance themselves further from wife and mother, they make fun of her, and shrugging their shoulders attribute [to the priest] the real reason for her great change.[45]

Belgiojoso's portrait ends with the wife and mother being dismissed by her sons and husband as "a woman of little brain completely dominated by priests."[46] By always accepting "the notion of her inferiority" this woman allows herself to be pushed to rebellion by another. Her rebellion is as ineffective as it is ridiculous. Belgiojoso's portrait of women's resentment ends with an all too facile male manipulation of dismissal of a woman's attempt to rebel. Here, she shows how anger and rebellion are not the solution. This woman's rebellion fails, Belgiojoso implies, because it is does not stem from a personal history of struggle and coming to consciousness, but is the result of the influence of a new absolute master over a "tortured and timid soul." [47] This slave speaks the language of her new master. Her rebellion leads merely to her further dismissal (if any further is possible). For women's resentment to be effective politically it must not just be a reaction to the moment, to the "now"; it must re-enter history, biography and temporality. For Belgiojoso, what is at stake is connecting women's resentment to a larger history of female resentment and to transform the personal and private resentment into a public and collective strategy. She examines women's profound unhappiness over the loss of everything they have ever had or loved but also responds to this unhappiness compassionately. Who can blame a woman, Belgiojoso writes, "for desperately trying to hold on to the shadow of her past beauty, if she tries to defend herself against aging, if she doesn't neglect anything in the attempt to preserve at least some aspect of her past self which is instead irremediably buried in the past?"[48]

Time

The question of time haunts Belgiojoso's writing. Hers is the time-trace of past beauty that a woman desperately seeks to hold onto, the trace-scaffolding of present time as the future is being built. Belgiojoso insists that traces of the past be understood as such and their influence on the present examined. Belgiojoso's imagined reform is all about making the traces, the "bricks" of the past, visible as they make up the future. By

[45] Ibid. (my emphasis).
[46] Ibid.
[47] Ibid.
[48] Ibid.

simply moving ahead in time or shedding the shackles of physical oppression one does not get rid of the past and its influence. In her treatise on the state of Italy, Belgiojoso points to the futility of simply wanting to destroy one's ties to the past. The past influences the present through cultural habits and education: "the past can be completely destroyed and transformed in a present completely opposite to it; but the traces of the past continue to exist in the character and in the popular practices [*abitudini*] in which they were formed ... our main work must be to shed ourselves of all the lethal influences of the past."[49] Thus, she urges Italians to reflect on their habits and their education under oppression to transform themselves and learn anew what it means to be free. This is the goal of her political treatise on Italy. Similarly, in her essay on women she seeks a path for undoing women's oppression not by forgetting it and leaving it behind through legal reforms or other declarations of freedom but by affectively moving both oppressed and oppressors to understand, see and feel the need for the just and radical end to oppression. From her perspective, there is important cultural and political work to be done. The very understanding of the relation between freedom and women must be examined and redefined. It is on this point that Belgiojoso positions herself most adamantly against the "deafening declamations" of the emancipationist discourse.[50] She asks, how can the majority of women want to be free when freedom is associated for women with "libertinage and vice?"[51] If most women, as she puts it, associate the word freedom with pleasure and sin or with the freedom to abandon their household duties, then, as she concludes, most respectable women must reasonably and responsibly reject and despise such emancipationist calls for freedom. Thus the very word emancipation, as she puts it, has negative connotations: "proffered so many times in those requests for a woman's freedom it has, and not without reason, something unpleasant and disgusting that excites the laughter of men and the disdain of many women."[52] What this word does, in her view, is allow men to dismiss women and to make "most" women unite against their own kind in a common feeling of superiority and disdain. Such feelings work to undermine the important work of detaching women's freedom from libertinage. Belgiojoso makes the point that the relation between woman's respectability and freedom has yet to be articulated and practiced. Thus, what needs to be made visible, articulated and transformed in the quiet but

---

[49] Belgiojoso, *Osservazioni*, 72.
[50] Belgiojoso, "Condizione," 20.
[51] Ibid.
[52] Ibid.

relentless transfer of bricks from one edifice to the other is the very meaning of freedom for women. Belgiojoso, in my view, does not seek to delay the process of emancipation. Rather, she understands it as a transitional process towards justice. Her concern is political, being governmental destabilization. Thus, when she evaluates emancipationist "requests for radical and immediate reforms, new norms and laws," she worries that they are "impossible" to implement unless one finds a "government friendly towards any novelty, sufficiently sure of itself to not care about public opinion and audacious enough."[53] Rather than demanding new reforms, Belgiojoso's political aim is to affectively change public opinion and to raise affective awareness of the injustice of women's oppression. Social and national destabilization would lead, in her view, towards an even further backlash against women. She writes: "I hold for certain that such an [emancipationist] experiment would turn back many years the satisfaction of the desires of those women who today ask for the emancipation of our sex."[54]

The time has come for ending oppression, Belgiojoso writes. It is time that "society, which is so anxious to banish all tyrannies and to extend a hand to all the oppressed (of which I bless and praise society) would remember that in every house, in every family, there are victims more or less resigned, absorbed in procuring the greatest dose of happiness to those who condemn her to a life of dependency and sacrifice."[55] It is time, she insists "that wives and mothers be taken seriously as reasonable creatures with intellectual abilities that might be different but equal to men."[56] But Belgiojoso desires that freedom be understood and defined by women rather than conceded to them by the political establishment and male confederacy. Here she more closely resembles contemporary feminist discussions than the practices of her peer emancipationists. Belgiojoso's wish, at the end of her essay, is that women will not have had to beg for freedom, and will not have had to fight their husbands for justice, nor will have had to separate themselves from men to affect power or come to reconciliation trials or acts of forgiveness.[57] There will be no need for

---

[53] Ibid.
[54] Ibid.
[55] Ibid., 15.
[56] Ibid., 15.
[57] Belgiojoso's questioning of the viability of emancipationist requests for women's freedom can appropriately be read alongside a more contemporary Italian feminist debate: "Freedom, as always, has a price and feminism in the seventies was mistaken in thinking that it did not, or that women could obtain freedom just by claiming it from society as a denied right: society is founded on female non-

division and alienation, resentment or forgiveness because both women and men, victims and oppressors, will have already have come to share in the same affective and political project of ending oppression. This wish, founded upon the desire for a freedom that stems from a cognitive and emotional experience of responding to injustice, marries with her equally strong wish that the Italian national-consolidation process and its future not be jeopardized by this freedom. Thus, Belgiojoso cautions against distracting politicians from their pressing governmental tasks. Truly revolutionary work against oppression, she suggests, must rise from the ground up, from women, rather than be dictated or bestowed from the male powers above.[58] This work begins with everyday practices: one woman who opens a door into the male confederate world holds open the door to another woman following in her footsteps. Foreshadowing the feminist call of the 1970s for the practice of entrusting (*affidament*), Belgiojoso understands the symbolic and affective importance of women looking towards other women as sources of authority.[59] In her concluding sentence, Belgiojoso writes: "Will the happy and honored women of the future think back from time to time to the pain and humiliation of those women who preceded them and remember with gratitude the names of those who opened and prepared the way to happiness never before experienced and perhaps only even dreamed about."[60] To read this statement, as previous critics have done, as merely revealing Belgiojoso's private feelings of resentment and memories of past humiliations is to diminish the import of her feminist insight into the symbolic value of linking women's ongoing process of defining freedom and of shedding the traces of patriarchal oppression through the making of a female genealogy.

---

freedom and therefore constitutionally has no need of female freedom and will not grant it." Luisa Muraro, Libreria delle donne di Milano, cited in *Italian Feminist Thought: A Reader,* eds. Paola Bono and Sandra Kemp, (Oxford, UK: B. Blackwell, 1991), 137.

[58] Reflecting on the relationship between emancipation and entrustment, Luisa Muraro writes: "here I would like to add my strongest argument against emancipation. It was available to me, and it attracted me, because of my human need for an autonomous existence. But every step I took was like taking something away from another woman or from all women ... I had impoverished them. It's not difficult to work out what was actually happening: faced with the social pre-eminence of the male sex I was denying my own sex its wealth; denying first myself and as a result all others whom I saw as similar to me. In this sense the relationship of entrustment is also, for me, a restitution." Muraro in *Italian Feminist Thought,* eds. Bono and Kemp, 126.

[59] See *Don't Think You Have any Rights*. La libreria di Milano.

[60] Belgiojoso, "Condizione," 24.

While I am certainly not claiming that Belgiojoso didn't experience resentment or sadness in reflecting on the future she would never see, I do not see her essay as medicalizing women's emotions of protest and resentment. Instead, she employs resentment to unleash a feeling meant to affect political desire for radical social change. Her image of the social edifices under construction, as I have argued, embodies and performs Belgiojoso's visualization and implementation of an emotional economy of resentment as, possibly, the only emotional and moral strategy able to lead to a sense of "equal satisfaction" by affording women, as the victims of oppression, justice, freedom and conciliation with their former oppressors. It is in this sense that the logic of resentment acts like a shadow economy of nineteenth-century normative expectations for women to be compassionate, forgiving and docile while empowering them to make their feelings of injustice felt by others. From Belgiojoso's perspective, female resentment garners power by finding energy in passivity, patience and tolerance. The masculine political agent fired up by revolutionary anger is displaced by women's resentment made political. Prior critical approaches have dismissed Belgiojoso's failure to call for immediate emancipationist action. In focusing on psychological meaning alone, critics have left Belgiojoso's proposed militant protest unread. Her proposal for an affective revolution meant, as her compatriot Niccolo' Tommaseo had suggested, "to move people to do prodigious things."[61]

Works Cited

Améry, Jean. "Resentments." *At the Mind's Limits: Contemplations by a Survivor on Auschwitz and Its Realities.* Bloomington: Indiana University Press, 1980.

Arendt, Hannah. *On Revolution.* New York: Viking Press, 1963.

Baeir, Annette C. "Hume on Resentment." *Hume Studies* 6 (2) (1980): 133–149.

Belgiojoso, Cristina. "Della presente condizione delle donne e del loro future." *Nuova Antologia di scienze, lettere e arti* 1 (1) (1866): 6–24.

—. *Osservazioni Sullo Stato Attuale Dell'italia e Sul Suo Avvenire.* Milano: F. Vallardi, 1866.

Bono, Paola & Sandra Kemp (eds.). *Italian Feminist Thought: a Reader.* Oxford, UK: B. Blackwell, 1991.

---

[61] Tommaseo, *Dizionario*. 422.

Butler, Joseph. *Butler's Fifteen Sermons Preached at the Rolls Chapel; and a Dissertation of the Nature of Virtue.* ed. J. H. Bernard and Tom Aerwyn Roberts. London: Society for Promoting Christian Knowledge, 1970.

Brudholm, Thomas. *Resentment's Virtue: Jean Améry and the Refusal to Forgive.* Philadelphia: Temple University Press, 2008.

Campbell, Sue. *Interpreting the Personal: Expression and the Formation of Feelings.* Ithaca, N.Y.: Cornell University Press, 1997.

Chiarito, D. M. "Gli scritti della vecchiaia." In *La prima donna d'Italia: Cristina Trivulzio di Belgiojoso tra politica e giornalismo,* edited by Mariachiara Fugazza and Karoline Rörig. Milano: F. Angeli, 2010.

Conti Odorisio, Ginevra. "La questione femminile nell'Ottocento e Cristina di Belgiojoso." In *Cristina di Belgiojoso: politica e cultura nell'Europa dell'Ottocento,* edited by Giverva Conti Odorisio, Cristina Giorcelli and Giuseppe Monsagrati. Casoria (NA): Loffredo University Press, 2010.

Crary, Jonathan. *Suspensions of Perception: Attention, Spectacle, and Modern Culture.* Cambridge, Mass: MIT Press, 1999.

Ferlito, Susanna. "Hysteria's Upheavals: Emotional Fault Lines in Cristina di Belgiojoso's Health History." *Journal of Modern Italy* 17 (2) (2012): 157–170.

Ferro, Marc. *Resentment in History.* Cambridge, UK: Polity, 2010.

Frye Marylin. "A Note on Anger." In *The Politics of Reality: Essays in Feminist Theory.* Trumansburg, N.Y: Crossing Press, 1983.

Gross, Daniel M. *The Secret History of Emotion: From Aristotle's Rhetoric to Modern Brain Science.* Chicago: University of Chicago Press, 2006.

Heiner, Brady Thomas. *The Passions of Michel Foucault.* Durham, NC: Duke University Press, 2003.

Hume, David. *An Inquiry Concerning Human Understanding: With a Supplement, An Abstract of a Treatise of Human Nature,* edited by Charles William Hendel. Indianapolis: Bobbs-Merrill Educational Publishers, 1955.

Kant, Immanuel. *Observations on the Feeling of the Beautiful and Sublime.* Berkeley: University of California Press, 1960.

Malvezzi dé Medici, Aldobrandino. *La principessa Cristina di Belgiojoso.* Milano: Fratelli Treves, 1937.

Muraro, Luisa. "Bonding and Freedom." In *Italian Feminist Thought: A Reader,* edited by Paola Bono and Sandra Kemp. Oxford, UK: B. Blackwell, 1991.

Nietzsche, Friedrich. *On the Genealogy of Morals; Ecce Homo,* edited by Walter Kaufmann. New York: Vintage, 1989.

Non credere di avere dei diritti: la generazione della libertà femminile nell'idea e nelle vicende di un gruppo di donne. Torino: Rosenberg & Sellier, 1987.

Nussbaum, Martha Craven. *Upheavals of Thought: The Intelligence of Emotions.* Cambridge: Cambridge University Press, 2001.

Scheman, Naomi. "Anger and the Politics of Naming." In *Women and Language in Literature and Society,* edited by Sally McConnell-Ginet, Ruth Borker & Nelly Furman, 174–187. New York: Praeger, 1980.

Sedgwick, Eve Kosofsky & Adam Frank. *Touching Feeling: Affect, Pedagogy, Performativity.* Durham: Duke University Press, 2003.

Showalter, Elaine. *The Female Malady: Women, Madness and English Culture, 1830–1980.* New York: Pantheon Books, 1985.

Smith, Adam. *A Theory on Moral Sentiments.* Edinburgh: J Bell, 1759.

Tommaseo, Niccoló. *Dizionario dei Sinonomi della lingua Italiana.* Milano Vallardi, 1848.

Tomelleri, Stefano. *La società del risentimento.* Rome: Meltemi, 2004.

Walker, Margaret Urban. *Moral Repair: Reconstructing Moral Relations after Wrongdoing.* Cambridge, UK: Cambridge University Press, 2006.

CHAPTER SIX

MECHANISMS OF COLLECTIVE RESENTMENT: GENDER WARS AND THE ALTERATION OF PATRIARCHY IN EIGHTEENTH-CENTURY RURAL FRANCE[1]

ELISE DERMINEUR

Historian Barbara H. Rosenwein has argued that people in the Middle Ages lived in "emotional communities," each having its own very particular norms of emotional values, expressions and gestures.[2] This study examines rural communities and their emotions with particular reference to the relation of debt and credit to the local economy from 1680 to 1785. I place a particular emphasis on resentment, a result of growing indebtedness, and how gender tensions within the community followed from this. The case study here is the *seigneurie* of Delle, a rural area located in the south of Alsace, on the border with the Swiss cantons, and only a few miles away from Basel. Here, peasants traded, exchanged and lived together in an "emotional community" as described by Rosenwein.[3]

The growing indebtedness of peasants is one of the features of the rural economy in the eighteenth century. As a consequence, exchanges in the

[1] The author gratefully acknowledges the support of a Bernadotte Schmitt Grant from the American Historical Association in 2011.
[2] Barbara H. Rosenwein, *Emotional Communities in the Early Middle Ages* (Ithaca: Cornell University Press, 2007).
[3] In 1659, Louis XIV, new lord of the old Habsburg possessions gained by the Treaty of Munster, gave the seigneurie of Delle, located in *Haute Alsace,* (along with others in the area) to his faithful minister and friend, Cardinal Mazarin. During the eighteenth century, the seigneurie was composed of about thirteen villages in which about 2,000 inhabitants lived in the 1760s. See Elise Dermineur, "Women in Rural Society: Peasants, Patriarchy and the Local Economy in Northeast France, 1650–1789" (Ph.D. Diss., Purdue University, 2011). 28–62.

local credit market became critical to these peasants. But more importantly, the rules governing these exchanges changed gradually to involve greater female participation, as we shall see. The goal of this article is to set both the economic changes and the social changes that occurred in the eighteenth century side by side, with particular reference to resentment. How did the growing indebtedness of peasants modify their individual and communal behaviour, and especially their social interactions? This essay contends that there was a correlation between the increasing weight of debt on rural households and changes in behaviour in eighteenth-century rural France. Resentment toward the growing and new economic power of women emerged as one of the social features in the area studied. This article therefore intends to answer the following questions: What was gender resentment and how was it triggered? What was the belief upon which gender resentment lay? What were the outcomes of gender resentment and did it alter the norms of cooperation within the society?

Resentment has a polymorphous definition. This feeling is described in traditional scholarly literature as an individual or collective sentiment towards one or several oppressive factors, individuals or groups of people who retain some sort of authority and power and who make others (agents) feel inferior, thus provoking their frustration and/or prompting a sentiment of injustice. The sense of having been treated unfairly, consequently the notion of injustice, is one of the features of this sentiment. The expression of resentment is rather discrete and therefore challenging to identify, mostly because of the agent's fear of repression and ostracism. Consequently, it is not only difficult for the agents to appropriately label their feelings but it is also complex for observers to identify resentment as such. Indeed, it seems that resentment could be made up of a multiplicity of negative feelings: anger, hatred, feelings of injustice or envy, and sometimes shame, disappointment, contempt, disgust, jealousy and the like.[4] Resentment as a sentiment is almost only identifiable when it takes the shape of reactions, when it bursts out as revenge. Resentment could also be defined as jealousy and a desire for revenge.

Peasants' emotions in the Old Regime constituted a set of complex and interrelated feelings and sentiments that shaped societal relations and regulated everyday life. Emotions *did* things, as Sara Ahmed put it recently, and should be analysed as historical objects in their own right.[5] In

---

[4] On the difficulty of appropriately labelling resentment, see especially Bernard N Meltzer and Gil Richard Musolf, "Resentment and Ressentiment," *Sociological Inquiry* 72 (2) (2002): 240–255.

[5] Sara Ahmed, "Affective Economies," *Social Text* 79 (2004): 117–139.

order to fully understand the mechanisms of resentment in the early modern period, I have chosen to consider resentment as an object of historical analysis. As such, resentment, as an emotion, emerged in a specific historical context within which various factors occurred and merged. In this specific region, indebtedness and changes in the patriarchal order modified relations between men and women. As an intrapersonal feeling or sentiment, resentment is difficult—almost impossible—to identify if it is not communicated to other agents. Most of the time, the term "resentment" is not used in the narrative describing the eruption of this emotion, although the word did exist in the early modern period. One of the reasons for this is that agents feeling resentment may not have been in a position to use the term without risking a break in social norms and may have feared retaliation. According to Jon Elster, "feelings of resentment and hostility do not lead to social conflict unless the object of these feelings appears as causally responsible for one's situation."[6]

Expressions of resentment that occurred publicly can be grasped and interpreted, but this step is probably the most difficult one for the historian, notably because of the necessary interpretation of the documents. As Mabel Berezin emphasizes, it is difficult to map triggering events or sequences of events.[7] Indeed, resentment was almost always represented as an intimate sentiment or feeling, only shared through actions, gestures and expressions that could take different shapes and significations. It is the historian's task to identify these demonstrations of resentment when sources might give only a few indications. Resentment fulfilled a social function that took different forms, as we shall see, as a vector of communication between agents, and came to disrupt the social norms of interaction within the community. I have chosen, therefore, an empirical and cross-analytical approach, using different quantitative and qualitative data, in order to capture in detail the manifestations of resentment. When resentment was expressed publicly, both the agent who expressed it and the target reacted to it. I also analyse the outcomes and social consequences of a display of resentment, with special reference to violence as one of the most common outcomes of resentment. In this case, violence was directed against women, leading to what I have called gender resentment.

---

[6] Jon Elster, *Making Sense of Marx* (Cambridge: Cambridge University Press, 1985), 338.
[7] Mabel Berezin, "Emotions and the Economy," in Neil J. Smelser & Richard Swedberg, *The Handbook of Economic Sociology* (Princeton: Princeton University Press, 2005), 109–127.

Fields such as philosophy and literature have richly explored resentment both as an emotion and a moral principle.[8] Historian Marc Ferro, for instance, has given many examples of resentment across time.[9] For example, the struggle between black and white people in the United States, especially before the civil rights movement, has been dissected and explained through the prism of racial resentment, eventually giving rise to the Civil Rights Bill. Some historians have partly explained the French Revolution as the class resentment of the bourgeois against the dominant elite, which materialized in the outburst of July 1789. The third wave of feminism has been explained through female resentment due notably to the lack of power women hold and through the prism of gender inequalities.[10] Gender resentment on the part of men has never been investigated, to my knowledge, in a historical perspective, and it is my goal to address this gap.

Various cross-referenced sources (such as loan contracts and judicial litigation) from one rural *seigneurie* inform us on peasant behaviour and emotions regarding credit and debt. The loan contracts, recorded by a notary, run from the 1730s to 1785 and stipulate the amount of money lent, the interest rate, the duration of the loan and the mortgage guarantee. They rarely reveal the purpose of the loan. I have consulted approximately two thousand loan contracts. Social changes occurring at the same time, and the emotions of the peasants involved, can also be tracked thanks to an analysis of local judicial records. I have consulted roughly 2,600 judicial cases for the *seigneurie* of Delle in Haute-Alsace, from 1680 to 1785, at the *Archives Départementales du Territoire de Belfort*. The local justice records I examined, called the "*registres d'audiences*," are one of the best sources for the study of rural communities. The seigniorial court was the first level of justice and peasants used this tool heavily. Historians, however, have not paid close attention to these registers; these types of sources are not usually used to examine emotions at all. Historians

---

[8] See, among others, Friedrich Wilhelm Nietzsche, *The Genealogy of Morals* (Toronto: University of Toronto Libraries, 2011); Max Scheler, *Ressentiment* (Milwaukee: Marquette University Press, 1994); John Rawls, *A Theory of Justice* (Oxford: Oxford University Press, 1973).

[9] Marc Ferro, *Le Ressentiment dans l'Histoire: Comprendre notre Temps* (Paris: Odile Jacob, 2008).

[10] Martha E. Gimenez, "Capitalism and the Oppression of Women: Marx Revisited ," *Science & Society* 69 (1) (2005): 11–32. Christa Reiser, *Reflections on Anger: Women and Men in a Changing Society* (Westport: Greenwood Publishing Group, 2001).

generally favour criminal records and/or autobiography and self-narratives, the latter being almost non-existent for peasants.

In order to examine the mechanisms of gender resentment, I first highlight the origins of resentment toward women through the prism of economic changes (growing indebtedness) throughout the eighteenth century. Then, I present a typology of the judicial cases and their chronological evolution, concentrating on those dealing with debt and ordinary violence, to demonstrate the chronological evolution of resentment. Finally, I focus on the outcomes of gender resentment both for men and for women. This project is not only a contribution to our understanding of rural communities but also, and more importantly, an ethnographic sketch, with a historical perspective, of a traditional society, contributing towards filling a gap in the historiography of emotions.

Origins of Resentment towards the Economic Power of Women—Growing Indebtedness and Economic Change

In the traditional historiography, social historians have demonstrated that economic changes were almost always echoed by social changes. In the early modern period, high inflation, for instance, led to a period of dearth and high mortality. On the other hand, periods of opulence and growth were met by social mobility. In the eighteenth century, the emergence of the market economy, the gradual monetization of exchange, and a relative economic growth modified the behaviour of a wide range of people, including ordinary people and peasants in particular.

In the eighteenth century, growing indebtedness was undoubtedly the most felt factor for the population and it had a wide range of economic and social effects. Throughout Europe, and in France especially, rural and urban dwellers borrowed money to finance their investments (land, tools, or shops etc.), their daily purchases (seeds, livestock, food etc.), and other expenses such as taxes. In the area under study, I noted a gradual increase in both the number of loans and the volume of the exchange in the credit market in the eighteenth century, with strong activity for the period 1760–1780. Inventories following deaths correspondingly mentioned the increasing indebtedness of peasants' households. This trend conforms to what has been observed elsewhere in Europe at the time. Borrowing money became increasingly common.[11]

---

[11] See, for instance, Jean-Laurent Rosenthal, "Credit Markets and Economic Change in Southeastern France 1630–1788," *Explorations in Economic History* 30 (2) (1993): 129–157; Philip T. Hoffman, Gilles Postel-Vinay & Jean-Laurent

Indebtedness appears to be cyclical in history and in this respect the eighteenth century seems to have been a dynamic period for credit markets throughout Europe. Conflicts between peasants over debt repayment have always been a feature of rural communities. Philip Hoffman mentions a conflict that took place in 1624 between two peasant families, where one individual was severely injured by another for the tiny amount of 10 sous.[12] Social conflict as a result of economic issues was certainly not new.

Women had the legal opportunity to borrow and lend money in the local credit market.[13] One should note that in this particular region, a woman could own property in her own name when she reached twenty-five years old. When she married, her husband managed her property but it remained in her name. Women regained full command of their belongings on becoming widows. A woman peasant could also inherit property from her family. As partible inheritance was the rule in the *seigneurie* of Delle, sisters theoretically inherited the same share of the inheritance from their deceased parents as their brothers. Women had capital to invest and could also be in need of money. In the *seigneurie* of Delle, for instance, women (unmarried, married women and widows) borrowed a little bit more than 51% of the total money exchanged in the credit market for the whole period, while they lent 23% of the total volume. Married couples borrowed 22% of the total volume in 1730–1739 but borrowed almost 50% in 1780–1789.[14]

Rosenthal, "Private Credit Markets in Paris, 1690–1840," *The Journal of Economic History* 52 (2) (1992): 293–306; Philip T. Hoffman, Gilles Postel-Vinay, & Jean-Laurent Rosenthal, *Priceless Markets: the Political Economy of Credit in Paris, 1660–1870* (Chicago: University of Chicago Press, 2000).

[12] Philip T. Hoffman, *Growth in a Traditional Society: The French Countryside, 1450–1815* (Princeton: Princeton University Press, 2000), 74

[13] For a discussion on women and credit in the early modern period see especially Dermineur, Elise M., "Female Peasants, Patriarchy, and the Credit Market in Eighteenth-Century France," *Proceedings of the Western Society for French History* 37 (2009): 61–84; James B. Collins, "The Economic Role of Women in Seventeenth-Century France," *French Historical Studies* 16 (2) (1989): 436–470; William Chester Jordan, *Women and Credit in Pre-Industrial and Developing Societies* (University Park: University of Pennsylvania Press, 1993); Beverly Lemire, Ruth Pearson & Gail Grace Campbell, *Women and Credit: Researching the Past, Refiguring the Future* (Oxford: Berg, 2001); Craig Muldrew, "'A Mutual Assent of Her Mind?' Women, Debt, Litigation and Contract in Early Modern England," *History Workshop Journal* 55 (2003): 47–71.

[14] Elise Dermineur, *Women in Rural Society*, 98–141.

The percentage of married couples who borrowed money increased from 1760 onwards, mostly because the mechanism of the credit market changed. Indeed, at the beginning of the eighteenth century, the data show that money was lent with large mortgage guarantees, mostly specific pieces of land. At the end of the period, land value did not seem as attractive as before, largely because much of it had been already mortgaged. In the 1730s and 1740s, most of the contracts contained specific mortgage guarantees, while at the end of the period the notary laconically inscribed on most contracts that the debtor(s) would mortgage *"tout ses biens tant meubles qu'immeubles."*[15] This does not necessarily mean that borrowers stopped putting their land on the deed as a mortgage guarantee. Rather, it indicates that the contracts became vague and that specific plots of land were not added to the deed. More importantly, borrowers had from now on to systematically bring with them a third-party underwriter, as we will see below.

In the meantime, women's lineage property became interesting to creditors, especially because of womens' dowries. Indeed, as noted previously, there was a dramatic increase in the number of married women who were involved in loan deeds after the 1760s. Husbands and wives borrowed together and therefore offered greater guarantees to their creditors. The structural economic patterns had changed, and this was expressed directly in the credit market; mortgaged lands no longer represented enough guarantees, and married women's property (mostly plots of land and cash, often earned as a rural domestic worker before marriage) now represented an additional and better guarantee. Furthermore, creditors could turn to the widow for her share in case of her husband's death. After 1760, peasants not only had to add their wives' lineage property to the deed, but also had to find, in most cases, a third-party underwriter; as Alexandra Shepard recalls "dependence on another man for help was a form of social stigma."[16] This is a key moment when patriarchy as a societal model began to erode.

In the context of strong indebtedness, men were no longer in command of their households. Their guarantors possessed external control over the household's husbandry, and their wives had to play a more critical role in the household's management. From then on, economic partnerships between spouses became even stronger. In addition to this, the proportion of female creditors in the credit market gradually increased throughout the eighteenth century, showing their gradual access to that market. Women's

---

[15] "All movable and immovable property".

[16] Alexandra Shepard, "Manhood, Credit and Patriarchy in Early Modern England c. 1580–1640," *Past & Present* 167 (2000): 75–106.

economic power, therefore, significantly increased in this period,[17] and this, we shall see, is what triggered gender resentment.

Because of these changes, men had to establish a better partnership with their wives and manage their households together. A married woman could decide to oppose the signature of a deed and, in theory, she could not be compelled to sign. If the deed became too risky, she had the option of withdrawing her lineage property and seeking, before the judge, a separation of her property from her husband's. The fact that her lineage property and assets were at stake did not represent a reinforcement of patriarchy, but rather a breach of it.

The gradual involvement of women in the local economy was not specific to the seigneurie of Delle. Here and there across early modern Europe, women progressively became key actors in the market. Sheilagh Ogilvie, Anne Laurence, Julie Hardwick and Allyson Poska, to name but a few, have underlined the increasing economic weight of women within their community.[18] None of them, however, has examined the eventual conflict with men over their economic participation.

The Expressions and Effects of Gender Resentment—
a Hypothesis

Economic changes, positive or negative, necessarily imply social changes in every society and in any historical period. Some historians have emphasized that economic contexts, particularly difficult ones, prepare the ground for tensions, conflicts and even violence. Daniel Vickers agrees, and defines debt as "an instrument of social power and, as such, [it] often became the focus of deep social tensions."[19] In the judicial cases examined, fights at the local tavern are likely to be the result of financial

---

[17] Julie Hardwick reaches the same conclusion. Julie Hardwick, *The Practice of Patriarchy: Gender and the Politics of Household Authority in Early Modern France* (University Park: Pennsylvania State University Press, 1998).

[18] Sheilagh Ogilvie, *A Bitter Living: Women, Markets, and Social Capital in Early Modern Germany* (New York: Oxford University Press, 2003); Laurence, Anne, Josephine Maltby & Janette Rutterford (eds.), *Women and Their Money, 1700–1950: Essays on Women and Finance* (London: Routledge, 2008); Julie Hardwick, *The Practice of Patriarchy: Gender and the Politics of Household Authority in Early Modern France* (University Park: Pennsylvania State University Press, 1998); Allyson M. Poska, *Women and Authority in Early Modern Spain: The Peasants of Galicia* (New York: Oxford University Press, 2006).

[19] Daniel Vickers, "Competency and Competition: Economic Culture in Early America," *The William and Mary Quarterly* 47 (1) (1990): 3–29.

issues and the most common insult was *"voleur"* (thief), referring mostly to someone dishonest in their business transactions.[20] Recently, discordant voices have challenged this argument. Zorina Khan, for instance, rejects "the hypothesis that markets eroded the social norms of cooperation that supposedly were a feature of small communities."[21] She contends that legal disputes over debt did not lead to genuine conflicts within the community. This argument is tenable because Khan analyses debt litigation by focusing only on the whole group, the community, and not on the individual, as a subject of analysis, and therefore she does not consider gender. According to my own research, growing indebtedness did not lead to more ordinary violence within the community—rather the contrary— but it did lead to more violence towards and on the part of women.

For the period 1680–1685 in the *seigneurie* of Delle, 16% of the cases brought before the judge were lawsuits over ordinary violence (insults and physical assaults). A century later, the proportion dropped to 3.65%. Not only did the proportion drop, but the nature of the cases of ordinary violence also changed—litigants defended their honour and the cases reported involved mainly insults in the public sphere (the most numerous cases), and fights among youths at the local tavern, which can be seen almost as a social ritual. Between 1680 and 1685, 13% of the plaintiffs in this type of case were female, usually represented by their husbands or their fathers at court, while a century later women accounted for 30% of the total, always named rather than being represented by a male relative. The number of female defendants also increased from less than 1% to 35% for the same period. We can only wonder how we can explain such violence against and on the part of women.

I would like to propose a hypothesis. Patriarchy, as the traditional societal model and one of the most important social norms within the community, entailed a series of expectations and rules.[22] One of these was the importance for the male head of the household to provide for his family by earning money honestly as a good husband, a good father and a

---

[20] Elise Dermineur, *Women in Rural Society.*

[21] B. Zorina Khan, "'Justice of the Marketplace': Legal Disputes and Economic Activity on America's Northeastern Frontier, 1700–1860," *The Journal of Interdisciplinary History* 39 (1) (2008): 1–35.

[22] On social norms, see especially Cristina Bicchieri, *The Grammar of Society: the Nature and Dynamics of Social Norms* (Cambridge: Cambridge University Press, 2006); Jon Elster, "Economic Order and Social Norms," *Journal of Institutional and Theoretical Economics* 144 (1988): 357–366.

good Christian.[23] His wife, on the other hand, was expected to behave according to the community's moral standards (sexual honour) and protect the household's provisions.[24] Men were sanctioned if they neglected their household duty through the separation of property, for instance, which almost always emphasized their failure as good providers. A change in these assigned social and economic roles would lead to a great imbalance in the division of labour, in marital roles within the household, and within the community.

Economic changes that allowed women to play a greater role not only within their community but also within their households could have nourished the rising sentiments of jealousy, envy, anger and resentment among men who, as a consequence, had lost their patriarchal authority. It seems that economic tensions such as inflation, fragmentation of land and the pressure of debt in eighteenth-century rural areas contributed to social tension, especially in the way in which men acted towards women, perhaps due to the loss of authority and control men exercised in marital relations (see my argument above about the position of women in the credit market).[25]

In the same way, the number of lawsuits for the separation of property increased in the last decade of the eighteenth century, while this type of case barely featured in the earlier period. Separation of property was a judicial means of sparing the wife's lineage property from the household's creditors, but in certain cases it could also be a way of withdrawing the economic authority of the husband over his wife's assets. Julie Hardwick argues that: "the prominence of indebtedness as a source of conflict between spouses was a striking illustration of the way that changing economic structures in early modern society impinged on family life."[26] In any case, requesting before the judge, an external party, the return of a dowry because of a husband's financial mismanagement probably altered patriarchal norms. In 1761, Marie Barré, a female peasant from the village of Joncherey, asked for a separation of property from her husband. She was granted the separation and was able to withdraw her dowry, amounting to 1,095 livres. Her husband was also required to reimburse her

---

[23] The expression "*bon père de famille*" was frequently employed to describe correct behaviour for a man.

[24] On this aspect see Alexandra Shepard, *Manhood, Credit and Patriarchy*, 83.

[25] See Elise M Dermineur, *Female Peasants, Patriarchy, and the Credit Market in Eighteenth-Century France*.

[26] Julie Hardwick, "Seeking Separations: Gender, Marriages, and Household Economies in Early Modern France," *French Historical Studies* 21 (1) (1998): 157–180.

for the lands belonging to her that he had sold.[27] Consequently, the new economic role of women within their community led to a relatively greater emancipation of women in their households (shown by the separation of property, for instance) and led above all to gender tensions as men became more violent toward women. As Robert Shoemaker commented on male Londoners in the eighteenth century, "men, as the superior gender, were expected to confirm their status by physically defending their integrity and reputation against all challenges."[28]

Through short examples, I would like to emphasize the link between economic changes and gender tensions. Before the judge, Jeanne Porchy asked for a separation of property from her husband Jacques Chaboudé, which she was granted in August 1780. This judicial step meant that her husband had to return her dowry to her. Porchy denounced the mismanagement of the household purse by her husband ("*la déroute des affaires*") and transferred, therefore, financial authority to the judge, who granted her the separation. She could then withdraw her assets from the community property, being about 289 livres. But a few months later, in June 1781, her sister-in-law, Marie Bouat, physically attacked her. We do not know the reason for this attack (economic perhaps?), but Bouat would certainly not have attacked her sister-in-law if the latter had not threatened the economic balance of the familial *domus*.

Margueritte Surgaud also asked for a separation of property from her husband and appeared repeatedly before the judge. In April and September 1780, Surgaud was in open conflict with her brother Georges Surgaud over their parents' inheritance. In April 1781, she summoned Dominique Théfine before the judge for the payment of a piece of land that she had sold to him and that he had refused to pay for. In August 1784, she summoned Francois Blanchard for the payment of another piece of land. In January 1783, she summoned Georges Macker before the judge for insult and physical assault.[29] After her separation, Surgaud was left helpless, with almost no protection. The fact that she had property and was very active in defending her rights and assets made her an easy target for physical attacks and insults.

Marie Eve Chavanne was a rural domestic working at Jean-Baptiste Galliat's farm. In July 1781, she came before the judge to claim the payment of her salary. Less than a month later, Melchior Galliat, brother of her former master, accused her of being a "slut and a slob" and

---

[27] ADTB 8B 130.

[28] Robert Shoemaker, "Male Honour and the Decline of Public Violence in Eighteenth-Century London," *Social History* 26 (2) (2001): 190–208.

[29] ADTB 8B 156, 157 and 159.

physically attacked her, perhaps because she had threatened the patriarchal order of the community by claiming her due in court.[30] The exact same thing happened to Anne Marie Huguelin from the village of Seppois le Haut. She had been working in Georges Surgaud's farm as a domestic. Her master owed her 6 livres and a muslin handkerchief, the remainder of her salary. In March 1762, she finally took the case before the judge who ruled in her favour. Two months later, when she ran into her former master, who had still not paid her, in the street, a fight between the two occurred. She claimed that Surgaud pulled her hair, knocked her down three times, and held her down while his new servant, Madelaine Burget, beat her head with a stick.[31] In these last two cases, claiming a salary in court could be seen as an infringement of the social hierarchy, but also, and more importantly, as an infringement of the patriarchal order, especially because the master was considered the head of the household, assimilated to a paternal image, for his servants. It is also interesting to note that some women within the community, such as the new female domestic servant in our last example, took sides and on most occasions did not support women in cases of violence but instead stayed on the side of traditional order.

Other cases, such as those above, can be found in the civil justice records.[32] Of course, due to the nature of our documents, it would be difficult to firmly attest that there was a link between the growing economic activity of women and ordinary violence towards them, but evidence seems to suggest that this was so. One important point is that peasant household issues remained strictly private, and complaints about domestic violence cannot be found for rural areas like the *seigneurie* of Delle.

Insults and physical attacks have always been a common feature of rural social life. But perhaps, as peasants entered upon the civilizing process described by Norbert Elias, the proportion of litigations concerning insult and battery dropped. It is a characteristic that has also been observed by Robert Shoemaker in the case of eighteenth-century London upper-class society and by Thomas Gallant in nineteenth-century rural Greece.[33] The proportion of women as defendants and plaintiffs in

---

[30] ADTB 8B 156.

[31] ADTB 8B 132.

[32] In looking at another rural seigneurie, I have reached the same conclusions.

[33] Thomas W. Gallant, "Honor, Masculinity, and Ritual Knife Fighting in Nineteenth-Century Greece," *The American Historical Review* 105 (2) (2000): 359–382; Robert B. Shoemaker, "The Taming of the Duel: Masculinity, Honour and Ritual Violence in London, 1660–1800," *The Historical Journal* 45 (3) (2002): 525–545.

criminal cases in England also dropped in the eighteenth century.[34] Everywhere, the rate of violence decreased. Going against the trend, the proportion of women involved as plaintiffs and defendants in this particular type of case in our region, however, rose dramatically after 1740–1745. One explanation could lie in the economic context (i.e. indebtedness) and in particular in the growing economic participation of women, which created social and, more importantly, gender tensions within the community. Alexandra Shepard argues that: "Violent conduct could also function to assert manliness."[35]

Tensions within the community were not unusual. After all, several peasant revolts took place in the French countryside and throughout Europe from time to time during the Middle Ages and in the early modern period. These peasant uprisings had strong economic motivations and were often the result of an intense feeling of class resentment, a model in which peasants felt unfairly financially oppressed by their lord.[36] Class resentment resulting from economic changes was also likely to affect relationships between the wealthy and the less wealthy members of the community, between the successful peasants and the less successful ones, for instance.[37] Class resentment and gender resentment are neither antagonistic nor exclusive and could have occurred at the same time, but class resentment would have been much more difficult to express publicly for at least two reasons. First, class and authoritative status were often paired in a model in which the lord had authoritarian means at his disposal. Punishment for crossing the line, in this case, could be financially burdensome and even life threatening. Second, class resentment between wealthy and not so wealthy peasants could threaten the norms of cooperation within the community, and could deprive the disadvantaged peasants of employment, credit and social and political support.

Expressing class resentment could be interpreted as rebellion against authority, as was the case for peasant rebellions, and the punishment for this would have had worse consequences than expressing resentment against women, especially in a traditional society. More importantly,

---

[34] Malcolm M. Feeley & Deborah L. Little, "The Vanishing Female: The Decline of Women in the Criminal Process, 1687–1912," *Law & Society Review* 25 (4) (1991): 719–757.

[35] Alexandra Shepard, *Manhood, Credit and Patriarchy*, 103.

[36] On peasant rebellions see especially, Yves-Marie Bercé, *Croquants et Nu-Pieds* (Paris: Gallimard, 1991).

[37] The literature on class resentment is extensive. Among recent research is J. M. Barbalet, "A Macro Sociology of Emotion: Class Resentment," *Sociological Theory* 10 (2) (1992): 150–163.

expressing class resentment could alter the norms of cooperation within the community; expressing gender resentment did not affect the norms of cooperation but called for a return to the traditional and social norm of patriarchy.

Women were not the direct cause of gender resentment; the blame lay with the invisible market economy and the growing pattern of indebtedness. Men could not challenge the emerging and uncontrollable laws of finance and indebtedness that deprived them of their traditional authority and social position. As Solomon points out, lack of power is one of the crucial components of resentment.[38] Resentment was not directly aimed at women but at the invisible mechanisms of the credit market, which deprived men of their traditional authority and which considerably altered the paradigm of patriarchy. The fact that male peasants lost control of their household and husbandry reflected on women, as the system (the market) gave them a greater economic role. In addition, men perhaps became aware of their loss of power and this self-consciousness could have triggered violence against women.

It is intriguing to note that resentment was expressed through physical violence and/or insults, but "resentment" was not identified as such by the agents. None of the male peasants involved in these cases defended themselves by arguing that their masculinity was threatened, or that their patriarchal role was challenged, by female economic participation. The question of the consciousness or otherwise of their actions is still pending.

Following my hypothesis, resentment at both the increased pressure of debt, and above all the greater participation of women in the economic sphere (here I would like to recall their growing positions as economic partners in their households, as described above), developed within the community as a shared emotion, especially among men. The peasants, as a group, reacted to the new role of women within the community through violence and defiance against them, perhaps from fear as traditional patriarchal roles were challenged. Female peasants in turn were also quicker to use violence to defend their interests, which might explain the increase in the proportion of female defendants. Resentment toward the new economic position of women described a change in the traditional social system in which patriarchy used to be the main social model of gender interactions. Its infringement by new economic patterns generated sanctions against women, expressed through ordinary violence. It is also

---

[38] Robert Solomon, "One Hundred Years of Ressentiment: Nietzsche's Genealogy of Morals," in *Nietzsche, Genealogy, Morality : Essays on Nietzsche's Genealogy of Morals*, ed. Richard Schnacht (Berkeley: University of California Press, 1994), 95–126.

interesting to note that resentment could be developed by some of the women in the community who were attached to the patriarchal order and therefore stood by men, or perhaps because patriarchy was such a strong social norm that they did not dare/think to challenge it.

The economic changes of the eighteenth century led to a greater economic role for women, not only within their households but also within their communities. Changes such as indebtedness provoked upheaval in the social tissue, profoundly affecting the old societal model of patriarchy. The new economic role of women meant that these female peasants had greater latitude in their actions. Becoming an incontrovertible economic partner to their husbands, and also to other men of the community, gradually endangered the traditional patriarchal pattern. Indebtedness certainly led to class resentment from those who suffered the heavy burden of debts towards those who were making profits. Nevertheless, this type of resentment stayed within the traditional limits of the social hierarchy, inherited from the feudal system and now one of the features of early modern society. It was probably impossible to make class resentment visible without altering the norms of cooperation within the society. But gender resentment emerged because the object of resentment—women— was traditionally an inferior agent in the social normative system of patriarchy. Actions against women in the market economy were not simple because of legal procedures, but actions against them in order to redress the patriarchal norm within the frame of social life were quicker and simpler.

It has to be said that assessing whether such violent behaviour directed towards women was the result of gender resentment rather than the consequence of other factors is a complex task, but the correlation between the increased violence between the sexes within the community and the greater economic participation of women reinforces this argument.

Conclusion

Pre-modern rural credit markets expanded gradually and dynamically in the eighteenth century in amounts never seen before. Credit, and consequently debt, turned out to be key in social relations within the community. As the credit market grew in the eighteenth century, litigations for debt repayment occurred more and more often. As a consequence, a "justicialization" of the economy took place and it seems that peasants spent more time, energy and money regulating their default of payment in court than in taverns or in the street attacking each other. They transferred their anger, hatred, bitterness and resentment towards this matter of debt payment to the judge, who decided on sanctions that did not involve violence. As a result, cases of ordinary violence decreased significantly in the eighteenth century, confirming Norbert Elias' theory of a civilizing process, i.e. Western society learned to refrain from violence—at least in public—and became more peaceful. According to Elias, the nobility began to follow new social standards of politeness and etiquette, which involved a decrease in blood feuds. As a result, the lower classes of society imitated the upper class and everybody became civilized. Unconscious mimicry, therefore, provoked a change in mentalities in Elias' theory. From my point of view, however, it was the economic changes, in particular indebtedness, that provoked a change in social behaviour and human interaction within traditional societies. It seems that a decrease in violence could be generally accepted as a social phenomenon, as individuals retained a certain control over their emotions and a state of self-discipline. Anger, for instance, came to be expressed through other means than physical violence. But if cases of ordinary violence decreased in the eighteenth century, violence on the part of women, and against women, rose significantly. Women's new economic role within society did not correspond to the traditional system of patriarchy in which their economic and social role was significantly reduced.[39] As this social norm was infringed, men perhaps tried to redress this pattern of patriarchy through violence, perhaps trying to reassert authority over women, unconsciously or not. One of our problems is that domestic violence in rural households is almost impossible to examine as few cases were reported to the bench.

This chapter has shown that we need to be attentive to emotions in economic mechanisms and changes as these reveal information about human interaction and also shed light on social change. Perhaps other studies in the future will inform us whether the challenge to patriarchy in the eighteenth century led to something of a rise in ordinary violence against women, as I suggest.

---

[39] This aspect can be applied to other societies in other times. In an article published on May 13, 2011 in the French newspaper *Le Figaro*, Laure Marchand describes the current changing social climate in Turkey, a country with a growing and dynamic economy. The journalist observes that women who are seeking and getting more independence and economic power become the target of violence on the part of men. Laure Marchand, "Turquie: la violence contre les femmes croît avec leur emancipation," *Le Figaro* 20, 770, Friday May 13, 2011.

Works Cited

Ahmed, Sara. "Affective Economies." *Social Text* 79 (2004): 117–139.

Barbalet, J. M. "A Macro Sociology of Emotion: Class Resentment." *Sociological Theory* 10 (2) (1992): 150–163.

Bercé, Yves-Marie. *Croquants et Nu-Pieds.* Paris: Gallimard, 1991.

Berezin, Mabel. "Emotions and the Economy." In *The Handbook of Economic Sociology*, edited by Neil J. Smelser & Richard Swedberg, 109–127. Princeton: Princeton University Press, 2005.

Bicchieri, Cristina. *The Grammar of Society: the Nature and Dynamics of Social Norms.* Cambridge: Cambridge University Press, 2006.

Collins, James B. "The Economic Role of Women in Seventeenth-Century France." *French Historical Studies* 16 (2) (1989): 436–470.

Dermineur, Elise M. "Female Peasants, Patriarchy, and the Credit Market in Eighteenth-Century France." *Proceedings of the Western Society for French History* 37 (2009): 61–84.

—. "Women in Rural Society: Peasants, Patriarchy and the Local Economy in Northeast France, 1650–1789." (Ph.D. Diss., Purdue University, 2011).

Elster, Jon. "Economic Order and Social Norms." *Journal of Institutional and Theoretical Economics* 144 (1988): 357–366.

—. *Making Sense of Marx.* Cambridge: Cambridge University Press, 1985.

Feeley, Malcolm M. & Deborah L. Little. "The Vanishing Female: The Decline of Women in the Criminal Process, 1687–1912." *Law & Society Review* 25 (4) (1991): 719–757.

Ferro, Marc. *Le Ressentiment dans l'Histoire: Comprendre notre Temps* Paris: Odile Jacob, 2008.

Gallant, Thomas W. "Honor, Masculinity and Ritual Knife Fighting in Nineteenth-Century Greece." *The American Historical Review* 105 (2) (2000): 359–382.

Gimenez, Martha E. "Capitalism and the Oppression of Women: Marx Revisited." *Science & Society* 69 (1) (2005): 11–32.

Hardwick, Julie. "Seeking Separations: Gender, Marriages, and Household Economies in Early Modern France." *French Historical Studies* 21 (1) (1998): 157–180.

—. *The Practice of Patriarchy: Gender and the Politics of Household Authority in Early Modern France.* University Park: Pennsylvania State University Press, 1998.

Hoffman, Philip T., Postel-Vinay, Gilles & Rosenthal, Jean-Laurent. "Private Credit Markets in Paris, 1690–1840." *The Journal of Economic History* 52 (2) (1992): 293–306.

—. *Growth in a Traditional Society: The French Countryside, 1450–1815.* Princeton: Princeton University Press, 2000.

Hoffman, Philip T., Gilles Postel-Vinay & Jean-Laurent Rosenthal. *Priceless Markets: the Political Economy of Credit in Paris, 1660–1870.* Chicago: University of Chicago Press, 2000.

Jordan, William Chester. *Women and Credit in Pre-Industrial and Developing Societies.* University Park: University of Pennsylvania Press, 1993.

Khan, B. Zorina, "'Justice of the Marketplace': Legal Disputes and Economic Activity on America's Northeastern Frontier, 1700–1860." *The Journal of Interdisciplinary History* 39 (1) (2008): 1–35.

Laurence, Anne, Josephine Maltby & Janette Rutterford (eds.). *Women and Their Money, 1700–1950: Essays on Women and Finance.* London: Routledge, 2008.

Lemire, Beverly, Ruth Pearson & Gail Grace Campbell. *Women and Credit: Researching the Past, Refiguring the Future.* Oxford: Berg, 2001.

Meltzer, Bernard N. & Gil Richard Musolf. "Resentment and Ressentiment." *Sociological Inquiry* 72 (2) (2002): 240–255.

Muldrew, Craig "'A Mutual Assent of Her Mind?' Women, Debt, Litigation and Contract in Early Modern England." *History Workshop Journal* 55 (2003): 47–71.

Nietzsche, Friedrich Wilhelm. *The Genealogy of Morals.* Toronto: University of Toronto Libraries, 2011.

Ogilvie, Sheilagh. *A Bitter Living: Women, Markets, and Social Capital in Early Modern Germany.* New York: Oxford University Press, 2003.

Poska, Allyson M. *Women and Authority in Early Modern Spain: The Peasants of Galicia.* New York: Oxford University Press, 2006.

Rawls, John. *A Theory of Justice.* Oxford: Oxford University Press, 1973.

Reiser, Christa. *Reflections on Anger: Women and Men in a Changing Society.* Westport: Greenwood Publishing Group, 2001.

Rosenthal, Jean-Laurent. "Credit Markets and Economic Change in Southeastern France 1630–1788." *Explorations in Economic History* 30 (2) (1993): 129–157.

Rosenwein, Barbara H. *Emotional Communities in the Early Middle Ages*, 1st ed. Ithaca: Cornell University Press, 2007.

Scheler, Max. *Ressentiment.* Milwaukee: Marquette University Press, 1994.

Shepard, Alexandra. "Manhood, Credit and Patriarchy in Early Modern England c. 1580–1640." *Past & Present* 167 (2000): 75–106.

Shoemaker, Robert B. "Male Honour and the Decline of Public Violence in Eighteenth-Century London." *Social History* 26 (2) (2001): 190–208.

—. "The Taming of the Duel: Masculinity, Honour and Ritual Violence in London, 1660–1800." *The Historical Journal* 45 (3) (2002): 525–545.

Solomon, Robert. "One Hundred Years of Ressentiment: Nietzsche's Genealogy of Morals." In *Nietzsche, Genealogy, Morality: Essays on Nietzsche's Genealogy of Morals*, edited by Schnacht Richard, 95–126. Berkeley: University of California Press, 1994.

Vickers, Daniel. "Competency and Competition: Economic Culture in Early America." *The William and Mary Quarterly* 47 (1) (1990): 3–29.

PART III:

LOOK BACK IN ANGER

CHAPTER SEVEN

RESENTMENT IN PSYCHOSOMATIC PATHOLOGY (1939–1960)[1]

PILAR LEÓN-SANZ

Introduction

From antiquity, emotions have had an outstanding role to play in medicine. Thus, for example, Greek rational medicine, apart from clearly beneficial effects for health, saw uncontrolled, intense emotions as the origin of certain diseases. Sadness and anger were, in this sense, paradigmatic emotions, and other, more complex ones became the centre of medical attention much later. This is the case for resentment, which had been explored extensively in the fields of philosophy, social sciences and psychology. However, less critical attention was paid to it from the point of view of the history of Medicine.

As has been said in another chapter in this volume, in the nineteenth century, it was Nietzsche who linked resentment to medicine.[2] This

[1] This study is the outcome of the research project "Emotional Culture and Identity," funded by the Institute for Culture and Society (ICS) at the University of Navarra. The research was finished at Harvard University (2011) with thanks to the sources of the Countway Library. I am most grateful to my colleagues, historians of Medicine, at the Department of Biomedical Humanities at the University of Navarra for their input and advice.
[2] For this author, weakness and illness arising from resentment was characteristic of the morale of slaves, in contrast with the energy and moral strength of gentlemen, which was clearly healthy. However, things are perhaps not quite as simple as they seem. Solomon considers that Nietzsche does not identify illness with weakness, his intention being to differentiate the two positions: that of the individual who struggles to overcome these difficulties, and that of he who yields and gives in. This is how we should interpret his celebrated aphorism: "What does not kill me makes me stronger." Robert C. Solomon, "One Hundred Years of Resentment. Nietzsche's Genealogy of Morals," in *Nietzsche, genealogy, morality: Essays on Nietzsche's Genealogy of Morals*, ed. Richard Sacht (Berkeley:

relationship was even closer in the Max Scheler's work (1874–1928). In the monograph he wrote on this emotion, we find a clear association between resentment and pathology. For Scheler the hatred that causes resentment may become pathological when it spreads in every direction and breaks away from its origins. He states that:

> When the repression is complete, the result is a general negativism—a sudden, violent, seemingly unsystematic and unfounded rejection of things, situations, or natural objects whose loose connection with the original cause of the hatred can only be discovered by a complicated analysis … Cases like this are confined to the domain of pathology.[3]

If the intensity of the resentment can produce illness, at other times the emergence of this emotion is a clear sign of mental alteration:

> In some psychoses, for example, in hysteria, we find a kind of "altruism" in which the patient has become incapable of feeling and experiencing anything "by himself." All his experiences are sympathetic, built on those o another person and *his* possible attitude and expectation, *his* possible reaction to any event. The patient's own existence has lost its centre and focus, he neglects all his affairs, is completely drawn into the "other's" life —and suffers from it. He eats nothing or injures himself in order to vex the "other."[4]

Thus we can categorically state that Scheler underlines that the exacerbation of resentment is both the cause and effect of illness.

In this chapter we intend to explore resentment form the history-medicine perspective (1939–1960). From that point of view, we will analyse the medical concept of resentment and revise the articles published on the subject in the *Psychosomatic Medicine* journal, which was, and still is, the official peer-reviewed journal of the American Psychosomatic Society (from 1939). Over the years we are interested in, we find that resentment is a recurring issue which appears in many articles. Most of these that we will consider deal with cases and patient stories which are very useful in understanding the etiopathogenic theories and therapeutic aspects of the doctor-patient relationship.

University of California Press, 1994), 95–127. On the other hand, and as we will observe later in more detail, resentment is described in historical figures considered as great and powerful.

[3] Max Scheler, *Ressentiment* (Milwaukee: Marquette University Press, 1974), 51.

[4] Scheler, *Ressentiment*, 101–2.

We will also suggest some reasons to explain why there were so many studies on resentment, both clinical and in laboratories, at a time when this emotion was not studied in general medicine.

Resentment in Psychosomatic Medicine

During the inter-war period, German medicine saw the beginning of what was called psychosomatic medicine, which associated elements belonging to Freudian psychoanalysis with internal medicine. Its development was conditioned by the great number of combatants who, after the two World Wars, suffered from many illnesses without any somatic cause.

However, the diaspora caused by World War II led some of the main promoters of this movement to move to the USA where they settled at the most important universities and developed ways and means to study the influence of psychology on somatics.[5] Their work and, especially, their articles, published in the journal *Psychosomatic Medicine*, are the basis for this study.

The presence of resentment can be found in the earliest issues of the journal, and it is studied from both the neurophysiological and clinical perspectives. From a bibliometric standpoint, we see that the attention paid to resentment was parallel to the progress of the Psychosomatic School, which increased greatly from the 1940s, particularly in the years following World War II, until the 1960s. In fact, over half of all the articles on the incidence of resentment (54.4 %) were published between 1945 and 1954, and many of the studies mentioned here include people who were affected by their participation in World War II, as research subjects.

More than 270 articles on resentment were published in *Psychosomatic Medicine* during the period selected, obliging us to focus on the analysis of the studies carried out, fundamentally, by the members of the Cornell University Medical College, given the interest and repercussions of this

---

[5] An historical analysis of this school can be found in Herbert Weiner, "Psychosomatic Medicine and the Mind-Body Relation: Historical, Philosophical, Scientific, and Clinical Perspectives," in *History of Psychiatry and Medical Psychology: With an Epilogue on Psychiatry and the Mind-Body Relation*, edited by Edwin R. Wallace IV and John Gach, 781–834 (New York: Springer, 2008). For the period here studied Dorothy Levenson, *Mind, body, and Medicine: a History of the American Psychosomatic Society* (Baltimore, MD: Williams & Wilkins, 1994).

group's research into the physio-pathological signs of resentment.[6] We will also consider the works of two members of the Editorial Board of Psychosomatic Medicine, Franz Alexander (1891–1964) and Helen Flanders Dunbar (1902–1959),[7] because of the importance of their contributions to the theoretical framework of the school of psychosomatic medicine in the USA. We also refer, due to the importance of their published works, to authors such as Avery D. Weisman, who practiced at the Department of Neurology and Psychiatry at Harvard Medical School and at the Massachusetts General Hospital, Leon J. Saul of the Chicago psychological school, and Irving D. Harris, who was a military physician, among others.

In the early 1930s, Harold Wolff (1898–1962) created one of the most influential centres of psychosomatic medicine, Cornell University Medical College at New York Hospital. Wolff, who was born in New York, received his medical degree at Harvard, and in 1923 returned to New York for house staff training. He then spent time with Stanley Cobb in Boston, Adolf Meyer at Johns Hopkins, Ivan Petrovich Pavlov in Moscow and Otto Loewi in Austria. While chief of neurology at New York Hospital, Wolff was appointed Professor of Neurology and Director of the Neurology Division at Bellevue Hospital.[8]

Dr. Wolff studied the connection between human problems and health and disease. With his colleagues, he published research on peptic ulcers, ulcerative colitis, hypertension, and a host of other bodily disturbances. Among those colleagues who co-authored studies on resentment with Wolff were Donald J. Simons, Robert M. Marcussen and George A. Wolf, Jr.

Of particular relevance for our topic is the work which Wolff carried out with the psychiatrist Bela Mittelmann who had emigrated from Berlin to the USA.[9] Mittelmann, Wolff and Keeve Brodman together devised the

---

[6] Levenson, *Mind, body, and medicine: a history of the American Psychosomatic Society*, 98.

[7] H. F. Dunbar was listed as managing editor of *Psychosomatic Medicine* and also as a member of the Editorial Board representing psychiatry. Franz Alexander, representing "psychoanalysis," was alphabetically listed first on the Editorial Board, and played a major part in the assembly of the first issue of the journal. See Levenson, *Mind, Body, and Medicine: a History of the American Psychosomatic Society*, 37.

[8] About Harold Wolff see Stewart Wolf, "In Memoriam," *Psychosom Med* 24 (3) (1962): 222–224.

[9] Mittelmann was born in Budapest in 1899. After receiving his medical degree in Prague, he completed an internship in Berlin and then emigrated to the United States. After some years in general practice in New York City, he completed a residency in psychiatry at Bellevue Hospital. From 1932 to 1938, he was an attending physician at the New York Postgraduate Hospital, and then became a

Cornell Indices for the quick assay of personality and psychosomatic disturbance. As well as his long-term studies on motility, Mittelmann wrote papers on Graves' disease, allergic pruritus, juvenile adiposogenital dystrophy and epilepsy. He pioneered the treatment of families, using techniques which were novel for the times, such as treating marital partners concurrently, and treating parents and children at the same time.

Thomas H. Holmes also worked with Harold Wolff at New York Hospital, and then moved to the Department of Psychiatry of the School of Medicine at the University of Washington in Seattle. They (Wolff with Holmes and Theodore Treuting) studied the effect of stress on the nasal passages and back pain.

Also working at the Departments of Medicine and Psychiatry of New York Hospital and Cornell University Medical School were Charles Brenner, Arnold P. Friedman, Sidney Carter, Charles H. Duncan, Ian P. Stevenson, Herbert S. Ripley, Saul Rosenzweig (1907) and Fred V. Rockwell.

As will be seen, the articles published in *Psychosomatic Medicine* show that the studies on the influence of resentment on pathology are formulated from a scientific and laboratory medical perspective; they are based on empirical data which, with objective, quantitative data, intends to express the holistic concepts of the psychosomatic school.

Resentment in Medicine

The American authors who addressed the subject of psychosomatic medicine stressed that situations of psychological origin must be recognized within the framework of psychology, as a global response of the organism to its surroundings: "The increasing knowledge of the relations of emotions to normal and disturbed body functions requires that for the modern physician emotional conflicts should become just as real and tangible issues as visible micro-organisms."[10]

The main contribution of psychoanalysis to medicine is the addition of the psychological microscope to the microscope technique as a procedure with which the emotional life of patients can be scrutinized in detail.

---

research associate with Harold Wolff's group at Cornell Medical College. During the 1940s and 1950s he served on the faculties of the New York Psychoanalytic Institute, City College of New York, New York University College of medicine, and Albert Einstein College of Medicine. Regarding this author, see Levenson, *Mind, Body, and Medicine*, 110–111.

[10] Franz Alexander, "Psychological aspects of Medicine," *Psychosom Med* 1 (1) (1939): 7–18.

The psychosomatic medicine school believed that, up to then, psychological symptoms were only considered insofar as they served for the classification of certain diseases, but no attempt was made to study their meaning. Moreover, they affirmed, the most numerous group of patients who benefited from the laboratory studies on emotions were not the mental patients, but rather those who had slight psychoneurotic symptoms, who also needed help. As Alexander programmatically announced in the first issue of the journal *Psychosomatic Medicine*, thanks to Freud, psychiatry, taken as the study of the morbid personality, would become the gateway for a more synthetic medical perspective. However, psychiatry could only carry out this function if it discovered the centrality of the study of personality.[11]

In the publications presented here, we have not found a theoretical development of the concept of resentment. In general, resentment appears to be linked to other emotions which are thought to be "negative," such as "insecurity, guilt and frustration";[12] it is also connected with shame, anger and, above all, anxiety. Each author repeatedly enumerates one type of association. Thus, for example, in the article published by Harold G. Wolff and Bela Mittelmann on peptic ulcers, they connect "severe anxiety, hostility, resentment, guilt and frustration."[13] The research studies the anatomical seat of resentment and how it interferes with the workings of the human being. Resentment causes physiological changes which finally have anatomopathological repercussions.

Another type of contemporaneous source is of use in establishing the medical concept of resentment. The Spanish physician Gregorio Marañón y Posadillo (1887–1960),[14] in his book *Tiberio: Historia de un resentimiento*,

---

[11] Alexander, "Psychological Aspects of Medicine," 7–18.

[12] Bela Mittelmann & Harold G. Wolff, "Emotions and Gastroduodenal Function: Experimental Studies on Patients with Gastritis, Duodenitis and Peptic Ulcer," *Psychosom Med* 4 (1) (1942): 5–61.

[13] Mittelmann & Wolff, "Emotions and Gastroduodenal Function: Experimental Studies," 53.

[14] Gregorio Marañón specialized in endocrinology and became professor of that specialty in the Complutense University in Madrid in 1931. He was also a member of the International Society for the History of Medicine. Marañón founded the Institute of Medical Pathology and was president of the Institute of Experimental Endocrinology and the Centre of Biological Research. He contributed to establishing a relationship between Psychology and Endocrinology. There is an abundant bibliography on this author. For example, Gary D. Keller, *The Significance and Impact of Gregorio Marañón: Literary Criticism, Biographies and Historiography* (New York: Bilingual Press, 1977); Pedro Laín Entralgo, *Marañón y el enfermo* (Madrid: Revista de Occidente, 1992); Juan Francisco

offers a theory on resentment. This volume was first published in 1939,[15] translated into German in 1952[16] and into English in 1956.[17] An in-depth analysis goes beyond the remit of this chapter, so we will merely make some comments on those aspects in Marañón's work which help to explain the clinical interest of the US school of psychosomatic medicine in resentment.[18]

Resentment, Marañón explained, comes from a biased perception of oneself and one's relationships with others. It is the bitter reaction produced in the resentful individual facing the contrast between a reality that assails them again and again, and "the happiness they think they deserve."[19] In the resentful individual, their deception with their surroundings turns into aggression which remains:

> Present in the depths of our consciousness, perhaps unknown to us. Down there, the resulting bitterness incubates and ferments. It infiltrates throughout our whole being; and it ends by becoming the director of our behaviour, of our slightest reactions.[20]

This feeling, which "has been retained and incorporated in our very soul," is resentment.[21]

Together with the external causes which unleash this passion, Marañón adds a personal predisposition, beginning in youth, which gives rise to the resentful personality:

> As a rule, this passion strikes root in minds predisposed to it during the period of adolescence; for it is then that the sense of competence or the

---

Jiménez Borreguero, *Gregorio Marañón: el regreso del Humanismo* (Madrid: Egartorre, 2006).

[15] Over the years there have been twelve editions in Spanish. The latest edition dates from 2006; Pozuelo de Alarcón (Madrid: Espasa, 2006).

[16] Gregorio Marañón, *Tiberius; Geschichte eines Ressentiments*, Übersetzung von Dr. Karl August Horst (München: Nymphenburger Verlagshandlung, 1952).

[17] Gregorio Marañón, *Tiberius: A Study in Resentment* (London: Hollis & Carter, 1956). In this chapter, we use the English first edition.

[18] In his theory of resentment, Marañón develops the following headings: Definitions; Resentment, Generosity, Affection; Intelligence and resentment; Envy, hatred and resentment; Timidity, gratitude and hypocrisy in relation to resentment; Social success and resentment; Age, sex, aesthetics and resentment; False virtue in the resentful man; Appearance and resentment; Humour and resentment; Success and the resentful man. Marañón, *Tiberius*, 9–19.

[19] Marañón, *Tiberius*, 11.

[20] Ibid., 9.

[21] Ibid., 9.

sense of incompetence, the source of resentment, originates, either at school or college, or during those first free steps in life that possess a clearly marked social significance.[22]

Dr. Marañón points out that resentment is a passion "of the mind; though, to be sure, it may lead to sin, and sometimes to passion or crime,"[23] a statement which we could compare with the explanation offered by Scheler. This also coincides with the earlier beliefs of the physicians of the psychosomatic school in its emphasis of a negative character.

Like Nietzsche, Marañón associates resentment with weakness. Marañón says: "On this plane of profound causes, in short, the resentful man is a human being poorly endowed with the capacity for affection; and, accordingly, a human being of mediocre moral quality."[24] Moreover, the resentful individual is uncongenial and "Uncongeniality increases in proportion as the person concerned outwardly exudes the repressed bitterness of resentment."[25] The resentful individual may be hypocritical and hide his passion, but "no passion shows itself so clearly as resentment in a man's looks, which are much less amenable to the discipline of caution than his words and his actions."[26] For Marañón, one example of the hypocrisy of the resentful individual is their penchant for anonymous letters: "Almost all such letters are written, not in hatred or in envy, but by the trembling hand of resentment." [27]

For Marañón there is no doubt that: "the virtue of generosity is the contrary of the passion of resentment."[28] And this opposition between resentment and generosity is fundamental, as it acquires an epistemic level and explains the idea of resentment.

In my opinion, the three most important characteristics to be underlined in Dr. Marañón's theory on this emotion are: the oversensitive reaction to surroundings at the origin of the resentment; the delayed reaction of the resentful person when facing what they consider to be aggression; and, finally, the social character of resentment. Resentment, Marañón declares: "is a passion which has much about it that is impersonal, much that is social."[29] It is impersonal because what causes it

---

[22] Ibid., 14.

[23] Ibid., 9.

[24] Ibid., 10.

[25] Ibid., 18.

[26] The resentful person is almost always wary and hypocritical. They rarely show their his inner bitterness to those close to him. Ibid., 13.

[27] Ibid., 13.

[28] Ibid., 131.

[29] Ibid., 12.

may not only have been another person, but simply "fate," illness or destiny, against which the resentful individual rebels.

Marañón analyzes "which characters are susceptible to its attack and which are immune from it,"[30] so we will also refer to the typology of the resentful individual. This classification was established by means of the study of "the resentful people we have known in the course of our lives, and also those who, because they suffered a similar impact, might have been so, but nevertheless were not."[31]

Sensitivity to Surroundings

Resentment appears as a disproportionate reaction to surroundings.

The resentful individual does not accept failure or is incapable of overcoming or forgetting it: "The mind of the resentful man, after its first inoculation, becomes more and more sensitive to fresh impacts";[32] hence, this passion may be due to causes that, for others, would be trivial, as "resentment does not depend upon the nature of the impact, but upon the make-up of the person who receives it."[33] This is why the passion can endure over time and be incurable:

> Everything, in his eyes, is an equivalent to an affront or comes into the category of an injustice. Indeed, the resentful man reaches the point of experiencing a morbid need for the causes that serve to keep his passion alive; a condition of masochistic thirst that makes him seek them out or invent them if they do not come his way.[34]

Everything, other people's behaviour or "life itself," have to do with the aggression felt. This kind of reaction is crucial and specific in the concept of resentment. It shows that one of the causes of resentment is non-adaptation to the milieu which, as we will see, is a key issue in the etiopathogenesis of the illness for psychosomatics. It also explains the importance of social aspects in resentment.

---

[30] Ibid., 10.
[31] Ibid.
[32] Ibid., 14.
[33] Ibid., 9.
[34] Ibid., 14.

A passion with delayed reactions

In resentment, the time passing between the aggression and the reaction is a peculiarity that distinguishes it from other emotions such as hatred, which almost always gives a swift response to an offence.

Resentment is a passion, as already stated, "of belated reactions." Only when resentment accumulates and completely poisons the spirit does it become obvious. The reaction to unjust punishment may cause humiliation, fleeting hatred or desire for revenge, "but scarcely ever resentment, unless it be frequently repeated and thus betrays a personal passion charged with specific injustice."[35]

That is to say, for the resentful individual the reaction is so important that it is never overcome or disappears, because it is not forgotten:

> The resentful man has a stubborn memory, impervious to time. When it does occur, the aggressive explosion of resentment is usually very belated; there is always a very long period of incubation between the offence and its revenge.[36]

Resentment, Marañón affirms, implies the continuity in time of the perceived vital aggression. And as we will see later on, this characteristic also has connections with the emotional etiology of the illness as suggested by psychosomatic medicine.

Social Failure

Marañón states that "resentment, though it looks very much like envy and hatred, differs from both. Envy and hatred are sins of a strictly individual cast,"[37] whereas resentment has a social component.

For Marañón, "all those causes which make social success difficult are the very causes that have the greatest, efficacy in creating resentment."[38] It is for this reason that the author considers resentment to be an urban emotion: "[it] is, for the most part, a passion that belongs to great cities." Because resentment crystallizes in contact with others it implies the assessment of the established society which gives value or merit to an action or a person. The resentful individual, according to Marañón, can be found "seeking refuge in the solitude of a village or wasting his time in fruitless travelling," but is always a "migrant from some city, and it is

---

[35] Ibid., 15.
[36] Ibid., 11.
[37] Ibid.
[38] Ibid., 13–14.

there that he fell sick."[39] This is why, in Marañón's opinion, the number of resentful people have multiplied. "In proportion as civilization advances and the struggle for success becomes more embittered, so the social significance of resentment increases."[40] This characteristic and the evolution of society would, for Marañón, explain the increase in the number of resentful individuals.

Marañón's "theory of resentment" coincides with what was written by the psychosomatic physicians when they stated that "side by side with causes of social significance, an important role is played by causes of a sexual kind." However, he differs from the psychosomatic authors when he deems that it appears "above all in the case of the man."[41] He justifies this opinion by referring to "the profound social repercussion which, in his case, is exerted by the sexual instinct,"[42] and because "sexual failure, in whatever form, exercises a depressing influence so great as to make essential its immediate concealment in the consciousness. Hence it transforms itself easily into resentment."[43]

According to Marañón, many resentful people are this way due to their social or sexual—or both simultaneously—inferiority:

> Created by some physical imperfection, especially some illness, difficult to conceal, which is offensive to the senses, or some defect, which people lacking in consideration are accustomed to regard as a matter for joking, such as a hump-back or a limp.[44]

Marañón's analysis of the social dimension of resentment also emphasises one of the most-studied facets of this emotion—its relationship with revolutions and social disorders.[45] There are many resentful men, he affirms with examples, who turn "to revolutionary confusion and play such a large

---

[39] Ibid., 14.

[40] Ibid.

[41] Ibid., 8, 15, 16.

[42] Ibid.,15.

[43] Ibid.

[44] Marañón's viewpoint on the resentful man or woman demands further contextualization and corresponds to a social structure unlike that of the period in the US. He states that "a large number of resentful men are sexually weak: they suffer from timidity, they are husbands unfortunate in their marriages, they are people affected by abnormal or repressed tendencies." Although he also comments that, "most resentful women are so in consequence of their specifically sexual failure: sterility or forced celibacy." Marañón, *Tiberius*, 16.

[45] On this issue of the analysis of resentment, there is ample, fundamental bibliography. See, for example, Marc Ferro, *Le ressentiment dans l'histoire: comprendre notre temps* (Paris: Odile Jacob, 2007).

part in its development." However, on such occasions they are to be
feared: "The most cruel of leaders often have antecedents that betray their
former timidity and show unequivocal symptoms of their present
resentment."[46] Such examples of this are Robespierre, Calvin or Tiberius.

Typology of the resentful man

In Marañón's opinion, "all the circumstances which favour resentment
often coincide with a definite physical and mental type."[47] Resentful
people are usually asthenic, tall, inclined towards inner life and the
affective frigidity that characterizes schizophrenics. At another point he
explains that: "the thin, reserved and egotistic man is more likely to be so
[resentful] than the plump, generous and sociable man."[48]

Other features of resentful individuals are their intelligence ("Almost
all great resentful men are talented") and shyness. According to Marañón:
"what is very characteristic of such men is not merely their incapacity for
gratitude, but also the facility with which they transform the favours
conferred on them by others into fuel for their resentment."[49]

The explanation of resentment as a characteristic of a certain way of
being and a type of person can also be seen in the psychosomatic medicine
view of illness. It implies a reciprocal and multiform relation—genetic and
configurative—between what is "personal" in the life of the patient
(understanding, life projects, moral responsibilities, etc.) and what is more
purely "physical."[50] The features of the personality of the resentful person
explain the physical consequences this passion unleashes in the affected
party, given that the psychological reality is seen as "psychic causality."

The Pathologization of Resentment

The psychosomatic approach to the symptoms of resentment meant a
re-thinking of the mind-body dichotomy; it launched the psychological
mechanism as the cause of illness and underlined the role emotions play in
somatic illnesses. "In the last two decades," said Alexander in 1939,
"increasing attention has been paid to the causative role of emotional

---

[46] Ibid., 12.
[47] Ibid., 17.
[48] Ibid., 18.
[49] Ibid., 13.
[50] Pedro Laín Entralgo, *Introducción histórica al estudio de la patología
psicosomática* (Madrid: Paz Montalvo, 1950), 123.

factors in disease and a growing psychological orientation manifests itself among physicians."[51]

In fact, all emotions are accompanied by physiological changes—fear goes with cardiac palpitations, anger with an increase in cardiac activity, higher arterial pressure and change in the metabolism of carbohydrates, etc. Physiological phenomena are the result of complex muscular interaction that occurs due to the influence of nervous impulses and the vegetative nervous system. Thus, the facial muscles and the diaphragm are modified by laughter, the lachrymal glands by weeping and the heart by fear, the suprarenal glands and the vascular system by rage, etc.[52]

For example, the study by Jule Eisenbud on the effect of repression on the somatic expression of emotion in vegetative functions shows that the function of repression varies directly with the excitement of the para-sympathetic branch of the autonomic nervous system. To prove this, the author tested this hypothesis using the gastric motility and parotid gland secretory rate as indices of autonomic nervous system function.[53]

According to the theories of psychosomatic medicine, the physical changes that usually accompany emotions are transitory, but they do produce physical alterations which can lead to functional disturbances, particularly when the influence of emotions is enduring. We know, for instance, of cases of so-called "conversion hysteria" within psychoanalysis. The condition appears when a person tries to restrain long-term and repressed emotions which, as we have seen, is the case for resentment.

---

[51] Alexander, "Psychological Aspects of Medicine," 7.

[52] Ibid., 14.

[53] Jule Eisenbud, "A Method for Investigating the Effect of Repression on the Somatic Expression of Emotion in Vegetative Functions: A Preliminary Report. Department of Psychiatry, New York State Psychiatric Institute and Hospital," *Psychosom Med* 1 (3) (1939): 376–387. Although, in Eisenbud's opinion, the results were "highly suggestive but require careful controls before a more definite impression can be gained. The hypothesis to be tested was that the function of repression varies directly with the excitement of the para-sympathetic branch of the autonomic nervous system. A method of testing this hypothesis, using the gastric motility and the parotid gland secretory rate as indices of autonomic nervous system function, is described. The results of the experiments with gastric motility are, as far as they go, in harmony with the hypothesis. The results of the simultaneous experiments with the parotid gland secretory rate are highly suggestive but require careful controls before a more definite impression can be gained. The method described can be used in plotting out the behavior of other autonomic functions in relation to the function of repression."

Moreover, a consistent thread woven through the tapestry of psychosomatic investigation is the idea that illness was related to events in a patient's life. Franz Alexander saw the events of infancy reflected in later illness. Others connected ill health to the stresses and strains of everyday adult life. This idea is reflected in Marañón's "theory of resentment," and he finds in the life of Tiberius (one of the historical figures who he considers best reflect this emotion) the events which made this emperor an good example.

Many researchers adopted the notion of tracking the events of a human life to ascertain, or even to predict, which circumstances were likely to produce illness. In the early years of the twentieth century, Adolf Meyer tried to convince physicians that they should consider both biological and psychological influences on illness. He constructed a chart to record the major life events, including the calendar years of the patient's life-span, important life events, the patient's emotional reaction to those events, and illness experiences through their lifetime. Meyer's chart was used and modified by others, including Stanley Cobb in Boston and Harold Wolff and Lawrence Hinkle at New York Hospital-Cornell.[54]

The problem of specificity in emotional etiopathogenesis

At least initially, the American Psychosomatic School noted that each emotion was related specifically to an organic disorder or disease.[55] However, from the first issue of *Psychosomatic Medicine* we can see the centrality of the debate on this point. In a study carried out on rats, Hunt concluded that: "no clear difference is shown … The hoarding reaction in rats is determined chiefly by deprivation, and that it is unaffected by the frustrating procedure employed."[56]

---

[54] Levenson, *Mind, body, and Medicine: a History of the American Psychosomatic Society*, 158.

[55] Franz Alexander, *Psychosomatic Medicine: its Principles and Applications*, (New York: W.W. Norton, 1950), 9, 14, 16.

[56] Joseph McVicker Hunt & R. R. Willoughby, "The Effect of Frustration on Hoarding in Rats," *Psychosom Med* 1 (1939) 1, 309–310, explains that "As there is no clear difference (and there certainly is no difference in favour of the frustrated group), it is concluded that the rats' hoarding reaction is determined mainly by privation, and is not affected by the frustrating procedure used."

In the same issue of the journal, Saul Rosenzweig points out that: "the treatment included a delineation of types of frustrating situations—privations, deprivations and conflicts, either external or internal to the organism in point of origin." Saul Rosenzweig, "Frustration as an Experimental Problem," *Psychosom Med* 1 (1) (1939): 199–200.

The works of Harold Wolff and his collaborators at New York Hospital-Cornell are also related to the problem of specificity: "Were certain diseases associated with specific personalities? Did specific childhood conflicts result in specific diseases in the adult?"[57] The experimental studies showed that only a certain degree of specificity can be mentioned because the same reaction may derive from similar emotions and psychological status and, on the contrary, people may react in different ways when faced with the same external stimuli:

> Individuals differ as regards the intensity and duration of the cardiovascular and respiratory responses to life situations. The fact that a single subject tends to react under different circumstances in many different ways suggests that the individual is manifesting a variety of ways of dealing with his environment as regards his cardiovascular and respiratory functions.[58]

Besides, the same reactions can be seen when facing emotions that are considered enjoyable or pleasurable. As I. Stevenson shows, "symptoms occurred during joy or elation as well as during such states as anxiety, resentment, and depression."[59]

Next, we will give examples of the introduction of resentment into the psychogenesis of the symptoms, and revise the main pathologies and diseases with which this emotion was associated—gastric disorders and cardiorespiratory diseases. Other studies link resentment with disorders such as headache or backache. Through these cases, we will see the relativity of the specificity between the emotions and the symptoms they cause.

---

[57] Lawrence E. Hinkle, William N. Christenson, Francis D. Kane, Adrian Ostfeld, William N. Thetford & Harold G. Wolff, "An Investigation of the Relation Between Life Experience, Personality Characteristics, and General Susceptibility to Illness," *Psychosom Med* 20 (4) (1958): 278–295.

[58] They also concluded that "fatigue as experienced by patients is a complex state dependent upon emotional attitude, the absence of a dominant motivation and the presence of a stress-producing life situation with accompanying inefficiency of cardiovascular and respiratory function." George A. Wolf, Jr. & Harold G.Wolff, "Studies on the Nature of Certain Symptoms Associated with Cardiovascular Disorders," *Psychosom Med* 8 (5) (1946): 293–319.

[59] Ian Stevenson, "Physical Symptoms During Pleasurable Emotional States," *Psychosom Med* 12 (1) (1950): 98–102.

Resentment and gastric changes

The military physician Irving D Harris claimed that resentment would appear in all types of diseases, in organic and other ailments which were defined as functional. However, in the opinion of this author, above all in gastric disorders: "… the hostility in these patients was not as freely expressed as it was in patients with gastric symptoms."[60]

As Avery D. Weisman summarised in 1956, there had been numerous studies of ulcers in military personnel during World War II. In general, as Mittelmann & Wolff reported: "specific effects of anxiety, hostility, resentment, guilt, and frustration, which occurred in their patients, resulted in an increase in gastric motility, secretion, and blood, whereas fear and sadness diminished these functions."[61] These findings were later confirmed by Wolff. He related periods of gastric hyperactivity, gnawing epigastric pain, and heartburn with anger and resentment.

Then again, Manuel Zane stressed:

> The high standards which compel ulcer patients to strive for unattainable perfection. The fear and resentment which occur when the patient feels required to act in a certain prescribed manner, despite a conviction of failure, result in the dissociation of physiological functions necessary for the development of ulcer.[62]

Let us have a more detailed look at this. Mittelmann y Wolff, in their extensive work published in 1942 on more than thirty patients, stated categorically that "reactions of intense anxiety, insecurity, resentment, guilt and frustration were obtained in all [the patients included]. Also, compensating efforts to bolster self-esteem by a show of independence, self-sufficiency, and perfectionism were common."[63] These data confirmed the hypothesis proposed by Alexander when he pointed out that "it was evident from the long duration of the personality disturbances that the mucosal lesion itself was not responsible for the major emotional

---

[60] I. D. Harris, "Relation of Resentment and Anger to Functional Gastric Complaints," *Psychosom Med* 8 (3) (1946): 211–13.

[61] Avery D. Weisman, "A Study of the Psychodynamics of Duodenal Ulcer Exacerbations with Special Reference to Treatment and the Problem of 'Specificity'," *Psychosom Med* 18 (1) (1956): 2–42.

[62] Manuel D. Zane, "Psychosomatic Considerations in Peptic Ulcer," *Psychosom Med* 9 (6) (1947): 372–380.

[63] Bela Mittelmann & Harold G. Wolff, "Emotions and Gastroduodenal Function: Experimental Studies on Patients with Gastritis, Duodenitis and Peptic Ulcer," *Psychosom Med* 4 (1) (1942): 5–61.

conflicts."[64] This is something we see as an example in the concept of resentment.

Mittelmann and Wolff gathered data on the behaviour and remarks of the subjects. Simultaneously, records were made of the motility and secretions of the stomach, as well as of finger temperature and respiration.[65] The experiments revealed that:

> Tension, anxiety, resentment, anger, guilt, obsequiousness and desperation, already present, accentuated or induced, were almost always accompanied by an increase in hydrochloric acid, mucous and pepsin secretions. Peristaltic activity became continuous, and contractions increased in magnitude. Respiration became more rapid and shallow, with frequent sighs. There was usually a drop in finger temperature. Often in patients with ulcers, pain of a burning and gnawing quality was precipitated and unusual amounts of bile and moderate amounts of fresh, unclotted blood appeared in the extractions. Similar changes occurred in a few instances during sleep following a period of affective stress. During and after interviews which engendered emotional security, functional over-activity decreased and approached normal levels. A comparison of the individual physiological and emotional changes in normal subjects with those of patients with ulcer, gastritis and duodenitis revealed similar patterns was carried out, but the changes in the pathological group were greater in magnitude and duration.[66]

In addition, "in situations which engendered feelings of emotional security and assurance, gastric function was restored toward normal and symptoms eliminated in those with symptoms and abnormal function."[67]

However, despite the spectacular nature of the results, Mittelmann & Wolff considered that they had not proved that resentment was the cause of the duodenal ulcer, as:

---

[64] Mittelmann & Wolff, "Emotions and Gastroduodenal Function: Experimental Studies," 58. They affirmed that "In all of the patients with peptic lesions it was possible to demonstrate a chronological parallelism between the onset, recrudescence and course of gastroduodenal symptoms, and the occurrence of untoward emotional reactions. The situations that prompted these reactions were not necessarily dramatic or in the nature of crises, but because of the existing emotional frame within which they occurred they had important effects on the patients." Ibid.

[65] In the research project, 165 observations were conducted on 26 subjects, 10 of whom had ulcers of the stomach or the duodenum, and 3 of whom had gastritis and duodenitis. Thirteen subjects were healthy and without complaints.

[66] Mittelmann & Wolff, "Emotions and Gastroduodenal Function: Experimental Studies," 53.

[67] Ibid.

In appraising the data of this study, the relation between the described emotions and the functional changes in the stomach was not interpreted as cause and effect. Instead, both affects and gastroduodenal changes were viewed as coincident aspects of biological behaviour in reaction to life situations; behaviour in some instances compatible with health, and in others resulting in disease.[68]

Fig. 7.1. Normal Male. Rise in acidity during induced resentment, anxiety and embarrassment. Source: Mittelmann & Wolff (1942).

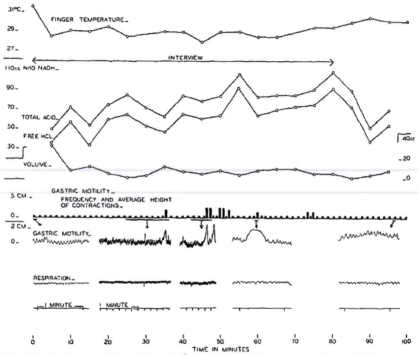

Fig. 2. Subject 1. Normal Male. Rise in Acidity during Induced Resentment, Anxiety and Embarrassment. (Cf. Fig. 1)

Once more, M. Zane confirmed the importance of the duration of the emotional conflict in the appearance of ulcers: "the ulcer diathesis resides in the basic character structure which readily thrusts the patient into the peptic-ulcer type of conflict situation. If the situation is of short duration,

---

[68] Mittelmann & Wolff, "Emotions and Gastroduodenal Function: Experimental Studies," 57.

the symptoms will also be brief; if sustained, they will be prolonged."[69] The prognosis also depends on this factor: "The best prognosis exists for patients with the longest intervals between attacks, implying as it does, adequate adjustment during the intervals ...the emotional reaction of the patient is held to be of greater significance than the particular diet or drugs utilized in treatment."[70]

However, he considers that fear and resentment produce dissociated reactions that can be identified: "When fear and resentment are experienced simultaneously, the reactions in the stomach are dissociated, often resulting in increased acid, motility, and vascularity, with decreased mucin." The problem is: "that during such dissociation other protective substances and mechanisms are likewise deficient in the presence of increased acid and pepsin ... such physiological concomitants to this conflict situation are highly conducive to the development of ulceration." Thus, "the peptic-ulcer conflict situation involves both fear and resentment, each of which has opposing effects on the stomach and duodenum."[71]

The research project that Weissman carried out on six male patients with exacerbations of chronic duodenal ulcers studied the concomitant psychological factors with ulcers. In his opinion, and in agreement with Zane: "the ulcer recurrence invariably developed in an atmosphere in which the patient vacillated between active seeking and passive yielding."[72]

The ulcer exacerbation was associated with no single factor operating alone, but required the integrated presence of the nuclear conflict, basic fear, special ego defences, and ambivalent interpersonal relationships.

However, he added three ways in which the stress of the conflict could act: "by a lack of fulfilment of passive-receptive wishes, by a transgression of the exaggerated ego ideal, and by fear of passivity itself." The basic affects were restrained resentment, angry guilt, and guilty fear. The patients were afraid of becoming helpless and submissive through a narcissistic injury, by depleting demands, or by loss of a source of strength or support.

Weissman discussed the meaning of specificity. In his opinion, the logical requirements for specificity were described in terms of equivalent and conditional forms and a distinction was made between disorder

---

[69] Zane, "Psychosomatic Considerations in Peptic Ulcer," 379.

[70] Zane, "Psychosomatic Considerations in Peptic Ulcer," 380.

[71] Zane, "Psychosomatic Considerations in Peptic Ulcer," 379.

[72] Weisman, "A Study of the Psychodynamics of Duodenal Ulcer Exacerbations with Special Reference to Treatment and the Problem of 'Specificity'," 40.

specificity and stress specificity. The specific psychosomatic formulation of the various categories of psychological factors was regarded as conditional stress specificity because a similar formulation could exist without necessarily entailing the development of a duodenal ulcer. It is therefore, he concluded, to be differentiated from equivalent stress specificity where a specific psychosomatic formulation may be applied if, and only if, a duodenal ulcer is present. Parallel psychological observations in other diseases are necessary in order to determine disorder specificity, which similarly may be either conditional or equivalent.[73]

Resentment and cardiorespiratory symptoms

Within the framework of the etiopathogenic specificity of resentment, nor were the cardiorespiratory symptoms and syndromes linked to resentment unequivocal.

Thus, for example, George A. Wolf, Jr. & Harold G. Wolff studied, over a period of almost a year, the symptoms and cardiovascular and respiratory functions of healthy human subjects. They concluded that there was as certain degree of specificity, as they found: "Dyspnea associated with inefficient pulmonary ventilation may occur in response to stress-producing life situations in association with anxiety, anger, guilt, rage, frustration, and tension."[74] Besides:

> palpitation associated with increased stroke volume may occur under similar circumstances ... heart pain in the presence of anatomical narrowing of the coronary arteries may result from increased work of the heart attendant upon prolonged elevation of the blood pressure and cardiac output in association with rage, resentment, anxiety, fear, and tension.[75]

In contrast:

> heart pain in the presence of anatomical narrowing of the arteries may result from a fall in the cardiac output and coronary blood flow in association with desperation and defeat ... Giddiness and faintness may result from cerebral anoxia attendant upon diminished venous return to the heart. Also, giddiness and faintness may result from hyperventilation, which is followed by cerebral vasoconstriction, impaired dissociation of

---

[73] Weisman, "A Study of the Psychodynamics of Duodenal Ulcer Exacerbations with Special Reference to Treatment and the Problem of 'Specificity'," 41.
[74] Wolf & Wolff, "Studies on the Nature of Certain Symptoms Associated with Cardiovascular Disorders," 317.
[75] Ibid.

oxyhemoglobin and cerebral anoxia. Both types of cerebral anoxia occur in response to stress-producing life situations in association with feelings of exhaustion, anxiety, fear, and during the early part of convalescence.[76]

On the other hand, C. H. Duncan, I. P. Stevenson & H. S. Ripley studied the circulatory dynamics at rest and after exercise in thirty-five subjects during different emotional states:

> A close correlation was found between the emotional state and the resting level of cardiac activity. Stressful life situations associated with attitudes of preparedness and feelings of anxiety or resentment were accompanied by cardiac hyperactivity, with heart rate and/or cardiac index increased in comparison to the values found during periods of security and relaxation.[77]

Situations evoking despair and discouragement were accompanied by cardiac hyperactivity, with the heart rate and cardiac index below the usual values.

A similar relationship was observed between the emotional state and the circulatory response to exercise:

> During periods of anxiety and resentment, exercise usually resulted in greater and more prolonged increase in heart rate and/or cardiac index than did the same exercise performed during periods of security and relaxation. This objective evidence of exercise intolerance was commonly accompanied by complaints of dyspnea, palpitations, weakness, or other discomfort on exertion. During mild life stress, the resting heart rate and cardiac index were sometimes unchanged but exercise tolerance impaired.[78]

---

[76] Ibid. These results indicate that, in a setting of adverse life circumstances and associated emotional reactions, performance in terms of respiration and work of the heart is costly. This high cost may manifest itself in cardiovascular symptoms which are not dependent alone upon gross structural heart disorder. This uneconomical performance may also manifest itself in impaired total efficiency of the individual, and short-term observations were made on selected patients displaying certain symptoms associated with cardiovascular disorders.

[77] Charles H. Duncan, Ian P. Stevenson & Harold G. Wolff, "Life Situations, Emotions, and Exercise Tolerance," *Psychosom Med* 13 (1) (1951): 36–50.

[78] Duncan, Stevenson & Wolff, "Life Situations, Emotions, and Exercise Tolerance," 49. The correlation between emotional state and circulatory dynamics at rest and after exercise was observed in all three groups of subjects. In the healthy controls the fluctuations in emotional state and in circulatory dynamics were relatively small, and symptoms of effort intolerance minimal. The patients with neurocirculatory asthenia exhibited greater variability in emotional state and in cardiac activity, and the association of pronounced anxiety, cardiac

For example:

> A 34-year-old housewife had had frequent attacks of paroxysmal
> tachycardia since childhood. During the past year she had felt under
> increasing tension in coping with her two children and in performing her
> housework in accordance with her perfectionist standards. Her frustration
> and resentment were accentuated by the failure of her husband to support
> her in her disciplinary measures or to afford her any sympathetic
> understanding. In this situation she noted marked fatigue, palpitations on
> exertion, weight loss, and increase in the frequency of her arrhythmias.[79]

The study on the influence of the emotional state on the dynamics of
blood circulation in repose and after exercise by Charles H. Duncan, Ian P.
Stevenson & Harold G. Wolff showed that, in all patients, both with and
without cardiac disease, intolerance to exercise was largely due to anxiety,
resentment and stressful life situations.[80]

Other pathological signs of resentment

Other studies associate resentment with discomforts such as headache,
backache or joint pain, which at the time were all considered "functional
disorders."

H. Wolff, in his early work on the anatomy and physiology of the
cerebral circulation, described the mechanism of migraine and other
headaches of vascular origin, while at the same time acknowledging the
influence of personality factors on the development of headaches. He went

---

hyperactivity at rest, and exercise intolerance was frequently observed. In the
subjects with structural heart disease effort intolerance was the product of the fixed
structural defect and the variable influence of life stress.

In all patients, both with and without structural heart disease, who presented
complaints of exercise intolerance, a significant portion of the symptomatology
was dependent on anxiety, resentment and cardiac hyperactivity incident to
stressful life situations. With the achievement of a state of relative security and
relaxation there was diminution in the cardiac activity at rest and improvement in
exercise tolerance.

[79] Charles H. Duncan, Ian P. Stevenson & H. S. Ripley, "Life Situations,
Emotions, and Paroxysmal Auricular Arrhythmias," *Psychosom Med* 12 (1)
(1950): 23–37.

[80] Duncan, Stevenson & Wolff, "Life Situations, Emotions, and Exercise
Tolerance," 49.

Fig. 7.2. Variation in exercise tolerance with change in emotional state.
Source: Duncan, Stevenson & Wolff (1951).

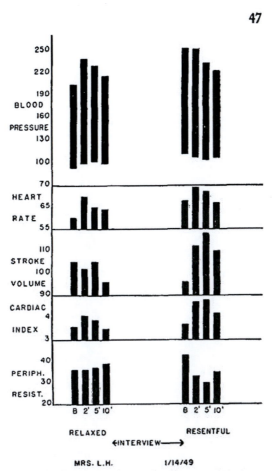

Fig. 9.—*Rapid Variation in Exercise Tolerance with Change in Emotional State* (Case 8). The values before (*B*) and after (*2'*, *5'*, and *10'*) the exercise are given. During an interview the patient became resentful and her blood pressure rose; exercise was then repeated. The second test showed impaired exercise tolerance as compared to the first, with a greater increase in the cardiac index and delay in its return to the resting level.

on to study pain as sensory experience, as related to personality and life experience.[81]

Wolff, together with Donald J. Simons, showed that chronic headaches resulted from sustained contraction of the skeletal muscles of the head and neck associated with the occurrence of sustained resentment, anxiety, frustration, tension and fear, and were sometimes augmented by noxious stimuli arising from abnormal healing and scar formation within the extracranial soft structures of the head and neck. In many instances the amount of muscle contraction was minimal and was the probable basis of the complaint because it was sustained and because of an abnormal preoccupation with the head. Since all of the patients in this study showed evidence of emotional disturbance, it was likely that they over-reacted to minimal head sensations which would otherwise be disregarded.[82] This shows a similar approach to what we have already seen in the etiopathogenesis of the gastric ulcer.

Other authors from the Cornell University Medical School (Charles Brenner, Arnold P. Friedman and Sidney Carter) published the results of a study carried out on several hundred patients with chronic headaches. They found that headaches were very often found in patients who had suppressed (or were unaware of) strong feelings of resentment or anger.[83]

The same group found quite similar results in research into backache using 65 patients and 10 healthy subjects:

> A pattern of skeletal muscle hyperfunction characterized by a generalized and sustained increase in motor and electrical activity was a common accompaniment of the reaction of subjects exhibiting the backache syndrome to situations which threatened their security and engendered apprehension, conflict, anxiety, and feelings of resentment, hostility, humiliation, frustration, and guilt.[84]

---

[81] Levenson, *Mind, body, and Medicine: a History of the American Psychosomatic Society*, 98.

[82] Donald J. Simons & Harold G. Wolff, "Studies on Headache: Mechanisms of Chronic Posttraumatic Headache," *Psychosom Med* 8 (4) (1946): 227–242.

[83] Brenner, Charles, Friedman, Arnold P. & Carter, Sidney, "Psychologic Factors in the Etiology and Treatment of Chronic Headache," *Psychosom Med* 11 (1) (1949): 53–56. A variety of other mechanisms have of course been observed: hysterical identification or conversion through symbolic displacement, satisfaction of a need for punishment, psychotic type hypochondriasis, high degree of secondary gain, etc.

[84] Holmes, Thomas H. & Wolff, Harold G., "Life Situations, Emotions, and Backache," *Psychosom Med* 14 (1) (1952): 18–33.

Fig. 7.3. Pattern of generalized skeletal muscle hyperfunction appearing as part of subject's reaction to a discussion of conflictual topics engendering feelings of resentment, hostility, frustration and humiliation. Source: Holmes & Wolff (1952).

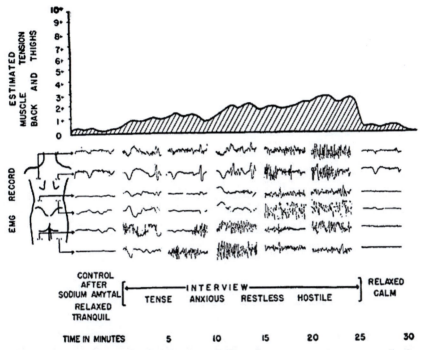

FIG. 2. Pattern of generalized skeletal muscle hyperfunction appearing as part of subject's reaction to a discussion of conflictual topics engendering feelings of resentment, hostility, frustration and humiliation.

The genesis of the backache syndrome appears to be related to the inappropriate utilization of a protective reaction pattern involving the participation of the skeletal musculature in an "action" pattern of behaviour designed to facilitate attempts at interpersonal and social adjustments.[85]

A very expressive image is reflected in the interview with a patient that reached a climax during the prolonged discussion of an accident: "The next night [after the accident] the boss came to see me in the hospital. I was in a stupor, but I recognized him ... in the latter part of the interview, as the subject's feelings of hostility and resentment reached peak intensity,

[85] Ibid., 29.

he became more restless and increased tension and electrical activity from the muscles was sustained."[86]

Drugs versus Psychotherapy against Resentment

Marañón categorically stated that "resentment is incurable" because it is a passion that "filters throughout the soul, and betrays itself in every action."[87] Resentment has to do with a way of being, so resentful individuals are not cured even when the failure or adversity which brought about this emotion has been overcome. This emotion is not like envy or hatred, which if "extirpated, may leave the soul intact."[88] For the Spanish physician "the sole antidote [to resentment] is generosity. But this noblest of the passions is born with the soul, it may therefore increase or diminish, but cannot be created in one who does not possess it."[89]

However, the psychosomatic physicians, as they linked resentment with the appearance of functional and organic symptoms and disorders, tried chemical remedies (agents) which would avert the ill effects produced by these "negative" emotions. Such was the case of F. V. Rockwell who studied the therapeutic uses of a sympatholytic drug, Dibenamine (N, N dibenzyl-beta-chloro-ethylamine). The work is based on the premise that the emotions of anxiety, fear, panic, resentment and anger are accompanied by the presence of increased amounts of adrenergic substances in the blood. It was further assumed that the increased concentrations of circulating adrenergic substances play a role in the production of certain symptoms and are of themselves detrimental to the patient.[90] The study concluded that: "the degree of therapeutic effectiveness has ranged from very mild to very marked," and therefore "Dibenamine has proved to be a valuable adjunct to psychotherapy."[91] A similar study

---

[86] Ibid., 21.

[87] Marañón, *Tiberius*, 12.

[88] Ibid.

[89] Ibid., 18–19.

[90] Fred V. Rockwell, "Dibenamine Therapy in Certain Psychopathologic Syndromes," *Psychosom Med* 10 (4) (1948): 230–237. Patients chosen for treatment with Dibenamine were those in whom anxiety, fear, panic, resentment, or anger, or the derivatives of these emotions, were prominent or leading features in the psychopathology. To date, about fifty patients have been treated. In any case in which the author and his colleagues accurately followed their own stated criteria for selection, the oral administration of Dibenamine has been of some therapeutic benefit.

[91] Rockwell, "Dibenamine Therapy in Certain Psychopathologic Syndromes," 237.

was presented by R. M. Marcussen and H. Wolff on the effectiveness of ergotamine tartrate on migraines.[92]

On the other hand, it is well-known that the psychosomatic therapeutic proposal of the American psychosomatic school stressed psychotherapy and the healing nature of the doctor-patient relationship.[93] According to Alexander, it was psychosomatic medicine that allowed the art of medicine to be considered scientific medicine. From that moment on, he stated, the influence of the doctor-patient bond could no longer be considered a mere addendum to the treatment, an artistic or personal touch, but rather the main therapeutic factor."[94]

The therapy, in the case of a process caused by resentment is based on what might be called the principle of "corrective emotional experience."[95] Helen Dunbar says something similar: "The physician's responsibility is to correct intraorganic dysfunction, but often this is possible only when he becomes the catalytic agent in restoring the patient's capacity for integration in society."[96] In this case, there must be intervention into what, for G. Marañón, is an essential condition for the genesis of resentment, a lack of comprehension, which creates in the resentful individual "a disharmony between his real capacity for success and what he *imagines* to be his capacity."[97]

The authors of the above-mentioned study on chronic headache stressed the great importance in psychotherapy of the physician-patient relationship:

> Even in those patients to whom formal psychotherapy is not given, the therapeutic results often depend in large measure on the psychological

---

[92] Robert M. Marcussen & Harold G. Wolff, "A Formulation of the Dynamics of the Migraine Attack," *Psychosom Med* 11 (1) (1949): 251–256.

[93] About this question: Pilar León Sanz, "El carácter terapéutico de la relación médico-paciente," in Cultura Emocional: Una Perspectiva de Análisis Social edited by Lourdes Flamarique and Madalena D'Olivera-Martins, 103–132 (Madrid: Biblioteca Nueva, 2013).

[94] Alexander, "Psychological Aspects of Medicine," 15.

[95] Alexander, *Psychosomatic Medicine: its Principles and Applications*, 112.

[96] Helen Flanders Dunbar, *Emotions and bodily changes; a survey of literature on psychosomatic interrelationships, 1910–1953* (New York: Columbia University Press, 1954), 685.

[97] Marañón, *Tiberius*, 14.

effect of the treatment situation on the patient and especially on the emotional relationship between patient and physician.[98]

Resentment in the doctor-patient relationship

The doctor-patient relationship itself can be an object of resentment, since this emotion is defined by its interpersonal character. Resentment expresses the repetition of a hostile emotional response from either the doctor or the patient. H. Dunbar believes that when the doctor is no longer capable of communicating properly with the patient, they become a "pathogenic agent," as they cause anxiety and fear and thus aggravate the state of the patient. Avery D. Weisman, in the aforesaid study on the duodenal ulcer, considered that:

> the therapist represented either an ideal, beneficent parent, or a demanding, exploiting, relentless, coercive force. In many respects the transference neurosis reflected the patient's relationship with the significant figures in his life.[99]

This particular relationship is therefore part of the pathology of the physician-patient relationship which includes resentment together with deception and seduction.[100] The studies connect the pathologization of the doctor-patient relationship with processes of chronic suffering or attention. Moreover, the authors differentiate between the ways in which resentment appears depending on the type of disorder or ailment. Thus, for example, the study on the Doctor-Patient Relationship carried out by means of Projective Techniques by M Thaler, H Weiner and Morton F. Reiser states that in disorders such as arterial hypertension or gastric ulcers the patients use the doctor's inability to cure them as a platform for resentment and provocation. However, they also state that there are differences between these two groups of patients. In the former, the origin of this resentment is real, while in the peptic ulcer group it is based on fantasy. In both cases, these conflicts are dependency related (as is the doctor-patient relationship)

---

[98] Brenner, Friedman & Carter "Psychologic Factors in the Etiology and Treatment of Chronic Headache," 55.

[99] Weisman, "A Study of the Psychodynamics of Duodenal Ulcer Exacerbations with Special Reference to Treatment and the Problem of 'Specificity'," 5. The author insists: "Ulcer symptoms recurred most often when the threat of depletion exceeded the promise of replenishment and the resulting angry protest was restrained," 40.

[100] Paul Freeling, "Pathology of Partnerships: Disappointments, Seductions, and Resentment," *British Medical Journal* (Clinical Research Edition) 284 (6318) (1982): 791–794.

and give rise to hostile impulses that lead to the development of defence mechanisms in the formation and establishment of relationships.[101]

The application of the experimental model leads to a search for biological markers which could be used to differentiate whether the patients' attitudes would be of collaboration, of "resistance" or even of hostility towards the physician. Thus, Alfred P. Solomon, Chester W. Darrow and Melvin Blaurock studied the results of simultaneous records of systolic blood pressure and palmar galvanic (sweating) responses during a standardized psychiatric interview.[102]

Conclusion—Somatization of Resentment in the Psychosomatic Medicine School

We can conclude that the American psychosomatic medicine school studied the consequences of resentment taken as the repeated experiencing and reliving of hostile emotional response reactions against someone else. It is a re-experiencing of the emotion itself which gradually pervades the core of the personality and becomes a generalized experience of suppressed wrath, hostility and hatred, largely independent of the activity of the ego that inspires numerous specific hostile intentions. In addition, resentment has a social factor, being connected with the comparisons which we make between oneself and another.[103] Marañón's "theory on resentment" supports the laboratory findings of the physicians of the school. To the external causes that provoke this passion, the author adds a personal predisposition, which gives rise to the resentful personality, and is what leads to the biased perception of oneself and one's relationships with others; to a bitter reaction to the surrounding reality, in contrast with an idealized version.

Moreover, psychosomatic medicine underlines the importance of individual psychology in the so-called "organic neuroses" which give rise to "biographical pathology," that is, the genesis and shaping of the morbid

---

[101] Margaret Thaler, Herbert Weiner & Morton F. Reiser, "Exploration of the Doctor-Patient Relationship through Projective Techniques: Their Use in Psychosomatic Illness," *Psychosom Med* 19 (3) (1957): 228–239.

[102] Alfred P. Solomon, Chester W. Darrow & Melvin Blaurock, "Blood Pressure and Palmar Sweat (Galvanic) Responses of Psychotic Patients before and after Insulin and Metrazol Therapy: A Physiologic Study of 'Resistant' and Cooperative Attitudes," *Psychosom Med* 1 (1) (1939): 118–137.

[103] We can find similar elements in the definition of resentment in other more present-day authors such as Patrick Masterson, "The Concept of Resentment," *Studies: An Irish Quarterly Review* 68 (271) (1979): 157–172.

process from the perspective of the "meaning" they have in the patient's biography. Psychosomatic medicine attempted to understand human illness scientifically, from the viewpoint of the patient's "human" or "personal" condition, and so tried to extend its scientific knowledge to the physical and mental dimensions of human nature.

The psychosomatic medicine school carried out in-depth analyses from a psychological and experimental viewpoint on the effects produced by resentment, consequences being produced by the reactive character of this emotion which are prolonged and so bring about physiological changes and also harmful ones.

The evolution of society and the medicalization that was, little by little, introduced, and is partly due to psychosomatic medicine, could explain the increase in medical references to resentment that seems to be linked to medicalization.

The medical concept of resentment seems to be connected with the somatization of emotions, which is part of a medical tradition going back to medieval Galenism when we find the first expression of a medical theory on the emotions based on the organic repercussions deriving from them, regardless of the philosophical or moral explanation.[104] However, this approach is not detached from the advent of new methods and techniques for the study of human reality which allowed for a scientific basis for numerous observations performed in clinical and research laboratories.

The numerous experimental studies carried out associated resentment with multiple ills, both organic and functional. Therefore, and in contrast with Alexander's initial theory, the Cornell University Medical College research showed that there is no specificity between resentment and illness. Resentment is part of a group of emotions like anxiety, sense of guilt or hostility, all of which can give rise to the same type of symptoms and organic disorders. A sign of the somatization of resentment is the proposal to control it by means of the drugs used to avoid the symptoms unleashed, such as adrenergic antagonists.

However, it was the psychological approach to the problems of life and illness that allowed for a synthesis between the internal biological processes of the body and the individual's relations with their social milieu. A detailed awareness of the emotional relationship with the life and body processes is demanded of the physician or therapist. This is why the relationship between the doctor and the patient is, in itself, of such

---

[104] Pedro Gil-Sotres, "Modelo teórico y observación clínica: Las pasiones del alma en la psicología médica medieval," in *Comprendere et Maîtriser la nature au moyen age. Mélanges d'histoire des sciences offerts à Guy Beaujouan*, edited by D. Jacquart, 181–204 (Genève: Droz - Hautes Etudes médiévales et modernes, 1994), 204.

importance. The establishment of this link is indispensable as a therapeutic resource, even though its consequences may be positive and negative, from both the practitioner and patient's perspectives.

From the social and ethical-philosophical perspective, it has been said that some emotions such as guilt, resentment, shame and anger may have a special role in the establishment of a range of "response-dependent" values and norms that lie at the core of moral life. One of the repercussions of the psychosomatic period was the significance attained by the emotional factor in medicine, which led to an emphasis on the importance of communication or the consideration of social-environmental factors, and contributed to the reshaping of the relationships between doctors and patients.

Works Cited

Alexander, Franz. "Psychological aspects of Medicine." *Psychosom Med* 1 (1) (1939): 7–18.

—. *Psychosomatic Medicine: its Principles and Applications.* New York: W. W. Norton, 1950.

Brenner, Charles, Arnold P. Friedman & Sidney Carter. "Psychologic Factors in the Etiology and Treatment of Chronic Headache." *Psychosom Med* 11 (1) (1949): 53–56.

Dunbar, Helen Flanders. *Emotions and Bodily Changes; a Survey of Literature on Psychosomatic Interrelationships, 1910–1953.* New York: Columbia University Press, 1954.

Duncan, Charles H., Ian P. Stevenson & Harold G. Wolff. "Life Situations, Emotions, and Exercise Tolerance." *Psychosomatic Medicine* 13 (1) (1951): 36–50.

Duncan, Charles H., Ian P. Stevenson & H. S. Ripley. "Life Situations, Emotions, and Paroxysmal Auricular Arrhythmias." *Psychosom Med* 12 (1) (1950): 23–37.

Eisenbud, Jule. "A Method for Investigating the Effect of Repression on the Somatic Expression of Emotion in Vegetative Functions: A Preliminary Report. Department of Psychiatry, New York State Psychiatric Institute and Hospital." *Psychosom Med* 1 (3) (1939): 376–387.

Ferro, Marc. *Le ressentiment dans l'histoire: comprendre notre temps.* Paris: Odile Jacob, 2007.

Freeling, Paul. "Pathology of Partnerships: Disappointments, Seductions, and Resentment." *British Medical Journal* (Clinical Research Edition) 284 (6318) (1982): 791–794.

Gil-Sotres, Pedro. "Modelo teórico y observación clínica: Las pasiones del alma en la psicología médica medieval." In *Comprendere et Maîtriser la nature au moyen age. Mélanges d'histoire des sciences offerts à Guy Beaujouan*, edited by D. Jacquart, 181–204. Genève: Droz - Hautes Etudes médiévales et modernes, 1994.

Jiménez Borreguero & Juan Francisco. *Gregorio Marañón: el regreso del Humanismo*. Madrid: Egartorre, 2006.

Keller, Gary D. *The Significance and Impact of Gregorio Marañón: Literary Criticism, Biographies and Historiography*. New York: Bilingual Press, 1977.

Harris, I. D. "Relation of Resentment and Anger to Functional Gastric Complaints." *Psychosom Med* 8 (3) (1946): 211–3.

Hinkle, Lawrence E., William N. Christenson, Francis D. Kane, Adrian Ostfeld, William N. Thetford & Harold G. Wolff. "An Investigation of the Relation Between Life Experience, Personality Characteristics, and General Susceptibility to Illness." *Psychosom Med* 20 (4) (1958): 278–295.

Holmes, Thomas H. & Harold G. Wolff. "Life Situations, Emotions, and Backache." *Psychosom Med* 14 (1) (1952): 18–33.

Hunt, Joseph McVicker & R. R. Willoughby. "The Effect of Frustration on Hoarding in Rats." *Psychosom Med* 1 (1) (1939): 309–310.

Laín Entralgo, Pedro. *Introducción histórica al estudio de la patología psicosomática*. Madrid: Paz Montalvo, 1950.

—. *Marañón y el enfermo*. Madrid: Revista de Occidente, 1992.

León Sanz, Pilar. "El carácter terapéutico de la relación médico-paciente." In *Cultura Emocional: Una Perspectiva de Análisis Social* edited by Lourdes Flamarique and Madalena D'Olivera-Martins, 103–132. Madrid: Biblioteca Nueva, 2013.

Levenson, Dorothy. *Mind, Body and Medicine: a History of the American Psychosomatic Society*. Baltimore, MD: Williams & Wilkins, 1994.

Marañón, Gregorio. *Tiberio: historia de un resentimiento*. Buenos Aires: Espasa-Calpe, 1939.

—. *Tiberius; Geschichte eines Ressentiments*. Übersetzung von Dr. Karl August Horst. München: Nymphenburger Verlagshandlung, 1952.

—. *Tiberius: A Study in Resentment*. London: Hollis & Carter, 1956.

Marcussen, Robert M. & Harold G. Wolff. "A Formulation of the Dynamics of the Migraine Attack." *Psychosom Med* 11 (1) (1949): 251–256.

Masterson, Patrick. "The Concept of Resentment." *Studies: An Irish Quarterly Review* 68 (271) (1979): 157–172.

Mittelmann, Bela & Harold G. Wolff. "Emotions and Gastroduodenal Function: Experimental Studies on Patients with Gastritis, Duodenitis and Peptic Ulcer." *Psychosom Med* 4 (1) (1942): 5–61.

Rockwell, Fred V. "Dibenamine Therapy in Certain Psychopathologic Syndromes." *Psychosom Med* 10 (4) (1948): 230–237.

Rosenzweig, Saul. "Frustration as an Experimental Problem." *Psychosom Med* 1 (1) (1939): 199–200.

Scheler, Max. *Ressentiment* (1915); translation by Lewis B. Coser, William W. Holdheim; introduction by Manfred S. Frings. Milwaukee: Marquette University Press, 1974.

Simons, Donald J. & Harold G. Wolff. "Studies on Headache: Mechanisms of Chronic Posttraumatic Headache." *Psychosom Med* 8 (4) (1946): 227–242.

Solomon, Alfred P., Chester W. Darrow & Melvin Blaurock. "Blood Pressure and Palmar Sweat (Galvanic) Responses of Psychotic Patients before and after Insulin and Metrazol Therapy: A Physiologic Study of 'Resistant' and Cooperative Attitudes." *Psychosom Med* 1 (1) (1939): 118–137.

Solomon, Robert C. "One Hundred Years of Resentment. Nietzsche's Genealogy of Morals." In *Nietzsche, Genealogy, Morality: Essays on Nietzsche's Genealogy of Morals*, edited by Richard Sacht, 95–127. Berkeley: University of California Press, 1994.

Stevenson, Ian. "Physical Symptoms During Pleasurable Emotional States." *Psychosom Med* 12 (1) (1950): 98–102.

Thaler, Margaret, Herbert Weiner & Morton F. Reiser. "Exploration of the Doctor-Patient Relationship through Projective Techniques: Their Use in Psychosomatic Illness." *Psychosom Med* 19 (3) (1957): 228–239.

Weiner, Herbert. "Psychosomatic Medicine and the Mind-Body Relation: Historical, Philosophical, Scientific, and Clinical Perspectives." In *History of Psychiatry and Medical Psychology: with an Epilogue on Psychiatry and the Mind-Body Relation*, edited by Edwin R. Wallace IV and John Gach, 781–834. New York: Springer, 2008.

Weisman, Avery D. "A Study of the Psychodynamics of Duodenal Ulcer Exacerbations with Special Reference to Treatment and the Problem of 'Specificity'." *Psychosom Med* 18 (1) (1956): 2–42.

Wolf, George A. Jr. & Harold G. Wolff. "Studies on the Nature of Certain Symptoms Associated with Cardiovascular Disorders." *Psychosom Med* 8 (5) (1946): 293–319.

Wolf, Stewart. "In Memoriam." *Psychosom Med* 24 (3) (1962): 222–224.

Zane, Manuel D. "Psychosomatic Considerations in Peptic Ulcer." *Psychosom Med* 9 (6) (1947): 372–380.

CHAPTER EIGHT

REPRESSING RESENTMENT: MARRIAGE, ILLNESS AND THE DISTURBING EXPERIENCE OF CARE

JUAN M. ZARAGOZA[1]

Introduction

The majority of my colleagues in this book have talked about resentment in several public contexts: in chapter one Paschalina Michou talked about the change in the meaning of the concept in the eighteenth-century British context when it became related to two strong emotions: injury and anger. Professor Patrick Lang discussed Max Scheler's thoughts about the role played by resentment in modern democracies; and Professor Elise Dermineur will explore in her chapter the role of resentment in what she calls "gender wars" in eighteenth-century France. These are just some examples of how the social role of resentment in the eighteenth and nineteenth centuries has been presented in this book. In these public contexts, resentment is sometimes a positive value, sometimes a negative one. Sometimes it is the cornerstone of the "politics of justice," sometimes it must be banished from the republic to (and through) oblivion.

In my chapter, however, I am going to analyse a less spectacular instance of resentment. There will not be any evident political implications in my chapter, neither revolutions, nor class-conflict. I will focus on an intuitive, everyday example of resentment—that between a husband and his wife. Resentment is tied to strong feelings such as anger, just as we

[1] The present text has benefitted from the economic support of the Basque Country Government, as part of its program for pre-doctoral research, and by the Research Project "Historical Epistemology: History of Emotions and Emotional Communities in the 19th and 20th Centuries," supported by the Ministry of Science and Innovation, Spanish Government.

have seen in Michou's chapter. The ambiguity of this emotion, the possibility of feeling "rightful anger," leads to the abovementioned ambivalence of resentment. But when we introduce "love" into the equation, the ambivalence disappears and resentment is always a negative emotion. There is no rightful anger against those we love. We are supposed to forgive and forget. The appearance of resentment is the symptom of a failure in the relationship, in the love of the resented, or even in the constitution of our inner selves.

In my chapter I will explore the difficult conciliation of love, resentment and guilt when one of the members of a marriage suffers a chronic disease. The narratives of the other part (the caregiver) show how this task is supposed to be the supreme proof of love, but at the same time we can detect how resentment and guilt are repressed, as something that could damage the very identity of the caregiver. I will use the word "love" to mean a normative ideology manifested largely as a practice within long-term relationships, present in Western culture at least since the nineteenth century.[2] As an essential part of "love" as ideology, there exists a normative expectation that lovers will subordinate their personal desires to a concern for the other,[3] especially when the other is ill. However, this subordination could be the source of negative feelings such as guilt, resentment and remorse. The arousal of these negative feelings could generate a crisis within a marriage, leading to the failure of the relationship or, in other situations, it could generate an identity crisis in one of the members of the marriage, putting his or her inner self at risk.

The care of a chronically disabled relative is a situation well-suited to prompt this kind of reaction. To the abovementioned expectation of lovers subordinating their desires to a concern for the other, we must add another kind of pressure from the very experience of care. I will argue that care is a multi-layered phenomenon, in which its different layers (caring as a human trait, a moral imperative, an affect, an interpersonal interaction, and an intervention)[4] interact to produce the experience of care. But this

---

[2] A history of marriage, as the main institution of this ideology, can be found in Stephanie Coontz, *Marriage, a History: From Obedience to Intimacy or How Love Conquered Marriage* (New York: Viking, 2005). A history of "romantic" love is traced in Eva Illouz, *Consuming the Romantic Utopia: Love and the Cultural Contradictions of Capitalism* (Berkely, Calif. & London: University of California Press, 1997). I am in debt to Dolores Martín-Moruno for Illouz's book and other relevant references. They form part of a long-running debate on the nature of care and the role of sacrifice.

[3] Daniel Miller, *A Theory of Shopping* (Cambridge: Polity Press, 2005), 19.

[4] J. Morse et al., "Comparative Analysis of Conceptualizations and Theories of

interaction is organized according to a very specific form[5]—that of sacrifice.[6] Resentment, in the context of care, will appear as the result of the interplay between the logic of sacrifice and the logic of the new model for social mobility—meritocracy.[7] The case study I will present in this chapter will help us to understand these complex dynamics.

The Letter

How dare you?—what do you mean by it?[8]

When Arthur Conan Doyle opened a recent letter from his mother in November of 1899, these were the very first words he read. Arthur was not

---

Caring," in *Qualitative Health Research*, ed. J. Morse (Newbury Park, CA: Sage, 1992).

[5] On the distinction between experience's forms and contents see Georg Simmel, "The Categories of Human Experience," in *On Individuality and Social Forms*, eds. Georg Simmel and Donald N. Levine (Chicago & London: University of Chicago Press, 1992). Another approach follows Dilthey in *The Anthropology of Experience*, eds. Victor W. Turner and Edward. Bruner, eds. (Urbana & Chicago: University of Illinois Press,1986). Javier Moscoso shows the historiographical strength of this approach in his recent *Pain: a Cultural History*, and the interest of Dilthey's distinction between "lived experience" and "structured experience" for the history of the emotions. See Javier Moscoso, *Pain: A Cultural History* (Basingstoke: Palgrave Macmillan, 2012).

[6] The literature on sacrifice and care is scarce. Even more so, self-sacrifice in the context of care has been characterized as a personality defect or as self-defeating behaviour. Some recent articles on the topic, from different points of view, stress the importance of a rethink on the role of sacrifice within the experience of care. I will elaborate on this point below, but I want to quote two of them, even if I do not totally agree with their approach: Howard M. Bahr & Kathleen S. Bahr, "Families and Self-Sacrifice: Alternative Models and Meanings for Family Theory," *Social Forces* 79 (4) (2001); Kaija Helin & Unni Å Lindström, "Sacrifice: An Ethical Dimension of Caring That Makes Suffering Meaningful," *Nursing Ethics* 10 (4) (2003). Without explicitly mentioning the term "sacrifice," but with a similar approach, is Sharon C. Bolton, "Who Cares? Offering Emotion Work as a 'Gift' in the Nursing Labour Process," *Journal of Advanced Nursing* 32 (30) (2000).

[7] The classic and critical study on meritocracy in Britain, originally published in 1958, is Michael Young's, *The Rise of the Meritocracy* (New Brunswick, N.J.: Transaction Publishers, 2008). A recent and cross-cultural analysis is by Livia Martins Pinheiro Neves, "Putting Meritocracy in Its Place. The Logic of Performance in the United States, Brazil and Japan," *Critique of Anthropology* 20 (4) (2000).

[8] Arthur Conan Doyle, *Arthur Conan Doyle: A Life in Letters* (London: Harper Press, 2007), 427.

a child. He was in his forties. He was a well-known writer and a rich man who supported all the family—his children and wife, but also his brother and sisters and, of course, his mother. Anyway, she was giving him a good telling-off, finishing with a mother's favourite words all around the world: "Do not go Arthur, that is my first and last word."

Conan Doyle's relationship with his mother was a complex one. He wrote her countless letters from 1868 (when he was sent to boarding school) until 1920, when she passed away. Sometimes he looked for her approval, sometimes he expressed opposed points of view, but he always respected her opinion and, if possible, tried to please her.

I'm not interested in the psychological details of these mother-and-son relationships. What it is interesting is the fact itself, the letter, and the response from Arthur. The first question we may ask now is: what kind of prank played by her forty-year-old "Dearest and very naughty son" gave rise to this angry answer? As we can expect from a man like Arthur, it was not exactly a prank.

The Second Anglo-Boer war had broken out October 11, 1899, and things were not going very well for the English army. Ladysmith, Mafeking and Kimberley, in South Africa, were under siege, and from the December 10–17 that year, a period dubbed "Black Week," the British army suffered three devastating defeats with almost three thousand casualties. Britain was ashamed and surprised.[9]

The reaction of public opinion was unanimous: Britain needed to win the war (because of the gold and the diamonds, but also because of its pride as a nation), and every man who considered himself a patriot should support the war effort. As John Westlake, at the time Whewell Professor of International Law at the University of Cambridge, stated in a lecture delivered on November 9 that it was a war between "two ideals":

> On one side you have the English ideal of a fair field for every race and every language, accompanied by a human treatment of the native races ... the other ideal, the Transvaal ideal, is racial, not only in its results if it should succeed, but in its objects.[10]

---

[9] The failure during the first stages of the war was a complex combination of an ill-prepared British army, unqualified officers and the guerrilla tactics employed by the Boer army. See Peter Warwick, *The South African War: The Anglo-Boer War, 1899–1902* (Harlow, Essex: Longman, 1980). On the Boer's guerrilla tactics see Peter Burke, *The Siege of O'okiep: Guerrilla Campaign in the Anglo-Boer War* (Bloemfontein: War Museum of the Boer Republics, 1995).

[10] John Westlake, *The Transvaal War. A Lecture Delivered in the University of Cambridge on 9th November, 1899* (London: C. J. Clay & Sons, Cambridge

The Anglo-Boer War, besides its global and economic implications, was understood by the British as a menace against the very idea of the British Empire as a civilizing force.[11] Volunteers were called for all around the country, and the response was overwhelming.

Arthur positioned himself in favour of the war, against his mother, and letters discussing the moral and economical issues of the war had been normal since the summer. Therefore, it was not a surprise that Conan Doyle supported the volunteer campaign.

But Mary Doyle never expected her son to volunteer himself. That was Arthur's "prank." He was determined to fight with the English army against the enemies of the Empire.[12] The question now is: Why? Arthur delayed the response to his mother's impassioned letter. Instead, he wrote to the Times, just after Black Week:

> Might I suggest that lists should at least be opened and the names of those taken who are ready to go if required—preference might be given to those men who can find their own horse? There are thousands of men riding after foxes or shooting pheasants who would gladly be useful to their country if were made possible for them. This war has at least taught the lesson that it only needs a brave man and a modern rifle to make a soldier.[13]

Mary Doyle answered this letter in very similar terms to the first:

> Mind you are not to go unless already bound in honour—your first duty is to your own family of which you are the one staff, prop, support, pride & glory.[14]

University Press, 1899), 4.

[11] Pradip Kumar Datta, "The Interlocking Worlds of the Anglo-Boer War in South Africa/India," *South African Historical Journal* 57 (1) (2007). Economical implications acknowledged by Westlake just some paragraphs later; Westlake, *The Transvaal War. A Lecture Delivered in the University of Cambridge on 9th November, 1899*, 5.

[12] On Arthur Conan Doyle and Imperialism see Douglas Kerr, "The Straight Left: Sport and the Nation in Arthur Conan Doyle," *Victorian Literature and Culture* 38, (1) (2010); Lawrence Frank, "Dreaming the Medusa: Imperialism, Primitivism, and Sexuality in Arthur Conan Doyle's Sign of Four," *Signs* 2 (1) (1996). On Arthur's war experience see Asher Dubb, "Arthur Conan Doyle and the Anglo-Boer South African War (1899–1902)," *Adler Museum Bulletin* 26 (3) (2000).

[13] Doyle, *Arthur Conan Doyle: A Life in Letters*, 432.

[14] Ibid.

Arthur was clear in his response: it was a matter of honour, and she was the one who taught him the importance of honour as a child. Therefore, even if she disliked the idea, he would volunteer anyway.

For his mother's peace of mind, the English army was not convinced about the value of mobilizing civilians, especially middle-aged ones like Arthur. Still, he was determined to serve by returning to his medical training if necessary. Mary Doyle was pleased with the British army's decision, and the idea of Arthur being a doctor, if not exactly what she wanted, was at least reassuring.

The following letters were in a completely different tone. In these, Arthur explained to her all his arrangements for the next departure, how he had written his will, and how he had left no loose ends. And then, in January of 1900, Arthur opened his heart to her:

> I know exactly what I am doing and why & there is lots of method in my actions. Nothing could fit into my life better. I have lived for six years in a sick room and oh how weary of it I am! Dear Touie! It has tried me more than her—and she never learns of it and I am very glad she does not. That is the restlessness of which Connie speaks.[15]

I would like to draw your attention to the structure of this paragraph. Arthur started reaffirming himself in front his mother: "don't worry, everything is OK, I know what I'm doing," and after that, he complained about the last six years of his life "in a sickroom," expressing his weariness. Then suddenly, he stopped. There is a silence, right there. We can perceive it. There is a doubt, a hesitant pause. His following words are: "Dear Touie!" We need to unravel this silence in order to understand Arthur's motivations.

The Disease

We are now in October 1893. Arthur and Louise (Touie) Doyle, his wife, had spent almost a year in Vienna, where he studied ophthalmology, and then some time in Switzerland, before coming back to London, to his brand new house in Tennyson Road, South Norwood. Within a few weeks of their return, Touie complained about a cough and pain in her side. The doctor was called, and the diagnosis was clear—tuberculosis.[16] Even more,

---

[15] Ibid., 438.

[16] Ironically, Arthur attended Koch's demonstrations in Berlin during this period, see Douglas Kerr, "Arthur Conan Doyle and the Consumption Cure," *Literature & History* 19 (2) (2010).

"galloping consumption." Doctors did not give her more than a few months to live. As Arthur wrote in his memories, that was "the great misfortune which darkened and deflected our lives."[17] "Galloping consumption" was an acute form of phthisis, very different from the chronic form. Richard Payne Cotton, in his book *On Consumption*, published in 1858, described it as follows:

> ... commences suddenly and proceeds rapidly, and assumes every other character of an acute disease. Shivering, succeeded by intense fever, quickness of pulse, anxiety of countenance, severe thoracic pains, dyspnoea, and cough, are its earlier symptoms. These rapidly increase, and are soon followed by those of depression, with hectic fever, profuse perspiration, or diarrhoea, under which the patient rapidly sinks into exhaustion.[18]

And continues:

> In the majority of cases, -probably in nearly all, it proves fatal. In one which fell under my own observation, it did so in less than five weeks from its commencement; and in another case, in about six weeks.[19]

As you can suppose, Arthur was devastated. But soon, a plan of action took form: he decided to fight against the disease:

> Lottie [his sister] Touie & I will start for St Moritz -which is rather higher than Davos. If Touie does well there we might have a run to Egypt in the early spring and come back by sea to England when the weather is warm ... That is, I think the best course we can adopt. Lottie returns tonight from Bournemouth and then we can talk the thing over again ... Well, we must take what Fate sends, but I have hopes that all may yet be well.[20]

Indeed, it was so much better than expected. Louise Doyle died in 1906, thirteen years after the first diagnosis.

Louise Doyle's therapy was a common one at the time against tuberculosis. They went abroad, looking for a climate that suited her better, such as high altitudes, and dry and warm weather. Sanatoriums in Switzerland, such as those in Davos or St. Moritz, were fashionable at the time. They were strongly recommended against these diseases; therefore,

---

[17] Arthur Conan Doyle, *Memories and Adventures* (London: Hodder and Stoughton, 1924), 120.
[18] Richar Payne Cotton, *On Consumption: Its Nature, Symptoms, and Treatment* (London: John Churchill, 1858), 162.
[19] Ibid.
[20] Doyle, *Arthur Conan Doyle: A Life in Letters*, 322.

there were plenty of rich bourgeois looking for recovery. This implied a busy social life of dinners, balls, theatres, variety shows, etc. As *The Graphic* published in September 14, 1889:

> The very word of a health-resort recalls to the remembrance of most of us long bills for dinners we have never eaten, for luxuries we have never enjoyed. Whether we return the better or the worse for our sojourn at Platz, Davos, St. Moritz, or in the Riviera, our pockets are sure to be the lighter; those palatial hotels, which spring up like mushrooms in all the places English doctors choose to favour, are arranged for millionaires ....

Arthur had talked about his "six years in a sick room," but if we read his letters and memories it is hard to believe that. While in Davos, he became the first English man to traverse an Alpine pass in winter skiing. After that, he travelled to America with his brother, and to Egypt with his wife, where he had: "plenty to do: golf, tennis, riding, billiards, with the dissipation of Cairo in the background, so don't picture us as castaways at all."[21] Lottie, Arthur's little sister, described to her mother one of these "to-dos":

> I was perfect! All these military balls are given in the Casino of Ghesireh Palace. The ball room itself is splendid and the big sitting-out room like a scene in a fairy pantomime, fountains & coloured lights, lovely screens & oriental rugs palms, bamboos & all sorts of beautiful plants compose a lovely picture. At the Gippy ball the gardens were all illuminated & one side of the place was thrown open so that one could step straight out onto the terraces. It was a beautiful sight with all the pretty dresses & smart uniforms—needless to say I danced every dance I always do and was very sorry when the end came.[22]

During their sojourn at Cairo, Arthur and Touie went on a cruise on the Nile, even if "those who knew best described it as a madness."[23] Straight afterwards, he worked as a correspondent during the war against the Mahdist forces, travelling with the army to Sudan, while his wife remained at Cairo with his sister. Back in England, he travelled constantly to London, eating in his club and sleeping in expensive hotels. He played cricket and rode horses ... there was a sick room, sure, but Arthur was not shut away in it.

---

[21] Ibid., 364.
[22] Ibid., 363.
[23] Ibid., 366.

The Mistress

Why then this sudden necessity to flee, since he was not trapped in the "sick room" he talked to his mother about?

Once we put aside Arthur's political ideas, and once we dismiss his supposed retreat in his wife's sickroom, we need to look for a new explanation. In April of 1899, Arthur wrote a letter to his mother; one of many. He talked to her about his last book (*A Duet*, the story of two newlyweds, at the beginning of their relationship), about everyday life at home, etc. There is interesting data in the postscript:

> J is well & happy in her new flat with her two comrades. Did I tell you that Mr & Mrs Leckie gave me a beautiful diamond and pearl pinstud for Xmas. It must have cost fifteen guineas at least.[24]

The mysterious "J" (mysterious at least for us, obviously not for his mother) was Jean Leckie, Mr and Mrs Leckie's twenty-seven-years-old daughter. The question here is: why is Arthur talking to his mother about a young woman in a new flat and about her parents? It is not clear when Arthur and Jean first met. What is clear is that Arthur fell in love with Jean almost instantly. The first mention in the correspondence was in a letter from February 1899. Arthur and Innes (his brother) went to Blackheath and lunched with "our friends the Leckies." We don't know if that was a second visit, with a chaperone this time, or if the relationship started later, but what we know now is that for all of 1899 Arthur had an extramarital relationship with Jean Leckie, and that his mother and his brother knew of it. Even more, we know that he was encouraged and supported by his mother. In 1900, just after his return from Africa, he and Jean encountered his sister Connie at Lord's Cricket Ground, in London, when they were watching some matches. Neither Connie nor her husband had any idea about his and Jean's relationship. Nor, when he explained, did they offer sympathy or understanding. It was Mary Doyle who wrote to her daughter on behalf of Arthur, expressing her support for this relationship.

From 1900, Jean became part of Arthur's public life. They were together at cricket matches and music soirees, and she was invited to the balls in Arthur's villa in Surrey. In 1901 they travelled together to Sussex, to the Ashdown Forest Hotel, to play golf. He wrote to his mother:

> I have been feeling rather run down lately so had the happy idea—or rather J had, for she is quite a guardian angel in such matters—to throw

---

[24] Ibid., 417.

everything up for a few days and come here with Hamilton and play golf all day."[25]

There was not any sickroom in Ashdown Forest Hotel, but sunny days, golf and a young, blonde and healthy guardian angel.

Resentment and Care

Can we identify the silence in Arthur's letter now? This silence between the "how weary of it I am!" and the "Dear Touie!" I think we can, and I think we can call this silence "resentment," as defined in the Oxford English Dictionary as: "a feeling of ill will, bitterness, or anger against a person or thing." Arthur was aware of the possibility of being accused of this "sin," and indeed he was, by his own mother in August 1900. He refused the accusation point black. No "Dear Mam" heading the letter, just "You":

> You must have misunderstood something which I said. I have nothing but affection and respect for Touie. I have never in my whole married life had one cross word with her, nor will I ever cause her any pain. I cannot think how I came to give you the impression that her presence was painful to me. It is not so.[26]

An obvious way to focus the research in cases like that of Arthur is Peter and Carol Stearn's "emotionology," defined in their classic 1985 article as "the attitudes or standards that a society, or a definable group within a society, maintains towards basic emotions and their appropriate expression."[27] If we follow this path, Arthur's silence and violent denial of the "charges" should be understood as directly pointing out these "attitudes or standards." Arthur's story opens the door to the study of the attitudes of nineteenth-century middle classes towards resentment. From this point of view, Arthur's inability to talk about his resentment against Touie was the consequence of the general understanding of this emotion as a negative one. The standard for resentment, in interpersonal relationships, should not be talked about; resentment should be kept secret, even from oneself. Self-deception was the only way to deal with resentment.

But this is not all the truth. Sir Henry Wellcome, founder of the Wellcome Trust, separated from his wife, Syrie Wellcome, formerly

---

[25] Ibid., 473.

[26] Ibid., 455.

[27] Peter N. Stearns and Carol Stearns, "Emotionology: Clarifying the Study of the History of Emotion," *American Historical Review* 90 (1985): 813–14.

Barnardo, four years later, in 1904. The letters of the period, both of Sir Henry and Syrie, are full of resentment, especially those of Syrie. In a letter to Alfred C. Fletcher, Henry Wellcome's friend, she wrote: "in spite of this, and my honestly sacrificing myself in a way I hated both to please him and to gather curios for ourselves I am treated in this way!"[28] Therefore, resentment could be expressed and discussed. There was not any kind of taboo regarding the expression of resentment, even in a husband and wife relationship. Arthur's problem was not to be married. The Matrimonial Causes Act was passed in 1857, and Arthur had not been the first insincere husband accusing his wife of adultery.[29] He even thought about divorce, but he wrote to his mother "I will never do this to Touie." Arthur's problem was not his wife, but his wife's disease.

Arthur was not just Touie's husband, but also her caregiver. I have pointed out above how "care" is a multi-layered activity. To "take-care-of" someone, involves practices so different among them such as bandage, feed, giving emotional support, time managing, etc.[30] These practices change with time, and what it was considered part of the phenomenon of care in that age, could be completely strange, even preposterous, to us. The following text is a good example: "We have had to get Touie's old room papered (she has taken the front room for the summer) the other had such a smell of carbolic and medicines about that it was no good."[31] Written by Caroline Doyle to her mother in May 1894, the letter assumes that to paper an old room was part of taking care of Touie. The assumption, based in well-known medical theories and popular books on the caring of the sick, sounds absurd to us. We do not think about papering a room as part of our care practices. We tend to think about it in relation to interior design or English pubs, but not, definitely, as something related with care. We need

---

[28] Frances Larson, *An Infinity of Things. How Sir Henry Wellcome Collected the World* (Oxford: Oxford University Press, 2009), 55.

[29] On Caroline Norton and the passing of the Matrimonial Causes Act see Mary Poovey, "Covered but Not Bound: Caroline Norton and the 1857 Matrimonial Causes Act," in *Uneven Developments: The Ideological Work of Gender in Mid-Victorian England*, ed. Mary Poovey (Chicago: The University of Chicago Press, 1988); For a general assessment of its application, Gail L. Savage, "The Operation of the 1857 Divorce Act, 1860–1910. A Research Note," *Journal of Social History* 16 (4) (1983).

[30] An interesting approach to the problem of time in Tanisha Jowsey, "Perceptions of Time: Chronically Ill Health Service Users and Their Family Carers," in *Making Sense Of: Health, Illness and Disease. Chronic Illness: The Borderlands Between Health and Illness*, ed. Maria Vaccarella and Rob Fisher (Mansfield College, Oxford, United Kingdom, 2011).

[31] Doyle, *Arthur Conan Doyle: A Life in Letters*, 335.

to keep this in mind when talking about Arthur as a caregiver. All the practices I have described in the previous sections (the travels, the parties, and the dinners) were part of the multi-layered phenomenon of care in late-Victorian Britain. All the costume balls, golf matches, and cruises on the Nile, were "in the sick room," about which Conan Doyle talked to his mother.

And resentment? Could we find resentment in the sick room also or only in Arthur's story? We have no data for the Victorian and Edwardian eras, but some recent studies stress how common caregiver's feelings of stress and anger are found even among spouses (leading to, among other emotions, resentment and always to family conflict).[32] Nancy W. Sheehan and Paul Nuttall conducted a survey among ninety-eight family caregivers for a frail or impaired elderly relative in an article published in *Family Relations* in 1988. In this article, they identified several negative emotions causing family conflict, and among the major sources of conflict they found resentment. They identified two different causes of resentment: (1) the disruption of family patterns and routines; and (2) the lack of involvement of other family members.[33] These two causes point directly to sacrifice as the major source of resentment. We can imagine the caregiver saying to their relative: "I sacrificed something (these patterns and routines) and you didn't."

Sacrifice

Howard and Kathleen Bahr wrote an article published in 2001 upholding the capital role of self-sacrifice for our understanding of family dynamics. According to their interpretation, self-sacrifice was neglected by social sciences, and a "recovery" of the concept was needed. They presented "sacrifice" (self-sacrifice, to be accurate) as opposed to the logic of "selfishness" and individualism, attached to the "logic of love," and being the cornerstone of family relationships. They define self-sacrifice as "the sacrifice of self or extensions of self, in the interest of priorities or

---

[32] Gordon MacNeil et al., "Caregiver Mental Health and Potentially Harmful Caregiving Behaviour: The Central Role of Caregiver Anger," *The Gerontologist* 50 (1) (2010); Betty J. Kramer et al., "Predictors of Family Conflict at the End of Life: The Experience of Spouses and Adult Children of Persons with Lung Cancer," *The Gerontologist* 50 (2) (2010); Amanda S. Barusch, "Problems and Coping Strategies of Elderly Spouse Caregivers," *The Gerontologist* 28 (5) (1988).
[33] Nancy W. Sheehan & Paul Nuttall, "Conflict, Emotion, and Personal Strain among Family Caregivers," *Family Relations* 37 (1) (1988).

persons whose needs we see more pressing than our own."[34] This is a precise description of what I have called "love as a normative ideology." In consequence, I agree with their interpretation of the role played by sacrifice in long-term relationships. Even more, I sustain that sacrifice is the structure giving form to the whole experience of care within this "normative ideology" we call "love." Todorov's identification of "sacrifice" and "caring" points in the same direction.[35]

The problem with Bahr & Bahr's lecture on selfless sacrifice appears in its conclusions. To support their aspiration of reintroducing self-sacrifice as the basis of family relations, they chose to reinforce the "positive" side of sacrifice; that is, the giver always receives something, and there are "positive benefits" to the giver.[36] Once again, I agree with Bahr & Bahr, even if they are unclear that sacrifice is a form of exchange.[37] I am following here Henri Hubert and Marcel Mauss' classic book on sacrifice. In this book, sacrifice is an act of exchange between the sacrifier[38] and the divinity, in which the first offers something to the last and expects something in return. It does not matter that he or she expects something for him or herself or for another person or thing, the sacrifier is always affected. He or she receives something in exchange; his or her moral status changes.[39] Even when the offer is just for the sake of the other (the one who receives the benefits of sacrifice) the sacrifier is affected, and receives something in exchange.[40] The problem with exchange is that it always creates value,[41] and when we talk about value, a different set of questions arise.

What does the caregiver receive in exchange? It can change—he/she can expect a religious reward, the support of the government, or just some kind of appreciation. But part of the logic of sacrifice is that he or she will receive something in exchange, here or in heaven, so what happens when nothing happens? What happens when the sacrifier does not receive

---

[34] Bahr & Bahr, "Families and Self-Sacrifice," 1232.

[35] Tzvetan Todorov, *Facing the Extreme: Moral Life in the Concentration Camps*, (New York: Henry Holt, 1996). Quoted by Bahr & Bahr, "Families and Self-Sacrifice,"

[36] Bahr & Bahr, "Families and Self-Sacrifice," 1255.

[37] Georg Simmel, "Exchange," in *On Individuality and Social Forms*, ed. Georg Simmel & Donald N. Levine (Chicago & London: The University of Chicago Press, 1992), 48.

[38] *"Sacrifier"* is a neologism coined by Hubert and Mauss' first translator.

[39] Henri Hubert & Marcel Mauss, *Sacrifice: Its Nature and Function* (London: Cohen and West, 1964), 9.

[40] Ibid., 10.

[41] Simmel, "Exchange," 47.

anything in exchange? Or when what he or she receives is not what he or she thinks they deserve? We can compare the value of what we sacrificed (patterns and routines) with the value of what we received in exchange, and maybe we can think that we have lost. Therefore, value is a problem for Bahr & Bahr's interpretation of selfless sacrifice, but that is not the point for us here. Our problem is different: could this sense of loss lead the *sacrifier* to resentment? I think the answer is yes, from the nineteenth century onwards.

As the majority of the contributions to this book emphasise, resentment should be interpreted as a modern emotion, emerging in the late eighteenth century (and I add) as the result of the promise of a meritocratic society.[42] A promise (supposedly) fulfilled during the nineteenth century with the rise of the bourgeois culture. The idea under meritocratic systems is quite simple—if you do the right thing, you will receive a fair and appropriate reward for your actions. That was Arthur's primary motivation in his career, first as a doctor; later as a writer, and that was Arthur's motivation in his private life, also, in deep contrast with his alcoholic and demented father. His entire life, such as the life of most of his contemporaries, was shaped by this promise.[43]

The similarities between the logic of meritocracy and the logic of sacrifice are quite obvious. Both of them are forms of exchange, they create value, and we can compare the value of our actions with the value of our reward. The problem is that the new logic of meritocracy introduced a new element into the older logic of sacrifice—you expect to receive the fair and appropriate reward for your actions. This latter expectation collides with the logic of love—you cannot expect anything from your sacrifice. Because the normative ideology we call "love" implies that the sacrifice must be disinterested. But even then, because sacrifice is a form of exchange you receive something with a value that you can compare with the value of that "part of your self" that you sacrificed. And, according to the logic of meritocracy, you expect a fair and appropriate reward ... exactly the kind of expectation that "love" does not allow. How

---

[42] I understand by "meritocracy" a political system premised on individual merits. As a political system, it appeared after the French Revolution and is strongly linked with the republican ideal of *egalité*. Meritocracy is used in the context of social mobility analysis, in which the meritocratic ideal is a society in which occupation and ability are perfectly matched, in what it is supposed to be a fair and just society. I am grateful to Prof. Javier Moscoso for calling my attention to meritocracy and its collision with the idea of care as sacrifice.

[43] A good example is Pip's story of social progress in Charles Dickens, *Great Expectations* (London: Chapman & Hall, 1861).

can we solve this problem? How can we solve the tensions and contradictions between these two logics?

Arthur was trying to find an answer to these questions. He did the right thing (move to Davos, live all his life in a health resort[44]); he receives something in exchange (Touie's wellbeing); and he found that what he received was not as valuable as he expected it to be, that he had sacrificed too much, and he believed that Jean could give him back what he lost. And, indeed, he was resentful; resentful against Touie. Resentment is always negative when we are dealing with people we love, and if the loved one is chronically ill, then the "sin" of resentment becomes even more serious. We must add selfishness and cruelty to resentment. It implies neither just the failure of the relationship, nor a failure in the love of the resented. It implies a failure in Arthur's subjectivity—he was not the kind of man he pretended to be.[45] That was the reason for the silence and self-denial, the reason for his voyage to South Africa, and the reason why Arthur and Jean's relationship remained a platonic one until Touie's death. It was the difference, in Arthur's own words, between "guilt and innocence."[46]

Conclusions

Arthur's story helps us to think about resentment as the result of deep cultural dynamics only possible after the rise of modernity. These cultural dynamics cross the well-established borders in the historical interpretation of the nineteenth century of the public/private dualism. Following Arthur, we have detected how the construction of his subjectivity was, at the same time, a public and private issue. Arthur's emotional turmoil was the consequence of the tensions between the logic of sacrifice and the logic of meritocracy, putting Arthur's subjectivity at risk.

However, Arthur's subjectivity was not just his business. Since he was offering himself as a model of "British manhood," that is, the kind of man that the Empire needed, any failure, any crack in the placid surface of Arthur's subjectivity would show the contradictions and tensions not just

---

[44] Doyle, *Arthur Conan Doyle: A Life in Letters*, 346.

[45] The role played by Conan Doyle in the definition of late-Victorian masculinity has been widely discussed. See Diana Barsham, *Arthur Conan Doyle and the Meaning of Masculinity* (Aldershot and Brookfield, VT: Ashgate, 2000); A discussion on the approach to care as something based in our "central identity" in Kristen Renwick Monroe, *The Heart of Altruism: Perceptions of a Common Humanity* (Princeton: Princeton University Press, 1996).

[46] Doyle, *Arthur Conan Doyle: A Life in Letters*, 454.

of his personality, but also of the late-Victorian culture he pretended to encapsulate. Arthur's story resonates with the concentration camps of the Boer War, the massacre of Australian aborigines, and with the disappearance of the Indian cotton industry.[47]

Arthur's negotiations, trying to solve his own contradictions, were the result, but also the symptom, of this mixed and thick confluence of factors. Resentment was the consequence of modernity's unsolved contradictions; the consequence of the distance between its promises and its effects. The consequence of the secret hidden in Westlake's "English ideal"; of the secret hidden in Arthur's public image of perfect husband and patriarch; the consequence of their inability to fulfil their promises.

But it was also the consequence of the inability of the normative ideology of "love" to fulfil its promises. As Stephanie Coontz points out, the "conquest" of marriage by love implied the promise of meeting spouses' needs for intimacy, affection and sex.[48] Unfortunately for Arthur, that was not the case for him. Touie's disease broke all these promises, and, just as we have seen, the result of sacrifice, that is, Arthur's profit of the process of exchange, was not the one he expected. This was quite terrible, because only a successful sacrifice would redeem "love" from its failure. Resentment emerges from this chain of failures as the proof of the fragility of these two modern institutions: love-based marriage and the meritocratic society.

Works Cited

Bahr, Howard M. & Kathleen S. Bahr. "Families and Self-Sacrifice: Alternative Models and Meanings for Family Theory." *Social Forces* 79 (4) (2001): 1231–58.

Barsham, Diana. *Arthur Conan Doyle and the Meaning of Masculinity.* Aldershot and Brookfield, VT: Ashgate, 2000.

Barusch, Amanda S. "Problems and Coping Strategies of Elderly Spouse Caregivers." *The Gerontologist* 28 (5) (1988): 677–85.

---

[47] Jenny de Reuck, "Social Suffering and the Politics of Pain: Observations on the Concentration Camps in the Anglo-Boer War 1899–1902," *English in Africa* 26, (2) (1999); Bruce Elder, *Blood on the Wattle: Massacres and Maltreatment of Aboriginal Australians since 1788* (Frenchs Forest, NSW: New Holland Publishers, 2003); B. M. Bhatia, *Famines in India: A Study in Some Aspects of the Economic History of India (1860–1965)* (Bombay: Asia Publishing House, 1967).

[48] Coontz, *Marriage, a History: From Obedience to Intimacy or How Love Conquered Marriage.*

Bhatia, B. M. *Famines in India: A Study in Some Aspects of the Economic History of India (1860–1965)*. Bombay: Asia Publishing House, 1967.

Bolton, Sharon C. "Who Cares? Offering Emotion Work as a 'Gift' in the Nursing Labour Process." *Journal of Advanced Nursing* 30 (2000): 580–86.

Burke, Peter. *The Siege of O'okiep: Guerrilla Campaign in the Anglo-Boer War*. Bloemfontein: War Museum of the Boer Republics, 1995.

Coontz, Stephanie. *Marriage, a History: From Obedience to Intimacy or How Love Conquered Marriage*. New York: Viking, 2005.

Cotton, Richar Payne. *On Consumption: Its Nature, Symptoms, and Treatment*. London: John Churchill, 1858.

Datta, Pradip Kumar. "The Interlocking Worlds of the Anglo-Boer War in South Africa/India." *South African Historical Journal* 57 (1) (2007): 35–59.

de Reuck, Jenny. "Social Suffering and the Politics of Pain: Observations on the Concentration Camps in the Anglo-Boer War 1899–1902." *English in Africa* 26 (2) (1999): 69–88.

Dickens, Charles. *Great Expectations*. London: Chapman & Hall, 1861.

Doyle, Arthur Conan. *Arthur Conan Doyle: A Life in Letters*. London: Harper Press, 2007.

—. *Memories and Adventures*. London: Hodder and Stoughton, 1924.

Dubb, Asher. "Arthur Conan Doyle and the Anglo-Boer South African War (1899–1902)." *Adler Museum Bulletin* 26 (3) (2000): 8–10.

Elder, Bruce. *Blood on the Wattle: Massacres and Maltreatment of Aboriginal Australians since 1788*. Frenchs Forest, NSW: New Holland Publishers, 2003.

Frank, Lawrence. "Dreaming the Medusa: Imperialism, Primitivism, and Sexuality in Arthur Conan Doyle's the Sign of Four." *Signs* 2 (1) (1996): 52–85.

Helin, Kaija & Unni Å Lindström. "Sacrifice: An Ethical Dimension of Caring That Makes Suffering Meaningful." *Nursing Ethics* 10 (4) (2003): 414–27.

Hubert, Henri & Marcel Mauss. *Sacrifice: Its Nature and Function*. (London: Cohen and West, 1964).

Illouz, Eva. *Consuming the Romantic Utopia: Love and the Cultural Contradictions of Capitalism*. Berkeley & London: University of California Press, 1997.

Jowsey, Tanisha. "Perceptions of Time: Chronically Ill Health Service Users and Their Family Carers." In *Making Sense Of: Health, Illness and Disease. Chronic Illness: The Borderlands Between Health and*

Illness, edited by Maria Vaccarella and Rob Fisher, Mansfield College. Oxford, United Kingdom, 2011.

Kerr, Douglas. "Arthur Conan Doyle and the Consumption Cure." *Literature & History* 19 (2) (2010): 36–51.

Kerr, Douglas. "The Straight Left: Sport and the Nation in Arthur Conan Doyle." *Victorian Literature and Culture* 38 (1) (2010): 187–206.

Kramer, Betty J., Melinda Kavanaugh, Amy Trentham-Dietz, Matthew Walsh & James A. Yonker. "Predictors of Family Conflict at the End of Life: The Experience of Spouses and Adult Children of Persons with Lung Cancer." *The Gerontologist* 50 (2) (2010): 215–25.

MacNeil, Gordon, Jordan I. Kosberg, Daniel W Durkin, W. Keith Dooley, Jamie DeCoster & Gail M. Williamson. "Caregiver Mental Health and Potentially Harmful Caregiving Behaviour: The Central Role of Caregiver Anger." *The Gerontologist* 50 (1) (2010): 76–86.

Miller, Daniel. *A Theory of Shopping*. Cambridge: Polity Press, 2005.

Monroe, Kristen Renwick. *The Heart of Altruism: Perceptions of a Common Humanity*. Princeton: Princeton University Press, 1996.

Moscoso, Javier. *Pain: A Cultural History*. Basingstoke: Palgrave Macmillan, 2012.

Morse, J., I. Bottoff, W. Neander & S. Sorberg. "Comparative Analysis of Conceptualizations and Theories of Caring." In *Qualitative Health Research*, edited by J. Morse, 69–89. Newbury Park, CA: Sage, 1992.

Pinheiro Neves & Livia Martins. "Putting Meritocracy in Its Place. The Logic of Performance in the United States, Brazil and Japan." *Critique of Anthropology* 20 (4) (2000): 333–58.

Poovey, Mary. "Covered but Not Bound: Caroline Norton and the 1857 Matrimonial Causes Act." In *Uneven Developments: The Ideological Work of Gender in Mid-Victorian England*, edited by Mary Poovey. Chicago: The University of Chicago Press, 1988.

Savage, Gail L. "The Operation of the 1857 Divorce Act, 1860–1910. A Research Note." *Journal of Social History* 16 (4) (1983): 103–10.

Sheehan, Nancy W. & Paul Nuttall. "Conflict, Emotion, and Personal Strain among Family Caregivers." *Family Relations* 37 (1) (1988): 92–98.

Simmel, Georg. "The Categories of Human Experience." In *On Individuality and Social Forms*, edited by Georg Simmel and Donald N. Levine, 36–40. Chicago & London: University of Chicago Press, 1992.

—. "Exchange." In *On Individuality and Social Forms*, edited by Georg Simmel & Donald N. Levine, 43–69. Chicago & London: The University of Chicago Press, 1992.

Stearns, Peter N. & Carol Stearns. "Emotionology: Clarifying the Study of the History of Emotion." *American Historical Review* 90 (1985): 813–36.

Todorov, Tzvetan. *Facing the Extreme: Moral Life in the Concentration Camps*. New York: Henry Holt, 1996.

Turner, Victor W. & Edward. Bruner (eds.). *The Anthropology of Experience*. Urbana & Chicago: University of Illinois Press, 1986.

Warwick, Peter. *The South African War: The Anglo-Boer War, 1899–1902*. Harlow, Essex: Longman, 1980.

Westlake, John. *The Transvaal War. A Lecture Delivered in the University of Cambridge on 9th November, 1899*. London: C. J. Clay & Sons, Cambridge University Press, 1899.

Young, Michael. *The Rise of the Meritocracy*. New Brunswick, N.J.: Transaction Publishers, 2008.

CHAPTER NINE

THATCHER AND THE POLITICS
OF CLASS RESENTMENT:
CULTURE, POWER AND SHAME
IN CONTEMPORARY BRITISH HISTORY

JOSEPH MASLEN

Introduction—Using Emotion in Contemporary
British History

Emotion represents an important factor in the biographical study of historical figures. Until recently, though, this was a significance mainly recognised outside the discipline of history. In biographical studies, as long ago as the 1980s and 1990s, there were approaches to life history which noted the centrality of emotion. Norman Denzin, for example, stated in 1989 that "the central postulate of the biographical method ... is that there is a 'real' person 'out there' who has lived a life ... and has probably deeply felt the human emotions of shame, love, hate, guilt, anger, despair, and caring for others."[1] Wilhelm Mader used the term "emotionality" to describe "if and how patterns of emotions determine and mold a life during its social intercourse and thus contribute to a unique profile and a biography."[2] These and other scholars such as Agnes Hankiss were considering the complex relationships between autobiographical self-

---

[1] Norman K. Denzin, *Interpretive Biography* (London: Sage, 1989), 22.
[2] Wilhelm Mader, "Emotionality and Continuity in Biographical Contexts," in *Aging and Biography: Explorations in Adult Development*, ed. James E. Birren (New York, NY: Springer, 1995), 51.

image and emotional well-being.[3] It has taken time for historians to catch up with these developments.

However, though historians were late to recognise the significance of emotion, historical reflection on the workings of the mind has a long history. It began in continental Europe with the discussions of Marc Bloch (1886–1944) and Lucien Febvre (1878–1956). In the 1920s these French historians, in their adjoining offices at the University of Strasbourg, founded the Annales school of problem-oriented, interdisciplinary and cultural history. Bloch studied the nature of collective belief-systems (writing on the traditional faith in the King's power to cure disease), while Febvre preferred to think in terms of the relationship between individual sensibility and social constraints.[4] Their work helped to constitute the "history of mentalities" as a field of historical research which, by the turn of the 1980s, could be described as "the new map of cultural history."[5] Pertinently for this chapter, the history of mentalities has also drawn on the concept of the modern "shame-threshold" advanced by the German-Jewish sociologist Norbert Elias (1897–1990), who argued that "the reasons for shame and for embarrassment aroused by the conduct of others" have become ever more "subtle" and "manifold" since the sixteenth century.[6]

Those ideas are the forerunners of the history of emotions. As Thomas Dixon has outlined, the first historical texts on "the emotions" appeared in the 1980s but the field only took off in the 2000s, accelerating after 2008.[7] Perhaps this field's major contribution has been to explore, with a thoroughness that the established branches of history (political, social, and cultural) had not previously attempted, the emotional climates of different historical settings. The state-of-the-art work within the field now seeks to

---

[3] Agnes Hankiss, "Ontologies of the Self: On the Mythological Rearranging of One's Life-History," in *Biography and Society: The Life History Approach in the Social Sciences*, ed. Daniel Bertaux (London: Sage, 1981), 206.

[4] Peter Burke, *The French Historical Revolution: The Annales School, 1929–89* (Cambridge: Polity, 1990), 2, 16, 18, 20.

[5] Patrick H. Hutton, "The History of Mentalities: The New Map of Cultural History," *History and Theory* 20 (3) (1981): 237–259.

[6] Norbert Elias, *The Civilizing Process: State Formation and Civilization* (1939), trans. Edmund Jephcott (Oxford: Blackwell, 1982), 293, 297.

[7] Thomas Dixon, "History in British Tears: Some Reflections on the Anatomy of Modern Emotions: A Lecture Delivered at the Annual Conference of the Netherlands Historical Association, Koninklijke Bibliotheek Den Haag, 4 November 2011," 11–13. The History of the Emotions Blog, Queen Mary, University of London, http://emotionsblog.history.qmul.ac.uk/wp-content/uploads/2012/03/History-in-British-Tears.pdf (accessed January 1, 2013).

reconsider political, social and cultural histories from the perspective of emotion, bringing new insights to bear on the historical discipline's central problems.[8] Yet, so far, historical topics such as the European Middle Ages and the American Revolution have been at the forefront of these developments, while contemporary Britain has been left behind.

This chapter provides an analysis of emotion, and particularly resentment, in relation to Margaret Thatcher, Conservative Prime Minister of the United Kingdom between 1979 and 1990. This is the first time that the history of emotions has been applied to Thatcher, yet emotion is clearly relevant to her political biography. Thatcher is known for being "abrasive" and causing "upset" as a political actor, projecting deviance and perversity onto opposing camps and inflicting humiliation on her adversaries.[9] Equally, the political attitude of herself and her supporters is known for its hostility to the traditional, Labour-supporting working class. In the 1970s, that class was breaking up, with the emergence of new, right-leaning social groupings such as the meritocratic "New Tories" who had joined the expanding middle class and the ambitious "midway class" of working-class home-owners. By the mid-1980s, left-wing commentators were noticing how, as a result, the "politics of class" were being reconfigured by emotions of shame and embarrassment. Those new social groupings, who idolised Thatcher, were seen to reject affinities with, and behave contemptuously towards, those below themselves who they viewed as culpable for their own poverty.[10]

In this chapter, however, I explore how Thatcher herself was a victim of shaming practices earlier in her career, and how those experiences were related to the resentment between social classes. I begin by outlining "The Emotional Politics of Class in Contemporary British History," which leads to a breakdown of "The Emotional Style of Thatcher as a Prime Minister." I then discuss "Class Resentment and the Politics of Resentment as Explanatory Concepts" and use these ideas as a framework for considering "The Emotional Context of Thatcher's Election in 1975" and "Emotion in the 1974–5 Food-Hoarding Controversy." This analysis culminates in my

---

[8] Jan Plamper, "The History of Emotions: An Interview with William Reddy, Barbara Rosenwein and Peter Stearns," *History and Theory* 49 (2010): 248–9.

[9] Dennis Kavanagh, "Thatcher, Margaret Hilda," in *A Dictionary of Political Biography*, ed. Dennis Kavanagh and Christopher Riches (Oxford: Oxford University Press, 2012). Oxford Reference Online http://www.oxfordreference.com/view/10.1093/acref/9780199569137.001.0001/ac ref-9780199569137-e-704 (accessed January 1, 2013).

[10] Margaret Jones, *Thatcher's Kingdom: A View of Britain in the Eighties* (London: Collins, 1984), 298, 301.

conclusion "Decoding the Emotionality of Thatcher's Britain." My contention is that the politics of class resentment were a formative part of Thatcher's relationship with British political culture, and are critical for understanding contemporary British history.

The Emotional Politics of Class in Contemporary British History

Friction between social classes is central to the politics of contemporary British history. Within Conservative politics, it has profoundly affected the relationship between the party's leaders and its supporters ever since Thatcher's resignation in 1990. Her administration is seen by critics as having successfully embodied the aspirations of "working families" for the trappings of middle-class success, such as home-ownership.[11] Her successors have sought to appease the apparent hostility of those voters towards the social security provisions available to those they left behind.[12] As a result, a particular version of social fairness (championing social mobility rather than "welfare") has become a core virtue for the party. The Conservative leader David Cameron, Prime Minister since 2010, has pledged to continue what he called, in a 2008 speech, "our commitment to social justice—a society made more equal by dispensing opportunity more widely, and more fairly."[13] Yet issues of unfairness have re-emerged under his leadership in ways that reflect social divisions within the Conservative Party.

2012 saw the development of a "class war" within the Party, with Cameron perceived by rank-and-file Conservative MPs as "upper-class" and out of touch with ordinary voters.[14] In March that year, in the wake of a chancellor's budget widely seen as increasing taxes on ordinary old-age

---

[11] Peter King, *Housing Policy Transformed: The Right to Buy and the Desire to Own* (Bristol: Policy, 2010).

[12] John Sergeant, *Maggie: Her Fatal Legacy* (London: Macmillan, 2005).

[13] Stephen Driver, "'Fixing Our Broken Society": David Cameron's Post-Thatcherite Social Policy', in *The Conservatives under David Cameron: Built to Last?*, eds. Simon Lee and Matt Beech (Basingstoke: Palgrave Macmillan, 2009), 89.

[14] Dominic Lawson, "Cameron is Facing Class War, in his Own Party: Many Tory Backbenchers Feel their Leader is Still at Heart the Old Etonian Upper-Class Bon Vivant," *Independent*, online edition (October 18, 2011) http://www.independent.co.uk/voices/commentators/dominic-lawson/dominic-lawson-cameron-is-facing-class-war-in-his-own-party-2372025.html (accessed January 1, 2013].

pensioners and cutting those of rich businessmen, a separate scandal emerged surrounding rich party donors' private influence over policy.[15] In April, Nadine Dorries, a Conservative MP from a low-income background, publicly accused Cameron and the Chancellor George Osborne of being "two arrogant posh boys who show no remorse, no contrition, and no passion to understand the lives of others."[16] If resentment at this perceived bias has the potential to "retoxify" the party's brand-image, as the liberal *Independent* newspaper has predicted, then it may have far-reaching consequences for the balance of power in British politics.[17]

This chapter locates the origins of this tension in the mid-1970s. The argument is that, during that time, Thatcher was the victim of what Dorries calls the failure to "understand the lives of others." In the months prior to the Conservative leadership election of 1975, which she won against her more upper-class rival, the former Conservative Prime Minister (1970-74) Edward Heath, her social background was portrayed negatively in Britain's most prestigious broadsheet daily, the *Times*. Focusing on its coverage of Thatcher's supposed endorsement of food-hoarding, I seek to explore: (a) the collective mindset of the cultural and political establishment with which Thatcher had to contend during her rise to power, and; (b) the effect of this attitude on the portrayal of Thatcher's personality during the *Times* food-hoarding controversy.

The Emotional Style of Thatcher as a Prime Minister

The relationship between Thatcher and the political culture that surrounded her leadership was the subject of several studies published during her career, such as Peter Jenkins' *Mrs Thatcher's Revolution* (1987).[18] However, the enquiry which most directly considers the relevance of emotion to that relationship was written by Anthony King, Professor of Government at the University of Essex. King's chapter on Thatcher's "style" in his book *The British Prime Minister* (1985) is remarkably prescient in foreshadowing one of the contemporary concerns

---

[15] Andrew Grice & Oliver Wright, "Most Voters See Tories as the Party of the Rich," *Independent* (March 27, 2012), 1; "Guess Who Came to Dinner: Bankers, Traders and an Oil Baron: Prime Minister's Private Guests All had One Thing in Common: Wealth," *Independent* (March 27, 2012), 4–5.

[16] "'Posh Boys' Come under Attack from Own MPs," *i* (April 24, 2012), 1, 4.

[17] "Tories Being 'Retoxified' as Details of Top Donors Emerge," *Independent* (March 27, 2012), 4.

[18] Peter Jenkins, *Mrs Thatcher's Revolution: The Ending of the Socialist Era* (London: Cape, 1987).

of the history of emotions. In 2012, "emotional styles" was the theme of Benno Gammerl's special issue of *Rethinking History*, which examined the "different ways in which women and men generated, handled and expressed emotions" in different historical contexts.[19] King describes Thatcher as a political actor with a distinctive emotional pattern and register. What he observes most of all is its stridency: "She stamps her foot, she raises her voice. For a British prime minister, she is extraordinarily assertive."[20]

King's description of Thatcher corresponds with Gammerl's approach, which seeks to link the behaviour of individuals to surrounding "communities and spaces."[21] King sees Thatcher's outlook as a response to the political realm: "Thatcher is in fact a remarkably cautious politician. Not only is she cautious, but she respects power and has an unusually well developed capacity for weighing it, for seeing who has it and who has not, for calculating who can damage her and who cannot."[22] Consequently, King views Thatcher's assertiveness not as a loss of control but as part of an emotional skill-set which is functional to the setting of politics. This relates to Gammerl's concept of "emotional patterns and practices" being an adjustment to "distinct spatial settings," each of which elicits an appropriate "emotional repertoire."[23]

However, this brings us to the limitations of King's account. Focusing on Thatcher's understanding of power, he describes her as a rational actor in the mould of what Gammerl calls the "free-willed and intentionally choosing" subject who acts "autonomously" outside "external influences."[24] King's description seems to draw on the image of Thatcher (a chemistry graduate) as, literally, a political scientist; a master of the study of political forces, reactions and elements. He concludes that emotion is not central to a true appreciation of her personality: "She is often described as an emotional person; in her ability to weigh power, she is more like a precision instrument."[25]

---

[19] Anthony King, "Margaret Thatcher: The Style of a Prime Minister," in *The British Prime Minister*, ed. Anthony King (ed.) (London: Macmillan, 1985), 96–140; Benno Gammerl, "Emotional Styles: Concepts and Challenges," *Rethinking History* 16 (2) (2012): 167.

[20] King, "Margaret Thatcher," 118.

[21] Gammerl, "Emotional Styles," 164.

[22] King, "Margaret Thatcher," 118.

[23] Gammerl, "Emotional Styles," 164.

[24] Gammerl, "Emotional Styles," 166.

[25] King, "Margaret Thatcher," 118.

Yet John Campbell's biography *Margaret Thatcher*, with its two volumes *The Grocer's Daughter* (2000) and *The Iron Lady* (2003), has helped to develop a more complex portrait of Thatcher's emotionality.[26] His focus on emotion echoes King's analysis, but comes at the topic from the opposite direction. Deliberately or not, it accords with some of the more advanced thinking in biographical studies and studies of Thatcher. Moving away from the concept of the individual's consistency over time, it considers the "contingent, evolutionary trajectory" of "'a life' as it is lived in its length, complexities, contradictions, shifts and changes."[27] The scope of Campbell's two volumes allows for this proper recognition that Thatcher was not made out of iron but was instead forged by events during her political life. He suggests at the outset that Thatcher's "legend" of a consistent selfhood founded in childhood, a legend cultivated by her autobiographical writings and subsequent biographies, "does not explain her aggression; or her anger."[28]

Class Resentment and the Politics of Resentment as Explanatory Concepts

The "politics of resentment" turns the social politics of conservatism on its head. It is associated not with traditional conservatism but with the radical "New Right" philosophy pursued across Western Europe and the US in the 1980s. As critics have shown, this philosophy was defined not by its distance from the working classes but by its "thunder" against elites within the "bureaucratic, centralized state," such as senior civil servants, police and magistrates. The New Right's "neo-liberal program" was based on a hostility to superiors, being "a political weapon against the established political institutions and their alleged monopolization of power," as well as "a movement of social protest" which "[sought] through

---

[26] John Campbell, *Margaret Thatcher, Volume One: The Grocer's Daughter* (London: Cape, 2000); John Campbell, *Margaret Thatcher, Volume Two: The Iron Lady* (London: Cape, 2003).
[27] Peter Kerr & David Marsh, "Explaining Thatcherism: Towards a Multidimensional Approach," in *Postwar British Politics in Perspective*, eds. David Marsh, Jim Buller, Colin Hay, Jim Johnston, Peter Kerr, Stuart McAnulla & Matthew Watson (Cambridge: Polity, 1999), 184; Liz Stanley, *The Auto/biographical I: The Theory and Practice of Feminist Auto/biography* (Manchester: Manchester University Press, 1992), 26.
[28] Campbell, *Margaret Thatcher, Volume One*, 3.

victory to regain lost status, to embarrass or humiliate their enemies ... and to regain control of the culture."[29]

What is new in my approach to Thatcher's New Right politics is that I link this programme to emotionality by identifying it with the "politics of resentment." There is already a strong awareness of how Thatcher was acting against the establishment in various ways, by "recasting the welfare state," "reconstructing the civil service" and "confronting local government' in 'economic liberal crusades.'"[30] Yet I contend that those acts were fuelled by a revolutionary morality based on a frustrated sense of inferiority.[31] The idea of overthrowing the permissive society and generous welfare system of the liberal elites, and replacing it with the "self-restraint" and "self-reliance" of the modest shopkeeper's daughter, was central to her sense of virtue.

A major dimension of Thatcher's crusade against such elites was social class. The relevant term here, "class resentment," was pioneered in sociology to describe how "unacknowledged shame, arising from rejection [by a higher social class], leads to anger."[32] Applying this sociological notion of class resentment to politics is an original innovation that fulfils a number of criteria in the history of emotions. First, it represents a contribution to the existing line of research on the political history of emotions which, as Susan Matt has argued, "is transforming notions of political change and how and why it has occurred."[33] Second, it treats this political history of emotions in relation to society, not in isolation from it. This is crucial because, as Joanna Bourke says, we "cannot ignore" both "power relations" and "social inequality" in explaining how emotion originates and is articulated.[34] Willemijn Ruberg has stressed the importance of the "structures that facilitate, entail or hide emotions" as well as the "explicit emotional utterances" by which "[historical] subjects"

---

[29] Hans-George Betz, "The New Politics of Resentment: Radical Right-Wing Populist Parties in Western Europe," *Comparative Politics* 25 (4) (1993): 418; Alan Crawford, *Thunder on the Right: The 'New Right' and the Politics of Resentment* (New York, NY: Pantheon, 1980), 149.

[30] Geoffrey K. Fry, *The Politics of the Thatcher Revolution: An Interpretation of British Politics, 1979–1990* (Basingstoke: Palgrave Macmillan, 2008), 105–179.

[31] See Georg Stauth & Bryan S. Turner, *Nietzsche's Dance: Resentment, Reciprocity and Resistance in Social Life* (Oxford: Blackwell, 1988), 110.

[32] J. M. Barbalet, "A Macro Sociology of Emotion: Class Resentment," *Sociological Theory* 10 (2) (1992): 155.

[33] Susan J. Matt, "Current Emotion Research in History: Or, Doing History from the Inside Out," *Emotion Review* 3 (1) (2011): 120.

[34] Joanna Bourke, "Fear and Anxiety: Writing about Emotion in Modern History," *History Workshop Journal* 55 (2003): 123.

articulate their feelings, and these structures of feeling are social as well as political.[35]

The Emotional Context of Thatcher's Election in 1975

As Theodore Zeldin said, "a rewriting of a piece of history from the point of view of a particular emotion" means considering what events and processes carry the most emotional weight in the lives of individuals.[36] For Thatcher, one such high-point of emotion was her election as Leader of the Opposition on February 11, 1975. Campbell emphasises that it was this event, not her election as Prime Minister four years later, that was the real turning point in her biography "when her life and her prospects really changed."[37] Before that day, her career in British politics seemed unlikely to have an upward trajectory. Reflecting on her position within her constituency on January 6, the *Times*' political correspondent John Groser could only offer the appraisal that: "Mrs Thatcher's majority of just under 4,000 last October, although down on the February figure, is an indication that her seat is still relatively safe and that she has a strong personal following."[38]

The main cause of prejudice against her, at a time when women were routinely belittled in popular culture and Thatcher was one of only twenty-three female MPs in an elected Parliament of 516, was gender. The *Times* columnist George Hutchinson spelled it out on December 14, 1974 in an article on the Conservative Party's leadership contest: "Mrs Thatcher—to her credit—is still willing to stand; but whether the Party is yet ready to elect a woman leader, however able, remains more than doubtful."[39] Bernard Levin, supporting Thatcher's candidacy, complained that: "Her chief problem is, or at any rate is supposed to be, that she is a woman."[40]

---

[35] Willemijn Ruberg, "Interdisciplinarity and the History of Emotions," *Cultural and Social History* 6 (4) (2009): 510; See also William M. Reddy, *The Navigation of Feeling: A Framework for the History of Emotions* (Cambridge: Cambridge University Press, 2001), 143.

[36] Theodore Zeldin, "Personal History and the History of the Emotions," *Journal of Social History* 15 (3) (1982): 344.

[37] Campbell, *Margaret Thatcher, Volume One*, p. xii.

[38] John Groser, "Mrs Thatcher Active amid Constituency Apathy," *Times* (January 6, 1975), 2.

[39] George Hutchinson, "Where have All Our Inspiring Leaders Gone?" *Times* (December 14, 1974), 12.

[40] Bernard Levin, "The Tories' Best Hope of Salvation," *Times* (January 23, 1975), 16.

Yet in the context of the Tories' claim to be a "one-nation" party, another issue was its ability to appeal across class divides. In January 1975, the Conservative MPs Hugh Fraser and Ian Gilmour (a supporter of Heath) both pledged allegiance to a "Conservative approach" that was "national and not class-based"; rooted in the party's "special moral, social and economic base" across a broad swathe of public opinion and not simply the Conservatives' "suburban" and "southern provincial" heartland.[41] As quoted by Groser, Gilmour's argument was that 'we have ... to be moderate in policy and moderate in conduct."[42] For Fraser, the "special Tory interests" at the heart of their "political identity" had to be supplemented with "policies and principles which in the national interest rise above class."[43]

It was in this context that, three months earlier on Thursday November 28, 1974, the *Times* had broken the story that Thatcher had advocated food-hoarding in an interview with the magazine *Pre Retirement Choice*. Under the heading "Mrs Thatcher's food store to beat inflation," the *Times* explained that Thatcher had, when:

> asked for practical advice for people approaching retirement age and worried about the pace of inflation', advised that they should buy and store tinned food: "People tend to think of storage these days in terms of deep freezing, but fresh meat won't keep in a deep freeze for more than a year," she said. "Tinned food on the other hand will keep for five, 10 and 15 years. What you collect are the expensive proteins: ham, tongue, salmon, mackerel, sardines."[44]

Thatcher at that time was the Conservative Party's spokesman on economic affairs, but was framed by the article in terms of home economics. The class politics of that perception of Thatcher will become more evident as we follow the story through the pages of the *Times*.

Emotion in the 1974–5 Food-Hoarding Controversy

The *Times* pursued the story over an extended period, all the while reinforcing this representation of Thatcher. On the following day, Friday

---

[41] John Groser, "Tory Monetarists Attacked by Mr Gilmour," *Times* (January 31, 1975), 2; Hugh Fraser, "Tories Need a New Leader to Heal the Wounds and Take the Party to Grass Roots," *Times* (January 31, 1975), 14.

[42] Groser, "Tory Monetarists Attacked by Mr Gilmour," 2.

[43] Fraser, "Tories Need a New Leader to Heal the Wounds and Take the Party to Grass Roots," 14.

[44] "Mrs Thatcher's Food Store to Beat Inflation," *Times* (November 28, 1974), 2.

November 29, the National Housewives' Association were said to have reacted angrily to Thatcher's reported statement by calling on her to give away her stock of tinned food to pensioners. This article, "Housewives protest at Mrs Thatcher's 'hoard'," describes how the association had "been given two tons of sugar by a national grocery chain, which it intends to distribute to old age pensioners," and was about to "suggest to Mrs Thatcher that she allows it to distribute her stock as well." The article positions Thatcher as part of a debate among housewives, such as "Mrs June Wall, a committee member of the association," who in the article is quoted as saying: "'We shall express our disgust at her hoarding'." Thatcher is depicted from this angle as basing her advice on preconceptions derived from an elevated social standing, with Wall reported as complaining that: "'Only the rich can afford to hoard food or have enough space to stockpile'."

There is significance in the *Times* alighting on this description of Thatcher "stockpiling" her food; as if Thatcher's "large quantities of food in the average household deep freeze" were her equivalent of a Cold War nuclear arsenal. The article concludes by suggesting how petty the affair must have appeared from the chauvinistically masculine and collectively unionised ranks of the working-class Labour Party. The final word is given to the former miner Dennis Skinner, a Labour MP for the coalfield district of Bolsover who had, according to the *Times*, "accused Mrs Thatcher of 'filching little tins of salmon from supermarkets and taking them out of the pensioners' mouths'."[45]

The debate was then continued in the *Times*' letters pages. In the following week, there were two days of correspondence on the topic. On Tuesday December 3, the *Times* printed two letters under the heading "Stocking up the larder," both of which reinforced the identification between Thatcher and housewives. One of them, from A. M. Lloyd of Greater Totham, Essex, criticised Thatcher for her supposed public commitment to "stock up two larders with tinned food": "What is she trying to do in publicizing this fact, get *other housewives* [my emphasis] to stock up and so create a shortage of tinned food?" The other letter, by the editor of *Pre Retirement Choice*, attempted to defend Thatcher by explaining that: "What she advocates is that we rediscover that old fashioned prudence practised by housewives of a previous generation."[46]

A longer letter, by Cecily Evans of the village of Copford, Essex, appeared on Wednesday December 4, under the heading "Mrs Thatcher's cupboard," and again defended Thatcher's old-fashioned housewifely

---

[45] "Housewives Protest at Mrs Thatcher's 'Hoard'," *Times* (November 29, 1974), 2.
[46] "Stocking Up the Larder," *Times* (December 3, 1974), 15.

virtues. This time, Thatcher was defined in class terms as an example of the hard-pressed suburban housewife as opposed to the gentrified countrywoman. As Evans explained, Thatcher had been forced by her station in life to buy pre-packaged produce at the supermarket rather than:

> go forth in due season and buy peas, beans, strawberries, raspberries, quarters of beef, carcases of lamb and all the other seasonable produce when they are severally at their least expensive ... I should have thought that Mrs Thatcher was exercising exactly the same housewifely instincts as her more fortunate sisters with time and space to pick, trim, blanch, bag and freeze the products of the countryside ... All honour to Mrs Thatcher for maintaining the—sadly—old fashioned virtues of forward buying on her housekeeping budget and keeping a well-stocked store cupboard.[47]

The *Times* continued with the story into January with a feature in which Groser interviewed women from Thatcher's constituency of Barnet in north London. The article tried to capture the reaction to Thatcher's hoarding locally and, above all, emphasised that Thatcher's constituents shared the same narrow-minded and class-bound mentality: "'If Mrs Thatcher can hoard, so can we,' one woman in a supermarket said." The conclusion to be drawn, according to Groser, was that the concerns of the respectable middle-class housewife were personal and not political: "The shopper was well-dressed and articulate but, like many of her fellows, totally preoccupied with providing for her family." Groser's overview offers Thatcher the backhanded compliment that, as a politician consumed by personal issues, she is the politician for non-political voters: "Politics may be a bore for them, but the locals are all in favour of Mrs Thatcher to lead the country out of its troubles."

There is also a sexist angle to this commentary. In Groser's view, such women were not emotionally involved with the man's world of British politics: "The wider issues of confrontation with the unions and the state of the economy concerned these women not at all." The world of these ordinary women was to be sharply divided from the grand world of "Mr Heath's advisors at Smith Square," a detachment summarised by Groser with a pithy quotation from a local woman: "In Victoria Park an old-age pensioner called Maud thought that things were very bad for pensioners. ... Did she think Mrs Thatcher would make a good leader of the Conservative Party? 'Oh, I don't know about that. Would they want to woman to lead them'?"[48]

---

[47] "Mrs Thatcher's Cupboard," *Times* (December 4, 1974), 17.
[48] Groser, "Mrs Thatcher Active amid Constituency Apathy."

Conclusion—
Decoding the Emotionality of Thatcher's Britain

This story of Thatcher and the food-hoarding controversy may be a historical footnote, but it takes us into the emotional heart of Britain's economic problems in the 1970s. The hyper-inflation of the early 1970s, exacerbated by the fourfold increase in the price of oil in 1973, brought concerns over the household economy into the centre of British political life. As the price of commodities such as eggs, cheese and beef almost doubled between 1970 and 1974, the free-market cost of basic groceries became a powerful political factor. The snap general election of February 1974, called in response to a coalminers' strike and its challenge to the government's authority, was fought over the housewife's purse. Heath was ultimately displaced, after a second election in October, by Labour's Harold Wilson and his promise to introduce state food subsidies and price controls.[49]

Culturally, these events coincided with what seemed to be a sudden change in the emotional "temper" of life in Britain. Kenneth O. Morgan's history of post-war Britain locates 1973/4 as the exact tipping point between the residual optimism of "the people's peace" and the emergence of "a growing mood of confrontation, with more than an undercurrent of violence."[50] Only a week before the *Times* broke the story of Thatcher's "food store," the Birmingham pub bombings of November 21, 1974 had killed twenty-one ordinary British citizens, heralding the terrorist Irish Republican Army's new strategy of attacking British civilians on the mainland. Referring to other issues from that era, such as football hooliganism and inner-city crime, Morgan posits "the erosion of an ethical system … withering away in confusion and doubt."[51] The meanness of Thatcher's alleged food-hoarding could be presented as yet another instance of the worrying lack of social cohesion.

In this emotional context of societal breakdown, the controversy took shape as a debate over Thatcher's identity as a politician capable of leading Britain out of its ethical impasse. Thatcher's persona was suspect not only because she was a woman but also because of her proximity, in gender and class, to the figure of the housewife. Not only was the housewife's purchasing, storing and preparing of food synonymous with the domestic sphere of everyday life as distinct from the practice of

---

[49] Peter Dorey, *British Politics since 1945* (Oxford: Blackwell, 1995), 127.

[50] Kenneth O. Morgan, *The People's Peace: British History, 1945–1989* (Oxford: Oxford University Press, 1990), 354.

[51] Morgan, *The People's Peace*, 357.

politics; the housewife was seen as being at odds with the collective solidarity required to remake Britain as a "united kingdom." The coverage of Thatcher's food-hoarding in the *Times* reinforced this sense of an emotional dichotomy between caring about food and caring about politics.[52]

That distinction was built on an old-fashioned idea of the public man; a concept laden with assumptions about class and emotion in politics.[53] Public figures were supposed to be elevated above want, and the emotion of fear created by it;[54] even in economic conditions in which the price of food was rising. The coverage of Thatcher's food-hoarding approached the problem from this perspective of plenty, and took shape as a social anthropology of those below. Its message was that food-hoarding was, or could be, a cause of shame and embarrassment; that Thatcher's relationship with politics was compromised by her place in the relationship between classes.

This analysis of the controversy relates back to the theoretical observations with which the chapter began. Because of the formidable image cultivated by and around Thatcher since 1975, we are not used to seeing her as a "real" person who has experienced emotional suffering. It is quite possible that Thatcher's political career reflected her "emotionality," her subsequent attacks on the ideals and privileges of the establishment being affected by resentment arising from earlier negative representations.

This chapter has addressed the question of Thatcher's emotionality indirectly. It has focused not on Thatcher's explicit emotional utterances but instead on the *Times* as an organ of the establishment intelligentsia; a structure with the capacity to produce emotion by describing individuals and groups in positive or negative ways. Perhaps the ability of the *Times* to generate hostility against the food-hoarding housewife contributed to a broader emotional climate of class-prejudice against Thatcher in the 1970s. Perhaps, too, this atmosphere was partly responsible for provoking Thatcher's "class politics of resentment" in the 1980s; her defence of

---

[52] See Michel de Certeau, Luce Giard & Pierre Mayol, *The Practice of Everyday Life, Volume 2: Living and Cooking* (1994), trans. Timothy J. Tomasik (Minneapolis, MN: University of Minnesota Press, 1998), 151, 153–4.

[53] Matthew McCormack, "Introduction," in *Public Men: Masculinity and Politics in Modern Britain*, ed. Matthew McCormack (Basingstoke: Palgrave Macmillan, 2007), 2, 3.

[54] Francis Dodsworth, "Masculinity as Governance: Police, Public Service and the Embodiment of Authority, *c.* 1700–1850," in McCormack, *Public Men*, 42–3.

housewifely virtues of "self-restraint" and "self-reliance" and her attacks on the perceived vices of the establishment.

This new concept of the "class politics of resentment" combines "class resentment," as developed in sociology, and "the politics of resentment," as found in studies of the New Right. Perhaps it is already popularly understood that the "politics of resentment" is a "politics of class"; if so, this chapter provides the necessary addition to our conceptual apparatus. Meanwhile, it applies the history of emotions for the first time to Thatcher. This innovation throws fresh light on her prime ministerial style, while contesting accounts of her politics that focus on its antagonism against those below, not above her in the social scale.

A warm thank you to Dr Dolorès Martin Moruno and, as ever, Emma Katz, along with the other editors/organisers and conference delegates in Geneva.

Works Cited

Barbalet, J. M. "A Macro Sociology of Emotion: Class Resentment." *Sociological Theory* 10 (2) (1992): 150–163.

Betz, Hans-George. "The New Politics of Resentment: Radical Right-Wing Populist Parties in Western Europe." *Comparative Politics* 25 (4) (1993): 413–427.

Bourke, Joanna. "Fear and Anxiety: Writing about Emotion in Modern History." *History Workshop Journal* 55 (2003): 111–133.

Burke, Peter. *The French Historical Revolution: The Annales School, 1929–89*. Cambridge: Polity, 1990.

Campbell, John. *Margaret Thatcher, Volume One: The Grocer's Daughter*. London: Cape, 2000.

—. *Margaret Thatcher, Volume Two: The Iron Lady*. London: Cape, 2003.

Crawford, Alan. *Thunder on the Right: The "New Right" and the Politics of Resentment*. New York, NY: Pantheon, 1980.

De Certeau, Michel, Luce Giard & Pierre Mayol. *The Practice of Everyday Life, Volume 2: Living and Cooking* (1994), translated by Timothy J. Tomasik. Minneapolis, MN: University of Minnesota Press, 1998.

Denzin, Norman K. *Interpretive Biography*. London: Sage, 1989.

Dixon, Thomas. "History in British Tears: Some Reflections on the Anatomy of Modern Emotions: A Lecture Delivered at the Annual Conference of the Netherlands Historical Association, Koninklijke

Bibliotheek Den Haag, 4 November 2011." The History of the Emotions Blog, Queen Mary, University of London http://emotionsblog.history.qmul.ac.uk/wp-content/uploads/2012/03/History-in-British-Tears.pdf (accessed January 1, 2013).

Dodsworth, Francis. "Masculinity as Governance: Police, Public Service and the Embodiment of Authority, *c.* 1700–1850." In *Public Men: Political Masculinities in Modern Britain*, edited by Matthew McCormack, 33–53. Basingstoke: Palgrave Macmillan, 2007.

Dorey, Peter. *British Politics since 1945*. Oxford: Blackwell, 1995.

Driver, Stephen. "'Fixing Our Broken Society': David Cameron's Post-Thatcherite Social Policy." In *The Conservatives under David Cameron: Built to Last?*, edited by Simon Lee and Matt Beech, 80–96. Basingstoke: Palgrave Macmillan, 2009.

Elias, Norbert. *The Civilizing Process: State Formation and Civilization* (1939), translated by Edmund Jephcott. Oxford: Blackwell, 1982.

Fraser, Hugh. "Tories Need a New Leader to Heal the Wounds and Take the Party to Grass Roots." *Times*. January 31, 1975.

Fry, Geoffrey K. *The Politics of the Thatcher Revolution: An Interpretation of British Politics, 1979–1990*. Basingstoke: Palgrave Macmillan, 2008.

Gammerl, Benno. "Emotional Styles: Concepts and Challenges." *Rethinking History* 16 (2) (2012): 161–175.

Grice, Andrew & Oliver Wright. "Most Voters See Tories as the Party of the Rich." *Independent*. March 27, 2012.

Groser, John. "Mrs Thatcher Active amid Constituency Apathy." *Times*. January 6, 1975.

—. "Tory Monetarists Attacked by Mr Gilmour." *Times*. January 31, 1975.

"Guess Who Came to Dinner: Bankers, Traders and an Oil Baron: Prime Minister's Private Guests All had One Thing in Common: Wealth." *Independent*. March 27, 2012.

Hankiss, Agnes. "Ontologies of the Self: On the Mythological Rearranging of One's Life-History." In *Biography and Society: The Life History Approach in the Social Sciences*, edited by Daniel Bertaux, 203–209. (London: Sage, 1981).

"Housewives Protest at Mrs Thatcher's 'Hoard'." *Times*. November 29, 1974.

Hutchinson, George. "Where have All Our Inspiring Leaders Gone?" *Times*. December 14, 1974.

Hutton, Patrick H. "The History of Mentalities: The New Map of Cultural History." *History and Theory* 20 (3) (1981): 237–259.

Jenkins, Peter. *Mrs Thatcher's Revolution: The Ending of the Socialist Era*. London: Cape, 1987.

Jones, Margaret. *Thatcher's Kingdom: A View of Britain in the Eighties*. London: Collins, 1984.

Kavanagh, Dennis. "Thatcher, Margaret Hilda." In *A Dictionary of Political Biography*, edited by Dennis Kavanagh and Christopher Riches. Oxford: Oxford University Press, 2012. Oxford Reference Online
http://www.oxfordreference.com/view/10.1093/acref/9780199569137.
001.0001/acref-9780199569137-e-704 (accessed January 1, 2013).

Kerr, Peter & David Marsh. "Explaining Thatcherism: Towards a Multidimensional Approach." In *Postwar British Politics in Perspective*, edited by David Marsh, Jim Buller, Colin Hay, Jim Johnston, Peter Kerr, Stuart McAnulla & Matthew Watson, 168–188. Cambridge: Polity, 1999.

King, Anthony. "Margaret Thatcher: The Style of a Prime Minister." In *The British Prime Minister*, second edition, edited by Anthony King, 96–140. London: Macmillan, 1985.

King, Peter. *Housing Policy Transformed: The Right to Buy and the Desire to Own*. Bristol: Policy, 2010.

Lawson, Dominic. "Cameron is Facing Class War, in his Own Party: Many Tory Backbenchers Feel their Leader is Still at Heart the Old Etonian Upper-Class Bon Vivant. *Independent*, online edition. October 18, 2011.
http://www.independent.co.uk/voices/commentators/dominic-lawson/dominic-lawson-cameron-is-facing-class-war-in-his-own-party-2372025.html (accessed January 1, 2013).

Levin, Bernard. "The Tories' Best Hope of Salvation." *Times*. January 23, 1975.

Mader, Wilhelm. "Emotionality and Continuity in Biographical Contexts." In *Aging and Biography: Explorations in Adult Development*, edited by James E. Birren, 39–60. New York, NY: Springer, 1995.

Matt, Susan J. "Current Emotion Research in History: Or, Doing History from the Inside Out." *Emotion Review* 3 (1) (2011): 117–124.

McCormack, Matthew. "Introduction." In Matthew McCormack (ed.), *Public Men: Masculinity and Politics in Modern Britain*, 1–12. Basingstoke: Palgrave Macmillan, 2007.

Morgan, Kenneth O. *The People's Peace: British History, 1945–1989*. Oxford: Oxford University Press, 1990.

"Mrs Thatcher's Cupboard." *Times* (December 4, 1974).

"Mrs Thatcher's Food Store to Beat Inflation." *Times*. November 28, 1974.

Plamper, Jan. "The History of Emotions: An Interview with William Reddy, Barbara Rosenwein, and Peter Stearns." *History and Theory* 49 (2010): 237–265.

"'Posh Boys' Come under Attack from Own MPs." *i* (April 24, 2012).

Reddy, William M. *The Navigation of Feeling: A Framework for the History of Emotions*. Cambridge: Cambridge University Press, 2001.

Ruberg, Willemijn. "Interdisciplinarity and the History of Emotions." *Cultural and Social History* 6 (4) (2009): 507–516.

Sergeant, John. *Maggie: Her Fatal Legacy*. London: Macmillan, 2005.

Stanley, Liz. *The Auto/biographical I: The Theory and Practice of Feminist Auto/biography*. Manchester: Manchester University Press, 1992.

Stauth, Georg & Bryan S. Turner. *Nietzsche's Dance: Resentment, Reciprocity and Resistance in Social Life*. Oxford: Blackwell, 1988.

"Stocking Up the Larder." *Times*. December 3, 1974.

"Tories Being 'Retoxified' as Details of Top Donors Emerge." *Independent*. March 27, 2012.

Zeldin, Theodore. "Personal History and the History of the Emotions." *Journal of Social History* 15 (3) (1982): 339–347.

PART IV:

COMING INTO CONFLICT: RESENTMENT, WARS AND REVOLUTIONS

CHAPTER TEN

TURNING BROTHERS INTO ENEMIES? RESENTMENT AND ATLANTIC REVOLUTIONS

MANUEL LUCENA-GIRALDO

Emotional categories are historical constructions. However, in history, some emotions have been related to "primitives" and others to "civilized" peoples. Space and geography provide fundamental explanations, because emotions are not universal, but framed within particular contexts until the present, even in globalized forms.[1] Cultural relativism does not solve the question. Which society in the centre, or in the periphery, tends to capture—or produce—resentment? Who and why is possessed by it, until it explodes in a ritual or violent form? The problem is deeply rooted in what we mean by "modernity." If the Enlightened fabrication of a progressive and linear sense of time has to be taken into account, resentment has acquired new meanings. It is not an emotion that suddenly appeared in the eighteenth century. In fact, it is very old in Western culture and others. In the biblical fight between Cain and Abel, whether the motive of the killing was pure jealousy, or involved the desire of women, or represented the somehow eternal fight between shepherds and farmers, it provides the explanation of the crime. At the same time it was the beginning of a sharp division sanctioned by God between what is "good" and "evil" in the field of emotions, contrary to the Greek tradition.[2] Having said that, something

---

[1] One good example of this geographies of emotions is the extension of regional resentment, between the South and North of given countries; James V. Carmichael, "Southern Librarianship and the Culture of Resentment," Cheryl Knott Malone, Hermina G.B. Anghelescu, John Mark Tucker (eds.), *Libraries & Culture. Historical Essays Honoring the Legacy of Donald G. Davis Jr.* (Washington: Library of Congress, Center for the Book, 2006), 123.

[2] "Adam made love to his wife Eve, and she became pregnant and gave birth to Cain. She said, 'With the help of the LORD I have brought forth a man.' Later she gave birth to his brother Abel. Now Abel kept flocks, and Cain worked the

new (literally) happened by the 1700s, a time when revolutions in a modern definition, including politics, where invented. The implications for emotions were huge, but as Marc Ferro puts it, "To what extent do revolutions constitute one of the extreme expressions of resentment?"[3] It is an important question. Resentment would acquire a distinctive, contemporary form after that encounter.

Old Politics

By means of explanation, we can argue there is a connection between certain emotions and the so-called—in different periods and cultures—"spirits of the age." That is, a social acceptance—and some would say a production of an atmosphere of political correctness—concerning some emotions, and a refusal of others. This adaptation of an emotional category to a concrete context can afford important explanations to what the emotions "are" and in fact "represent" and/or convey in different situations. The study of emotions in the eighteenth century can give us a glimpse of the emotional transition from the *Ancien Regime*, based on traditional hierarchies of religion and nobility, to modern societies and individuals, based on citizenship and individuality. The role of resentment in this debate concerns the idea of political revolution as the modern, utopian and, for some, desirable way human societies could change. However, that possibility has developed through a historical pattern. Revolution could and can happen in a sudden, but the presumption of tradition was not the only source of political wisdom that took centuries to be conceivable. At least in the Western world, what we mean by "change" could only be framed until that century of enlightenment by way of reform. That is, restoration of old virtues, as only moral values could be imagined. The very idea of novelty did not even exist. In the most extreme circumstances, innovation was possible in statecraft if something "new" was similar to an undisputable model from the past. The influential Spanish

---

soil. In the course of time Cain brought some of the fruits of the soil as an offering to the LORD. And Abel also brought an offering—fat portions from some of the firstborn of his flock. The LORD looked with favor on Abel and his offering ... Now Cain said to his brother Abel, 'Let's go out to the field.' While they were in the field, Cain attacked his brother Abel and killed him" (*Genesis*, 4); "The classical Greeks did not have the concept of evil; for Christians, evil is the central category of human existence," Pal W. Kahn, *Out of Eden. Adam and Eve and the Problem of Evil* (Princeton: Princeton University Press, 2007), 3.
[3] Marc Ferro, *Resentment in History* (London: Polity Press, 2010), 21.

"Dictionary" of Covarrubias (1611) defined "novelty" as "something new and non accustomed, it is usually dangerous because it implies a change of old custom."[4] "Real" life was eternal, and life in this world a mere transit. Everybody was given a place at birth by God, and it was forever with the exception of "His" decision to take direct and mysterious action in human history by means of providentialism. That is, an election to provide and confront errors and sins through direct action and concrete actors. Conformity was something natural. Social mobility was related to the acceptance of rules and justice as an individual aspiration could be fulfilled, if any, through the mercy of the powerful or negotiations of loyalty. If it was not obtained in this world due to sinning, or the misconception or misinformation of kings and judges, in the next life God would no doubt provide adequate compensation (or punishment). Even in the extreme case of slaves, resentment was separated from the narrative of change, a problem of the human condition, but not of objects. Such emotion was usually considered (and punished) as excess of pride or haughtiness. They were affected by lack of rationality, moral weakness and natural inferiority. As the "benevolent" Marquise of Yolombó puts it in a Colombian novel by Tomás de Carrasquilla (1858–1940), coming from oral sources, slaves were negligent and unhappy, set apart from moral progress, ready to attend her compassion.[5]

Revolts, *jacqueries* and mutinies were, first and utmost, an offence against God and the natural order of the world, an act of madness. Sometimes, explanations and remedies due to the mercy of kings and queens could arrive, but always after the restoration of order had been achieved. It is important to take into account that the *post factum* narrative of revolts in the *Ancien Regime* saved the role of the monarchs. "Long live to the king, down with bad government" was commonly shouted in revolts in Europe and the Americas between 1500 and 1800. Ministers and officers were always guilty, not kings, although social contract could be affected if they had forgotten his sacred duties governing through favourites or "*validos.*" In other words, kings, if well-informed, were expected to be fair; if not, justice in the

---

[4] Sebastián de Covarrubias, *Tesoro de la lengua castellana o española* (Madrid: Luis Sánchez, 1611), 565; Alvarez de Miranda, Pedro, *Palabras e ideas: el léxico de la ilustración temprana en España, 1680–1760* (Madrid: Real Academia Española, 1992), 621.
[5] Ángela Uribe Botero, *Perfiles del mal en la historia de Colombia* (Bogotá: Universidad Nacional, 2007), 129.

next life would be fulfilled. Despots, however, were sinners by definition.

Revolutions happened in the stars and the planets, not on earth. In the narrative of political change, injustice, sin, corruption or greed uncover what would in modern times be resentment. Bad government was the result of the breakdown of a wise and divine monarchy, the only fair form of government as dictated by God, due to the passing of time and the weakness of human nature. Some cases of tyranny could even justify the killing of the tyrant by good Christians, roughly the argument for the murder of the Jesuit father Mariana (1536–1624), one of the most celebrated, indeed prosecuted, political philosophers of the Spanish Golden Age. In *De Rege et Regis Institutione,* published in Toledo in 1599, he justified (and explained) the unthinkable—"the capricious will of the king and the desires of the few" provided an excuse.[6]

The fascination in the Renaissance with figures like Emperor Nero exhibits the absolute madness of absolute power, but, as goes the moral tale, he was punished. He was helped to commit suicide by his secretary Epaphroditus, just before new authorities arrived. Tradition and common sense restored order. The killing of a king represents in this context the "impossible resentment" of the *Ancien Regime* as something inconceivable. Take the case of Henry IV of France, murdered in the streets of Paris on May 14, 1610. He takes a carriage to visit Sully the minister to check the decoration for the arrival of the queen, Mary of Medici. In the Rue de la Ferronnerie, a mob stops them, and a red haired man stabs the king. In Mexico, on the other side of the world, Domingo de San Antón Chimalpahin, an Indian author of a diary in nahuátl, the language of the Aztecs, explains that the killer was a servant: "To kill the king he gave him a letter and then stabbed him in the neck. Nobody knows why."[7] François Ravaillac killed the king, it came to be known, because he wanted to save France from the Huguenots. He was tortured, burnt with lead and sulphur, and dismembered, his body turned to ashes. But what is important for a history of emotions is the interpretation by Catholics of his behaviour as insane, in a global sense. His resentment was not conceivable, and far less explained or justified what he did.

---

[6] Harald Braun, *Juan de Mariana and Early Modern Spanish Political Thought* (London: Ashgate, 2007), 56.
[7] Serge Gruzinski, *Les Quatre Parties du Monde. Histoire d'une Mondialisation* (Paris: Editions de La Martinière, 2004), 23.

Changes in Ideas about Liberty

By the end of the seventeenth century, the so-called "Battle of the books" in England, the *"Querelle"* of the Ancients and the Moderns in France, and the discussions about the *"novatores"* or lovers of the new in Spain, changed once and for all the framework of political virtues and languages. If the pre-eminence of Ancient Greeks and Romans over the "people of an enlightened age" was no longer accepted, tradition would not be venerated in the same fashion as before. Everything was put into discussion in a century with a public sphere for the first time in history. Ancients were not necessarily wiser than moderns, it seemed, and did not provide an indisputable model. At least, not without proper comparisons in time and space, and debates in academies and publications in different languages. The evaluation of the present as a time for optimism and progress, the victory of the modern, destroyed the tradition of the imitation of classics as the only source to establish a fair political regime. Something really new could be imagined, and the political meaning of revolution—out of the stars, but on earth—began to be conceived. If imitation of tradition was not an obligation, and the modern was a "dwarf on the shoulders of ancient giants," out of tradition, revolution was possible. There was a virtuous past but a present could be conceived out of imitation. In practical terms, for sure, consequences took time to be seen, but the replacement of monarchies and republics was suddenly a possibility. In this context, resentment opened up a new "modern" emotional space, a "second nature" necessary for the relocation of relations between political agents.[8]

The age of resentment had begun by 1750, a key element in the explanation of the justice and opportunity of any cause. As none other than Nietzche puts it, a "vendetta spirituale" was ready to serve social mobility.[9] From then on, resentment conveyed individuality, built up public opinions, or expressed the aspirations of political communities. Resentment explains revolution, working as a self-fulfilling prophecy to justify destruction of traditions and any previous *status quo*. Revolution invented historical and social discontinuity,[10] but it must be taken into account that generalizations are difficult. At least three different

---

[8] Marc Angenot, *Les ideologies du ressentiment* (Montreal, XYZ Éditeur, 1997), 17.

[9] Luisa Villa, *Figure del Risentimento. Aspetti della costruzione del sogetto nella narrativa inglese ai margini della "decadenza"* (Pisa: ETS, 1997), 18.

[10] Kevin M. F. Platt, *History in a Grotesque Key. Russian Literature and the Idea of Revolution* (Stanford: Stanford University Press, 1997), 187.

meanings of liberty were established at the time of the Atlantic revolutions. In a classic historiographical definition, it is the period of foundation of political liberties in the Western world. It goes from the independence of United States in 1776, to the French Revolution, the Haitian Revolution that ended in 1804, and the revolutions of independence in Spanish and Portuguese America which ended in 1824, including the peaceful independence of Brazil.[11]

First there was the liberty of ancient Greece and Rome, defined as the right to elect governments and magistrates, obviously an attribution of a very small number of citizens and "paterfamilias." In an Atlantic context, this "ancient liberty" was often explained with reference to an origin in a European political community, a kingdom, city-state, or republic, destroyed by despotism. The pilgrims who "founded" the United States, even the conquistadores of Spanish America, all first colonists, were the source of such an idea of liberty. The difference in the place of origin after a couple of generations was important, because it gave a sense of location and a difference in genealogy. The reference was European, but American too. In the construction of resentment as a political revolutionary emotion, it marked the beginning of a new narrative. Europeans would have "betrayed" their liberties of ancient times. Nonetheless, in the Americas was born an opportunity for freedom as well as happiness. By 1775, "widespread belief in the idea of a lineal right to liberty, begun in the ancient republics and passed through generations of free-spirited Britons," was being left behind. "Ministerial butchers" and mongrels were alien to "a true English spirit."[12] In order to save this spirit, another political, independent, entity had to be established in the colonies.

Secondly, there was the definition of liberty of the estates connected to specific laws and prerogatives of corporations, merchant guilds, military personnel, nobles and priests. Liberties proper of institutions, typical in what is now called "civil society," do not explain the change in the status of resentment after 1750. However, it must be said that new political agents, men and women, had in corporations, clubs or "Sociétés des Amis" a unique place to plot and fabricate resentment in a scale never seen before. Political parties appeared at that time. Finally,

---

[11] Jacques Godechot & Robert R. Palmer, "Le problème de l'Atlantique du XVIIIe. au XXe. Siècle," in *Actas del X Congreso Internacional de Ciencias Históricas*, vol. 5. Storia contemporanea (Florence: IAHS, 1955), 173–239.

[12] Nicole Eustace, *Passion is the Gale. Emotion, Power and the Coming of the American Revolution* (Williamsburg: University of North Carolina Press, 2008), 431.

there was the sense of modern liberties connected to new sovereign entities—representative government, the separation of powers, division between the public and the private, elections, constitutions, the definition of citizenship and equality under the law. All this was the result of revolutions, but at the same time the product and the proof of the success of new definitions of resentment.

Revolutions at Work

"The throwing off of those who would treat us as slaves"—Jefferson's account of revolution explains the sense of sacrificial act that founds a political order.[13] Although the emotional history of revolutions is a matter of research and a work in progress, the classical theory of revolutions applied to the Atlantic World helps us to understand the importance of resentment as a key element in their results. In fact, I would argue that resentment was the prevalent emotion, especially at the beginning of political changes. It is the emotion that provides a sense of undisputed justice. It conveys separation from tradition and the justification of a new political time as an aspiration of order out of despotism. Whether in the United States, France, Haiti, or Spanish and Portuguese America, revolutions began after a reformist period. In a period of growth in population, opportunities declined and social mobility decayed. Aristocratic luxuries were displayed to an insane scale in courts and extravagant palaces. Austerity was not fashionable for courtiers. At the same time, especially between urban and educated classes—small plantation owners and *petit blancs* in Saint Domingue, lawyers and Creole preachers in Spanish America, artisans and shopkeepers in Massachusetts, craftsmen, teachers, doctors and lawyers in provincial France—there was a common feeling. New and unfair forms of taxation were destroying their way of life and corrupting their hope in the future.[14] It must be said that reforms were an ambivalent experiment. It was the *Ancien Regime* learning from experience, changing what was needed to stay the same. After the end of the Seven Years War in 1763, reformers in Great Britain, France and Spain, coming from a cosmopolitan and bureaucratic elite, mostly with "nobility of merit" of bourgeois origin, but without much in the way of resources or wealth, tended to make general accusations of laziness or corruption against older, local and aristocratic elites. The changes in the

---

[13] Kahn, *Out of Eden*, 169.

[14] Philip G. Nord, *The Politics of Resentment. Shopkeeper Protest in Nineteenth Century Paris* (New Brunswick: Transaction, 2005), 9.

use of language prepared the revolutions. A number of American and French revolutionaries announced that "their revolutions would regenerate their respective languages and that their regenerated language would contribute to the regeneration of society."[15] Before revolutions, reformers tried to solve the financial problems by negotiating rules, social status and taxation. Their criticism of the past to justify new rules and measures opened up a door to express resentment as a way of serving monarchies and kings. By the end of the 1770s, as the situation deteriorated, corrupt governments tended to be seen as the norm. But to what extent did failed reforms produce revolutions in the Atlantic context?

No doubt there was a glorious moment for resentment in all revolutions. In the French revolution, Camille Desmoulins mocks and denounces the atmosphere of general suspicion linked to the victory of resentment, borrowing from Tacitus:

> Does a citizen enjoy a certain popularity? He is a rival of the prince, who could ignite a civil war—Suspect.
> Does he, on the contrary, flee popularity and keep to himself? This retired way of life makes you noticeable, makes people treat you with respect—Suspect.
> Are you rich? There is an imminent danger of the people being corrupted by your generosity—Suspect.
> Are you poor? Well, then, we have got to keep an eye on this man. There is nobody so enterprising as someone who has nothing—Suspect.[16]

Before such a situation, related to the "radical period" of revolutions, resentment found a means of expression through certain typologies of documents. The so-called "memorials of grievances" expressed and ignited the first stages of revolutions, characterized as a succession of reform, privileged revolt, moderate period, radical period, counter-revolution and dictatorship. It served to fabricate the case of the deposition of ministers or governors. In some cases of extreme violence, collective acts of sadism and brutality were justified. One famous case in the French revolution was the killing of the Princess of Lambaye, a friend of queen Marie Antoinette, and as she was so hated she was executed, her body dismembered and the head shown to the multitude on a pike. In Spain in 1808 such grievances against governors

---

[15] Mathew Lawzon, *Signs of Light. French and British Theories of Linguistic Communication, 1648–1789* (Ithaca: Cornell University Press, 2010), 217.
[16] Ferro, *Resentment*, 29.

famously produced serial depositions followed with the body of the victims dragged in the streets until death.[17] In the bureaucratic tradition of the *Ancien Regime*, memorials of grievances were expositions of acts of injustice deserving retribution. It was not in any sense a revolutionary document, but the negotiation of a pact, an appeal for justice and restoration of order. It was not about a radical change, but about conservation. The declaration of independence of the United States in 1776 can be seen as the expression of such grievances, but no doubt at the same time it is one of the first documents in history expressing new, revolutionary, resentment. Patriot leaders made a solemn declaration and established: "a vehement brand of emotion that burnished the power of passion." The process of elevation of resentment to patriotic duty turned resentful arguments into sacred texts: "The spirit of liberty arose from the careful blend of genteel feeling and popular passion. Consisting of a heavy blend of civic love, mighty anger, and communal sympathy and public grief ... Liberty belonged to all American citizens."[18]

It is interesting to contemplate the influence of the declaration of independence of the United States, not as a document related to the will of constitutional liberty, but as a case of ambivalent narrative and traditional opposition to despotism. Take the case of the Viceroyalty of New Granada. Camilo Torres (1766–1816) was in 1809 an obscure lawyer from a province, "born in a distinguished family, although poor." He wrote a text in the name of the city of Santafe de Bogota, a report about unfulfilled promises, crisis and despotism. He included a reference to the mischievous conduct of the British monarchy towards the American subjects to explain the independence that, according to the ideas of the text, could have been avoided.[19]

In the case of Spanish America, the government of "ministerial despotism," with favourite Manuel Godoy (1792–1808) as prime minister, included the propagation of resentment. The Haitian case was different. The beginning of the revolution of slaves against their masters (85% of the population in French Saint-Domingue by 1790) came, as always, with a disillusion about justice. After July 1789 in Paris, a

---

[17] José María Cardesín, "Motín y magnicidio en la Guerra de independencia: La voz de "arrastrar" como modelo de violencia colectiva," *Historia Social* 62 (2008): 27–47.

[18] Eustace, *Passion,* 387.

[19] Camilo Torres, *Representación del cabildo de Bogotá, capital del Nuevo Reino de Granada, a la suprema junta central de España en el año de 1809* (Bogotá: Imprenta de N. Lora, 1832), 4.

rumour extended in the plantations. The "good" king of France Louis XVIII, a father for his slaves, decided to set them free, but the owners of the plantations, *grand blanc et petit blanc*, did not want to obey. Some Jamaican slaves, dangerous and organized people, plotted a revolt to begin in Bois Caiman on August 14, 1791. It was the beginning of the revolution, with ethnic resentment on an unprecedented scale. Blacks against whites, mulattoes against whites and blacks, whites against mulattoes, in a guerrilla war which, for some authors, resembles the holocaust due to the industrial scale of the killings. This ended in 1804 with the foundation of Haiti.[20]

What happened with resentment in the radical stages of Atlantic revolutions? No doubt it was used to justify some of the politics we now call "ethnic cleansing." The resentment "produced during centuries of injustice" justified the expulsion or killing of peninsular Spanish in Venezuela, or Portuguese in Brazil. The last whites were killed in Haiti after the "machete war" between blacks and mulattoes. The regime of terror in France has been seen as a kingdom of resentment, the world upside down, the victory of bad emotions, murder and killing, out of any sense of justice. The famous (or infamous) Charlotte Corday, after her killing of Jean-Paul Marat in July 1793, was asked about her motives. She talked about a sense of justice, of revenge. Resentment was not an emotion of revolutionaries, of course. According to her declarations, she cautiously kept in her soul the will for revenge and killed him "to save thousands." The Corday case gives us a glimpse into the evolution of resentment in revolution. The organization of revolutionary regimes and instability change the social conditions of resentment, and it turns out to be revolutionary ideology at work, once and for all.

Conclusions

In the age of Atlantic revolutions, from the independence of the United States in 1776 to the French Revolution in 1789, for the Haitian Revolution and the foundation of the first "Black republic of the world" in 1804, or the independence of Portuguese and Spanish America, concluded in 1824, resentment was a prevalent political emotion. Certainly, in the *Ancien regime* there was a channel to express resentment without breaking the rules. The foundational tradition of the

---

[20] Laurent Dubois, *A Colony of Citizens. Revolution and Slave Emancipation in the French Caribbean, 1787–1804* (Williamsburg: University of New Carolina Press, 2004), 85.

"memorial of grievances" expressed a fault in the social contract through the actions of unfair rulers. The declaration of the independence of the United States was a memorial of grievances and sufferings of the colonists under the government of the British King George III. It is the first document with elements of modern, revolutionary resentment. Rebellion was organized and justified to make justice, but tradition was still there. The king broke the contract, the Atlantic constitution of the British Empire. In the end, political independence was obtained in 1783. The virtuous foundation of a republic of planters and traders did not affect the social model; on the contrary, it was reinforced. The French revolution was a different matter; strong social issues were in the agenda.

Between 1789 and 1793, the revolution was against the king, the aristocrats, and the rich.[21] Violence and revenge were justified by resentment, an emotion in principle appropriated by revolutionaries, and then by those opposed to changes, counter-revolutionaries and, when defined as political movement, the so-called "ultramontanes," very modern in their approach to emotions in politics. The Haitian case was different because on the other side of the Atlantic ethnicity was a key element. Resentment could not explain anything, because nothing was in need of explanation for rebel slaves or their masters. Social mobility or negotiation did not exist in proper sense, although there was a small group of free (and rich) mulattoes. Finally, resentment in the revolutions of independence of Spanish and Portuguese America was based on a combination of political and social issues. On the one hand, it served the Creole elites, after the imperial crisis in the centre, to explain and justify a rebellion against the peninsular government, and after a period of time against the king and the monarchy. This Creole resentment was related to supposedly postponements and injustices. On the other hand it served mixed races, free blacks, slaves and poor whites, to convey their political aspirations to social, and not only political changes. Brothers would not be brothers any more, but enemies, because resentment destroyed once and for all the fiction of social stability.

---

[21] Ferro, *Resentment,* 20.

Works Cited

Alvarez de Miranda, Pedro. *Palabras e ideas: el léxico de la ilustración temprana en España, 1680–1760.* Madrid: Real Academia Española, 1992.

Angenot, Marc. *Les ideologies du ressentiment.* Montreal, XYZ Éditeur, 1997.

Anghelescu, Hermina, G. B. Tucker & John Marck (eds.). *Libraries Culture. Historical Essays Honoring the Legacy of Donald G. Davis Jr.* Washington: Library of Congress, Center for the Book, 2006.

Braun, Harald. *Juan de Mariana and Early Modern Spanish Political Thought.* London: Ashgate, 2007.

Cardesín, José María. "'Motín y magnicidio en la Guerra de independencia: La voz de "arrastrar" como modelo de violencia colectiva." *Historia Social* 62 (2008): 27–47.

Dubois, Laurent. *A Colony of Citizens. Revolution and Slave Emancipation in the French Caribbean, 1787–1804.* Williamsburg: University of New Carolina Press, 2004.

Eustace, Nicole. *Passion is the Gale. Emotion, Power and the Coming of the American Revolution.* Williamsburg: University of North Carolina Press, 2008.

Ferro, Marc. *Resentment in History.* London: Polity Press, 2010.

Godechot, Jacques & Palmer, Robert R. "Le problème de l'Atlantique du XVIIIe. au XXe. Siècle." In *Actas del X Congreso Internacional de Ciencias Históricas,* vol. 5. Storia contemporanea, 173–239. Florence: IAHS, 1955.

Gruzinski, Serge. *Les Quatre Parties du Monde. Histoire d'une Mondialisation.* Paris: Editions de La Martinière, 2004.

Lawzon, Mathew. *Signs of Light. French and British Theories of Linguistic Communication, 1648–1789.* Ithaca: Cornell University Press, 2010.

Kahn Pal W. *Out of Eden. Adam and Eve and the Problem of Evil.* Princeton: Princeton University Press, 2007.

Nord, Philip G. *The Politics of Resentment. Shopkeeper Protest in Nineteenth Century Paris.* New Brunswick: Transaction, 2005.

Platt, Kevin M. F. *History in a Grotesque Key. Russian Literature and the Idea of Revolution.* Stanford: Stanford University Press, 1997.

Torres, Camilo. *Representación del cabildo de Bogotá, capital del Nuevo Reino de Granada, a la suprema junta central de España en el año de 1809.* Bogotá: Imprenta de N. Lora, 1832.

Uribe Botero, Ángela. *Perfiles del mal en la historia de Colombia.* Bogotá: Universidad Nacional, 2007.

Villa, Luisa. *Figure del Risentimento. Aspetti della costruzione del sogetto nella narrativa inglese ai margini della "decadenza."* Pisa: ETS, 1997.

CHAPTER ELEVEN

ARTIFICIAL HATRED[1]

JAVIER ORDÓÑEZ

Dangerous Emotions

War seems to exploit a large reservoir of emotions. To some extent, wars operate as managers of different kinds of emotions, although it is easy to make the mistake of imagining war only as a catalyst for emotional sacrifice. It is true that much of its legitimizing rhetoric is expressed in terms of heroism, dedication, sacrifice, the need to give one's life for a cause, juxtaposed with the terminology of revenge, hatred and retaliation. However, the roots of war are not just emotional. Nevertheless, this chapter is going to explore some of the emotions that underlie the development of war. Often, resentment is suggested as one of the possible conditions that may nourish a war, and those who analyze the origins of such conflicts generally have good reasons to consider this to be so. However, to understand the wars of the twentieth century, resentment is perhaps too insubstantial emotion, and it was found necessary to intensify it. The societies involved in these conflicts substituted the natural, instinctive and rather shallow resentments with a powerful emotional chemistry, in the same way that in an ersatz culture the natural is replaced by the artificial. This chapter, part of a broad investigation into the origins of modern war, introduces some of the basic concepts of this viewpoint.

[1] This study is an outcome of the research project *Wars and Norms*, which is being undertaken at the Max Planck Institut for the History of Science (Berlin), and by the Research Project "Historical Epistemology: History of Emotions and Emotional Communities in the 19th and 20th Centuries," supported by the Ministry of Science and Innovation, Spanish Government.

On the Concept of War

If we are permitted to provisionally blur the boundaries between the concepts which express the qualities of nature and those which belong to the sphere of culture, or, better still, if we are allowed to situate them in the same category so that culture permeates nature, then we can establish some affinities between concepts such as heat and war.

Following Bachelard's suggestions,[2] we would say that both of them are too close to us, in the sense that they are internally incorporated and that they live within us. We do not see ourselves as capable of sufficiently detaching ourselves from these two concepts in order to view them with clarity. Due to this, heat was the last general physical effect to be incorporated into the physical sciences, and similarly we endeavour to talk about war as little as possible because mentioning it tends to invoke it. On few occasions has war been the material for direct reflection in classical writers' philosophical works. War soon became the first uncomfortable truth.

We will leave the parallel here with one last point—up until the nineteenth century it was believed that little could be known about heat because our bodies are thermal systems and any measurement of the heat of bodies would include our own body heat, which would contaminate the measurement, creating more doubts than certainties. The same occurs when we attempt to talk about war. We find that our language and culture is full of bellicose expressions and references; war is disseminated in our language in such a way that we appear to be incapable of ridding ourselves of it. Given that it is present within our language, there is the temptation to cite the inevitability of war as a manifestation of our intrinsic or natural tendency towards it. Facing this conviction, the point of view which this chapter will maintain defends the benefits of talking about war, perhaps to distance it from the world of events which we consider to be inevitable.

Taxonomies

Therefore, let us talk about war. Leaving to one side the number of expressions alluding to war within our daily language, when we go in search of past and present wars in order to reflect upon them, we find that they proliferate in number and typology. To create a natural history of wars would be little short of impossible if criteria were not established,

---

[2] Bachelard, Gaston *Etude sur l'évolution d'un problème de physique: la propagation thermique dans les solides* (Paris: Vrin, 1928), 9.

albeit basic ones, to help us differentiate between them. One criterion that is often used is that which considers wars according to their admissibility; making a distinction between just and unjust wars. This distinction expresses the character of wars well; the same war can be just and unjust depending on the point of view of the respective sides. In the majority of instances, it is clear that no contender accepts that they have provoked an unjust war, and all victors assume that they have won because theirs was the just cause. As there is rarely a neutral arbiter to determine whether a war is just or unjust, and this discussion tends not to issues of justice but of legality. As a result, matters such as whether a preventative war is legal or not are considered, and parliaments debate over the legality of actions which can be carried out in the context of war. Perhaps it would be better to accept that there is no such thing as a just war; that all are unjust and that war is precisely the scenario in which unjust actions are performed.

This chapter attempts to contribute some suggestions regarding the possible classifications of wars. What if an emotional criterion was proposed instead of a legal one? It would only serve to characterise them, it is true, but perhaps it would be of use, or perhaps no more useless than other criteria. Our objective would be to analyse war according to the emotions which either made them possible or which directly caused them, focussing on enthusiasm, resentment and fear, all of which are emotions present in war.

Temporal Horizons

It is advisable to not expect to categorise history in its entirety. It is certain that wars have grown and developed at the same time as culture. Given that war represents one of the most radical and profound behavioural features of the human species it is better not to take it as a whole. It is radical because it forms part of our way of confronting, not the world, but our own fellow human beings; it is profound because its contemplation immerses us in an abyss from which we often do not know how to emerge. War grows alongside us, feeds off us and, at the same time, we feed it with the forms of our culture. If history is conceived as progress, without doubt war progresses with us. All of the indicators which chart an improvement in our standard of living in terms of health, education and employment could also be used to signal the good health of war which, up to a certain point, is one of the most significant demonstrations of our culture. Therefore, we have to look for the changes in the character of war in the same places where cultural changes are produced. In the same way that we are inheritors of political, social and ethical values conceived and introduced during the French revolution, we can search there for modifications in the way of waging wars.

Fourcroy's words are eloquent proof of this new philosophy of war:

> The war is a barbarism of kings, and it is only fair for a people to recover their rights with their freedom. The war has become for the French Republic a fortunate occasion to develop all the power of its arts, to realize the genius of scholars and artists, and to consecrate their usefulness in ingenious ways.[3]

The Republic could wage a legitimate war precisely due to its capacity to cultivate the arts and sciences, and because a society of citizens possesses the right to enter a war—not a natural right, but a "cultural" one. In this text, the origin of the legitimisation of many of the colonial wars can be found, which were waged as civilising military campaigns. But we can also find the seed of a new form of resentment, introduced during the wars carried out by the French Republic and the Napoleonic Empire.

Emotions

There is a difference between the emotions that cause a war and those produced by war. Wars involve human groups—entire societies, kingdoms, states, alliances. They are not conflicts between individuals but between collective groups, and individual emotions cannot be transferred directly to the collective. An eloquent example is that of fear; individuals' fear of death, or the fear of soldiers in battle, citizens' fears of being wounded in military campaigns—none of these classes of fear cause or maintain a war. The fear which causes a war can be named a "Delian fear," or a fear of the state. Thucydides [1881, par 84–116][4] explains that in the Peloponnesian wars, Athens asked the inhabitants of Melos to join the alliance it was leading, but the Milians declined the request as they wanted to remain neutral. Subsequently, Athens decided to annihilate the city due to the fear that this example would spread amongst other cities in the alliance. Athens' fear was a fear of the state. This fear can be found in many decisions of war, but it appears in a particular way in the same

---

[3] Fourcroy, Antoine-François 1794 *Texte du Rapport et projet de decret de Fourcroy du 7 vendémiaire an III (28 de septembre 1794)* (Paris: Imprimerie du Comité de Salut Publique, 1794), 32

[4] Thucydides, *History of the Peloponnesian War*, Benjamin Jowett, Ed. Volume 1 (Oxford: Clarendon Press, 1881), 84–116

period that I have previously mentioned, in the transition from the nineteenth to the twentieth century. At that point the Athenian's words gained their full import[5]: "But you and we should say what we really think, and aim only at what is possible, for we both alike know that in the discussion of human affairs the question of justice only enters where there is equal power to enforce it, and that the powerful exact what they can, and the weak grant what they must."

Emotions do not present themselves as isolated in the theatre of war. They are dominated by the enthusiasm to believe that the civilising cause is just in such a way that a certain harmony is produced between exaltation and resentment, between the jubilation of the civilising enterprise on the one hand, and on the other the irritation of the citizens who are offended by their treatment as vassals wanting to be finally liberated from the affront which pushed them into submission. This relation between war and resentment is not new for anyone who knows the work of Marc Ferro. However, it is convenient to differentiate periods where the action of resentment turns out to be much more efficient for the maintenance of the conflict. Sometimes it happens that, as much in the past as in the present, bellic conflicts between groups are created that have a profound axiological asymmetry, different social values and different categories of emotions. A clear example is the Napoleonic wars where different emotional value systems confronted one another. Not only were the armies that faced each other different but also the adversary towns, which we call "civilians," felt different emotions with respect to the war. It was a period of transition which culminated in a process of identification which we now denominate as a national process. It could be said that at the same time that the revolutionary conquest *par excellence*—the metric decimal system of French origin—was being disseminated throughout Europe, the emotions that made war possible were being normalised. In short, resentment was normalised. The resentments became similar and for this reason it is so surprising that the colonial ventures, the foreign interventions of European countries, are valid, including the Americans' campaigns in their own territory. Science, technology and resentment are three ingredients that create empires. In this case the resentment could be light or from reasons looked for by the contenders, which occurred in the opium wars or the US intervention in Japan, but it is not advisable to eliminate this third factor.

---

[5] Thucydides, *History of the Peloponnesian War*, 89.

Colonies and Nations

Perhaps the emotions of war that dominate the nineteenth-century can be said to be enthusiasm and resentment. Both thrived on the revolutionary fervours which sporadically took root in Europe and America. Enthusiasm stemmed from the excitement of feeling a sense of belonging to a nation, and resentment was due to nations' antipathy towards the other nations who were limiting their own growth. Nothing new, one would think, given that this dynamic had existed before, and it would have been an old dynamic if it had taken place in societies which did not look at the heart of their culture, if they had not believed that technological and scientific development legitimised their superiority. Other emotional agglutinations had certainly occurred in the past. For example, monotheistic religions had always projected the emotion of enthusiasm in the form of divine delirium in their groups of believers, which led to protracted and cruel wars. In the first decades of the nineteenth century, the Germanic countries still recalled the Thirty Years' War which eliminated at least a third of the inhabitants of those countries. However, in the nineteenth century enthusiasms were kindled that were either new or that possessed a renewed passion to form new nations or to legitimise the old ones. On some occasions this spirit produced centrifugal movements and desegregations from the old political systems, such as the creation of the mosaic of nations in the Balkans and in Eastern Europe, and the independence movements in the old Spanish viceroyalties in America. On other occasions, this eagerness resulted in centripetal movements which tended towards the creation of new nations on the memories of the old empires, as was the case with Italy and Germany.

The principal political parties—the most powerful ones amongst those born in this movement—cultivated a form of war that was fundamentally colonial, if this does not stop the internal political conflicts from being called wars. Emotions are not the only cause of the wars, it is certain, but they always accompany bellicose developments. In the colonial wars of the nineteenth century, the metropolises used the question of honour as *casus belli* with frequency, at least as an explicit *casus belli*, where the offences were caused to their own citizens or to the governments that sent envoys. To not receive an ambassador, to humiliate them, or to maltreat a citizen of the empire was considered to be just cause to provoke a conflict. It may be that there were underlying political and economic causes to provoke a colonial war, but the public trigger, that which would be wielded before the empire's people, often had an emotional nature. Great humiliation and wounded dignity would be caused if the European empires failed in trade negotiations with distant towns, and matters such as this formed part of the rhetoric of internal political discussions. Perhaps it is not necessary to mention all the nations that were implicated in this process, but it is not sufficient to simply talk of the British, the French and the Dutch, as the Germans and the Italians also participated in the colonial wars, and the Russian empire did not stay on the sidelines either. Even a new country such as Belgium managed to procure a fragment of Africa, although it was only as a direct property of the king. The old Baroque empires of Spain and Portugal developed into small empires which desired to maintain an international presence. The political doctrines which allowed the colonial campaigns employed the patriotic emotions to assert their cultural superiority. Victorian Parliamentary discourse is an eloquent example of this attitude. The emerging united states of North America advocated the Monroe doctrine, which used the previous colonies' resentment to propose a form of liberation and leadership, which established itself as a control of North America's new power.

Not many problems arose while this was a foreign matter, and frictions between the empires provoked few foreign conflicts. In the interior of Europe, political parties employed a French style of patriotic reinforcement, using the amalgamation of jubilation and resentment born from past problems of competition between regions. Sharing history during centuries always creates wells of resentment at one's disposal, which are frequently capable of provoking a conflict, but without doubt the empires were emotional escape valves. Some of them were bad businesses with reference to their economies, but they were very good forms of founding emotional projects. What was learned in the colonial wars? Apart from the importance of technical and scientific knowledge as tools of command, it was the ability to consider the enemy as a true alien, which did not necessarily prompt the desire for restraint. The result was that authentic massacres could be caused by acting on a superiority manifested by the technological resources. There are many examples of this disregard for life, but it is enough to mention that the first occasion in which grenades were launched from an aeroplane were dropped on civilians, in a skirmish carried out by the Italian army in Africa in 1909. This is only one symptom, but an illustrative one.

The Birth of Hatred

Resentment is characterised by history as a possible source of war. However, when looked at in depth, resentment is too volatile to explain what happened in those societies which were apparently too refined, too cultured, too scientific, and too embellished with all of the virtues of reason to enter into long, destructive and enormously cruel wars, such as those which occurred in the twentieth century. There were previous examples which could have enabled this cruelty to be predicted, such as the American civil war and the Franco-Prussian war. Attention could also be drawn to the new guests to assume the Western axiology, such as the Meiji empire, which knew how to effectively exploit resentment during the Russo-Japanese war and during the wars between Japan and China.

In order to study the many nuances of resentment which played a part in the Great War it is necessary to highlight the force with which it became entrenched in civil society. Previously, I have referred to the volatility of collective resentments. In reality, they are emotions which in their collective form prove to be fickle and of little lasting strength. This is how civil populations have behaved in wars throughout the course of history, although examples can always be brought to mind which demonstrate the adhesion of a certain group to a constant idea. There are examples, but they are not typical—in general, societies have gone wherever the wind of opportunity has blown them, and resentments have switched sides as much as loyalties. It is interesting to confirm that, during the course of the nineteenth century, resentments grew at the same rate as the increase in the wealth of communities, and the idea of identification, fundamental for resentment "against the other," was fossilised, becoming heavier, denser and more concrete. It became necessary that the patriot not only loved as expressed in the revolutionary songs of Paris at the end of the seventeenth century (I refer to the late eighteenth century in the French Revolution), but also that they hated, or at least that were willing to hate.

It has been frequently emphasised that the Great War was perversely related with the colonial wars of the preceding century. According to this perspective, it was a confrontation between potential colonies which applied the strategies of their past wars, but this time amongst themselves. In this sense, and only in this sense, it was a perfect war—there was no asymmetry at the starting point, as had occurred in previous wars. There was no nemesis which terrified the enemies with the mere presence of a technological superiority. Perfect in its symmetry, the Great War did not bring armies but societies into conflict and its consequences transformed them until they were beyond recognition. The casualness with which the first enlistments were carried out, emptying industries and universities, as much in the islands as on the continent, suggested that this would be a short conflict with a negotiated end, as if it were another colonial war. However, the rapidity with which the military resources, prepared over decades, ran out, and the frequency with which the carefully laid plans of the larger states failed (always underestimating the duration of the invasions into the adversary's territory) changed the nature of the war, which became unexpectedly difficult and gruelling. Six months after starting the conflict, the progress of the war was so bogged down that the war in the trenches became the perfect metaphor for the conflict itself. Entire societies were within those trenches; the frontiers were expressed there and the conflict became a global one. Even Costa Rica, a country without an army, entered the war, declaring itself in support of the Central Powers, the German and Austrian empires. The war was no longer a military question but a civil one, and it was necessary to boost society's feelings of resentment in order to conserve people's willingness to carry out sacrifices. Therefore, in the same way that they had prepared their armies, political leaders manipulated their societies, by encouraging resentment to become hatred: using it as a social weapon, an antipathy always on call.

Resentment can be a diffuse emotion, as can enthusiasm, and as such one that is quite contagious. However, hatred is an extreme form of resentment, with a more radical expression, and as contaminating as any emotion can be that can draw in groups or "masses," a term which would be used in the first decades of the twentieth century to express the form of a society of identical beings, who wholeheartedly embrace the lack of a singular denomination. The process of the transformation of those citizens who had been full of revolutionary fervour to individuals who desired above all to subsume their identity in the collective group had taken place throughout the course of the century. In the following points, I will try to analyse the characteristics of this hatred; the most powerful weapon of those societies which participated in the conflict.

The Chemistry of Emotions, or Emotions as a Social Chemistry

Perhaps the most immediate lesson learned in the Great War was that its cruelty was conceived outside of the trenches, in civil society. As much as the war was global, it took place intensely in very determined spaces, such as the battle lines that were established on the European continent for months, in some cases for years, whilst the seas became the location of the first war waged against civilians. However, the cruelty was not forged in these settings but in the adversaries' political and social spaces. In this way, all the societies which had played a leading role in scientific and technological developments confronted one another; they were proud of these developments and considered themselves to be the apex of civilisation. Furthermore, such developments were often considered to be linked to the supposed collective characteristics of these societies called nations. Even today, there is still this tendency to talk of knowledge according to supposed national capacities, as if determined communities were naturally gifted in the development of specific scientific knowledge.

Amongst all of the knowledge inherited in the eighteenth century, chemistry has been the language most used to exemplify emotions. Who does not remember the theoretical problem of the "elective affinities" which served as a bank of metaphors to explain chemical reactions, in other words, the tendency of substances to combine with some determined substances and not with others? There appeared to be within nature a "love" and a "rejection" in the same way as could be observed between humans; the propensity to love or to dislike, causing attraction or repulsion, or even indifference. A writer as influential as Goethe used this question of affinity to introduce conflicts between humans in *Die Wahlverwandtschaften*, as can be seen in the conversation quoted below; in the context of the narrative the parallel has a certain metaphorical weight, and perhaps Goethe can be criticised for being too opportunistic and literal in establishing so close an analogy between loving emotions:

"... what we call limestone is a more or less pure calcareous earth in combination with a delicate acid, which is familiar to us in the form of a gas. Now, if we place a piece of this stone in diluted sulphuric acid, this will take possession of the lime, and appear with it in the form of gypsum, the gaseous acid at the same time going off in vapour. Here is a case of separation; a combination arises, and we believe ourselves now justified in applying to it the words, 'Elective Affinity'; it really looks as if one relation had been deliberately chosen in preference to another ... You mean me by your lime; the lime is laid hold of by the captain, in the form of sulphuric acid, torn away from your agreeable society, and metamorphosed into a refractory gypsum". To this, Charlotte replies: "... man is raised very many steps above these elements ... Unhappily, we know cases enough where a connection apparently indissoluble between two persons, has, by the accidental introduction of a third, been utterly destroyed, and one or the other of the once happily united pair been driven out into the wilderness." Edward concludes with the following comment: "Then you see how much more gallant the chemists are. They at once add a fourth, that neither may go away empty."[6]

---

[6] Wolfgang Goethe (1885), Works Vol. 5, *Elective Affinities* (Philadelphia: G. Barrie), chapter 4.

However, despite the exaggeration, the literature of alchemy and chemistry is full of allusions to emotional contexts that serve to make plausible explanations for the behaviour of the different substances in chemical combinations.

Throughout the course of the nineteenth century the spell of affinity was cast off and more materialistic theories were preferred to explain the connections between the elements. However, frequently chemistry was alluded to in order to explain the emotional resonances of communities. Resentment was used by illustrious philosophers to explain the miseries of the emerging bourgeoisie, although from Nietzsche to Strawson it is considered that resentment was a problem generated by the behaviour of individuals and their treatment of one another. The liberation of resentment in an individual, and its transformation into sympathy and affection requires reaching a certain aristocracy of the spirit according to Nietzsche, while Strawson points out with admirable sharpness that it requires the acceptance that such a sentiment is only the manifestation of conflicts of low intensity. In both cases it appears that resentment remains confined to the personal sphere, although it is worth recognising Strawson's perceptiveness in suggesting how it would arise in a collective manner.

Here it is not individual resentment that interests us, as although it is produced in large communities, we are interested in the resentment which affects the groups themselves. For this reason the work of seeing how this emotion of resentment is transformed into something collective still remains to be done; it remains to be determined how it is used in communities, by them and against them as appears to occur in war. This paper only endeavours to bring forward some considerations of a broader project, which tries to delve into the question which I denominate as "emotional chemistry," if I am allowed to make a perhaps overly risky analogy.

It is not easy to track the emotional characteristics that would come into play in the Great War before they were produced; it is more tempting to talk of afterwards, when the emotions were already observable. However, it is better to explore the comfortable societies of the end of the century, and to do that we can find many traces of how resentment gradually turned into bitter antipathy. Although authors such as Stefan Zweig argue that no one believed a conflict between civilised countries possible (how can gentlemen fight beyond the boundaries of limited dispute?), it did not seem that the hostile emotions between the different continental powers, more or less underground movements, would have given in.

At least between the French Republic and the central empires there was a public and well-known animosity since the end of the Franco-Prussian war. However, German industry was present at the trade fairs in Paris and many German patents were applied in French industry. Philosophy crossed the Rhine in both directions, as well as the musical and artistic culture. It is certain that few French people went to German universities to study for their doctorates, despite the fact that these Central European institutions were the most cosmopolitan in the world during the three decades preceding the Great War. There was also an abundance of publications in which the "German character" was demonised. It is not necessary to look far to find popular novels of the age where this conflict was noticeable. An author as popular as Jules Verne published in 1879 *Les Cinq cents millions de la Bégum,* which exemplified the degeneration of two people, one French and the other German, both inheritors of great fortunes. Utopia or dystopia? It is not easy to know if the novel was a sounding board of the Parisian preoccupations or a transmission centre of resentment against the recently created German empire.

The bitterness of the defeat is present in the story and is transformed into a literary metaphor to explain the difference between national "attributes." In the first months of the war in 1914–1918 the medium of fiction came to demonstrate the need to justify these differences philosophically. In the same way that a significant number of German scientists sided with the military theories of Kaiser Wilhelm, prestigious French philosophers undertook to distinguish between ways of understanding science and civilization in the countries in conflict on both sides of the River Rhine. And so, Henri Bergson went to great lengths to explain the differences between the "organic" civilisation of French culture and the "mechanical" or "mechanistic" culture of the Germans.[7]

There was no shortage of texts which tried to stimulate resentment in the decades leading up to the war on all sides. Emphasis is often placed on the importance of propaganda, but it is anachronistic to place it in these years. Propaganda, understood as a mechanism to stimulate resentment, was more a phenomenon of the inter-war period, a discovery made subsequent to the Armistice. Its success could be founded in the radical increase of resentment due to other causes, which are not easy to determineIn the present we tend to explain events which took place before Goebbels' arrival to history from the point of view of Goebbels' propaganda model and this does not help us to understand the phenomenon of extreme resentment which made the Great War possible,

---

[7] Bergson, H. *La signification de la Guerre* (Paris, Bloud et Gay Editeurs, 1916), 8–9.

the master of the wars of our time

Instead of searching anxiously for the causes, if we depart from the analysis of the circumstances and we try to give them an adequate emotional dimension, perhaps we will find clues to support a perspective which allows us to understand the chain of wars of the twentieth century, and those of the twenty-first, in a more fruitful or beneficial manner.

Therefore, maybe it is convenient to highlight that the principal states that entered into conflict had some or quite a few similarities, as well as the differences leading to the insults with which they criticised one another. These were "normalised" states, in other words states that had found the creation of standards advantageous, such as a common language of communication. The industries worked well, they cooperated with success because standards had been advocated in the manufacture of objects. But furthermore, daily life was marked by standardised timetables; a large part of the population acquired the rail culture, with precise hours which disseminated the necessity to measure time in an unequivocal manner. This chronological standardisation was not banal, which regulated working life, transport times and even leisure time. Less intense was the influence of the telegraph standardisation because it was a less accessible means of communication, but all the newspapers' information depended on this new language.

I wish to focus on chemistry, the industry *par excellence* of this period. It was an industry which commenced the demolition of the idea of nature, due to the challenge caused by the synthesis of new substances. Standardisation and synthesis are two categories which forged the culture of these well-developed societies. What had begun in the mid-nineteenth century, with the artificial anilines for ink manufacture, continued its inexorable path. With the turn of the century, chemistry seemed to be an unstoppable conqueror. One figure suffices—the year before the First World War, Bayer had 10,000 employees and close to 8,000 patents. Could chemical synthetic processes substitute nature?

This led to "substitute" philosophy, dreamed about, aspired to, constantly searched for and, in certain cases, simply tolerated. The necessity to find things with which to fill a deficiency is an impulse of the human condition that is much older than it might appear at first sight. It is a longing which can be summed up by commonly-used expressions such as "if men could fly" or "if we could achieve the impossible." *Ersatz* is a German word used across a multitude of European languages. This is somewhat surprisingly, and is maybe due to the fact that this term is more than a simple noun which exists in all languages to refer to determined products. In effect, it is an enormously powerful concept, the spinal cord of a whole "philosophy" which emerged in Germany at the end of the nineteenth century and the beginning of the twentieth. It is a dream, one of replacing the arbitrary powers granted by nature, never sufficiently bountiful, for the fruits created by human ingenuity; the dream of non-dependence, of omnipotence; of man's unlimited capacity to create according to his necessities, and the real and genuine possibility of achieving it. Not only this, but it is a dream also of the convenience, the necessity, the exhortation to carry this out in a systematic and programmed way, and the assignation of positive values, in the concept of progress, due to the fact of having achieved it. Without a shadow of doubt, Germany was, and continues to be, the champion and the vanguard of this conviction. Is it perhaps due to this that European languages consider it opportune to conserve all of the concept's power in the German language?

Did Emotions follow the same Path as these Products?

It is not as easy to follow the trail left by emotions as it is to follow those left by industrial products. But also in this case, we can request that we are allowed to blur the differences between one and the other in order to find connections which will permit us to understand resentment's degeneration, its intensification and transformation into hatred, as well as its durability throughout the years of the Great War and subsequent ones: the period (1917-1945) which Nolte denominates as the great European Civil War.

The Ersatz of natural products followed a parallel path to the emotional one. The adversary societies, above all the central empires and more concretely the second German Empire, became aware of the possibilities during the Great War. Yet it was after this conflict and during the inter-war period that the politics of Ersatz turned into state politics in all of the states, especially in the Weimar Republic and during the Nazi period. Today, we can understand that the realisation was preceded by a space of time before the war where this conviction was forged; it can even be interpreted within an ideology which could be summed up in these words: "standardisation in order to fight better."

The exponential increase of resentment, which had emerged in interwar Europe and had already been converted into the highest quality hatred, can be interpreted in the same way. It had already reared its head during the Great War, but its roots are found in the same period as the processes of standardisation referred to earlier. It is not a new idea to establish a parallel between the industry of synthetic products and other cultural signs. Esther Leslie published an essay in 2005 entitled "Synthetic Worlds, Nature, Art and the Chemical Industry," full of suggestions for readers who desired to have a more complete idea of the interwar period. Its analysis also blurs the boundaries between the different cultural patterns which make up the mosaic of a period which is often excessively simplified.

This work aims to delve deeper into these nuances, although emotions are more elusive than the products of industries which manufactured colourings, aniline and nitrogenous products. Nor are they works of art, objects as concrete as paintings or photographs, which can be created and destroyed. Emotions are often expressed through words. It is not their only channel of communication, of course, but it is normally the first. Words can be deposited in many different places. If I am permitted to make the analogy, words are the atoms of emotions, atoms of meaning, or of quasi-meaning. In a scientific language, the propositions are the important part; in a language with high emotional content, the words are the elements which make up a large part of the sentiments expressed.

The necessary resentment to maintain a war such as the Great War could not be left to the chance of a natural growth, in the same way that the natural rubber tree was not enough to feed the machinery of war. Synthetic rubber and synthetic resentment—synthetic rubber was of a better quality than that extracted from trees, more resistant, harder and could be replaced more easily. In the same way, a more durable resentment was needed which would support the horrors of war and which would avoid being worn down as quickly as personal emotions. It was clear that it was necessary to assure that the civil population was part of the conflict. This process of identification was forged over decades and only half awoken in WWII to once more become absorbed in the hypnosis of the cold war, and again now in the seduction of terrorism. The interwar propaganda machines worked with this hatred, a raw material of the highest quality, but they did not invent it.

My problem is to find to where the production of this cascade of words can be traced, these words which allowed such quantities of hatred to be readily available. What I present here is not the solution to the problem, but its approach; I can tell you where I have looked, and an outline of what I have been able to make out.

Although it seems that the realms of literature (understanding literature as fictional texts and essays, including journalism) and industry are very separate spheres, in reality they are profoundly implicated in the period prior to the Great War. For this reason, it is convenient to attentively read the texts that deal with the conflict, some of which reflect the emotional reaction before the war. Furthermore, it is advisable to pay attention to the texts written just on the brink of the declaration of war, on all of the battle fronts. Many of the texts, of which there is a huge number, can be found catalogued and available for the reader. After the professional armies had annihilated themselves with a professional efficiency, in the same way that young people had waited in line in the conscription centres to be sent to the front, almost all writers, journalists, philosophers and classes of intellectuals inundated the newspapers and publishing houses with texts about war. The idea of "the others" was almost always discussed. The others were represented as something which could be detested, and rightly so. Few maintained the sufficient distance to adopt a less belligerent and embittering stance. They were soldiers of the pen who desired to form part of an army efficient in their role of maintaining the conflict. In the same way that associations of ladies prepared packages for the front, in order to comfort and nourish the soldiers, this army of writers fabricated a hatred of the highest quality.

During my enquiries I consulted many of these texts to uncover a general panorama of the embittering effects that they achieved. However, now I want to conclude this chapter with a couple of meaningful allusions. The first, that of a prolific Austrian writer who always wrote in excess, whose impertinence condemned him simultaneously to fame and isolation, but who at the moment of the declaration of war, fell silent. I am referring to Karl Kraus, author/editor/bard/actor, illustrious representative of Viennese impertinence. He fell silent, and the whole world clamoured for his word. Only six months after the start of the conflict he published an article in his magazine, entitled *In dieser grossen Zeit*, ("In this great age"), in which he analyses elements of the conflict. (I say "his" magazine because he was the only author, editor and proofreader, although not the only reader.) In this text he does not talk of the soldiers, but of the society that wages war:

> In the kingdoms deprived of imagination, where human beings die of a lack of spirituality without perceiving their soul's hunger, where the pen is dipped in blood and the sword in ink, we have to become what we do not believe, but what we believe on our own is unutterable. Do not expect from me a single word of my own. Even less could I say something new: in the room in which one writes there is so much noise; and it is not the hour to decide if it comes from animals, from children or from mortars.[8]

Years later, Kraus would write naming a multitude of agents who took the affirmation of Kurt Tucholsky, *"Sprache ist eine Waffe"* ("language is a weapon") seriously. I will follow this clue, the same that Siegfred Sassoon

---

[8] Kraus, Karl. *In dieser großen Zeit—Aufsätze 1914–1925.* (Hamburg: Tradition).

highlights in his relationship with Russell, and the same revealed by Gravriel Chevalier. Following these clues, I will continue this research.

Although it is not easy to trace the path of the generation of those emotions that allow the continuance of war, in this chapter some ideas have been proposed to help identify the sources of the resentment by means of which war may be maintained.

Works Cited

Bachelard, Gaston. *Etude sur l'évolution d'un problème de physique: la propagation thermique dans les solides.* Paris: Vrin, 1928.

Bergson, Henri. *La signification de la Guerre.* Paris, Bloud et Gay Editeurs, 1916.

Fourcroy, Antoine-François. *Texte du Rapport et projet de decret de Fourcroy du 7 vendémiaire an III (28 de septembre 1794).* Paris: Imprimerie du Comité de Salut Publique

Ferro, Marc. *Le ressentiment dans l'histoire.* Paris: Les Éditions Odile Jacob, 2008.

Goethe, Wolfgang. Works Vol. 5 *Elective Affinities.* Philadelphia: G. Barrie 1885.

Kraus, Karl *In dieser großen Zeit—Aufsätze 1914–1925.* Hamburg: Tredition, 2012.

Leslie, Esther, *Synthetic Worlds, Nature, Art and the Chemical Industry.* London: Reaktions Books, 2005.

Nietzsche, Friedrich. *On the Genealogy of Morality*, edited by keith ansell-pearson, translated by Carol Diethe. Cambridge: Cambridge University Press, 2006.

Nolte, Ernst Der Euroäische Bürgerkrieg 1917–1945 Ntionalsozialismus und Bolschewismus. München, Herbig VBH, 1997.

Strawson, Peter, *Freedom and resentement and other essays.* London: Methuen & Co, 1974.

Thucydides. *History of the Peloponnesian War.* Edited by Benjamin Jowett. Volume 1. Oxford: Clarendon Press, 1881.

Verne, Jules. *Les Cinq cents millions de la Bégum.* Paris: Hachette, 1915.

CHAPTER TWELVE

FRENCH RESENTMENT AND THE ANIMALIZATION OF THE GERMANS DURING THE FIRST WORLD WAR

BEATRIZ PICHEL

Introduction: The Enemy of the Man of Resentment

In 1886, a poster called "*la revanche*" (the revenge) was published in France.[1] It showed a big, monstrous octopus wearing a pointed helmet, expanding its tentacles from the German Empire in the direction of France, Great Britain, Russia, Northern Europe and the Austro-Hungarian Empire. This monster encounters the resistance of only a French soldier and a Russian soldier, who are trying to fight him with swords.

Like others belonging to the same collection, this poster recalled the Franco-Prussian War (1870–1871) when the Prussian army had defeated France. As a result, Prussia had occupied parts of the regions of Alsace and Lorraine and became part of the German Empire. However, this poster does not make an explicit reference to this conflict, but to the German expansion. The reason for the French rebellion in this image is not a particular Prussian action of the past, but the menacing present and likely expansion of the empire.

Moreover, the interest of this poster lies in the way in which it pictures this confrontation. It materializes the French viewpoint of the unequal relationship between French and German soldiers. While the German people are represented by a huge monster, the French is a small soldier. At

---

[1] Ici on lit "La Revanche" Imp. Levy rue des Petits Champs, Affiche lithographie (42x56 cm), 1886. It is available online at gallica.fr
http://gallica.bnf.fr/ark:/12148/btv1b9004374w.r=ici+on+lit+%22la+revanche%22.
langES.

sight, the monstrous octopus could seem more powerful than the soldier because of its bigger size. But its strongest point is precisely the point of its weakness. Even if it is bigger, the German is an animal, not a human being.

This chapter aims to examine this paradoxical construction of the German as a powerful enemy and as an animal in the French visual culture during the First World War (1914–1918). It claims that this characterization is the typical one of the enemy created by the man of resentment. Following Nietzsche's texts and Solomon's ideas, this chapter understands resentment as the powerless reaction to unfair treatment.[2] This emotion is essentially directed towards an enemy, regarded by the subject as the cause of their unfair state, which is usually domination. The man of resentment thinks that he does not deserve this dominance and humiliation; he wants to reverse the situation, achieving the power held by the enemy, but he recognizes the superiority of his enemy, feeling impotent in facing him. In order to reverse the situation, the enemy is characterized as the opposite of the subject, who presents itself as the beholder of a different and superior morality. Therefore, resentment involves a paradox as the enemy is hated because of its domination but also envied because of its empowerment.

This chapter will show that the representation of the German in French newspapers during the Great War followed this very logic. In line with the aforementioned poster, German soldiers were presented as militarily and technologically superior, but at the same time as animals guided by their lowest instincts.

Therefore, this research deals with the representation of resentment in a very particular way. Instead of focusing on the man of resentment, it addresses the question of the construction of his enemy. This analysis has three purposes. First, it claims that the study of resentment through the enemy enlightens the analysis of the historical and cultural characteristics of that emotion. Both the condemned and the envied features attributed to this enemy are interpreted as manifestations of the cultural codes in which resentment is embedded into.

Second, this chapter vindicates the active role that visual culture plays in the social construction of resentment. This particular case study shows that the effectiveness of this "enemy" in revitalizing resentment depends on its visual representations, and images, and photographs in particular will be regarded as political artefacts rather than simple illustrations.

---

[2] Friedrich Nietzsche, *The Genealogy of Morals* (New York: Dover Publications, 1887/2003); Robert C. Solomon, *The Passions: Emotions and the Meaning of Life* (Indiana: Hackett Publishing Company, 1993).

Third, it aims to show the relevance of focusing on emotions when studying a cultural history of war. Joanna Bourke has remarked that "history is saturated with emotions," and so too is historiography.[3] An increasing number or works deal with emotions to enlighten certain cultural aspects of the First World War. The best example in this regard is the commemoration of the dead, which has been analysed through the construction of mourning.[4] From a broader point of view, Michael Roper's *The Secret Battle* is the first work that explicitly focuses on the emotional experience of soldiers at the front.[5] This chapter is in line with these works, but differs from them in one essential point—its sources are not texts, but visual documents. These photographs change the way in which history is elaborated, providing new aspects for the study of war, and a new approach to emotions. The analysis of the revitalization of resentment through the photographs published in official albums implicitly considers emotions as practices configured in the inter-subjective space.[6] Resentment is not presented as an inner-state owned by a subject, but as a subject reaction mediated by objects. Thus, this chapter claims that resentment is not only a prism through which we can study the soldiers' war experience, but also a case study for the dynamics of the emotions in war.

Revenge or Resentment?

One of the reasons for the cause of the First World War most spoken of is that France wanted revenge on Germany because of the defeat in 1871 that resulted in the loss of Alsace and Lorraine. However, recent historiography has shown that claims of revenge between 1871 and 1914 were in the minority. Historians such as Jean Jacques Becker, Stéphane Audoin-Rouzeau, and Bertrand Joly have argued that France did not seek

---

[3] Joanna Bourke, "Fear and Anxiety: Writing about Emotion in Modern History," *History Workshop Journal* 55 (2003): 111–133.

[4] Jay Winter, *Sites of Memory, Sites of Mourning The Great War in European Cultural History* (Cambridge: Cambridge University Press, 1995); Stéphane Audoin-Rouzeau, "Qu'est-ce qu'un deuil de guerre?" *Revue Historique des Armées* (2010): 259.

[5] Michel Roper, *The Secret Battle: Emotional Survival during the Great War* (Manchester: Manchester University Press, 2009).

[6] Sarah Ahmed, *The Cultural Politics of Emotion* (Edinburgh: Edinburgh University Press, 2004); Jo Labanyi, "Doing Things: Emotion, Affect and Materiality," *Journal of Spanish Cultural Studies* 11 (3–4) (2010): 223–233.

revenge, even during the months just after the defeat.[7] According to them, even if the idea remained in public discourse at least until 1905 (and Becker recognizes that "we did not forget for all that"), neither French international politics, nor its military plans were preparing to retake Alsace and Lorraine.[8] The reason is, according to Becker, the change of the economic, international and national situation of France over the period from 1871–1914. First, the French economy had risen and was on the way to prosperity, partly because of its colonial Empire, which was one of the biggest in the world. Second, the new nationalism was blamed on the Communards, not the Germans, for the decadence of France. Finally, and more importantly, France, Russia, and Great Britain had become allies, replacing the country in the international political arena.[9] Therefore, in this new context, France stopped worrying about the German menace of war. Delcassé, the ministry of Foreign Affairs, had indeed tried to renew political relations with Germany through their colonial interests during the period from 1898–1905.[10]

In conclusion, the outbreak of the First World War cannot be interpreted as the fulfilment of military or political desires for revenge, and neither did the discourse of revenge re-emerge during the war. On the contrary, war was presented as a German action, not a French one. Even in 1917, a Ministry of War publication referred to the First World War as the "German War," remarking that France had not started the fight.[11] The position of France was a defensive one, and that became the main argument that propaganda services developed for supporting the war.

However, this absence of the idea of revenge does not mean that French people had forgotten about the war against Germany. The monuments dedicated to the fallen in the Franco-Prussian War erected

---

[7] Jean-Jacques Becker, "1905: la menace de guerre est-elle à l'origine d'un renouveau nationaliste?" *Mil neuf cent. Revue d'histoire intellectuelle* 19 (1) (2001) : 19–25; Jean-Jacques Becker et Stéphane Audoin-Rouzeau, *La France, la nation, la guerre, 1850–1920* (Paris: Sedes, 1995) ; Bertrand Joly, "La France et la Revanche (1871–1914)," *Revue d'histoire moderne et contemporaine Revue d'histoire moderne et contemporaine*, avril–juin, 325–347.

[8] Becker, 22. He and Audoin-Rouzeau also state that "the great military effort accepted within the frame of national defence, does not present an offensive character," 153.

[9] "At the level of the facts, there is not question for revenge. The foreign police are that of 'reverence.' France recalls its defeat, not by means of a new war, but through appeals to peace," Becker and Audoin-Rouzeau, 153.

[10] Becker, 23.

[11] Section Photographique de l'Armée (SPA), *1917: La victoire prochaine du droit* (Paris : E. Paul, 1917), 1.

between 1871 and 1914 stood as living memories of the outrage.[12] This chapter claims that these monuments, and photographs published during the war, materialized a more complex and subtle emotion than revenge because it was grounded on memory.

Resentment, or rather, *ressentiment*, is a *longue durée* emotion. The man of resentment "understands remaining silent, not forgetting, waiting," Nietzsche says.[13] In the same way, Somolon describes resentment as "the most obsessive and enduring of emotions, poisoning the whole of subjectivity with its venom."[14] According to this, we should not see the defeat in 1871 as the only cause of French resentment. Only one outrage does not lead to *ressentiment*, but to revenge. Marc Ferro precisely interprets the traditional tension between France and Germany as an alternation of resentments.[15] Therefore, the defeat of 1871 happened in a context of rising international tension, where both sides had reasons to blame the other. In this sense, the French writer Paul Chocquer accused Prussia of starting the war of 1870 because of unfair desires for revenge. For him, "this furious people, who have only sowed resentment, will harvest fair punishment."[16] Paul de Saint Victor expressed a similar idea in 1871. In his book dedicated to *"Barbarians and Bandits*,*"* that is, Prussia and the Communards, Saint Victor described Prussia as the "perfidious and cruel enemy for whom our resentment will never level the insult."[17]

Both texts refer to a great affront that cannot be reduced to a sole action, but they present resentment in different ways. Choquer's notion of resentment is closer to revenge, as it foresees a "fair punishment." However, Saint Victor denounces that Prussian actions are so cruel that fair punishment would be impossible. This idea reflects a conscious inferiority towards the enemy typical of *ressentiment*. This is clearer in a poem written in 1914 by Ernest Raynaud. For him, "despite all, the resentment of the defeated, the protest of the diminished race, whose pride has been wounded, woke up from the obscure depth of my being."[18] The year when the war broke out, he recognizes the feeling of impotence and inferiority regarding his enemy. More important, it is not an individual

---

[12] Antoine Prost, *Republican Identities in War and Peace* (Oxford/New York: Berg, 2002).

[13] Nietzsche, 15.

[14] Solomon, 290.

[15] Marc Ferro, *Le ressentiment dans l'histoire* (Paris: Odil Jacobs, 2007).

[16] Paul Chocquer, *La Revanche* (Paris: P. Dupont, 1874), 8.

[17] Paul Saint-Victor, *Barbares et Bandits* (Paris: M. Lévy-Frères, 1870), 1.

[18] Ernst Raynaud, *Les deux Allemagne: poèmes* (Paris: Mercure de France, 1914), 7.

feeling, but a collective one—it was the French that felt insulted by the Prussians.

From the start of the war, French propaganda and other discourse abandoned the word "resentment," as well as "revenge." However, this does not mean that resentment totally disappeared. In 1915, the American professor Edward Raymond Turner remarked that:

> it may be seen that the causes which led to the cataclysm had long been in operation. They must be sought in the curse of militarism, the spoliation and resentment of France, the envy and apprehension of England, the arrogance and prosperity of Germany, the weakness of Austria, the rise of the Balkan states and the glowering menace of Russia.[19]

In this kind of distribution of emotions among the belligerent nations, France is linked to resentment and Germany to pride. Moreover, both nations are the only ones described in economic terms—France has been spoiled and Germany has prospered. This was precisely the idea spread by French propaganda and public discourse from 1914. The Germans had been spoiling France and stealing its natural wealth both before and during the war and this was the reason for both the prosperity of Germany and the decadence of France.

Therefore, France did not seek revenge, and did not explicitly use the term "resentment" in public discourse, but it can be seen implicitly in the way in which France presented the war as the occasion to reverse the unequal relations of power in the realm of international politics. National propaganda enthusiastically claimed that war was serving France to recuperate its former and natural position. However, this recuperation was being done not through military actions, but in the spiritual and moral realm. This is the essential point of the argument. France recognized the military and technological superiority of Germany, and this had been presented as the reason for their victory in 1871, and it was again argued as the reason why they had occupied Belgium and Northern France so quickly in the first few months of the war. However, paradoxically, militarism was not regarded as a positive quality during the war. Reigniting the old opposition between "Kultur" and "civilization," France distinguished between the "military" and the "warrior":

> The French is warrior, but the German is military. In the first case, the courage, devotion and sacrificial spirit are combined with a kind of individual instinct for the fight necessities. He adapts to the most difficult

---

[19] Edward Raymond Turner, "The Causes of the Great War," *The American Political Science Review* 9 (1) (1915): 16–35.

situations and inspires the cleverest solutions. In the second case, only the discipline, the passive obeisance and the automatism can galvanize its apathetic, soft, amorphous nature.[20]

France felt itself to be both militarily and technologically impotent in facing the Germans. The previous text was intended to condemn the Germans; however it started praising the military facts accomplished by them:

> God saves me from denying that the Germans have not accomplished astonishing actions during this war. The successive waves of attacks under the fire, moving almost in perfect order like in a parade, provoked cries of admiration even among their adversaries.[21]

This military inferiority was overcome by a moral superiority. French propaganda's strategy was to claim that war was not a military issue, or even a political one, but a moral one, in which the future of the whole humanity was at stake. Saurès described in these very terms the Battle of Verdun in his poem *Ceux de Verdun* when he says:

> By means of your dead, your mourning and your sacrifice,
> Saints of Verdun, burning torches, the entire world stopped being blind;
> It brightens; it understands that Germany is the matter
> and France the soul of the humankind.[22]

The French fight was presented as a noble one, whose aim was the defence of the civilized world. Another propagandistic text published by the SPA entitled *"Le monde avec la France pour la liberté"* (*"The world with France for Freedom"*) claimed in 1917 that:

> A century ago, France gave the essential features to modern society. Now, the great nation testifies the sign of historical choice that made of it the armed personification of mankind, the adopting country of the free spirits, the law and the hope of those who vindicate a higher ideal than the predominance of force, and a more noble law than that of collective egoism.[23]

---

[20] SPA, *1917: leur armée* (Paris: Émile Paul, 1917), 1.

[21] Ibid.

[22] André Suarès, *Ceux de Verdun* (Paris: Émile Paul, 1916), 32.

[23] SPA, *1917: Le monde avec la France pour la liberté* (Paris: Émile Paul, 1917), 1.

These kinds of moral arguments aimed to reverse power relations. The French strategy to counterattack the military superiority of the Germans was to diminish them in the moral realm. That was the aim of expressions such as "the most perfect machine is impotent against a solid heart."[24] In these kinds of affirmations, the powerless were the German soldiers, precisely because of their technology. The French turned the German strongest point (the military and technological superiority) into their weakness.

The basis of this moral argument was the French appropriation of the concept of humanity.[25] These texts presented the French soldiers and France as the defenders of humanity while at the same time denying this characteristic to the Germans. This dehumanization happened through two features. On one hand, the Germans were presented as mechanical and disciplined people; too engaged with technology and science. But on the other hand, they were reduced to animals, behaving according to their lower instincts. This paradoxical character, half machine half animal, reveals the typical traits of resentment as it is a combination of the qualities most admired (technological power) and the most despised (instinctive behaviour).

The illustrated albums published by the French official photographic section, the *Section Photographique de l'Armée* (SPA), are excellent examples of the animalization of the Germans. The SPA was created in March 1915 with the aim of promoting the French cause among the French population and the neutral countries. Therefore, the images they produced were intended to be the official image of the war. The propagandistic rhetoric of these albums relied both on the texts and the photographs. These images increased the power of the words because they were presented as objective documents. Photographs "bring the war home," as John Carteret stated in 1916.[26] Therefore, they supposedly allowed the spectator to "live every moment of this great work, which is the evidence and glory of the soldiers of the Republic."[27]

---

[24] SPA, *1917: l'hommage de l'Italie* (Paris: Émile Paul, 1917), 1.

[25] John Horne and Allan Kramer have argued that dehumanization was a strategy shared by French and German propaganda in *German Atrocities 1914: A History of Denial* (Yale: Yale University Press, 2001). This chapter tries to specify the particularity of the French appropriation of the concept of humanity by means of claims such as the following: "Humanity, it is that, even if it is a hazy word, what summarizes the essential features of the French tradition!" SPA, *1917: Le bon soldat de la France* (Paris: Émile Paul, 1917), 1.

[26] John Carteret, *Verdun: Images de Guerre* (Paris: Chapelet, 1916), 16.

[27] SPA, *1917: les soldats de la France* (Paris: Émile Paul, 1917), 1.

This chapter focuses on two kinds of photographs. First, the pictures of the German prisoners captured by the French army reveal the way in which this process of dehumanization happened through the representation of weakened bodies. Second, the pictures showing crimes committed by the Germans, in particular the destruction of churches, allows the animal characteristics of the Germans against the humanity of the French to resonate deeply.

The Body of the Enemy—Prisoners

The first thing to remark regarding the photographs of prisoners is that they were published in almost all the SPA publications, and most of them represented German soldiers. Austrian or Bulgarian prisoners, as well as their cadavers, were hardly pictured. This focus on German bodies is similar to the rhetoric of the previous texts in which the enemy of France is reduced to the German army, omitting any other nationality. For example, the mentioned SPA publication *"Leur armée"* (their army) did not need to clarify that it was the German army it referred to, because it was evident. This reveals that they were not occasional enemies but historical ones.

Just like the trophies, the prisoners were presented as the booty at the end of the day.[28] Their imprisonment was seen as a great achievement because of their technological superiority. Therefore, prisoners were the material evidence of the efficacy of the French army, which had been able to capture these soldiers.

However, the main function of these photographs was to introduce the enemy to the French public, presenting the "nature and mentality of the average German soldier."[29] With this aim, one page of the album *La Bataille de Champagne* explicitly referred to the German animality as that, "which is so developed that the feeling of material satisfaction predominates in him, even the most refined German."[30] The images show dozens of prisoners queuing for bread. The previous page represented the prisoners smiling and having lunch. According to the text, they were happy because they were eating and no longer in danger. Therefore, "the war is over for them," and they enjoy telling this truth to anyone.[31] In this regard, they

---

[28] "Nous arrivons maintenant a la conclusion de l'action: la capture des prisoniers et son evacuation," SPA, *La Bataille de Champagne* (Paris: Ed. Flambeau, 1917), 15

[29] SPA, *1917: leur armée*, 1.

[30] SPA, *La bataille de Champagne*, 23.

[31] SPA, *La bataille de Champagne*, 23.

were characterized as cowards, the opposite of the French soldier, who "accepts his death for the beauty of one idea."[32]

These images were especially relevant because, as one commentator remarked in *Les soldats de la France*, the morality of both French and German people were materialized on their physiognomy. According to him, "the diversity [between French and German soldiers] is so different that it strikes … [the] diversity of types, gestures, attitudes and gazes."[33] In this regard, each kind of body represented a national and moral character. In the case of the Germans, photographs like that published in *Le sang n'est pas de l'eau* showed weakened bodies whose uniforms were too large.[34] Weakness could be interpreted as the result of life conditions at the front. However, in this context, these weakened bodies represented more than the physical effects of the war. They were intended to reveal the actual nature of the Germans, which remained hidden behind their technology. This photograph, published in *1917: leur armée*, was done so with this purpose.[35] It shows a group of several German soldiers whose bodies and attitudes contrast with those of the French, pictured to the back.

These photographs were intended, then, to correct the previous image of the Germans as a powerful, monstrous octopus, or the "bull with two horns of pride and science."[36] In these descriptions, the scientific and technological development made them proud of themselves. However, it was "the science without conscience, and the colossal pride, the pride of the bad angels."[37] This is why the German were not depicted as military men with weapons, as the French were. By means of recuperating the Barbarian myth, the Germans were identified with unconscious animals without theoretical or superior knowledge.

The pictures of prisoners supported this myth as they represented the Germans after having lost their military technology and pride. Without their weapons, they were weak, herded like animals, often surrounded by fences, as in the images published in *La Bataille de Champagne*.[38] Once

---

[32] SPA, *1917: L'hommage de l'Italie*, 1.

[33] SPA, *1917: Les soldats de la France*, 2.

[34] "Types of prisoners," *1917: Le sang n'est pas de l'eau* (Paris: Émile Paul, 1917), 19.

[35] Prisoners in France," *1917: Leur armée*, 38. Reproduced under authorizartion of the Bibliothèque Nationale de France.

[36] Suarès, *Ceux de Verdun*, 18.

[37] "à savoir la bêtise à front de taureau… la science sans la conscience, l'orgueils des mauvais anges" SPA, *1917: le bon soldat de la France*, 1.

[38] SPA, *La Bataille de Champagne*, 21.

they had been captured they were no longer strong animals like the bull or the big octopus.

Fig. 12.1. "Prisoners in France." *1917: Leur armée*, 38.

Source gallica.bnf.fr / Bibliothèque nationale de France

This chapter suggests that these images also reveal French resentment. First, they turned the most envied features of the Germans (their technology and military knowledge) into their weakness. Second, this transformation was done by means of dehumanizing them. Unlike the few photographs of Bulgarian prisoners, for example, these pictures focused on their weakened bodies or on their primary needs, stressing their decadence. Another picture published in *1917: Du langage renommé et de la photographie*, showed a group of German prisoners fighting among themselves for drinking from a barrel of wine which had fallen on the other side of the wire.[39] The German were under the control of the "diminished" race, which fed them, surrounded them with fences and even forced them to pose in front of the camera.

---

[39] SPA, "in a prisoners' camp," *1917: Du langage renommé et de la photographie* (Paris: Émile Paul, 1917), 8.

The Actions of the Enemy—Ruins

This animalization was completed by means of the photographs showing brutal German acts. As animals, they acted following their lower instincts, which were linked to crime. According to the French, the satisfaction of their primary needs included eating and getting drunk, as well as raping and stealing. Indeed, *Leur armée* denounced that "this war was impatiently expected because it allowed the turning to pillage, gluttony and violation."[40]

This criminalization started at the beginning of the war, when the Germans were accused of committing atrocities in the occupied regions of Belgium and Northern France, such as shooting civilians, raping women and even cutting the hands of Belgian children.[41] During this period, one of the main representations of the Germans were the kinds of illustrations that emphasized the brutality and the animalistic character of these soldiers, e.g. threatening an imploring young woman.[42] As Ruth Harris remarked, these images of rape symbolized the suffering of the nation rather than that of the individual woman.[43] Thus, at the beginning of the war, France depicted itself as a defenceless woman.

However, the photographic albums of 1916 and 1917 give a different image of France. In the album most explicitly directed against the Germans, *Ce qu'ils ont fait*, France is not depicted as a woman but is represented through artistic patrimony and the fruits of the land.[44] This album displayed the German destruction of the cities, the fruit trees, the churches and even some desecrated graves. As a result, what seemed to be threatened by the war were the Catholic religion and future nourishment of the nation. The proliferation of these pictures, published in almost all the albums, sought to confirm that the Germans were the enemy of civilization.

These photographs were shown as evidence of German brutality, materializing their animal and barbaric characteristics in the occupied territories. Therefore, these images were the counterpart of the previous ones. While the pictures of prisoners sought to reveal the actual nature of the Germans, their weakness, these photographs of ruins aimed to mobilize

---

[40] SPA, *1917:Leur armée*, 2.

[41] See John Horne and Allan Kramer, *German Atrocities*.

[42] Escaudier and Richepin (comps), *Livre rouge des atrocités allemagnes*, drawing 17 by G. J. Duomerge Extracted from Ruth Harris, "The 'Child of the Barbarian': Rape, Race and Nationalism in France during the First World War," *Past & Present* 141 (1993): 170–206.

[43] Harris, 175.

[44] SPA, *Ce qu'ils ont fait* (Paris: documents de la SPA, 1917).

the spectator. The image of the destruction of the very essence of France was a way to revitalise resentment, more powerful than any text could be. These photographs bore witness to the continuation of the French humiliation by the Germans.

However, the combination of these two images not only created resentment. The animalisation of the German under French domination represented the possibility of victory. These photographs show that, despite the material destruction provoked by the Germans, they were powerless. This idea was essential to guarantee the civilian support for the war effort.

Conclusions

In conclusion, this chapter has analysed the role of visual culture in the construction of resentment. Photographs became essential propagandistic tools because they were supposed to depict facts, that is—what happened in the way it had happened. The denial of humanity to German soldiers through the pictures of their weakened bodies and their criminal actions were intended to present an enemy who deserved to be defeated, and that victory was possible.

The interpretation of this dehumanisation as the materialisation of a historical French resentment allows us to delve deeper into the question. On one hand, the analysis of the construction of the German enemy in light of *ressentiment* has enlightened the symbolic importance of defeating the Germans. On the other hand, it has explained why the war was not seen as revenge but as a German attack.

Finally, this chapter is an attempt to study the emotional experiences of war. The focus on photography has allowed a shift from individual emotions to collective ones. The question here was not to examine how individual people felt resentment, but how resentment was constructed in the inter-subjective space. Photography has revealed itself as a powerful means to materialize and mobilize emotions as it does not only represent emotions, but also configures them through its particular uses.

Works Cited

Ahmed, Sarah. *The Cultural Politics of Emotion*. Edinburgh: Edinburgh University Press, 2004.
Audoin-Rouzeau, Stéphane. "Qu'est-ce qu'un deuil de guerre?" *Revue Historique des Armées* (2010): 259.

Becker, Jean-Jaques & Audoin-Rouzeau, Stéphane. *La France, la nation, la guerre, 1850–1920.* Paris: Sedes, 1995.

Becker, Jean-Jacques. "1905: la menace de guerre est-elle à l'origine d'un renouveau nationaliste?" *Mil neuf cent. Revue d'histoire intellectuelle,* 19 (1) (2001): 19–25.

Bourke, Joanna, "Fear and Anxiety: Writing about Emotion in Modern History." *History Workshop Journal* 55 (2003): 111–133.

Chocquer, Paul, *La Revanche.* Paris: P. Dupont, 1874.

Ferro, Marc. *Le ressentiment dans l'histoire.* Paris: Odil Jacobs, 2007.

Grand- Carteret, John. *Verdun: Images de Guerre.* Paris: Chapelot, 1916.

Harris, Ruth. "The 'Child of the Barbarian': Rape, Race and Nationalism in France during the First World War." *Past & Present* 141 (1993): 170–206.

Horne, John & Kramer, Allan. *German Atrocities 1914: A History of Denial.* Yale: Yale University Press, 2001.

Joly, Bertrand. "La France et la Revanche (1871–1914)." *Revue d'histoire moderne et contemporaine,* avril–juin (1999): 325–347.

Labanyi, Jo. "Doing Things: Emotion, Affect and Materiality." *Journal of Spanish Cultural Studies* 11 (3–4) (2010): 223–233.

Nietzsche, Friedrich. *The Genealogy of Morals.* New York: Dover Publications, 1887/2003.

Prost, Antoine. *Republican Identities in War and Peace.* Oxford/New York: Berg, 2002.

Raynaud, Ernst. *Les deux Allemagne: poèmes.* Paris: Mercure de France, 1914.

Roper, Michael. *The Secret Battle: Emotional Survival in the Great War.* Manchester: Manchester University Press, 2009.

Saint-Victor, Paul. *Barbares et Bandits.* Paris: M. Lévy-Frères, 1870.

Solomon, Robert C. *The Passions: Emotions and the Meaning of Life.* Indiana: Hackett Publishing Company, 1993.

Section Photographique de l'Armée. *La Bataille de Champagne.* Paris: Ed. Flambeau, 1917.

SPA. *1917: Les soldats de la France.* Paris: Émile Paul, 1917.

—. *1917 : La victoire prochaine du droit.* Paris: Émile Paul, 1917.

—. *1917: Du langage renommé et de la photographie.* Paris: Émile Paul, 1917.

—. *1917: l'hommage de l'Italie.* Paris: Émile Paul, 1917.

—. *1917: Le bon soldat de la France.* Paris: Émile Paul, 1917.

—. *1917: Le monde avec la France pour la liberté.* Paris: Émile Paul, 1917.

—. *1917: Le sang n'est pas de l'eau.* Paris: Émile Paul, 1917.

—. *1917: Leur armée.* Paris: Émile Paul, 1917.

—. *Ce qu'ils ont fait.* Paris: Documents de la Section Photographique de l'armée, 1917.

Suarès, André. *Ceux de Verdun.* Paris: Émile Paul, 1916.

Turner, Edward Raymond. "The Causes of the Great War." *The American Political Science Review* 9 (1) (1915): 16–35.

Winter, Jay. *Sites of Memory, Sites of Mourning. The Great War in European Cultural History.* Cambridge: Cambridge University Press, 1995.

PART V:

RESENTMENT AND COLLECTIVE IDENTITIES

CHAPTER THIRTEEN

THE SOCIOLOGY OF RESENTMENT

STEFANO TOMELLERI

Introduction

It is typical nowadays to interpret problems of social structuring as if the solutions were up to the individual person. As already stated by Wright C. Mills back in the 1960s, most problems of collective order can be traced back to the framework of the individual's vital spaces and to face-to-face interactions. The predominant orientation is that of providing a mainly psychological explanation for an entire series of critical and contradictory situations of a systemic and structural nature. This "intimation" of social processes is so broadly widespread in common sentiment that social players find it more and more difficult to imagine intersecting spaces between their private lives and the great transformations of historic and institutional scenarios.

In particular, if the specific case of affective life is considered, it seems nowadays that everything depends on the individual, their competences, abilities, personal aptitudes, and mostly their close relationships. On the one hand, the effect of this flattening onto the individual can be understood by the gap between individual biographies and the problems of social structuring; on the other hand, by the abandonment of the subjects to the solitude and incapacity to critically examine the entire society in which they live.

There is, however, a very close bond between the feelings and great historic transformations which, although hard to rebuild in the collective imagination, continues even now to profoundly modify the life projects of the social players. The sociology of emotions and resentment acts on an attempt to reconstitute this bond, which seems to be unravelling into an incurable divide, even though in reality it is itself, as we shall see, the offspring of the social transformations that are marking this difficult endemic crisis.

Resentment, in particular, is not a merely intra-individual psychic content, but a social relationship, with a dynamic and procedural nature, culturally and societally located. Beginning with a critical examination of F. Nietzsche and M. Scheler's account of individualistic and vitalistic resentment, I consider the emotional patterns of resentment in daily interactions, in social inequality and in relation to the institutional evolution that has occurred with modernity. Resentment depends on a structural contradiction typical of capitalistic and democratic societies, where by definition "socially unjust" situations continue or even worsen in a cultural scenario that strongly proclaims competitive individual desires. The promises of the broad range of choices for ever more ambitious and individualistic desires are often followed by frustrations at being denied the opportunities to achieve biographical projects. The consequence is rapidly spreading resentment, an invading emotion not limiting itself to contaminating the private life, but also invading, in a more or less underground way, the public sphere that is progressively less recognisable as such.

The Genesis of Resentment

What is resentment? Friedrich Nietzsche is known to have considered it a reaction inseparable from the moral revolt of slaves that: "From the beginning says no to an 'out' and to a 'not me': and this 'not' is the action creating it. This reversal of judgment that establishes values ... relates to resentment ... action is fundamentally a reaction."[1] It is a prerogative of weak individuals, an impotent hate leading to the most explosive and insidious violence. It is substantially the expression of impotence when faced with the true enemy, to whom one is more or less enslaved because of one's own mediocrity. A person's capacity to self-determine, to affirm themselves, to be autonomous and free from social conditioning, according to Nietzsche, coincides with the development of their strength: it will be active in the aristocratic type, and reactive and weakened in the plebeian slave type.[2] A vicious cycle is thus created, a double knot between being resentful and the capacity to be self-determining—resentful because one is not capable of affirming oneself, yet incapable of affirming oneself because one is resentful.

---

[1] Friedrich Nietzsche, *On the Genealogy of Morality* (Cambridge: Cambridge UP, 1994), 24.

[2] Gilles Deleuze, *Nietzsche et la philosophie* (Paris: Press Universitaire de France, 1962).

The genesis of resentment therefore resides in the individual's lack of emancipation, a sign of their minority status, of maturity still to come. But this unfulfilled desire for revenge, provoked by a sense of inferiority, is typical of the specific Judeo-Christian culture, which Nietzsche believes has taken on the secularised forms of socialism and democracy in the modern era. The philosopher seizes upon: "The *great* danger of humanity, its most sublime temptation and seduction—and toward what? Toward nothing? ... the beginning of the end, the moment it comes to a halt, the tiredness looking back, the will revolting against life, the last disease that gently and sadly takes hold," he sees "in the morality of compassion ... the most upsetting symptom of our European culture."[3] The true spiritual disease of our time, the morality of compassion, is the offspring of the misrepresentation of the values maneuvered by resentment. Because of the incapacity to confront the real enemy, the resentful seek to change the world, to transform every value and: "legitimise revenge in the name of justice —as if justice were nothing other than another development of the feeling of the person feeling offended—and afterwards to honour the effects of the reaction with revenge."[4]

The evangelical revelation and the cultural tradition which it inspires would have legitimated the misrepresentation of values, sanctioning the affirmation of impotent men. Christ's message has progressively led men to admire common individuals, more than heroes and wise men, who have respected, understood and loved others, and because of this they have sacrificed the desire for glory and social success. The secularised principles of Christianity, neighbourly love, solidarity, compassion, principles of equality and equal dignity for all men, are the signs of deep crisis fuelled by resentment, according to Nietzsche.

Nietzsche is credited with having translated the nature of resentment into scientific terms and with having shown the efficacy of this emotional condition in understanding modernity. You could appropriately speak of a Nietzschean model of resentment, with the distinctive features that define the object being the desire for revenge, the types of people, and the misrepresentation of values. These distinctive features are: the energetic and vitalistic idea of strength at the foundation of the moral construct and the misrepresentation of values; individualistic psychology, for which the incapacity to self-determine of some individuals taken singularly is the cause of resentment, and; the condemnation of the morality of compassion, the true spiritual disease of modern era.

---

[3] Nietzsche, *Genealogy of Morality*, 7.
[4] Ibid., 60.

The Resentment between False Egalitarianism
and Social Inequalities

The Nietzschean analytic model of resentment has been adopted and elaborated in its definition by the sociologist and phenomenologist Max Scheler who, in his essay entitled *Das Ressentiment im Aufbau der Moralen*, critically resumes and develops the thesis maintained in *Genealogy of Morals*. Scheler recognises that: "if we take a look at the history of Europe, we see resentment used to build morality in surprising activity."[5] But he distances himself from Nietzsche's opinion on resentment's participation in the construction of Christian morality, sustaining that: "the meaning of Christian values degenerates into resentment with extraordinary ease and has often have been understood in this latter sense, although, on the other hand, the nucleus of Christian ethics did not grow on soil of resentment."[6]

For Scheler, evangelical revelation expresses noble love toward another, which is ascended and seeks perfection, and not the flattening of values, which is the tendency of resentment. Christian love is fullness and vigorous active strength, which is not fuelled, as sustained by Nietzsche, by the incapacity of the individual to self-affirm. Resentment is instead fertile ground for the roots of modern bourgeois morality, of humanitarian culture, of the altruistic sociology of Auguste Comte, the political economy of Adam Smith and Ricardo, the democratic utilitarianism of Bentham. This is wherein the Nietzschean misunderstanding lies— according to Scheler, Nietzsche confused Christian love for bourgeois morality. Resentment would be generative of a *de facto* structure through which a reading of the world could be made, or a *Weltanschauung*. There are three distinctive principles of that conception of the world: the "democratisms"; the priority of that which is useful over that which is vital, and; the negation of the principle of solidarity. All three signs have in common the intrinsic incapacity of resentful men to conceive of an authentic judgment, independently of the conditioning of others, about the hierarchy of life values.

"Democratisms" only hide "the desire to lower those who are higher from a value perspective, those who are worth more, to the level of those below."[7] The principle of utility, to which we shall return in the next paragraph, levels off any difference in values. If every human relationship is reduced to its utility, to a mere economic relationship or a convenience,

---

[5] Max Scheler, *Ressentiment* (New York: Free Press of Glencoe, 1961), 74.
[6] Ibid., 75
[7] Ibid., 110.

other values of the social life are flattened and debased. In the same way, denying solidarity and esteem for others is a way for diminishing the vital connection uniting men, to not recognise the value of nobler men and of the higher spirit.

Scheler's phenomenological critique of the Nietzschean conclusion therefore rests on a very precise judgment—Nietzsche confused the nobility of Christianity with the mediocrity of bourgeois morality. However, if the Schelerian thesis is viewed at a distance, historically from the Nietzschean analyses, it does in any case constitute a coherent and in-depth application of the theoretical model proposed by Nietzsche from a psychological standpoint.

The basic nature of the phenomenological model of resentment is, as with Nietzsche, impotence, the incapacity of the common person to be self-determining and to act independently of social and cultural conditioning, for which:

> The feeling of revenge, envy, spite, wickedness, the joy of hurting and evil come into play in the formation of resentment only when they are neither followed by moral mastery ... nor by an action: an adequate expression of emotion in external manifestations ... and precisely when this consequence does not occur as such action or expression is stopped by an even more explicit awareness of one's own impotence.[8]

A resented person imagines themself as inferior or a loser, and this poisoning of self-image leads them to denigrate the value of others they recognise as winning and superior. This denigratory action is the peculiarity of the misrepresentation of values manoeuvred by resentment. This is visible, for example, in the case of a person who belittles the values of others who oppress them or, in the case of do-goodism, when in the name of false egalitarianism they want to level and nullify hierarchic differences.

The phenomenological analysis proposed by Scheler adopts and develops the main points of the Nietzschean model—the uniquely reactive nature of resentment, the belonging to a weak typology of men, and the reversal of values (beyond the fact that the reference values for the two authors are entirely different). However, Scheler has further contributed to the understanding of the phenomenology of resentment, structuring a principle essential for us not only to interpret modernity, but also, as we shall see below, late modern society.

---

[8] Ibid., 149.

Scheler deduces that in modernity the common man has been invited to immerse in a land of fun, where everyone is apparently considered equal, free to make their individual aspirations come true, but also where the real possibility of making them come true is strongly bound by social determiners.[9] Therefore, according to Scheler: "The maximum load of resentment will be possessed by a society in which political rights and other nearly identical types, along with a publicly recognised formal social equality, go hand in hand with the great differences of real power, real possession of assets and real cultural formation."[10]

Resentment is not so much fuelled by egalitarianism, as by the acute contradiction between expectations of equality and structural inequality, of systemic antagonism between "formal social equality" and "great differences in de facto power." Scheler holds that the manifestation of resentment can more exactly be the result of the contradiction between the development of these egalitarianisms and the continuation of inequality, along with the incapacity (in the absence of individual and collective ways) to overcome social disparity.

Mimesis of Resentment

Nietzsche's genealogical analyses and Scheler's phenomenological study define resentment as a privileged interpretive key of modern times, which can be useful to understanding many problems. Resentment highlights connections that emerge from the replication, in highly diverse contexts, of reconstruction strategies of the sense and identity which have surprisingly analogous aspects and which the two great scholars—at the end of the 1800s and at the beginning of the 1900s—summarised into a theoretical model for interpreting the close relationship between affective life and the historic and social processes of modernity.

Nevertheless, said analysis did not receive much attention from social science scholars during the first half of the 1900s. Many studies have injected new vigour into the study of resentment and phenomenology in the last fifteen years or so. In particular, René Girard, with his mimetic theory of desire, proposed the theme again in an anthropological and relational key through a critical analysis of the Nietzschean model.[11]

The mimetic theory can be outlined in the expression *desire selon l'autre*. The desiring subject is anthropologically bound to the other for

---

[9] See Lewis Alfred Coser, "Introduction" in M. Scheler, *Ressentiment*.
[10] Scheler, *Ressentiment*, 145.
[11] Renè Girard, *Things Hidden Since Foundation of the World* (Stanford, CA: Stanford University Press, 1987).

forming and transforming themself over social interactions. By definition, they are lacking, are not autonomous or self-sufficient, but their condition of incompleteness is generative, an expression of openness and potentiality, and not a sign of lower worth or weakness, as maintained by Nietzsche and many other scholars. It is a dynamic and relational condition that makes the other a model to be imitated in order to be able to desire. The model is those who imitated the ways, tones, gestures, styles and desires up to the point of desiring according to the other, and finally wanting to be them.

Mimetic desire requires a review of the Western conception of desire and imitation.[12] In fact, it is not the urge of a subject, who by nature desires, that is important. It is not even the fascination exerted by some objects, which appear desirable because of social or cultural conditioning imagined as external, to activate our desire. Not even an object becomes desirable because of its economic scarcity or because of its intrinsic qualities. Desire returns to the intersubjective relationship which delineates in triangular forms when the subject sets their eyes on an object because the model is looking at it. Mimetic desire is a triangular desire between the subject, the model and the object. The object can be a symbol, an artifact, a social status or even another person, and it is the third which acquires value in the eyes of the subject, because it is desired by the model.

The model is desired, but as such it is also the reason for competition, because it will always be near the object of desire. It will also be the rival who desires that which the subject desires. This is the most innovative aspect of the mimetic theory, but also the hardest to accept, which is at the base of the mimetic analysis of resentment; the constituent ambivalence of desire is at the same time generative openness and destructive potentiality.

Girard maintains that the genesis of desire is in the action reflected by the desire of the other. He argues for the original and counter-intuitive aspect, showing that the relationship between the subject and the other is so constituent of the subjective identity that it paradoxically ends up concealing the rivalry first and the resentment thereafter. The risk of conflict and rivalry risks becoming inevitable when desirous eyes meet on a single object, like two hands that, converging on a single object, inevitably collide.

When desire is at one with the rivalry (and is fuelled by it), the drift toward resentment and violence is always possible. Rivalry mounts like a river in flood, because the object will never satisfy a desire that, due to its nature, aspires to the rival's existence, now identified as the enemy,

---

[12] Paul Dumouchel, *Èmotions* (Paris: Les empêcheur de penser en rond, 1995).

projected in the other's background by oneself. In this extreme action of separation between the subject and its model—now rival—the maximum confusion and loss of the differences is now experienced, such as in Escher's drawing hands. The relationship becomes recursive, making contrary instances cohabitate as a double reciprocal implication—the rival coincides with the model and vice versa. The need again arises to draw up a difference between the subject and their enemy because of the resentment of just when a unique, clear and singular identity can no longer be distinguished of oneself, confused as it is with the model-rival.

It is here, in the intricacy of the rivalry, in the immediacy with which each is a model and rival for the other, that the resentment "form of life" takes shape, which is: "That which the imitator feels with regard to his model when the model obstructs his efforts to possess the object over which both converge."[13]

Resentment, from a Girardian point of view, is not ascribable to any intra-psychic category, whether it is vital strength, incapacity for self-affirmation or index of a subjective reaction to humiliation experiences. Rather, it is an active construct that is socially built over the course of the interaction with the other relying on social and structural order. Resentment takes shape at the heart of human rivalry in the anthropological condition of reciprocal interdependence, contemporaneously finding restraining forms in the social organisation.

From the heritage of Emile Durkheim, Girard recognises that resentment was channelled through rituals in archaic communities, and that the mythical imagination of tendentially hierarchic order restrained possible emerging rivalries.

However, contrary to the great French sociologist, Girard insists on the crucial relevance that the figure of the sacrificial victim takes on in archaic social order. The rituals were peacemaking mechanisms centred on the figure of the scapegoat. On the one hand, the scapegoat indicates an innocent victim who, polarising the discontent on and around itself, saves the community from internal rivalries generated from the overflow of rivalry. On the other hand, the sacrificial victim, through their own death, draws an overwhelming difference between themself and the surrounding world. Herein lies the sacred, the great narration which inscribes the victim into a new order transcending the community. According to this ultimate narration, mythical to be precise, they who first was the generative cause of the crisis becomes the creator of a new harmonious order.

---

[13] René Girard, *Il Risentimento* (Milano: Raffaello Cortina, 1999), IX.

The hunt for the scapegoat in the evolutionary history of human societies has worked extraordinarily well for a long time, but it has been made progressively ineffective by the work of evangelical revelation over the course of the last two millennia, according to Girard, by bringing the violent nature of sacrifice to light, and by the subsequent secularising trends of modern times. Not that human societies have stopped generating scapegoats within them (Jews, blacks, Gypsies, the disabled, etc. have been tragic examples in recent history), but the peace making mechanism does not seem to work as it once did in archaic societies. A consequence of these radical transformations of ancient human expectations to find pacification of conflicts in the ritual killing of a victim is that resentment has deeply pervaded the souls of humans.[14]

This type of aspect of Girardian analysis, summarised schematically herein, re-adopts the Nietzschean idea, as above, according to which Christian anthropologists would have favoured spreading the desire for rivalry in every sector of public life. However, Girard, contrary to Nietzsche, and in agreement with Scheler, does not condemn Christianity. On the contrary, he maintains that it has given men the possibility to pacify their conflicts in a radically new way compared to the past, in a way that renounces violent demands as a necessary condition for reconciliation.

This important anthropological change, even before moral, naturally does not eliminate the risk that men will continue seeking scapegoats, according to Girard. They find themselves thus liberated from sacrificial mechanisms, but this liberation does not come without a price. The price to be paid depends on the mimetic nature of the desire which, liberated from the constraints of the past, manoeuvres undisturbed, generating great opportunities, but also great frustrations:

> Our society is the only one, or so it is said, that can trigger mimetic desire in a large number of sectors without fearing the irremediable collapse of the system ... We owe the prodigious "achievements" of the modern world, its inventive genius, etc. to the unexpected capacity to promote competition within limits that always remain socially, if not individually, acceptable. The price of all of this is not always extreme aggravation, but certainly the democratisation and spread of that which are called neurosis, connected in any case, it seems, to the reinforcement of competitive tension and to the "metaphysics" of these tensions.[15]

---

[14] Stefano Tomelleri, "Are we Living in a Society of Resentment?" in Wolfang Palaver, Petra Steinmair-Posel, Eds, *Passions in economy, Politics, and the Media* (Wien: Lit Verlag, 2005).

[15] René Girard, *Things Hidden Since Foundation of the World* (Stanford, CA: Stanford University Press, 1987), 387.

For Girard, contrary to Nietzsche, resentment therefore does not constitute an independent reality and an autonomous object of research. Rather, it corresponds to a specific dynamic of desire in modernity, which can take on different and complex forms. Therefore, this does not have to do with a true phenomenon in and of itself, but the term would lead back to certain specific aspects of historically located human interactions.

The importance of Girard's work is that it shifted from a definition of resentment in moral and psychological terms, which makes those who are crushed by its weight both victims and the guilty, and shifted it toward a more anthropological and sociological definition for certain aspects, when he conceived of resentment as an emotional tonality contained by historically determined social structures, which no longer confine it between the perimeter of the weak, the poor, and the petty bourgeois.

For a Sociology of Resentment

An analysis of Nietzsche's and Scheler's definition of resentment, filtered in particular by Girard's mimetic theory, offers the scholar of social sciences the possibility of an explicative model of resentment as a relational form generative of the modern social reality and, at the same time, as a relational form generated by specific historic processes, capable of highlighting the dynamic and circular nature of interaction dynamics between subjects, from micro and macro, between intra-psychic and social, and between order and disorder.[16]

This explicative model is defined firstly by three mutually complementary historic processes, generative of the main cultural transformations of modernity: the crisis of the hierarchy, the individualization of social manoeuvring, and the liberalization of desire. Secondly, it takes on social inequality as a structural condition intrinsic to modern social and late modern order.

The crisis of hierarchy. Competition progressively spread over the 1800s and 1900s, even in regard to the secularisation process, as an indisputable value of social action. Its diffusion in every part of public and private life has led to a loss of hierarchy, intended as a sense of limitation between that which is socially allowed to be expected and that which is not in a social relationship. The hierarchy indicates the subdivision

---

[16] Stefano Tomelleri, *Identità e gerarchia. Per una sociologia del risentimento* (Roma: Carocci, 2009).

between superior and inferior, and more generally remembers the limit between the parts and the whole of a relational and institutional relationship. The ideological and cultural foundation of the competition is a discussion on disconnection, the proliferation of fragmentation, and the precariousness of the existential and social condition. The perversion of the competition indicates that, when attributing a value to social action, the competition is the only parameter which annihilates any other dimension of action. Collaboration, justice, solidarity and trust in the other evaporate, taking on the rhetorical smoke of good intentions. It becomes a priority to have a congruent advantage to win the competitive challenge in relationships, and social relationships tend to take on an instrumental value. Not only is the competition pursued for a value, but the idea of an efficient performance is also central in the sense of the speed at which that which is needed is obtained. Social contexts require a speed of execution regarding the objectives imposed or urged in every sphere of life, which leaves little time for delays, contingencies, gratuitous events and social, listening and sharing moments, etc. In addition to competition and speed, it is also required to respond to rigorous standards, which establish universal criteria to be faster and more efficient (in fact, more competitive) to reach results. The metaphor of the docile robot immediately renders the meaning that tends to be attributed to productive process optimisation.[17] This is the inhuman technology, reproducible in series, where the social and artisan size of work continuously risks being reduced to a standardized and anonymous procedure.[18] The human element of the gesture tends to be transformed into an impersonal, replicable, mechanical component for fast precision of a useful and punctual action that does not allow for approximation or improvisation outside of protocol schemes. The historic affirmation of exasperated competition produces that which Lacan has analysed as a transformation of the owner (the hierarchic principle being the rule, the law, the order, the universally consolidated norm) in capitalistic discourse. If the owner's discourse asserts a hierarchic concept of power, instead the capitalistic discourse promises false democracy and egalitarianism. The promise for happiness is not only a resolution of the lack thereof, but a creation of a multiplication of possibilities and their achievement. However, when there is less of a sense of limitation, the risk is a flattening of differences and diffusion of social insecurity. People feel

---

[17] Charles Wright Mills, *The Sociological Imagination* (New York: Oxford University Press, 1959).

[18] Richard Sennett, *Microsociology: Discourse, Emotion and Social Structure* (Chicago: Chicago University Press, 1990); Richard Sennett and Jonathan Cobb, *The Hidden Injuries of Class* (New York, NY: Knopf, 1972).

ever more blocked in their aspirations, because exasperated competition exposes them to the risk of defeat and failure. The more interactive contexts there are and the more competitive they are (entry into formation paths, into the workplace, into the planetary market, etc.) the more the capacity to act is put into crisis. This produces intolerance, which makes the planning and designing of your own biography and professional career ineffective. Competition exposes the competitors to the uncertainty of not knowing how long they will be capable of continuing the challenges they faced with. When the number and type of possibilities, and the number of players to consider, multiplies, the choice—and the consequent achievement of dreams—becomes a less and less stable solution and ever more the beginning of a transitional event, often critical, within a fragmented, dynamic network of relationships and events in which the individual only governs a minimal part. The semantics of choice becomes enriched with the vocabulary of a selective and individualized reality, where the individual not only feels that one option excludes another, but also knows that they will not have a certain outcome, because there will always be a rival against whom to measure a situation, leading to a feeling of failure and resentment.

Individualisation. Exasperated competition makes nearly all promises of happiness in vain, and no longer regards collectivism as a whole but as an individual, which becomes the measure of all things. In good and bad, the individual has become the solitary terminal of social contradictions.[19] The deep cultural matrix of the configuration of the individualistic ideology has been brought to light by the study of the history of ideas by Louis Dumont. The French anthropologist showed that the affirmation of the individual in the modern West has a historic characteristic of exceptionality whose roots are found in the Judeo-Christian tradition:

> Where Nietzsche spoke of resentment, he would have attempted to see envy as the psychological concomitance of egalitarian revenge. Instead we are facing an essential perception: the quality of Christians makes all men equal and places the integral essence of man in each of them, so to speak. This is why they are justified, or better, are called on to oppose any affirmation of humanity not derived from their own interiority.[20]

The anthropological conception of the evangelical revelation places the individual on a transcendental plane in regard to the world and its institutions. The individual progressively becomes a measurement of all

---

[19] Ulrick Beck, *Risikogesellschafti* (Frankfurt am Main: Verlag, 1986).
[20] Louis Dumont, *Essais sur l'individualismei* (Paris: Seuil, 1983), 108.

things, thanks to a privileged condition of the individual-in-relation-to-God, which implies a reversal of the hierarchy at the base of the entire history of social order of human societies that, exalting a holistic totality, subordinated the individual entirely to it. From this reversal of the value hierarchy, which has always been considered a natural given, that dualism was created between the individual and the society that characterises the Western world and allows for the affirmation of economic and individualistic conceptions of good and value, for which:

> The modern scenario is well known. In the first place, modern conscience prevalently attributes the concept of value to the individual and philosophy deals mostly with individual values ... Furthermore in language, the word value, which in Latin means vigour, strength, and in Medieval times designated the courage of a warrior, today mainly symbolises the power of money as a measurement for all things.[21]

However, this individualistic shift is not the only characteristic feature of contemporaneous biographies, as the positive side of the individualization processes must not be forgotten. Individuals feel free from every rigid form of control, planning and rationalising their beliefs and behaviour models. They learn to build a more and more singular and dynamic personal and professional knowledge which consents them to make flexible and responsible actions in regard to action spaces that are no longer pre-determined. The modern idea of autonomy, self-achievement and possible achievement of the individual and only life project continues, bearing fruit in the individual conscience. On the other hand, this evolutionary side of the individualisation process continues (in a sometimes sneaky way) being close to the borderline of failure. Each individual feels free to "make a career," to "be successful," to "restart living from zero in social relationships," claiming independence from others; however, this risks denying every value of the connection of mutual trust and interdependence, which is the indispensable condition for achieving individual life projects, concretely lived, not only abstractly conceptualized. The centrality of the individual then risks taking on a persona of highly problematic, if not pathological, connotations, according to which, in various ways, is called "the era of sad passions," "the solitude of the global citizen," and "the difficulty of being oneself."[22] This is, in fact, a resentful society.

---

[21] Dumont, 263.

[22] Darian Leader, *The New Black: Mourning, Melancholia and Depression* (London: Pinguin 2009), 183.

Liberation of desires. The process of individualisation liberates and multiplies desires. The rationalisation of individual biographies has gradually taken the place of religious finality, creating a space of liberty where desire is no longer mediated in its achievement by a hierarchic order founded on divine law. Achieving desires is the task that each person autonomously acquires. Desire is triggered in many sectors without fearing any limitations, and the generative creativity of the modern world, with its extraordinary achievements, but also the progressive commercialisation of the social life, is due to this unprecedented promotion of desire. Each person is offered a plurality of choices and possibilities, which in traditional communities were unimaginable. A typical characteristic of modern liberation of desires is that the path to power and richness is potentially open to all, regardless of your starting point. This breeds frenetic social activity, a blending of work and jobs, continuous agitation, a desire to continue exceeding oneself. Richness, access to prestigious professions, a high standard of living, are the aspirations of an ambitious desire, which is willingly imagined to accomplish great things. The achievement of a desire presents itself as the capacity to negotiate the multiple possibilities offered by the commercialisation of human relationships, meaning an exploratory process of different possibilities experienced one at a time in the great supermarket of possible choices, which more often than not turn out to be improbable illusions more than opportunities.

The price to pay for this "liberation" is the risk of spreading frustrations bound to the reinforcement of competitive tensions. The emancipation of ancient automatic obedience to transcendental collective norms does not only liberate desires, but also exposes them to alienation. The individual no longer finds the reasons for their own desire elsewhere or outside of themselves, in the potent agencies of the magical or religious imagination, but in the imminent dimension of their own subjectivity:

> Today, so to speak, everything reduces down to the individual. It is up to the individual to establish that which he is capable of doing, to take that capacity to the extreme limit and choose the ends to which that capacity can be better applied, meaning the greatest possible satisfaction.[23]

The idea of an individualistic desire without the limits imposed by social hierarchies broadens the field of possible achievement of desires, but also contemporaneously broadens exposure to the risk of humiliation,

---

[23] Zygmunt Bauman, *Liquid Modernity* (Cambridge: Polity Press, 2000), 68.

paradoxically encouraging the chase toward ever more unattainable goals. The surprising richness of material wealth accessible made by the commercial economies of advanced capitalism is not sufficient to satisfy a desire which is more and more often the source of spiritual suffering.

Social inequality. Despite promises for a radiant future and unstoppable progress, modern and late modern times have been marked by structural conditions of actions characterised by a worsening of social and economic inequalities. The advantages of mass industrial production, consumerism, scientific and technological medical progress and other things have made the life of the common Westerner enviable for most inhabitants of the world in every historic time. However, access to resources, knowledge and opportunities remains seriously unequal, and in some situations the gap between the strata of the population is so broad that within the same opulent society of the north of the world you can find forms of discomfort similar to the more tragic of the south.[24] Whoever aspires to their own individualistic self-achievement, on the heels of a desire to seek unlimited goals, must pass the extremely difficult test of meeting all of the conditions to access the market of offers before choosing in a most right and favourable way. Late modern society, as already rightly stated by Scheler regarding modernity, is egalitarian with respect to proclaimed values, but unequal not only for the great differences of power between the governing classes and the masses, but also for a renewed, growing inequality of real possessions of material and immaterial wealth. Simultaneously competitive and unequal social relationships spread which, as seen in Scheler's phenomenological analyses, are the most favourable conditions for spreading resentment. An unease inseparable from the tireless tension toward achieving one's desires that always self-propagates as individualistic, is ever more exasperated in the paradoxical combination between growing competition among equals and a structural inequality no less growing, therefore condemned because of the unfulfilled desire, and for the desire for revenge, to which there is no response.

The analysis of resentment highlights the interweaving of affective life and the cultural transformations of Western societies. It shows the dark side of the falsely egalitarian, frenetically competitive disconnect promoting individualistic metaphysics, and the increasing resentment of a useful scientific category to include the generative nucleus of contemporaneous emotionality, both intrinsically social and relational.

---

[24] Jack M. Barbalet, "A Macro Sociology of Emotion: Class Resentment," *Sociological Theory* 10 (2) (1992): 150.

The Crisis of Social Regulation Devices of Resentment

Resentment is not an emotion like anger, hate, or fear, but a specific form of social relation, a way of viewing the world with "bitter blood," which arises in egalitarian and competitive societies with growing self-reflective capacities. Resentment can remain hidden, especially in those personal and psychological histories in which it is lived as a failure and moral fault, just as Nietzsche rightly asserted. But as a social relationship, resentment manifests in clearly manifested public violence.[25] The interesting point is that the individual and the social level are not separate fields, and not only do they interact, there is also continuity.

Resentment is a radically "ambivalent social relationship," potentially open to destructive shifts and generative possibilities; not only is it the source of discontent, but it also constitutes, as Nietzsche stated, an extraordinary creative push. A spring that can trigger the transformation of dissatisfaction and discontent in projects, creative work, the achievement of conditions of greater social justice, fraternal shifts in vital daily relations, etc. Over the course of history, resentment has been the reason for social aggregation as much as it has been cause for social division.[26]

Considering this intimate ambivalence, it will be clearer that the concrete outcome of resentment in carrying out social interactions is never predetermined. It can transfigure, so to speak, for better or for worse, even according to the binds and possibilities that the institutions and cultural repertories offer to individuals and their relations. The action of transfiguration is not only a transformation of frustrations into higher ends, in a sense of moral elevation and spiritual conquest, but is also the search, not necessarily aware, for self-regulating social systems, conflictual tensions and transformation to new expressive forms of that feeling of frustration.

In the contemporaneous societies there has been a rapid weakening of the symbolic public space; a process leading to a crisis of the legitimacy of resentment-transfiguration devices. The processes of mass society and commercialisation of human relations menace the culture of solidarity, colonising the public sphere and actively running to erode autonomy. The ever more interiorised subjectivity, the pursuit of profit or well-being on the horizon of a present without long-term planning, the aspirations for self-achievement within homogeneous and self-referential social circles, the solidarity of the group, the clan, the private company and often the private-social, pervade an ever more empty sense of sharing and binding

---

[25] Paul Dumouchel, *Le sacrifice inutile* (Paris: Flammarion, 2011).
[26] Marc Ferro, *Le ressentiment dans l'histoire* (Paris: Odile Jacob, 2007).

the public sphere, increasingly made up of frenetically elusive false encounters.[27]

The emphasis on individual self-affirmation fuels separation between the individual player and the overall relations and social institutions which orient the action. In this situation the social players mature an abstract concept of the individual, which leads to devaluing relational and societal points of reference, indispensable for personal self-achievement, and paradoxically ends up negating individual concrete subjectivities.

Works Cited

Barbalet, Jack M. "A Macro Sociology of Emotion: Class Resentment." *Sociological Theory* 10 (2) (1992): 150.

—. *Emotion, Social Theory and Social Structure. A Macrosociological Approach.* Cambridge: Cambridge University Press 1998.

Bauman, Zygmunt. *Liquid Modernity.* Cambridge: Polity Press, 2000.

Beck, Ulrick. *Risikogesellschaft.* Frankfurt am Main: Lit Verlag, 1986.

Coser, Lewis Alfred. "Introduction." In M. Scheler, *Ressentiment.* New York: Free Press of Glencoe, 1961.

Deleuze, Gilles. *Nietzsche et la philosophie.* Paris: Press Universitaire de France, 1962.

Dumont, Louis, *Essais sur l'individualisme.* Paris: Seuil, 1983.

Dumouchel, Paul. *Le sacrifice inutile.* Paris: Flammarion 2011.

—. *Èmotions.* Paris: Les empêcheur de penser en rond, 1995.

Ferro, Marc. *Le ressentiment dans l'histoire.* Paris: Odile Jacob, 2007.

Gans, Eric. *Signs of Paradox: Irony, Resentment, and Other Mimetic Structures.* Stanford: Stanford University Press, 1997.

Girard, René. *Il Risentimento*, edited by Stefano Tomelleri. Milano: Raffaello Cortina, 1999.

—. *Things Hidden Since Foundation of the World.* Stanford, CA: Stanford University Press, 1987.

Leader, Darian. *The New Black: Mourning, Melancholia and Depression.* London: Pinguin 2009.

Mills, Charles Wright. *The Sociological Imagination.* New York: Oxford University Press, 1959.

Nietzsche, Friedrich. *On the Genealogy of Morality.* Cambridge: Cambridge UP, 1994.

---

[27] Richard Sennett, *Together. The Rituals, Pleasures and Politics of Cooperation* (New Haven & London: Yale University Press, 2011).

Sennett, Richard. *Together. The Rituals, Pleasures and Politics of Cooperation.* New Haven & London: Yale University Press, 2011.

—. *Microsociology: Discourse, Emotion and Social Structure.* Chicago: Chicago University Press, 1990.

Sennett, Richard & Cobb, Jonathan. *The Hidden Injuries of Class.* New York, NY: Knopf, 1972.

Tomelleri, Stefano. "Are we Living in a Society of Resentment?" In *Passions in economy, Politics, and the Media*, edited by Wolfang Palaver & Petra Steinmair-Posel. Wien: Lit Verlag, 2005.

—. *Identità e gerarchia. Per una sociologia del risentimento.* Roma: Carocci, 2009.

CHAPTER FOURTEEN

HIDDEN INJURIES:
CLASS RESENTMENT IN WESTERN
DEMOCRACIES[1]

MARÍA GÓMEZ-GARRIDO

After World War II, humanities went through a fragmentation between political philosophy, social theory and phenomenology. With some exceptions, like various feminist critiques, social and political theory conceived subjects without bodies; power, cooperation and conflict were theorised as if agents were only minds and were often invested with only one kind of rationality. The renewed interest in emotions, particularly noticeable since the 1990s, indicates a demand to reintroduce experience into social theory and political philosophy. Any research on, for example, the formation of collective identities, or political mobilisations, needs to bring back the experiences of suffering, enthusiasm, hope, fear or anxiety of those groups we study. At the same time, research on the role of "emotions" needs to incorporate social and political theory in order to avoid a too-simplistic psychologisation of those social processes.

A reflection on resentment places us in front of the various difficulties entangled in the study of any passion or emotion. There is a wide body of research, from neuroscience to some theoretical trends in sociology, like structuralism, which studies emotions as if these were natural kinds. These otherwise heterogeneous approaches build theories that establish causal relations in the dynamics of emotional experiences.

From a perspective more sensitive to history and culture, emotions are seen as being traversed by symbols, memories, rules and values.[2]

---

[1] I am grateful to Jesús Izquierdo, Dolores Martín-Moruno and Peter Wagner for their useful comments and remarks on previous versions of this chapter. Unfortunately, I have not been able to introduce all their suggestions.

According to it, emotions cannot be of a universal, univocal nature, as they are necessarily embodied in a human being, subjected and vulnerable to discourse. Moreover, our vocabularies, referred to those experiences we call "emotions," are tinged with connotations of old usages and new meanings. Consequently, on the one hand, we sometimes have one label to refer to emotional experiences which are nevertheless different (we can think of the many variations of "love": romantic love, courteous love, erotic love, maternal love),[3] and on the other, we have different historical labels which have denoted very similar experiences (like sixteenth-century melancholy, and twenty-first-century depression, although arguably the active role of psychiatry and pharmacology has changed the meaning and experience of the latter).[4]

Most sociologists—even those who try to do physics of the social world—admit that there are some kinds of emotions, called "secondary," which are not innate, but the result of socialisation and subjected to historical variation.[5] Seen from any classificatory principle, resentment constitutes one of these "secondary" emotions which are not simply instinctive but the result of social and historical processes. Resentment is also of particular interest as some authors attribute to it an alleged repression of other emotions, like hatred or rage.

Nietzsche and Scheler elaborated a theory of resentment which became the most widely accepted interpretation in political philosophy. For these authors, *ressentiment* was a distressing experience that expressed the

---

[2] Sergio Moravia, "Esistenza e passione," in Silvia Vegetti Finzi and Remo Bodei, *Storia delle passion* (Roma: Laterza, 1995), 3–38.
[3] There is certainly the Christian distinction between *eros* and *agape*, which constitutes an interesting chapter in the history of emotions.
[4] Allan V. Horwitz & Jerome C. Wakefield, *The Loss of Sadness* (New York: Oxford University Press, 2007). An interesting cross-cultural research about the vocabularies of emotions in Anna Wierzbicka, *Emotions across Languages and Cultures* (Paris: Cambridge University Press, 1999).
[5] The classification of emotions in different kinds can be traced back to Simmel. The German sociologists distinguished between primary emotions, which were the direct cause of sociability; and secondary emotions, which were the result of interactions with others. Primary emotions were love, hate, *philia*. Secondary emotions were gratitude, shame. Today many sociologists, following Kemper, maintain some sort of classification between "primary" emotions (fear, anger, depression and satisfaction, for Kemper), which are considered innate and therefore universal, and "secondary" emotions, which are the result of processes of socialization and consequently depend on symbolisation and narration (guilt, pride, shame). Theodore D. Kemper, "How many emotions are there?" *The American Journal of Sociology* 93 (1987): 263–289.

inability of those placed at the bottom of a social scale to assert their own value, or to admire those placed above. For Nietzsche, *ressentiment* was embodied by the champions of Judeo-Christian culture with their coronation of the weak; for Scheler it was an emotion experienced in liberal democracies by those, like the petty bourgeoisie, who were placed in relatively subordinate positions, who stubbornly demanded equality. For both authors *ressentiment* was pathological: first, because its characteristic repression of other emotions, like anger or hatred, inflicted an acute damage on those who suffered it; secondly, because in its devaluation of those outstanding and placed above *ressentiment* manifested the insanity of those who embodied it.

With the term *ressentiment*, Nietzsche and Scheler actually resignified previous uses of resentment in political theory. If, in their hands, *ressentiment* becomes a degrading emotion that betrays the unworthiness of those who embody it, Hume and Smith had previously considered that *resentment* was not only a legitimate passion, but the safeguard of justice.[6] In this chapter I want to briefly revise Nietzsche's and Scheler's interpretation of *ressentiment* to find some similarities in the theory of Relative Deprivation, which is a well-established explanation of social distress in sociology. Against this perspective, I want to explore how resentment, and in particular class resentment, can be understood differently through the framework of a theory of recognition. I end by posing some notes on the malleable nature of emotional experience. In the context of democratic societies, the pain associated with being treated with contempt may be universal but the concrete forms this pain takes (an individual sense of failure; a collective sense of indignation) depend on the political processes that represent, mediate and transform those individual experiences. These metamorphoses show the absence of any natural or automatic development of the emotion.

---

[6] Hume considered it a condition of justice that those excluded from a community "made us feel their resentment"; *Enquiry, cf.* Annette C. Baier, "Hume on Resentment," *Hume Studies* 6 (1980): 133–149; For Adam Smith this emotion was "the safeguard of justice and the security of innocence," *The Theory of Moral Sentiments* (Oxford: Clarendon Press, 1976), 70; The violation of justice creates injuries and becomes what Smith considers the proper object of resentment.

Comparison and Envy—the Alleged Miserable Roots of *Ressentiment*

In the *Genealogy of Morals* [1887],[7] Nietzsche explored the conditions that have made *ressentiment* possible in the history of humanity. He emphasized how a certain doctrine, and a culture associated to it, encouraged a particular *ethos*, a series of values and attitudes which had a direct correlation in the emotional experiences of certain groups. According to his definition, *ressentiment* was a psychological state resulting from suppressed feelings of anger and hatred whose origins lay in a consciousness of inferiority with regards to others. When becoming conscious of their inferior position, those below want to make everything equal, blurring the lines of distinction that mark those above. For Nietzsche, Judeo-Christian culture represented the paradigmatic embodiment of this emotion – it gave to those who were inferior in society, because they lacked the will to assert and to dominate their own and other's lives, a moral justification for their lowness.

In 1915 Max Scheler published a phenomenology of *ressentiment* in democratic societies clearly inspired by the work of the philosopher. He presumed envy and a repression of emotions as its main components.[8] For Scheler, the roots of *ressentiment* lay in a comparison with others in which the person felt in disadvantage because (s)he did not have access to the same goods, or could not enjoy the same status. Nietzsche's sharp despise for Christianity was carefully neglected by Scheler, who focused his critique on the value of equality that permeated European democracies. Both, however, shared an aversion towards those doctrines that blurred the lines of distinction, considering them to be proof of a hidden hatred.

Scheler remarked one important premise that was fundamental in his interpretation of *ressentiment* as the core emotion of liberal democracies—that the experience of inequality is not necessarily painful; *ressentiment* proliferates under specific conditions, namely when equality is formally assumed, whereas important situations of inequality actually persist:

> *Ressentiment* must be especially strong in a society where formal social equality, publicly recognized, goes hand in hand with wide factual differences of power, property and education. While each has the right to compare himself with everyone else, he cannot do so in fact. Quite

---

[7] I have worked with the Spanish translation: Friedrich Nietzsche, *La genealogía de la moral* (Madrid: Alianza, 1972).
[8] Max Scheler (1915), *Ressentiment* (Milwaukee Winsconsin: Marquette University Press, 1998).

independently of the characters and experiences of individuals, a potent charge of *ressentiment* is here accumulated by the very structure of society.[9]

In contrast to Nietzsche, therefore, Scheler suggested in some parts of his work that *ressentiment* is an emotion emerging under certain social and cultural conditions. Paradoxically, though, the insidious mechanism of *ressentiment* lay for Scheler in the doctrine of equality and not in the actual situations of inequality that contradicted it.

> The postulate of equality—be it moral, social, political, ecclesiastical equality or equality of property—seems harmless, but who does not detect behind it the desire to degrade the superior persons, those who represent a higher value, to the level of the low.[10]

Ressentiment was the manifestation of the tensions resulting from a culture of equality in a society of naturally unequal persons. Though Scheler placed *ressentiment* in a social context (the particular tensions of liberal democracies where the values of equality are in contradiction with actual inequalities), he followed Nietzsche in providing a radically asocial interpretation of this emotional experience—the situation of those below is due to their own (in)abilities and not to the dynamics of the social structure. And *ressentiment* was for him, as for Nietzsche, a degrading emotion that betrayed the unworthiness of those who embodied it.

The resentful is at the opposite ends of Nietzsche's master—the aristocrat, the man of high standards, is someone who only considers his own values and deeds and takes his own purposes as a guide for action. In this romantic idealisation there is no mirror from which to figure an image of oneself, only self-purpose, self-assertion. Nietzsche and Scheler saw in the act of comparison the drama of *ressentiment*, the essence of its degrading character.

Twentieth-Century Sociology and the Concept of Relative Deprivation

What in Nietzsche and Scheler serves a normative purpose—the moral criticism of those who compare themselves with the groups standing above, and demand equal value of all—becomes a fundamental analytical principle in one of the most accepted theories of social distress in

---

[9] Ibid., 33.
[10] Ibid., 104.

twentieth-century sociology. In the theory of Relative Deprivation, the drama of comparison is also the scene in which this painful experience is articulated. Resentment appears in the writings of Robert Merton and Walter Runciman in close association with this concept, defined as "the discrepancy between actors' value expectations and their value capabilities."[11] The theory of Relative Deprivation does not presume any intrinsic superiority of some groups over others; inequalities are due to socio-structural factors, and not to the natural abilities or attitudes of the individuals in those groups. But uneasiness is felt when comparing with others, and the theory focuses in large part in analysing which is the reference group, or the group one compares with: "most often those we have direct interaction with, but also those who are of our same status [even if we do not have direct relation with them], or some others we just compare with because of different circumstances."[12]

The concept of Relative Deprivation, like Scheler's phenomenology of *ressentiment*, relates this experience not so much to a painful past of offences[13] as to a present of unfulfilled expectations. Two important elements constitute this theory. First, it emerges in the context of Western democratic societies where the idea of equality and social mobility among the citizenry opens the frame of reference (i.e. the groups of reference) that condition the experience of grievance of the subjects. Second, expectations are conceptualised in this theory under a utilitarian framework, according to which class is a social position that allows a certain lifestyle and the possession of certain goods. Frustration emerges when: "individuals who

---

[11] Ted R. Gurr, *Why Men Rebel*, (Princeton: Princeton University Press, 1970), 24. The concept is particularly developed in Robert Merton, *Social Theory and Social Structure* (New York: Free Press) and Walter Runciman, *Relative Deprivation and Social Justice: A Study of Attitudes to Social Inequality in Twentieth-century Britain* (London: Routledge, 1966).

[12] Robert Merton, *Social Theory and Social Structure*, 233. The concept of reference group is in Herbert Hiram Hyman, "The psychology of status," *Archives of Psychology* 269 (1942): 5–91, and Tamotsu Shibutani, "Reference groups as Perspectives," *American Journal of Sociology* 60 (1955): 562–569.

[13] Past offences mark the experience of "rancour." Indeed, it may be argued that Jean Améry's heart-breaking essay *"Ressentiments"* deals in fact with rancour rather than resentment. His painful experience and consequent hatred are very clearly expressed. Besides, his situation is not just that of someone who is undervalued, but of a victim of atrocious violence, a subject I am not dealing with here. As I will suggest, the experience of offence is present in resentment, but in connection to misrecognition.

lack something compare themselves with those who have it, and in so doing feel a sense of deprivation."[14]

The role of comparison and frustration had been underlined by Thomas Humphrey Marshall in his theory of class conflict. Following this, Barbalet develops a theory of class resentment in which he relates this emotion to structural determinants. Resentment is the: "feeling experienced by social actors when an external agency denies them *opportunities or valued resources* (including status) that otherwise would be available to them"[15] [italics are mine].

The interpretation of resentment under the framework of the theory of Relative Deprivation shares a utilitarian perspective with some theories of class conflict, in which the individual is supposed to suffer frustration because they cannot enjoy certain preferences or utilities that others enjoy.[16] Although intuitively acceptable, the argument about comparison misses an important anthropological dimension that makes resentment more intelligible—the human need for recognition.

On the Emotional Experience of Misrecognition— Shame and Resentment

The need to obtain a favourable image in the eyes of others was considered a constitutive axis of human nature by most thinkers of the Scottish Enlightenment. Our humanness was characterised not so much by our ability to reason as by our need to get a favourable judgement from others. Lack of recognition leads to a painful experience, but this can adopt different colours. The most common, succinctly studied by Hutcheson, is "shame":

> There is a determination of our minds as natural as that of gratitude and love to our benefactors which is to delight in the good opinion and love of

---

[14] John Scott & Gordon Marshall, *A Dictionary of Sociology* (Oxford: Oxford University Press, 2009).

[15] Jack M. Barbalet, "*A Macro-Sociology of Emotion: Class Resentment*," *Sociological Theory* 10 (1992): 153.

[16] This utilitarian interpretation inherent to the theory of relative deprivation is also proposed as the roots of different forms of collective protest, from riots to well-articulated political mobilisations. In this frustration-aggression model, social groups are supposed to mobilise the higher the intensity of the frustration felt, frustration being defined as "an interference with goal-directed behaviour." Gurr, *Why Men Rebel*, 9.

others, even when we expect no other advantage from them, except what
flows from this constitution, whereby honour is made an immediate good
… On the other hand, we are by nature subjected to grievous sensations of
misery, from the unfavourable opinions of others concerning us, even
when we dread no other evil from them: this we call *shame*; which in the
same manner as honour, is constituted an immediate evil.[17]

According to Hutcheson, we have by nature a moral sense of virtue,
which is placed above the importance of honour. But at the same time,
external signs of honour (wealth, prosperity in general) tend to be
collectively associated to an alleged virtue. The objects that constitute the
bases of honour may be completely arbitrary, having no intrinsic value,
but only that with which they are invested by a human group. However,
they have an impact on our affections. We search for those valued objects
as a way to obtain public esteem. In his *Essay on the Nature and Conduct
of the Passions and Affections* (1728), Hutcheson developed this idea:

The laws or customs of a country, the humour of our company may have
made strange associations of ideas, so that some objects, which of
themselves are indifferent to any sense by reason of some additional
grateful idea, may become very desirable; or by like addition of an
ungrateful idea may raise the strongest aversion. Thus many a trifle, when
once it is made a badge of honour … a monument of some great action,
may be impatiently pursued from our desire of honour. When any
circumstance, dress, state, posture is constituted as a mark of infamy, it
may become in like manner the object of aversion, though in itself most
inoffensive to our senses … Thus dress, retinue, equipage, furniture,
behaviour and diversions are made matters of considerable importance by
additional ideas. Nor is it in vain that the wisest and greatest men regard
these things; for however it may concern them to break such associations
in their own minds, yet since the bulk of mankind will retain them, they
must comply with their sentiments and humours in things innocent, as they
expect public esteem.[18]

External signs of honour symbolise a better kind of humanity as a higher
expansion of capacities, but those signs are different in each society.
Historical research can shed light on the specific social processes that
created one particular recognition order over others (whether on the basis

---

[17] Francis Hutcheson, *An Inquiry into the Original of Our Ideas of Beauty and
Virtue,* (Hildesheim: George Olms Verlagsbuchhandlung, 1971), 200. I have
turned to Hutcheson inspired by Pizzorno's reference to the author.
[18] Francis Hutcheson, *Essay on the Nature and Conduct of the Passions and
Affections* (Hildesheim: George Olms Verlagsbuchhandlung, 1971), 9–10.

of land property, education, or on the basis of ascetic self-discipline, to mention some examples).[19] However, as humans we are shaped by the symbolic order that establishes the attributes worthy of respect in a society, and we constitute ourselves as subjects of worth by the recognition we obtain from the social group.[20]

Lack of recognition causes, as Axel Honneth has remarked, a moral grievance experienced as a painful injury by the unrecognised subject.[21] But what emotional tone does this suffering take? The author mentions the possibility of experiencing shame, but his concern is namely the

---

[19] Note that the society that Hutchetson is describing already has some of the signs—like wealth and "dress"—that twentieth-century capitalist democracies consider to be of value. Other historical societies have had very different signs of honour. For example, in some Jewish and Christian communities self-discipline and austerity have been seen as a badge of honour; In peasant societies, like that of Castile in the sixteenth and seventeenth-centuries, the contribution to the community was a requisite to be included and recognised as a member. Hierarchical relations were incorporated by a series of rules of reciprocity, and it was expected from the rich peasants to contribute to the common good as a sign of respect for the community. Jesús Izquierdo Martín, *El rostro de la comunidad* (Madrid: Consejo Económico y Social, 2001). Empirical research therefore needs to explore not only the different signs that have marked social recognition (wealth, education etc.), but also the different social norms that establish the recognition order. Pizzorno classifies up to four forms of recognition (more specifically, he uses the term "reputation"): excellence (among equals), credibility (the ability to make promises and be trusted), conformity (being compliant with the norms of a closed group and obtaining recognition by belonging to the group), and visibility (when the judgement depends on a public of spectators). Alessandro Pizzorno "Dalla reputazione alla visibilità," in *Il velo della diversità. Studi sulla razionalità e riconoscimento* (Milano: Feltrinelli, 2007), 228–247.

[20] This process is explored by and large by Alessandro Pizzorno who uses the term 'circles of recognition'. His work, however, goes beyond the scope of this essay, as he also inserts the variable of time. The value of our actions depends on the stability of the group that will assess them in the future. That is why we sometimes may fight first for the stability of that group, as our self depends on it. In turn, our *selves* may change over time as the groups that recognize and sustain our identity change. "Some other kind of otherness. A Critique of 'Rational Choice' Theories," in *Development, Democracy and the Art of Tresspassing: Essays in the Honor of Albert O. Hirschman*, edited by Alejandro Foxley, Michael S. McPherson and Guillermo O'Donnell. Notre Dame: University of Notre Dame Press, 145 – 184.

[21] Axel Honneth, *The Struggle for Recognition. The Moral Grammar of Social Conflicts* (London: Polity Press, 1995); and "Redistribution as recognition. A response to Nancy Fraser," in *Redistribution or Recognition: A Political-Philosophical Exchange*, edited by Nancy Fraser and Axel Honneth (New York: Verso, 2003).

indignation felt by those aggravated that will lead to social struggles in as much as they are able to name their indignation collectively. Honneth cautiously avoids taking the statement regarding social struggles as an anthropological yardstick, and reminds us that the concrete expectations of recognition vary historically. Nevertheless, he assumes in the large part of his work an ahistorical notion of disrespect from which subjects will always embark on a social struggle.

Challenging this view, empirical research developed by Pierre Bourdieu has shown that the established order is usually assumed as a natural course of things by those dominated, and seldom challenged.[22] The acceptance of the established order does not alleviate the possible experiences of suffering or uneasiness, but these will not necessarily be transformed in anger or indignation towards those above.[23] As a third possibility, the processes of "moral boundary drawing" have recently been observed; that is, the processes by which social groups distinguish themselves from others in terms of moral differences, claiming for themselves certain virtues which others lack, for example "we are down-to-earth, they are pretentious; we are cosmopolitan, they are parochial."[24] In the next section I want to present some excerpts of several empirical works on the experience of class in Western democratic societies in the twentieth-century, paying attention to its emotional tonality.[25]

---

[22] Pierre Bourdieu, *Distinction: A Social Critique of the Judgement of Taste* (New York: Harvard University Press, 1984); Pierre Bourdieu and Jean-Claude Passeron *Reproduction in Education, Culture and Society* (London: SAGE, 1990).

[23] In fact, when resentment emerges it is sometimes addressed towards other groups who are also in a marginal position. Pierre Bourdieu et al., *The Weight of the World: Social Suffering in Contemporary Society* (Standford: Standford University Press, 1999).

[24] Michelle Lamont, *The Dignity of Working Men: Morality and the Boundaries of Race, Class and Imagination* (New York: Russelll Sage Foundation at Harvard University Press, 2000); Andrew Sayer, "Class, Moral Worth and Recognition," *Sociology* 39 (2005): 947–963.

[25] I believe the kind of experiences narrated in these research works are common to all working classes in western democratic societies. But the cases provided are drawn from the United Kingdom and the United States. So I admit that there may be other experiences according to specific national working class traditions and history which I have overlooked here.

The Case of the Working Classes and Low Status Groups in Western Democratic Societies

In democratic societies, despite embracing the idea of unique human nature, inequalities between social classes persist and go in hand with unequal public estimation. As Bourdieu revealed, there are a series of signs that order the world and establish hierarchies between those with more and those with less capital (whether economic, social, or cultural). Ideas like "merit" or "taste," for example, hide inequalities originating from birth and help to exercise a symbolic violence over those who do not possess cultural capital. The interactions of those above with those below tend to be patterned by these marks of distinction. The particular recognition order created has an impact on the lives of those without badges of honour. Even worse, given that this recognition order is constructed over the foundations of an individualist ideology—that is, badges of honour allegedly recognise an individual's effort and achievement—it is particularly difficult to make the collective dynamics that place some social groups over others visible.

The distressing experience lived by those who are supposed to lack "merit" or "taste" does not necessarily bring resentment inside them—the categories and hierarchies established in a society are usually assumed by those below as a natural division in the world. Like the Fanonian black who sees themself through the eyes of the white order,[26] the dominant figuration enters the self-image of those below, weakening them.

The examples provided by empirical research are many. Elias & Scotson, in their seminal essay based on a neighbourhood in a British industrial town in the 1950s, examined how the political principles of equality had not precluded the development of an emotional distance towards those below, aided by all kinds of figurations on whom they were. The sociologists analysed how the established made their rules prevail over the outsiders and cast a slur on them. A rank order based on no other objective sign than antiquity of arrival was created between two of the three groups living in the neighbourhood studied, both of a working class origin, with similar rents and educational level. This imaginary order became naturalised as different virtuous and scornful attributes were figured on each of them. As the authors noted, we often forget that "lower status, to put it bluntly, can go hand in hand with degradation and suffering."[27]

---

[26] Frank Fanon, *Black Skin, White Masks* (New York: Grove Press, 1967).
[27] Norbert Elias & John Scotson, *The Established and the Outsiders. A Sociological Inquiry into Community Problems* (London: SAGE, 1994), 148.

In the 1970s an important body of research registers persistent experiences of disrespect among the working classes in both Britain and the United States. Seminal works like those by Lilian Breslow Rubin in Britain, or by Sennett & Cobb in the United States, show that in spite of having achieved a certain level of living standards the working classes were still traversed by a painful experience. But this suffering was not a self-inflected pain, or a consuming envy when looking at those unachievable middle class life-styles. The long interviews of manual workers carried out by Sennett and Cobb indicate that this pain had to do with how these groups saw themselves through the eyes of other, better-situated groups. The increasing contact of the working classes with the middle and upper classes has often mirrored a contemptible picture. Their uneasiness was not the result of envy towards others' possessions or positions, but the experience of being treated with contempt, and sometimes the grim belief that they deserved less because, lacking "badges of ability," in Sennett's pertinent expression, they felt worthless.

Research carried out in those same countries in the late 1990s indicates that the lines separating social classes had not blurred, and that this had emotional consequences on those below. In a 1997 publication, Walter C. Runciman reports how the rise in living standards among the British population, and the generational mobility that accompanied it, has not yet eliminated the unequal esteem attached to the different occupational roles. For Runciman: "liberal ideology has to confront the differences in the respect accorded by the members of some status-groups to the members of other status-groups on their ascriptive grounds."[28]

The differences in social respect and esteem granted for each social status bring experiences of social suffering. This pain is not that of the objects not possessed but rather the attributes unrecognised. Objects and attributes go hand in hand in a symbolic relation that expresses who one is. As these research works show, the painful experience of being misrecognised is lived as a form of shame. As Simon J. Charlesworth's phenomenological study has depicted, lacking the symbolic resources, the self-image of the subject of working class conditions becomes devalued: "One's perceptions of the world become ever more threatening, and seem to bite deeper at the core of self-hood, violating the realm upon which one's status as moral being for oneself depends."[29]

---

[28] Walter G. Runciman, *A Treatise on Social Theory* (Cambridge: CUP), 284.

[29] Simon J. Charlesworth, *A Phenomenology of Working-Class Experience* (Cambridge: Cambridge University Press, 2000).

Empirical research, like that carried out in North America by Gorman,[30] detects that many working class adults suffer from a lack of self-confidence. The mixture of embarrassment and shame when interacting with persons of a middle-class origin becomes stained with resentment:

> Still today I hold resentment for [white collar and college educated people]. I call them "suits." I think they look down on me because I work with my hands and not sit behind a desk. I think this country would be in bad shape if everybody wanted to sit behind a desk (male, 34, unemployed bridge painter, high school).[31]

The social gap felt between those with a college education and those without is particularly strong. Against this, some of the workers interviewed remarked on the value of what they did over those owing to the credentials of higher education:

> The way I look at it, if you want to have an easy life, have money in your pocket, and do no work, go to college. That aggravates me. College makes them feel above other people intelligence wise [sic] even though they just know a few fancier words, along with that comes the dress and the posture. They basically get in the way. If you took [us] and you took the people who went to college and you made two little separate cities, who's going to be living right? Who's going to build the houses and the plumbing? I am right. Let's face it, the college people need people like us more than we need them (male, 40, maintenance worker).[32]

Gorman asks himself what makes his working-class respondents "angry," and he finds three foci: middle class language, middle-class clothing and middle-class attitudes. According to Gorman, several working-class respondents voiced their resentment at, for example, attempts by middle-class college graduates to showcase their language skills in a way that becomes insulting for those who do not have those skills.

In the narration of the class experiences presented by all these research works, shame sometimes shifts towards resentment. Indeed, a resentment that shares some of the components that Nietzsche and Scheler described for *ressentiment*—in the midst of the painful experience of feeling inadequate, a denial of the value represented by those above emerges, but

---

[30] Thomas J. Gorman, "Cross-Class Perception of Class," *Sociological Spectrum* 20 (2000): 93–120.

[31] Ibid., 107.

[32] Ibid., 103.

it is not collective rage. Resentment, as a hidden emotion, emerges only after careful inquiry by the researcher.

As all these works show, shame and resentment are two experiences frequently experienced in capitalist democracies by the working classes who lack the badges of honour valued by these societies. While they are entitled to them, they very often have no conditions to access them. However, shame and resentment, as two experiences derived of misrecognition, are clearly different. Shame is an intense emotion under which one accepts the dominant view and "sees oneself through the eyes of a scornful other."[33] Under resentment, however, there is a feeling of injustice, which does not express itself in collective anger, but more often in individual (and only verbal) expressions of devaluation of those above. There is no logical rule by which we will experience shame or resentment; only the concrete historical and political processes tell us how those experiences are lived and transformed. But certainly both shame and resentment lose their pathological character when framed under the social dynamics of recognition. On the contrary, Nietzsche's idealisation of the aristocrat—someone with no mirror from which to picture himself— becomes a romantic dream far from any historical experience.[34] Indeed, can we really imagine a world of auto-referential badges of honour? Hardly.

Some Closing Remarks—On the Socio-Political Dimensions of Emotions

Nobody stands out through any kind of honourable or virtuous ability in solitude—that honour is always conferred by others. Lack of recognition causes suffering which, even if perceived as an individual experience, has a social and political dimension. The aim of this chapter has been to understand the experiences of shame and resentment of the working classes in democratic societies through the framework of the need for recognition. The excerpts from the research works show that those resented do not perceive the situation as legitimate, but that their "anger"

---

[33] Thomas J. Sheff, *Microsociology* (Chicago: University of Chicago Press, 1990), 122.

[34] Whether one looks at the Greek warriors, or the medieval knights studied by the historian George Duby, one always finds a tight order based on the articulation of mutual recognitions and obligations. The knights needed to proceed according to a series of community rules (loyalty, participation in the wars to defend their "family") which were very far from fancy or self-assertion.

is only expressed after inquiry by the interviewer rather than articulated in a form of social protest.

The feeling of moral grievance, manifested in the form of resentment, is not a universal condition, but rather an experience mediated by collective referents, like the value of equality. As historical research indicates the experience of injustice, and above all the possibility to articulate (express, represent, name) it, it is related to a collective frame of reference.[35] It this sense, resentment in twentieth-century democracies has often been explained in the form of a teleological argument, assuming that hierarchical societies inhabit less resentment than democratic societies, as in the latter the value of equality would make expectations rise. This renewal of Sheler's *ressentiment* in the interpretation of late modern societies[36] needs first to face those empirical cases that indicate signs of resentment in hierarchical societies.[37]

Secondly, the very individualist foundation of democracies in late capitalism clearly makes the creation of collective sites from where to enunciate injustice, reject established values or create new ones difficult. The situation is not so much that of a world of increasing expectations and fluid spaces,[38] but rather one of broken solidarities and unstable social bonds.

And still, in the midst of unstable and fragmented circles of recognition some social movements at the moment are expressing a feeling of

---

[35] A classical work on these questions is certainly that by Edward Palmer Thompson on the origins of the workers movement. His research revealed that the naming of injustice by the workers was supported, among other things, by an existing order of collective customs that was being broken by capitalism. Edward Palmer Thompson, *The Making of the English Working Class* (London: Victor Gollancz Ltd, 1963).

[36] This is one of the arguments developed in the fine work by Stefano Tommelleri, *Identità e gerarchia. Per una sociologia del risentimento* (Urbino: Carocci, 2009); Also, Bryan S. Turner, "Max Weber and the Spirit of Resentment," *Journal of Classical Sociology* 11 (2011): 75–92.

[37] Parish has studied how low-caste Newars in Katmandu share narratives (in the forms of moral tales) that invert the value order. These dissident narratives disclose the discomfort that low-caste Newars express when directly asked about concepts like karma or the impurity attributed to them. Steven M. Parish, "Narrative Subversions of Hierarchy," in *Selves in Time and Place: Identities, Experience and History in Nepal*, edited by Pach III Skinner and Holland (Lanham: Rowman & Littlefield Publishers, 1998), 51–85.

[38] Turner, "Max Weber and the Spirit of Resentment," 90.

uneasiness. The *indignados*[39] have proposed a political definition of various social injuries. In this way, the suffering stops being an individual experience, becoming a collective, public problem. The very act of political mobilisation restores the dignity of those suffering and resented, transforming their individual experiences. But that is part of different subject.

Works Cited

Améry, Jean. "Resentimientos." In *Más allá de la culpa y la expiación. Tentativas de superación de una víctima de la violencia.* Valencia: Pre-Textos, 2001.

Baier, Anne. "Hume on Resentment." *Hume studies* 6 (1980): 133–149.

Barbalet, Jack M. "A Macro-Sociology of Emotion: Class Resentment." *Sociological Theory* 10 (1992): 150–163.

Bourdieu, Pierre. *Distinction: A Social Critique of the Judgment of Taste.* New York: Harvard University Press, 1984.

—. *Weight of the World: Social Suffering in Contemporary Society.* Stanford: Stanford University Press, 1999.

Bourdieu, Pierre & Jean-Claude Passeron,. *Reproduction in Education, Society and Culture.* London: Sage, 1990.

Charlesworth, Simon J. *A Phenomenology of Working-Class Experience.* Cambridge: Cambridge University Press, 2000.

Elias, Norbert & John L. Scotson. *The Established and the Outsiders. A Sociological Enquiry into Community Problems.* London: SAGE, 1994.

Fanon, Frantz. . *Black Skin, White Masks.* New York: Grove Press: 1967.

Gorman, Thomas J. "Cross-Class Perceptions of Class." *Sociological Spectrum* 20 (2000): 93–120.

Gurr, Ted R. *Why Men Rebel.* Princeton: Princeton University Press, 1970).

Honneth, Axel. *The Struggle for Recognition. The Moral Grammar of Social Conflicts.* London: Polity Press, 1995.

---

[39] I am referring to the movement that sprang from Madrid on the May 15, 2011, and which has other important manifestations like *Occupy Wall Street*. These are cross-class based movements, but clearly express the indignation of many with the economic and political organization of Western societies, which are becoming much less democratic than they presume to be. One of the challenges these movements have is to tackle the persistent problem of misrecognition of those with less resources.

—. "Redistribution as Recognition. A Response to Nancy Fraser." In *Redistribution or Recognition? A Political-Philosophical Exchange*, edited by Nancy Fraser and Axel Honneth, 110–159. New York: Verso, 2003.

Horowitz, Allan V. & Jerome C. Wakefield. *The Loss of Sadness. Has Psychiatry Transformed Normal Sorrow into Depressive Disorder?* New York: Oxford University Press, 2007.

Hutcheson, Francis. [1725]. *An Inquiry into the Original of our Ideas of Beauty and Virtue*. In Fabian, B. (ed.) *Collected works of Francis Hutcheson*. Hildesheim : Georg Olms Verlagsbuchhandlung, 1971.

—. [1728]. *Essay on the Nature and Conduct of the Passions and Affections*. In Fabian, B. (ed.) *Collected works of Francis Hutcheson*. Hildesheim : Georg Olms Verlagsbuchhandlung, 1971.

Hyman, Herbert H. "The Psychology of Status." *Archives of Psychology* 269 (1942): 5–91.

Izquierdo Martín, Jesús. *El rostro de la comunidad: La identidad del campesino en la Castilla del Antiguo Régimen*. Madrid: Consejo Económico y Social, 2001.

Kemper, Theodore D. "How Many Emotions are There? Wedding the Social and the Autonomic Components." *The American Journal of Sociology* 93 (1987): 263–289.

Lamont, Michelle. *The Dignity of Working Men: Morality and the Boundaries of Race, Class and Immigration*. New York: Russell Sage Foundation at Harvard University Press, 2000.

Merton, Rorbert K. *Social Theory and Social Structure*. New York: Free Press, 1949.

Moravia, Sergio. "*Esistenza e passione*." In Vegetti Finzi, Silvia and Bodei, Remo, *Storia delle* passioni, 3–38. Roma: Laterza: 1995.

Nietzsche, F. [1887]. *La genealogía de la moral: un escrito polemic*. Madrid: Alianza, 1972.

Parish, S. M. "Narrative Subversions of Hierarchy." In *Selves in Time and Place. Identities, Experience and History in Nepal*, edited by D. Skinner, A. Pach III and D. Holland, 51–85. Lanham: Rowman & Littlefield Publishers, 1998.

Pizzorno, A. "Some Other Kind of Otherness." In *Development. Democracy and the art of trespassing. Essays in honor of Albert Hirchman*, edited by Foxley, A. Notre Dame: University of Notre Dame Press, 1986.

—. 2007. "Razionalità e riconoscimento." In *Il velo della diversità. Studi sulla razionalità e riconoscimento*, 109–197. Milano: Feltrinelli.

Runciman, Walter G. *Relative Deprivation and Social Justice: A Study of Attitudes to Social Inequality in Twentieth-century Britain*. London: Routledge, 1966.

—. *A Treatise on Social Theory*. Cambridge: CUP, 1997.

Sayer, Andrew. "Class, Moral Worth and Recognition." *Sociology* 39 (2005): 947–963.

Sheff, T. J. *Microsociology. Discourse, Emotion, and Social Structure*. Chicago: University of Chicago Press, 1990.

Scheler, M. [1915], *Ressentiment*. Milwaukee Winsconsin. Marquette University Press, 1998.

Scott, J. & G. Marshall. "Relative deprivation." In *Oxford Dictionary of Sociology*, 2009.

Shibutani, T. "Reference Groups." *American Journal of Sociology* 60 (1955): 562–569.

Smith, A. [1759]. *The Theory of Moral Sentiments*, edited by D. D. Raphael and A.L. Macfie. Oxford: Clarendon Press, 1976.

Thompsom, E. P. [1963]. *The Making of the English Working Class*. London: Victor Gollancz, 1965.

Tommelleri, S. *Identità e gerarchia. Per na sociologia del risentimento*. Urbino: Carocci, 2009.

Turner, Bryan S. "Max Weber and the spirit of resentment: The Nietzsche legacy." *Journal of Classical Sociology* 11 (2011): 75–92.

Wierzbicka, Anna. *Emotions across Language and Cultures. Diversity and Universals*. Paris: Cambridge University Press, 1999.

CHAPTER FIFTEEN

RESENTMENT AS AN EMOTION REGULATION STRATEGY IN INTERNATIONAL POLITICS: THE LEBANESE-SYRIAN RELATIONSHIP

ELISABETH MEUR

Introduction

World politics provides a great pool of potential resentment. Indeed, the absence of a world government means that international relations (IR) are characterized by anarchy and existential struggles. States' identities are always at stake on the international stage. The absence of any formal inter-state structure has several implications in terms of disparities and status hierarchy.[1] The imbalanced structure of the international system and attempts to preserve or to impose one's identity can generate anger, feeling of unfairness, frustration, humiliation and envy in other states. For instance, the appetite for a revisionist power could result in policies of domination towards a weaker actor. IR can provoke emotions. Simply put, conflicts are motivated by fear and anger while cooperation is encouraged by love and trust. Generally speaking, emotions have a critical impact on perception, judgment and decision-making in IR. At the same time, the "international community," a moving set of identities and norms, provides a degree of constraint to the emotional experiences of decision-makers. In summary, on the one side, IR, due to states disparities and status claims, are a great source of diverse emotions, and on the other side, IR constrain emotional experience and expression. This paradoxical environment is particularly well-suited for resentment deployment.

This chapter examines a counter-intuitive hypothesis of resentment, arguing that it can prevent large-scale violent conflicts. In most literature,

---

[1] Marie-Claude Smouts, Dario Battistella & Pascal Vennesson, *Dictionnaire des relations internationales* (Paris: Dalloz, 2006), 470.

resentment is usually linked with danger and hostility. It resembles a "perverted desire of revenge"[2] and is associated with displays of extreme violence.[3] It can be argued that this emotion plays a pivotal role when explaining the specific origin of wars, ethnic violence and genocides. The historian Philippe Burrin argues that Adolph Hitler's personal resentment towards the Jewish people was what motivated the Holocaust. The history of IR abounds with examples of resentment, such as Germany against France, former colonial states against their colonizers, Arab countries against Israel and the United States, etc.[4] An American sociologist, Roger Petersen, proposes an analysis of the conflicts in former-Yugoslavia in terms of resentment. In each case, resentment is presented as a highly destructive emotion. However, under specific circumstances, it can be argued that resentment relieves other fierce, heated and destructive emotions. Therefore, resentment can preserve a kind of "negative peace."[5]

In the case of the Lebanese-Syrian relationship, the Lebanese political leaders could not, for moral and military reasons, "react" (in the Nietzschean sense) to the pain and humiliation induced by thirty years of Syrian occupation, nor to the 2005 assassination of the charismatic Sunni leader, Rafic Hariri. Rumination, the desire for revenge, and symbolic measures, as part of the resentment sequence, helped alleviated their feelings of injury when they were not in a position to react directly. Functional mechanisms of resentment allow, through petty retaliatory and, most of time, symbolic measures, to keep a mental equilibrium. Resentment reduces anger and pain intensity through cognitive and emotional processes. As a result, vengeful policies and discourses become strategies to cope with threatening events. Finally, resentment provides the

---

[2] Slavoj Zizek, "La colère, le ressentiment et l'acte," *La Revue Internationale des Livres et des Idées,* 2008. http://www.revuedeslivres.net/articles.php?idArt=104 (September 7, 2011).
[3] See Thomas Scheff & Suzanne Retzinger, *Emotions and Violence: Shame and Rage in Destructive Conflicts* (Lincoln: iUniverse, 2002); Philippe Burrin, *Ressentiment et apocalypse. Essai sur l'antisémitisme nazi* (Paris: Seuil, 2004); Roger Petersen, *Understanding Ethnic Violence. Fear, Hatred and Resentment in Twentieth Century Eastern Europe* (Cambridge: Cambridge University Press. 2002).
[4] See Marc Ferro, *Le ressentiment dans l'histoire* (Paris: Odile Jacob, 2007).
[5] Johan Galtung explains that negative peace refers to the absence of violence while positive peace is related to the restoration of relationships, the creation of social systems and the constructive resolution of conflict. Johan Galtung, *Peace by Peaceful Means: Peace and Conflict, Development and Civilization* (London: Sage, 1996), 32.

ability to cope with a negative stimulus event while lowering its negative impact on the psycho-physiological well-being.[6]

By relying on emotion regulation theory, this chapter seeks to present a balanced view of resentment in world politics. Resentment proceeds through the regulation of its basic affects in order to cope with helplessness and can be adapted to the international environment of inter-state relationships. It introduces a secondary appraisal in order to match socially satisfactory emotional behaviour.[7] Moreover, resentment is a social emotion which often translates a pain from the re-consideration of an emotional attachment. Therefore, mixing the imperatives of the psychological and social life in a functional perspective, emotion regulation is at the junction of psychology and social sciences. This chapter is based on two main arguments: on the one hand, the resentment is central to IR and on the other, resentment can sometimes ease a serious crisis.

This chapter uses the backdrop of the Lebanese-Syrian case to establish a model for analysis of political resentment in IR. Following the lineage of Petersen, it is argued that, in addition to the micro-psychological foundations of individual resentment, the macro-structural context matters as well. Since the collapse of the Ottoman Empire, the Lebanese-Syrian history has been marked by: "a tormented combination of attraction and repulsion, of love and hate."[8] This paradoxical situation has generated resentful developments. The fundamental issue is to understand how this social emotion contributes to the international political environment. In other words, how does resentment impact foreign policies and social relationships?

The chapter is organized in three sections. The first presents the theoretical model of political resentment in international relations. The second shows how and under which circumstances resentment can relieve high political tensions, and in this way demonstrates how resentment contributes to international security. The last section illustrates the specific ways resentment has operated in the Lebanese-Syrian history and has affected their relationship.

---

[6] Richard Lazarus & Susan Folkman, *Stress, Appraisal and Coping* (New York: Springer Publishing, 1984), 196.
[7] Olivier Luminet, *Psychologie des Emotions. Confrontation et Evitement* (Bruxelles: de boeck, 2008), 217.
[8] Youssef Chaïtani, *Post-Colonial Syria and Lebanon* (New York: I.B. Tauris, 2007), IX.

Resentment at the Core of International Politics

Usually, literature has stressed one aspect of resentment; namely, violence. With different perspectives, Erich Fromm, Hannah Arendt, Norbert Elias and Thomas Scheff have all been interested in the role of resentment in Nazism.[9] Direct witnesses of violence have stressed the dialectic of resentment and forgiveness after genocides.[10] A number of political scientists have focused on the role of resentment in ethnic violence and nationalism.[11] In these few examples, and as is shown in this section, resentment is used to explain hostility, violence and wars. However, it would be a great mistake to consider that resentment exists only in obviously violent periods.[12] Moreover, as demonstrated by Nietzsche and endorsed by Pierre Ansart, resentment is plural[13]. Political resentment is defined here as a pain experienced by national ruling elites in reaction to an offence or a humiliation attributed to a foreign state. This pain has endured through its being remembered. It provokes a desire for revenge against those who are blamed for being responsible for the "unfair" suffering (a foreign country or a political entity). Finally, the resentful actor cannot fully express its anger and cannot act because of norms and the material constraints of IR.

This chapter develops the argument of the link between IR and political resentment. In order to do that, it is necessary to present the sources of resentment in IR. Then, its development and its cognitive and behavioural consequences can be demonstrated. As an introduction, the two main premises of this research are explained.

The first premise considers resentment as a complex social emotion, a process over time that involve cyclical stages in which information generates emotional responses that generate new information, and so on. Secondly, we are interested in the "collateral consequences" of emotional experiences.[14] The emotional experiences, through their visible consequences,

---

[9] Pierre Ansart, *Le ressentiment* (Bruxelles: Bruylant, 2002), 2.

[10] See for example Jean Amery and Esther Mujawayo.

[11] See, for example, Petersen, *Understanding Ethnic Violence*, and also Liah Greenfeld, *Nationalism: Five Roads to Modernity* (Cambridge: Harvard University Press, 1992).

[12] Ansart, *Le ressentiment*, 3.

[13] Friedrich Nietzsche, *La faute de la mauvaise conscience et ce qui leur ressemble: Deuxième dissertation, extrait de La Généalogie de la morale* (1887), eds. Dorian Astor & Seloua Boulbina (Paris: Folio Plus Philosophie, 2006).

[14] James Gross, *Handbook of Emotion Regulation* (New York: The Guilford Press, 2007), 473.

reveal the goals, expectations and worldviews of political leaders. Therefore, our focus is on the long-term impact of resentment on perceptions and, as a result, the subsequent security interactions.

IR can be both a source of and a force for constraint on emotional experiences. Basic sites of pain contributing to the emergence of political resentment are related to state identity management concerns (role and status) and to state relationship threats. About identity concerns, entities are not equal in the international society. Richness, status, size, natural resources, stability etc. contribute to power disparities and the establishment of a variety of state hierarchies. These disparities—endorsed by leaders as socio-psychological realities—are potentially a great source of emotions. In some cases, there is a gap between the self-assigned status of a country and its actual status (as recognized by the international community). This situation may cause negative emotions like humiliation, envy and resentment. The political ambitions of the leader of a country can be granted or contested by other states. International politics has a mix of satisfied powerful actors, actors who contest the status of others, and actors unsatisfied by their own status. These kinds of social relations generate resentment.[15] In other words, resentment addresses status/self-esteem discrepancies, and the resentful actor will try to redress the perceived imbalance of status hierarchies.[16]

Not only status but also roles define a state identity. The roles in IR are related to the way people (here state leaders) perceive themselves and would like to be perceived by others. For instance, Iran perceives itself as a major regional and Islamic power and not as a "rogue state." Roles are also defined in relation to the other party as the friend, the rival, the protector or the enemy. For instance, Lebanon and Syria signed a Fraternity Treaty in 1989 in which they considered themselves brothers.[17] However, when they are contested, self-assigned roles can generate resentment.

Finally, roles and status can be synthesized in a self-image. This image is both a source of emotions and a constraint. A state which embodies the role of a peaceful democratic nation is not able to attack another state without strong justifications. Even after the installation of Russian missiles in Cuba, Kennedy needed to preserve the image of the USA as an innocent

---

[15] Jeff Goodwin, James. M. Jasper & Francesca Polletta (eds.), *Passionate Politics. Emotions and Social Movements* (Chicago: The University of Chicago Press, 2001), 63.

[16] Petersen, *Understanding Ethnic Violence*, 29.

[17] "Syrian Lebanese Higher Council,"
http://www.syrleb.org/about.asp (January 9, 2013).

victim of the communists and not as an aggressor. Kennedy therefore had to regulate his anger and humiliation due to the USA's identity.[18]

The ontological sources of resentment are also located in social relations threats, as the state of bonds between nations has emotional consequences. Engulfment (we-self), isolation (I-self) and solidarity (I-we balance) are the three types of social relationships.[19] Therefore, resentment is characterized by the clash of the engulfment and isolation aspirations of two states. It means that over the duration of a relationship, the relational desires of two states can diverge. The historian Georg Simmel stated that "The deepest hatred grows out of broken love."[20] When disputed, separation leads to conflict and conflict deepens separation.[21]

Resentment sheds light on an unsatisfying and/or asymmetric relationship. Political elites feel that their relation with the other state is unsatisfying and that their foreign counterparts dominate them unfairly. For instance, some Lebanese feel rancour toward Syrians because they think that Syria despises them. In the same way, some Syrians feel rancour toward the Lebanese because they think that the Lebanese consider them to be uncultured. In these two cases, the devaluated relation wounds self-esteem and produces negative social emotions.

How can resentment be conceptualized in IR? Most of the time, resentment addresses insecure state identities and this is the case for the two actors that are the basis of this study. Lebanon, after being called "the Switzerland of the Middle-East," disintegrated during nearly three decades of civil war.[22] Today, its state institutions are still weak and the nation is divided along sectarian lines. Syria, after its independence, was the theatre of several *coups d'état* and alleged that some were organized from Lebanon. After this period of unrest, it was able to consolidate itself as a sovereign state but only at the price of establishing an authoritarian regime, which at the time of writing is collapsing. Resentment starts with an event which causes a feeling of unfairness and anger. The continuous presence and interference of the Syrians in Lebanon after the end of the civil war (in 1991), but even more so following the Israeli withdrawal (in 2000), became painful for many Lebanese. Here, anger coexists with frustration because of the inability to cope with or to resolve the problem.

---

[18] Jean Barréa, *Théories des relations internationales* (Namur: Erasme, 2001), 67.

[19] Thomas Scheff, *Bloody Revenge. Emotions, Nationalism and War* (Lincoln: An Authors Guild Backinprint.com, 2000), 18.

[20] Cited in ibid., 2.

[21] Scheff & Retzinger, *Emotions and Violence*, 2.

[22] Georges Corm, *Le Liban contemporain* (Paris: La Découverte, 2005), 39.

Impotence is crucial for resentment. Lebanon, due to its own divisions and its weakness, could not confront Syria.

Resentment has clear cognitive and behavioural consequences. The resentment's structure will shape future perceptions and interactions in precise and negative directions. For example, it will focus attention both on the alleged culprit of each subsequent suffering event and on dispositional factors. It means that the resentful actors will attribute a continuing harmful intent to the subject. This was the case a few hours after Hariri's assassination (February 14, 2005) when the Lebanese political leaders focused exclusively on the Syrian regime.

The "value revaluation," theorized by Nietzsche, is another cognitive consequence of resentment. Resentment's pattern glorifies something with the purpose of depreciating something else. Syria's glorification of the Arab nation denies, in a certain way, the legitimacy of the independent Lebanese entity.

Political resentment also has behavioural consequences. Due to the inability to act, the resentful actor will produce symbolic, indirect or minor security actions. Even if Syria, in an angry reaction, had wished to forcefully restore its military presence in Lebanon, this would not have been possible because of its perceived role (protector of Lebanon) and the refusal of the international community. In other terms, resentment will not cause violent actions but rather punctual and limited retaliation policies.

In this section, we have tried to demonstrate the centrality of resentment in IR through two processes—state identity management and state relationship threats—and have shown that world politics are a great source of potential resentments. Secondly, looking at the consequences of resentment, we have shown how this emotion impacts IR and security interactions. To sum up, IR can generate emotions which have to be regulated due to material and normative constraints.

We will now look at the regulation process of resentment and its consequences on IR.

The Contribution of Resentment to International Security—the Emotion Regulation Process

Since the very beginning, emotions have had a special—often paradoxical—status in politics, being dangerous in certain respects and helpful in other circumstances. Plato and Aristotle considered that passions should be governed by reason. In a cynical way, Thomas Hobbes considered that it was elites' responsibility to teach citizens to fear certain items. The sovereign should transmit a fearful obedience to the population.[23] The seventeenth-century philosophers Descartes and Spinoza have both examined the dualism of mind. In Descartes' view, reason should absolutely dominate the passions, and he made a clear distinction between body and mind, emotion and rationality. In his lineage, Pascal and Kant claimed the superiority of reason over emotion. Since then, reason and emotion are not only separated but also unequal. However, even if Descartes' influence on Spinoza's view is evident, his understanding of emotions is quite different and amazingly perceptive. More recently, the influential sociologist Max Weber argued that rational action could not be emotional.[24]

Regarding emotion regulation, it is interesting to focus on Spinoza's writings. Firstly, Spinoza denies an absolute control over our passions, arguing that it is impossible for the human mind to be autonomous in the way Descartes held, an assertion which would be confirmed four centuries later by neurosciences. Secondly, Spinoza linked emotion and morality saying that: "... the knowledge of good and evil is nothing else but the idea of the pleasure or pain, which necessarily follows from that pleasurable or painful emotion."[25]

In this way, Spinoza explained the origins of moral values and he is quite close to Nietzsche's considerations about the sources of morality. Finally, Spinoza explained what it is at stake in resentment—the regulation of pain by other emotions and cognitions: "An emotion can only be controlled or destroyed by another emotion contrary thereto, and with more power for controlling emotion."[26]

How can the lessons taught by all these philosophers be summarized? Firstly, Descartes' dualism and rationalism have deeply influenced the research agenda in social sciences. Secondly, this vision has also impacted the way political actors behave, and use and express emotions. The French President, François Hollande, stated: "I have sensibility ... but I do not express my emotions publicly."[27] Political actors have been constrained to make as if they always act rationally, understood as dispassionately. Lastly, Spinoza's proposal about the way people can manage their

---

[23] Corey Robin, *Fear: The History of a Political Idea* (Oxford: Oxford University Press, 2004), 8.

[24] Goodwin, Jasper & Polletta, 2.

[25] Baruch Spinoza, *Ethics* (1677) (MTSU Philosophy WebWorks Hypertext Edition, 1997), Part IV, Prop VIII.
http://frank.mtsu.edu/~rbombard/RB/Spinoza/ethica-front.html (January 9, 2013).

[26] Spinoza, Prop VII.

[27] Interview, *Sept à huit,* TF1, October 23, 2011.

detrimental emotions by other emotions foreshadows the emotional regulation process.

Therefore, it is crucial to think about IR in terms of elites' emotions and regulation. This is the reason why resentment should be viewed in IR as a multi-layered emotion endowed with a regulation process. Contrary to the automatic effects of basic emotions such as fear, resentment systematically introduces a secondary appraisal between the eliciting event, the situation and the emotional response.

Now it is necessary to look at how resentment—due to its regulation—releases tensions and the escalation of violence. In order to do that, the first step is having an understanding of emotional regulation and international security theories. Then, a model of the contribution of resentment to security will be presented.

Emotion regulation is the process:

> ... by which individuals influence which emotions they have, when they have them, and how they experience and express these emotions.[28]

And:

> ... by which individuals assess (evaluate), control, and modify their spontaneous emotional reaction in order to achieve their goal or to express socially adequate emotional behavior.[29]

Emotions have always had a double-face: "they can hurt us as well as help us."[30] Sometimes, emotions can be maladaptive when they appear at the wrong time, the wrong place, or the wrong intensity level. Individuals—acting as decision-makers—feel emotions that they cannot freely and totally experience and express due to the culture and norms of IR.[31] Strong negative emotions, like fear or hatred, can be more dangerous when they appear in IR due to the potential destructive power of a state. Emotion regulation will not block, for instance, the ability to feel angry with someone but it will block the action tendency associated with it,

---

[28] James Gross, "Emotion Regulation," In *Handbook of Emotions*, edited by Michael D. Lewis, Jeannette M. Haviland-Jones and Lisa Feldman Barret (London: The Guiford Press, 2008), 497.

[29] Luminet, *Psychologie des Emotions*, 217.

[30] Lewis, Haviland-Jones & Feldman Barret, *Handbook of Emotions*, 498.

[31] James Gross, *Handbook of Emotion Regulation* (New York: The Guilford Press, 2007), 487.

namely aggression.[32] Therefore, emotion regulation in IR contributes to security.

Security perceptions are conditioned by norms and identities and are shaped by the emotional patterns which underlie them. Norms—shared expectations about appropriate or legitimate behaviour by actors with a particular identity—are crucial to understanding security policies and the regulation process.[33] International norms impose a regulation of affects. Moreover, in IR, the need for self-esteem will encourage socially-valued actions. Because the resentment transforms humiliation into an intentionally unfair action, the resentful actor becomes a victim. This victimization changes the actor's role and therefore impedes large-scale and overt violence.[34]

Nietzsche stressed two important aspects of regulation inside resentment: the powerlessness of the resentful actor and the transformation of values. The relative powerlessness of the resentful actor—regarding the constraints and norms of IR—can be overcome through symbolic actions and retaliatory measures. A positive status or the restoration of self-esteem can be regained through the changing roles and values. Therefore, the model of resentment regulation strategy runs as follows—a political leader experiences the pain of a humiliation; based on the situational and normative constraints of the international community, the politician cannot fully express their suffering. Moreover, sadness is not helpful in the pursuit of their goals, namely the restoration of their self-esteem and of a positive state identity; to regulate the sadness and frustration, they transform it into anger and a desire for revenge; they attribute a responsibility and an intention to the other party; finally, they try to find social support. In order to do that, they carry out a reassessment of values and undertake a role change; the other party is recategorized as the enemy and themselves as the innocent victim of an injustice. Due to the new role and values, they cannot engage in large-scale violent actions. Therefore, when resentment leads to violence it is the signal that its regulation mechanism has failed.

In this section, we have shown how state identity and international norms constrain emotional experience and, accordingly, have an impact on

---

[32] Keith Oatley, Dacher Keltner & Jennifer Jenkins, *Understanding Emotions* (Oxford: Blackwell Publishing, 2006), 240.

[33] Matt McDonald, "Constructivism." In *Security Studies. An Introduction,* ed. Paul D. Williams (New York: Routledge, 2010), 63.

[34] We consider that contemporary international culture values peaceful actions and diplomacy between actors. The UN charter is the main reference in terms of norms of political actions.

emotion regulation. Following this, we have demonstrated how the resentment and its regulation functions can decrease the risks of immediate and large-scale violence. Now, we will apply the emotion regulation process to the Lebanese-Syrian relationship.

The Lebanese Resentment towards Syria

The regulation process operates at each step of the resentment sequence, from the psychologically relevant situation, to the subsequent appraisals, and the emotional responses.[35] The purpose is to show how resentment has played in Lebanon as a regulation process to relieve some strong and destructive affects. Before analyzing the case study, we will clarify the context, the actors, the events and the object of the Lebanese resentment against Syria.

The historical legacy of the Middle East is based on the shared experience of colonization and decolonization with the consequence that some states are shallow-rooted and weak. In this context, the Lebanese and Syrian regions, parts of the same French mandate, do not have a real tradition of state in a region which was dominated by empires and provincial governorates.[36] Moreover, Syria and some people in Lebanon started their post-independence life with the idea of a pan-identity, based on Arabism. This idea was quickly frustrated by France which established two independent states: Syria and the "Great Lebanon."[37] From that time, anger and mistrust against colonial France and its Christian Lebanese allies was very real. Syrians thought that they had been sacrificed and had to pay for the cost of their independence while the Lebanese, and particularly the Christians, were favoured. From Lebanon's point of view, the fear of being swallowed up by Greater Syria has been a major component of the Lebanese-Syrian relationship.[38] These feelings permeate current historical and political visions of the construction of the two states. Indeed, the prevailing interpretation, both in Syria and in Lebanon, considers Lebanon to be an artificial creation of French imperialism. Therefore, Lebanon experiences the guilt of being separated from its big brother and Syria the rancour of being robbed of a part of its natural territory. Since the Lebanese civil war in 1975, Lebanon and Syria have developed an asymmetric relationship with a clear domination by the authoritarian and repressive Syrian Ba'ath regime of el-Assad over the

---

[35] Gross, *Handbook of Emotion Regulation*, 5.
[36] Corm, *Le Liban contemporain*, 33.
[37] Ibid., 49.
[38] Chaïtani, *Post-Colonial Syria and Lebanon*, 9.

fragile, multi-confessional and divided Lebanese democracy. Their respective statuses were clearly imbalanced and Syria presented itself as the only actor able to stabilize its neighbour. From the beginning, these two actors showed identity troubles. To sum up, we are confronted with two states with insecure identities, imbalanced relationships and historical roots of rancour.

The political context of Lebanese resentment since 2000, after the Israeli withdrawal from Lebanon and Hafez el-Assad's death, has been characterized by a growing feeling of annoyance over the Syrian presence. The actors at this time were mostly the Christian community, later joined by some Sunnis and Druzes groups. This formation is named after March 14, 2005 (the date of the massive demonstration against Syrian presence in Beirut), the anti-Syrian coalition. The eliciting situation at the origin of the Lebanese resentment against Syria is, generally speaking, the continuous presence of Syrian troops in Lebanon and the daily political interferences by Syrians in Lebanese domestic politics. This regional background has been disrupted by a set of negative emotional events, such as the extension of the presidential mandate of the pro-Syrian Emile Lahoud in 2004, the attempts and the assassinations of anti-Syrian personalities and, in particular, the murder of the charismatic former Prime minister, Rafic Hariri on February 14, 2005. The object of the Lebanese resentment was the Syrian systematic opposition to real Lebanese independence and sovereignty and the establishment of a balanced relationship with the Cedar Republic.

With regards to the macro-structural context, Lebanon and Syria have always had particular and close relations—they were under French mandate; they had the same currency and a customs union; Lebanese superior officers were trained in Syria; Syria intervened in the Lebanese civil war and prolonged its presence in Lebanon for nearly thirty years; the Taëf agreement (1989) and the Fraternity Treaty (ratified in 1991) formalized privileged relations; Syria was the only means of access for the Lebanese to the Arab markets; they had mutual economic and geopolitical interests; and finally the Syrian and Lebanese people had close family and personal ties. This means that despite the negative emotional climate, Lebanon and Syria both perceived their relationship as important.

Negative emotions have complex and subtle consequences at different levels and can be regulated at each of these levels.[39] Therefore, we will look at the regulation in the resentment sequence between the Cedar Republic and Syria since 2000. A first step in the regulation process is about the situation modification. There was a change of perception about

---

[39] Gross, *Handbook of Emotion Regulation*, 472.

Syria and the Syrian-Lebanese relationship which began during the mandate of the contested President Emile Lahoud (1998–2007). During the years 2000–2007, Christian Camp, the Druze leader, Walid Joumblatt, and other political personalities from the Left clearly expressed their opposition to Syrian occupation. This was perceived in Syria as an affront and a threat, and it provoked an authoritarian state of tension.[40] The extension of Lahoud's mandate in 2004 triggered a dramatic shift of the Syrian image in Lebanon. Instead of the role of protector, Syria was now considered a threat for Lebanon. In situations such as these, strategies to change the situation can involve military, diplomatic or other indirect uses of soft power. In order to keep one's reputation and depending on the material means available, a country will choose one or another solution. Some Lebanese leaders lobbied Western governments and sought the support of great powers like the USA and France.[41] The Syrian withdrawal from Lebanon in 2005 forced Damascus to adapt its domination policy to the new reality. This was done, for instance, by systematically poisoning the political game in Lebanon, transferring arms to pro-Syrian groups in Lebanon, etc. In the same way, after 2005, the new Lebanese government (an "anti-Syrian" majority) tried to restore balanced relations with Damascus but their efforts were clumsy and the wounds were still open.

The eliciting event, considered by many Lebanese as a cataclysm, was Hariri's assassination on February 14, 2005. In the regulation process, the cognitive change implies the meaning attributed to the emotional situation. The pain which first appeared following the bombing of Hariri's convoy was transformed into anger. The reappraisal focused on the other party's responsibility. In other terms, the cognitive transformation involved the recategorization of the event that had produced the emotion.

Let's examine the way affective and cognitive changes have worked in Lebanese resentment towards Damascus. After the assassination, sadness, anger and terror were quickly transformed into political claims. A few hours after the death of the former Prime minister, the Lebanese political leaders pointed to Syrian accountability, asking at the same time for truth, independence and sovereignty. Hariri's relatives explained that the former Prime Minister was dead because of his commitment to independence, sovereignty and unity. The Druze leader, Walid Joumblatt, said to the

---

[40] Caroline Donati, *L'exception syrienne entre modernisation et résistance* (Paris: La Découverte, 2009), 170.

[41] As a result of this lobbying, USA and France initiated the 1559 UNSC resolution which was adopted one day before Lahoud's extension (September 2, 2004). This resolution asked for the withdrawal of Syrian troops and the respect of Lebanese sovereignty.

press on the following day: "We have to hold out, it (the Syrian regime) is a regime of murderers." In another declaration, Joumblatt called on the Lebanese to express their anger. Koraytem camp (the Christian opposition) immediately called for the Syrian withdrawal, an international investigation and declared that the Lebanese and Syrian governments were responsible for Rafic Hariri's death. Some Lebanese media expressed not only Lebanese pain but also an insidious, or sometimes direct, call for revenge. The Editorialist of L'Orient le Jour explained that this event had freed all muted frustrations and cemented people in their pain. The emotional reactions of the political leaders and people were huge. To sum up, the main perceptions of the murder were accusatory and vengeful. The main reason evoked for the assassination was a message from Damascus against the Lebanese will for independence. There was a clear attribution bias focusing exclusively on Syria and on dispositional factors—the Syrian will to hurt and punish Lebanon's desire for autonomy. On March 14, 2005 there were massive demonstrations in Beirut,[42] and the political discourses and posters were vengeful and fierce. Later on, Syrian migrant workers were attacked in different regions of Lebanon. Others burned portraits of Bachar in symbolic revenge against Syrian regime.

Thirdly, the attentional deployment in resentment means that attention is redirected on thoughts and feelings associated with the emotion-eliciting event.[43] This attention bias refers here to "rumination." The rumination on past events increases the duration and intensity of the associated negative emotions. The rumination in Lebanon took a public form through the commemorations of the anti-Syrian "martyrs," and especially the charismatic Sunni leader Rafic Hariri. Several years after his assassination, Rafic Hariri's image is still regularly shown on television, on posters, on memorials etc.

Finally, the response modulation is often translated into expressive suppression. Examples include efforts to hide sadness before an acquaintance to preserve one's honour, or efforts to hide anger against a political enemy during a political show to preserve one's reputation as being a moderate. In the Lebanese resentment, the modulation used sadness and despair to enhance the unfair treatment imposed by Syria in order to gain empathy and support as a victim. This resulted in, after a preliminary international investigation, the creation of a special tribunal for Lebanon by the UN on May 30, 2007 in Leidschendam, Netherlands.

This regulation process allows Lebanon to be internationally recognized as an innocent victim with reasonable and legitimate requests

---

[42] Nearly a quarter of the Lebanese population took to the streets.
[43] Lewis, Haviland-Jones & Feldman Barret, *Handbook of Emotions*, 503.

of independence, sovereignty and security. In this way, Lebanon was able to manage a positive state identity. Some Lebanese political leaders regulated their long-lasting and fierce anger against the Syrian regime in indirect security claims and international lobbying. The political agenda at this time was influenced by a resentment pattern. Therefore, each action or discourse from Syria was interpreted through a negative lens as further evidence of Damascus' ill feelings and bad intentions. However, and despite a significant cooling of the Lebanese-Syrian relationship, they never totally broke their links.

Conclusion

Due to international norms, political leaders have to show restraint towards other states. If a national political actor feels humiliated or frustrated, the psychological need to manage a positive self-identity will promote social value actions and a convincing victimization discourse. The consequences are a public rumination process and a re-evaluation of values. Therefore, resentment in IR can release high tensions and immediate risks of violence. The political impact of resentment can be summed up in five points. Firstly, the resentment establishes an asymmetric relationship defining a strong party (the wrongdoer) and a weak party (the victim). Since 2000, Syria was gradually presented as a major threat to the Lebanese democracy, independence and sovereignty. Then, the resentment directs threat perception by imposing an atmosphere of mistrust. Political discourses in Lebanon did not solely focus on direct security threats from Syria but also on economical threats. The accusations of political terrorism and arms smuggling were accompanied with the denunciation of Syrian migrant workers, pillaging and corruption. At this time, the dialogue between Damascus and Beirut was frozen. Thirdly, resentment focuses responsibility on a party for the wrong suffered. The Lebanese political attacks were concentrated on Syrian regime but they omitted to talk about their past soft attitude toward Syrian authorities, their own failures, and their inability to rebuild state institutions. Finally, resentment engenders retaliation policies, targeting symbols like icons, symbols of military or economic power, or political leaders.[44] Lebanese political discourse became harsh and insulting toward Syria. Despite this verbal violence, physical violence was limited and the relationship between Beirut and Damascus was never totally broken. Political leaders

---

[44] Oded Lowenheim & Gadi Heimann, "Revenge in International Politics." *Security Studies* 17 (4) (2008): 692.

as well as citizens were still attached to their relation with Syria. Their emotional ties, their common historical legacy, but also political, geopolitical and economical concerns make them inseparable.

When people feel very angry with someone else, depending on the context, they will insult this person, shout at them, sometimes hit them, even to the point of harming themselves. Most of the time, the consequences will be minor. Now, imagine if the angry person is the leader of a nuclear country and the subject of their emotion is another state. Will they launch a nuclear bomb against this state as a reaction of their anger? We hope not. Therefore, in some specific cases, resentment and its regulation mechanisms can be helpful. Resentment is an affect which synthesizes emotion and reason, automatic responses and normative constrains, human psychology and social identity. For these reasons, this emotion is particularly well suited for political life. This study has not exhausted the richness of this human emotion but rather has demonstrated its centrality for national ruling elites and IR. Resentment is pivotal in world politics due to state relationship threats and the need to manage one's state identity. Resentment has an impact both on foreign policies and states relationships. It encourages indirect actions, minor retaliatory policies, and passionate discourses. However, in postponing the action tendency of anger and other basic and negative emotions, resentment relieves tensions and preserves the inter-states' relationship at the lowest level. Therefore, even if it precludes an immediate reconciliation process, resentment, contrary to anger, hatred or shame, allows the building of a "negative peace." In the long term, resentment can always be overcome by the recognition of respective past suffering and the establishment of mutual fulfilling relations.

Works Cited

Améry, Jean. *Par-delà le crime et le châtiment. Essai pour surmonter l'insurmontable*. Paris: Actes Sud, 1995.

Ansart, Pierre. *Le ressentiment*. Bruxelles: Bruylant, 2002.

Barréa, Jean. *Théories des relations internationales*. Namur: Erasme, 2001.

Burrin, Philippe. *Ressentiment et apocalypse. Essai sur l'antisémitisme nazi*. Paris: Seuil, 2004.

Chaïtani, Youssef. *Post-Colonial Syria and Lebanon*. New York: I.B. Tauris, 2007.

Corm, Georges. *Le Liban contemporain*. (Paris: La Découverte, 2005).

Donati, Caroline. *L'exception syrienne entre modernisation et résistance*. (Paris: La Découverte, 2009).

Ferro, Marc. *Le ressentiment dans l'histoire.* Paris: Odile Jacob, 2007.

Galtung, Johan. *Peace by Peaceful Means: Peace and Conflict, Development and Civilization.* London: Sage, 1996.

Goodwin, Jeff, James. M. Jasper and Francesca Polletta (eds.). *Passionate Politics. Emotions and Social Movements.* Chicago: The University of Chicago Press, 2001.

Greenfeld, Liah. *Nationalism: Five Roads to Modernity.* Cambridge: Harvard University Press, 1992.

Gross, James. *Handbook of Emotion Regulation.* New York: The Guilford Press, 2007.

—. "Emotion Regulation." In *Handbook of Emotions,* edited by Michael D. Lewis, Jeannette M. Haviland-Jones & Lisa Feldman Barret, 497–512. London: The Guiford Press, 2008.

Lazarus, Richard & Susan Folkman. *Stress, Appraisal and Coping.* New York: Springer Publishing, 1984.

Lewis, Michael D., Jeannette M. Haviland-Jones and Lisa Feldman Barret. *Handbook of Emotions.* London: The Guildford Press, 2008.

Lowenheim, Oded & Gadi Heimann. "Revenge in International Politics." *Security Studies,* 17 (4) (2008): 685–724.

Luminet, Olivier. *Psychologie des Emotions. Confrontation et Evitement.* Bruxelles: de boeck, 2008.

McDonald, Matt. "Constructivism." In *Security Studies. An Introduction,* edited by Paul D. Williams, 59–72. New York: Routledge, 2010.

Mujawayo, Esther & Souad Belhaddad. *La fleur de Stéphanie. Rwanda entre réconciliation et déni.* Paris: Flammarion, 2006.

Nietzsche, Friedrich. *La faute de la mauvaise conscience et ce qui leur ressemble: Deuxième dissertation, extrait de La Généalogie de la morale* (1887), edited by Dorian Astor and Seloua Boulbina. Paris: Folio Plus Philosophie, 2006.

Oatley, Keith, Dacher Keltner & Jennifer Jenkins. *Understanding Emotions.* Oxford: Blackwell Publishing, 2006.

Petersen, Roger. *Understanding Ethnic Violence. Fear, Hatred and Resentment in Twentieth Century Eastern Europe.* Cambridge: Cambridge University Press, 2002.

Robin, Corey. *Fear: The History of a Political Idea.* Oxford: Oxford University Press, 2004.

Scheff, Thomas. *Bloody Revenge. Emotions, Nationalism and War.* Lincoln: An Authors Guild Backinprint.com, 2000.

Scheff, Thomas & Suzanne Retzinger. *Emotions and Violence: Shame and Rage in Destructive Conflicts.* Lincoln: iUniverse, 2002.

Smouts, Marie-Claude, Dario Battistella & Pascal Vennesson. *Dictionnaire des relations internationales*. Paris: Dalloz, 2006.

Spinoza, Baruch. *Ethics* (1677). MTSU Philosophy WebWorks Hypertext Edition, 1997. http://frank.mtsu.edu/~rbombard/RB/Spinoza/ethica-front.html (January 9, 2013).

Zizek, Slavoj. "La colère, le ressentiment et l'acte," *La Revue Internationale des Livres et des Idées,* 2008. http://www.revuedeslivres.net/articles.php?idArt=104 (September 7, 2011).

—. "Syrian Lebanese Higher Council," http://www.syrleb.org/about.asp (January 9, 2013).

CONTRIBUTORS

ELISE DERMINEUR is currently a postdoctoral research fellow at Umeå University in Sweden. She previously held a Max Weber fellowship at the European University Institute in Florence, Italy. Her research interests range widely, from the history of justice and economics to gender and women's history. Above all, she is deeply interested in the study of rural communities in early modern Europe. She is currently completing her first book provisionally entitled *Women in Rural Society: Peasants, Patriarchy, and the Local Economy in Early Modern France.*

SUSANNA FERLITO is Associate Professor of Italian at the University of Minnesota. She earned a PhD in Comparative Literature from the University of California, Los Angeles. Her latest publications are: "Hysteria's Upheavals: Emotional Fault Lines in Cristina di Belgiojoso's Health History" (2012) and a chapter forthcoming on Enrichetta Caracciolo's attempted suicide in *Voglio morire! Suicide in Italian Literature, Culture, and Society 1789-1919* (2013). She is currently working on a book-project on 19th century Italian women's responses to injustice.

MARÍA GÓMEZ GARRIDO is professor of Sociology at the *Universitat de les Illes Balears.* She obtained a BA in History at the *Universidad Autónoma de Madrid* and a PhD in Social and Political Sciences at the European University Institute. She has studied the history of the statistical objectification of unemployment in Spain, looking at the intersections between social history and the history of sciences. She is currently engaged in two research projects, one on the history of neurasthenia as a cultural phenomenon and a medical category, the second on the main discourses on sex, love and intimacy in western societies by paying particular attention to the challenge represented by prostitution.

PATRICK LANG is graduated in economics, doctor and *agrégé* in philosophy from the University of Munich. He is also associate professor of ethics, phenomenology, and philosophy of music at the University of Nantes (France). He has recently published "À la fois réalité et idéal. Sur l'histoire philosophique de la liberté" (2013), *Gedichte und Erzählungen.*

Texte aus dem Nachlass (2012), and "Statut et signification des développements sur l'affectivité et la valeur" (2012).

PILAR LEÓN SANZ is Associate Professor of the History of Medicine and Medical Ethics at the University of Navarra. She was Research Fellow at the Wellcome Trust Centre for the History of Medicine at University College London, Visiting Scholar at Harvard University member of the Steering Committee Phoenix European Thematic Network on Health and Social Policy. She is member of the Project "Emotional Culture and Identity". Her research interests include topics related to medicine in eighteenth-century Spain, especially about music therapy, and the practices and health care professionals during 19th and 20th centuries. Her publications include *Health Institutions at the Origin of the Welfare Systems in Europe* (2010) and *La Tarantola Spagnola. Empirismo e tradizione nel XVIII secolo* (2008).

MANUEL LUCENA GIRALDO is Senior Research Fellow in the Spanish Council for Scientific Research and PhD in History of the Americas. He was Visiting Scholar at Harvard University, Lecturer BOSP in Stanford University, and Visiting Professor at Tufts University, Javeriana University (Bogotá, Colombia), IVIC (Venezuela), Colegio de México, Universidad Complutense and SAM in St. Antony´s College (Oxford). His publications include a number of books on travels, scientific expeditions, and images of nations, empires and Globalization. His last books are *Naciones de rebeldes. Las revoluciones de independencia latinoamericanas,* and *Francisco de Miranda. La aventura de la política.*

JOSEPH MASLEN is Lecturer in History at the University of Central Lancashire. He has published elsewhere on contemporary British history in special issues of *Biography* such as "Personal Narrative and Political Discourse" (2010) and "Challenging Dominant Discourses of the Past: 1968 and the Value of Oral History" (2013).

ELISABETH MEUR is a PhD student in International Relations at the Belgian National Fund for Scientific Research (FNRS) and a research fellow at the Tocqueville Chair in Security Policies. She is the author of *Liban-Syrie : inextricables destins?* (2012). Her focus is on the Middle East and especially on Lebanon and Syria where she did fieldwork between 2006 and 2012. She is interested in security studies and emotions. In 2010, she attended the political psychology summer school at Stanford University.

LINA MINOU is a PhD student at Loughborough University. Her main interests lie in eighteenth-century prose fiction, the history of passions and sentiments, and the history of medicine. Her current research focuses on the intersection, rather than the incongruity, between morally disapproved or irascible passions and the novel of Sensibility. She has presented papers on relevant topics such as anger in Richardson's *Clarissa*, envy and pathology in eighteenth-century fiction and eighteenth-century advice literature on anger and sociability.

JAVIER MOSCOSO is Research Professor of History and Philosophy of Science at the Institute of Philosophy of the Spanish National Research Council (CSIC), PhD. Along with several monographs, and many publications in scientific journals, he has also paid special attention to what is now called "knowledge transfer" and public engagement. He has been the curator of different exhibitions: on imaginary monsters at the Spanish National Library in Madrid; on the history of pain at the Science Museum in London, and more recently, on the cultural history of human skin at the Wellcome Collection Gallery, in London. His latest book, *Pain: A Cultural History*, has been published in Spain, by Taurus, in October 2011. The English version, by Palgrave-Macmillan, was published in 2012.

JAVIER ORDÓÑEZ is Professor of Logics and Philosophy of Science at the *Universidad Autónoma de Madrid* (UAM), where he teaches history of sciences. He has published several books on the field of history of science and technology, such as *Historia de la Ciencia*, *Teorías del Universo* (2004) and *Ciencia, tecnología e historia: Relaciones y diferencias* (2001). His recent research has turned to the history of war and, particularly, the ways in which civil society engaged with war during the First World War in Germany.

YAMINA OUDAI CELSO is a Balzan Prize Research Fellow. She was awarded with a PhD at Ca' Foscari University of Venice, where she held a lectureship in History and technique of philosophical dialogue. She also has been lecturer in History of Psychology at Bicocca University of Milan and she spent some short research stays in Paris (Paris Sorbonne I). Her research interests concern the relationship between philosophy and psychological disciplines with a special reference to the work of Freud and Nietzsche. She has published *Freud e la filosofia antica. Genealogia di un fondatore* (2006).

BEATRIZ PICHEL received her PhD in Philosophy at the *Universidad Autónoma de Madrid* with a thesis entitled, *Photography and Death in War. Objects, practices and representations during World War I in France*. Her research focuses on the relationships between history and theory of photography, the history of emotions, and the history of medicine. She has been visiting fellow at the Birkbeck College, the Queen Mary University of London and the *École des Hautes Études en Sciences Sociales*. She is working now on a new project, which examines the impact of photography in the shape of popular and medical knowledge on emotions during the second half of the 19th century.

STEFANO TOMELLERI is Associate Professor of Sociology at Bergamo University. He obtained a degree in Philosophy and a PhD in Sociology from Parma University. Since several years he has been studying the social phenomenology of resentment and its possible applications in the fields of social science and process counseling for organizations. Some of his publications are: *La società del risentimento* (2004), and *Identità e gerarchia. Per una Sociologia del risentimento* (2009).

JUAN MANUEL ZARAGOZA BERNAL is graduated in Philosophy and also in Information Sciences at the University of Murcia in 2006. He was awarded his PhD in History and Philosophy at the *Universidad Autónoma de Madrid* with a thesis entitled *Terminal patient's as an interactive class. Incurable patients in Spain (1850-1955)*. He was visiting scholar at the Wellcome Trust Centre for the History of Medicine, the Department of History and Philosophy of Science, Cambridge University, and the Centre for the History of The Emotions, Queen Mary University of London. His main research areas are the history of medicine from the patient's point of view, the material culture of experience, and the history of care. His new research project, *Material cultures of care and emotion in Britain and Spain, 1890-1940*, has been awarded with a Marie Curie Intra-European Fellowship, to be carried out at the Centre for the History of the Emotions of the Queen Mary University of London.